Fodor's

BIG ISLAND OF HAWAI'I

3rd Edition

D1008129

Fodor's Travel Publications   New York, Toronto, London, Sydney, Auckland
www.fodors.com

Be a Fodor's Correspondent

Your opinion matters. It matters to us. It matters to your fellow Fodor's travelers, too. And we'd like to hear it. In fact, we need to hear it.

When you share your experiences and opinions, you become an active member of the Fodor's community. That means we'll not only use your feedback to make our books better, but we'll publish your names and comments whenever possible. Throughout our guides, look for "Word of Mouth," excerpts of your unvarnished feedback.

Here's how you can help improve Fodor's for all of us.

Tell us when we're right. We rely on local writers to give you an insider's perspective. But our writers and staff editors—who are the best in the business—depend on you. Your positive feedback is a vote to renew our recommendations for the next edition.

Tell us when we're wrong. We're proud that we update most of our guides every year. But we're not perfect. Things change. Hotels cut services. Museums change hours. Charming cafés lose charm. If our writer didn't quite capture the essence of a place, tell us how you'd do it differently. If any of our descriptions are inaccurate or inadequate, we'll incorporate your changes in the next edition and will correct factual errors at fodors.com immediately.

Tell us what to include. You probably have had fantastic travel experiences that aren't yet in Fodor's. Why not share them with a community of like-minded travelers? Maybe you chanced upon a beach or bistro or B&B that you don't want to keep to yourself. Tell us why we should include it. And share your discoveries and experiences with everyone directly at fodors.com. Your input may lead us to add a new listing or highlight a place we cover with a "Highly Recommended" star or with our highest rating, "Fodor's Choice."

Give us your opinion instantly at our feedback center at www.fodors.com/feedback. You may also e-mail editors@fodors.com with the subject line "Big Island Editor." Or send your nominations, comments, and complaints by mail to Big Island Editor, Fodor's, 1745 Broadway, New York, NY 10019.

You and travelers like you are the heart of the Fodor's community. Make our community richer by sharing your experiences. Be a Fodor's correspondent.
Aloha!

Tim Jarrell, Publisher

FODOR'S BIG ISLAND OF HAWAI'I

Editor: Rachel Klein

Editorial Contributors: Bill Harby, Katie Young Yamanaka
Production Editor: Evangelos Vasilakis
Maps & Illustrations: Henry Colomb and Mark Stroud, Moon Street Cartography; David Lindroth, Inc., *cartographers;* Bob Blake, Rebecca Baer, *map editors;* William Wu, *information graphics*
Design: Fabrizio La Rocca, *creative director;* Guido Caroti, Siobhan O'Hare, *art directors;* Tina Malaney, Chie Ushio, Ann McBride, Jessica Walsh, *designers;* Melanie Marin, *senior picture editor*
Cover Photo: (Lava from Kilauea volcano enters the Pacific): Roger Ressmeyer/Corbis
Production Manager: Angela L. McLean

3rd Edition

ISBN 978-1-4000-0441-6

ISSN 1934-5542

SPECIAL SALES

This book is available at special discounts for bulk purchases for sales promotions or premiums. Special editions, including personalized covers, excerpts of existing books, and corporate imprints, can be created in large quantities for special needs. For more information, write to Special Markets/Premium Sales, 1745 Broadway, MD 6-2, New York, New York 10019, or e-mail specialmarkets@randomhouse.com.

AN IMPORTANT TIP & AN INVITATION

Although all prices, opening times, and other details in this book are based on information supplied to us at press time, changes occur all the time in the travel world, and Fodor's cannot accept responsibility for facts that become outdated or for inadvertent errors or omissions. So **always confirm information when it matters,** especially if you're making a detour to visit a specific place. Your experiences—positive and negative—matter to us. If we have missed or misstated something, **please write to us.** We follow up on all suggestions. Contact the Big Island editor at editors@fodors.com or c/o Fodor's at 1745 Broadway, New York, NY 10019.

PRINTED IN CHINA

10 9 8 7 6 5 4 3 2 1

CONTENTS

Fodor's Features

MAPS

ABOUT THIS BOOK

Our Ratings

Sometimes you find terrific travel experiences and sometimes they just find you. But usually the burden is on you to select the right combination of experiences. That's where our ratings come in.

As travelers we've all discovered a place so wonderful that its worthiness is obvious. And sometimes that place is so experiential that superlatives don't do it justice: you just have to be there to know. These sights, properties, and experiences get our highest rating, **Fodor's Choice**, indicated by orange stars throughout this book.

Black stars highlight sights and properties we deem **Highly Recommended**, places that our writers, editors, and readers praise again and again for consistency and excellence.

By default, there's another category: any place we include in this book is by definition worth your time, unless we say otherwise. And we will.

Disagree with any of our choices? Care to nominate a place or suggest that we rate one more highly? Visit our feedback center at ⊕ *www. fodors.com/feedback*.

Budget Well

Hotel and restaurant price categories from ¢ to $$$$ are defined in the Where to Eat and Where to Stay chapters. Real prices are listed at the end of each restaurant and hotel review. For attractions, we always give standard adult admission fees; reductions are usually available for children, students, and senior citizens. Want to pay with plastic? **AE, D, DC, MC, V** following restaurant and hotel listings indicate if American Express, Discover, Diners Club, MasterCard, and Visa are accepted.

Restaurants

Unless we state otherwise, restaurants are open for lunch and dinner daily. We mention dress only when there's a specific requirement and reservations only when they're essential or not accepted—it's always best to book ahead.

Hotels

Hotels have private bath, phone, and TV, unless we state otherwise. We always list facilities but not whether you'll be charged an extra fee to use them, so when pricing accommodations, find out what's included.

Listings

★	Fodor's Choice
★	Highly recommended
⊠	Physical address
↔	Directions or Map coordinates
⌂	Mailing address
☎	Telephone
🖶	Fax
⊕	On the Web
✉	E-mail
⧉	Admission fee
☉	Open/closed times
Ⓜ	Metro stations
▭	Credit cards

Hotels & Restaurants

▥	Hotel
⇱	Number of rooms
♨	Facilities
¶⊙¶	Meal plans
✕	Restaurant
⌕	Reservations
🏛	Dress code
↘	Smoking
₿♀	BYOB

Outdoors

🏌	Golf
⛺	Camping

Other

℃	Family-friendly
⇨	See also
⊠	Branch address
☞	Take note

Experience
Big Island

WHAT'S WHERE

1 Kailua-Kona. A seaside town packed with tons of restaurants, shops, and a busy waterfront bustling with tourists along the main street, Ali'i Drive.

2 The Kona Coast. An area the stretches a bit north of Kailua-Kona and much further south includes the gorgeous Kealakekua Bay. This is the place to come for world famous Kona Coffee to take farm tours and taste samples.

3 The Kohala Coast and Waimea. The sparking coast is where all those long, white sand beaches are found, and the expensive resorts to go with them. Ranches sprawl across the cool, upland meadows of Waimea, known as paniolo (cowboy) country.

4 Mauna Kea. Climb (or drive) this 13,796-foot mountain for what's considered the world's best stargazing, with 13 telescopes perched on top.

5 The Hāmākua Coast. Waterfalls, dramatic cliffs, ocean views, ancient hidden valleys, and rainforests and the stunning Waipi'o Valley are just a few of the treats that await you here.

6 Hilo. Known as the City of Rainbows for all its rain, Hilo is often skipped by tourists in favor of the sunny Kohala Coast. But for what many consider the "real" Hawaii, as well as incredible rainforests, waterfalls, and the best farmer's market on the island, Hilo can't be beat.

7 Puna. This section of the island was most recently covered by lava, and so it has brand-new jet-black beaches with volcanic hot springs.

8 Hawaii Volcanoes National Park and Vicinity. The land around the park is continually expanding, as the active Kilauea Volcano sends lava spilling into the ocean. The nearby town of Volcano provides a great base for exploring the park.

9 Ka'ū and Ka Lae (South Point). Round the southernmost part of the island for two of Big Island's most famous beaches–Green Beach, and Black Beach.

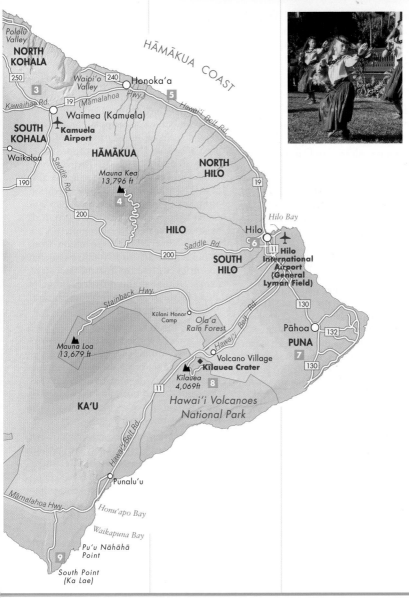

Poloʻlu Valley

NORTH KOHALA

250

3

Waipiʻo Valley

240

Honokaʻa

5

HĀMĀKUA COAST

19 (Māmalahoa Hwy.)

Kawaihae Rd.

Waimea (Kamuela)

✈ **Kamuela Airport**

SOUTH KOHALA

Waikoloa

190

Saddle Rd.

HĀMĀKUA

▲ *Mauna Kea 13,796 ft*

4

Hawaiʻi Bell Rd.

NORTH HILO

19

200

HILO

Saddle Rd.

200

SOUTH HILO

Hilo

Hilo Bay

6

11 ✈ **Hilo International Airport (General Lyman Field)**

Stainback Hwy.

Kūlani Honor Camp

Olaʻa Rain Forest

Hawaiʻi Bell Rd.

130

Pāhoa

132

PUNA

7

130

Volcano Village

▲ ◆ **Kīlauea Crater**

▲ *Mauna Loa 13,679 ft*

Kīlauea 4,069ft

8

11

Hawaiʻi Volcanoes National Park

KAʻU

Hawaiʻi Bell Rd.

Punaluʻu

Māmalahoa Hwy.

Honuʻapo Bay

Waikapuna Bay

Puʻu Nāhāhā Point

9

South Point (Ka Lae)

BIG ISLAND AND HAWAI'I TODAY

You could fit all the other Hawaiian Islands onto the Big Island and still have a little room left over—hence the clever name. Locals refer to the island by side: Kona side to the west and Hilo side to the east. Most of the resorts, condos, and restaurants are crammed into 30 mi of the sunny Kona side, while the rainy, tropical Hilo side is much more local and residential.

Hawaiian culture and tradition here have experienced a renaissance over the last few decades. There's a real effort to revive traditions and to respect history as the Islands go through major changes. New developments often have a Hawaiian cultural expert on staff to ensure cultural sensitivity and to educate newcomers.

Nonetheless, development remains a huge issue for all Islanders—land prices are skyrocketing, putting many areas out of reach for the native population. Traffic is becoming a problem on roads that were not designed to accommodate all the new drivers, and the Islands' limited natural resources are being seriously tapped. The government, though sluggish to respond at first, is trying to make development in Hawai'i as sustainable as possible.

Sustainability

Prior to Western contact, Hawai'i's native dwellers were 100% sustainable. For a place so well endowed with the richest natural resources, contemporary Hawai'i is a far cry from its past. This great challenge also presents a great opportunity. Hawai'i's climate and renewable resources—the sun, the wind, and the waves—can be developed for the greater good and provide almost every conceivable kind of alternative energy.

Although sustainability is an effective buzzword and authentic direction for the island's dining establishments, 90% of Hawai'i's food and energy is imported. Most of the land is used for monocropping of pineapples or sugarcane, which have both severely declined in the past decades. Sugarcane is now only produced commercially on Maui, while pineapple production has dropped by half. Dole, once the largest pineapple company in Hawai'i, closed its plants in 1991, and after 90 years, Del Monte stopped pineapple production in 2008. The next year, Maui Land and Pineapple Company also ceased its Maui Gold pineapple operation although about one-third of its crop was taken over in early 2010 by a group of execs who created a new company. Low cost of labor and transportation from Latin American and Southeast Asian countries are factors for the industry's demise. Although this proves daunting, it also sets the stage for great agricultural change to be explored.

Back to Basics Agriculture

Emulating how the Hawaiian ancestors lived and returning to their simple ways of growing and sharing a variety of foods has become a statewide initiative. Hawai'i has the natural conditions and talent to produce far more diversity in agriculture than it currently does.

The seed of this movement thrives through various farmers' markets and partnerships between restaurants and local farmers. Localized efforts such as the Hawai'i Farm Bureau Federation are collectively leading the organic and sustainable agricultural renaissance. From home-cooked meals to casual plate lunches to fine-dining cuisine, these sustainable trailblazers enrich the culinary tapestry of Hawai'i and uplift the island's overall quality of life.

Tourism and the Economy

The over-$10 billion tourism industry represents a third of Hawai'i's state income. Naturally, this dependency causes economic hardship as the financial meltdown of recent years affects tourists' ability to visit and consume. One way the industry has made changes has been to adopt more eco-conscious practices, as many Hawaiians feel that planning shouldn't happen without regard for impact to local communities and their natural environment.

Belief that an industry based on the Hawaiians' *aloha* should protect, promote, and empower local culture and provide more entrepreneurial opportunities for local people has become more important to tourism businesses. More companies are incorporating authentic Hawaiiana in their programs and aim not only to provide a commercially viable tour but also to ensure that the visitor leaves feeling connected to his or her host. The concept of *kuleana*, a word for both privilege and responsibility, is upheld. Having the privilege to live in such a sublime place comes with the responsibility to protect it.

Sovereignty

Political issues of sovereignty continue to divide the natives of Hawai'i with myriad organizations, each operating with separate agendas but collectively lacking one defined goal. Ranging from achieving complete and utter independence to solidifying a nation within a nation, existing sovereignty models remain fractured and their future unresolved. The introduction of the Native Hawaiian Government Reorganization Act of 2009 attempts to set up a legal framework in which Native Hawaiians can attain federal recognition and coexist as a self-governed entity. Also known as the Akaka Bill after Senator Daniel Akaka of Hawai'i, this pending bill has been presented before Congress and is still evolving at the time of this writing.

Rise of Hawaiian Pride

After Hawai'i received statehood in 1959, a process of Americanization transpired. Traditions were duly silenced in the name of citizenship. Hawaiian language and arts were banned from schools and children were distanced from their local customs. But Hawaiians are resilient people, and with the rise of the civil rights movement they began to reflect on their own national identity, bringing an astonishing renaissance of the Hawaiian culture to fruition. The people rediscovered language, the hula, the chant or *mele*, and even the traditional Polynesian art of canoe building and wayfinding (navigation by the stars without use of instruments). This cultural resurrection is now firmly established in today's Hawaiian culture, with a palpable pride that exudes from Hawaiians young and old.

The election of President Barack Obama has definitely done its share of fueling not only Hawaiian pride but also ubiquitous hope for a better future. The president's strong connection and commitment to Hawaiian values of diversity, spirituality, family, and conservation have restored confidence that Hawai'i can inspire a more peaceful, tolerant, and environmentally conscious world.

BIG ISLAND PLANNER

When You Arrive

The Big Island's two airports are directly across the island from each other. Kona International Airport on the west side is about a 10-minute drive from Kailua-Kona and 30 to 45 minutes from the Kohala Coast. On the east side, Hilo International Airport, 2 mi from downtown Hilo, is about 40 minutes from Volcanoes National Park. A 2½-hour drive connects Hilo and Kailua-Kona.

Visitor Information

Before you go, contact the Big Island Visitors Bureau to request a free official vacation planner with information on accommodations, transportation, sports and activities, dining, arts and entertainment, and culture. The Hawai'i Island Chamber of Commerce has links to dozens of museums, attractions, bed-and-breakfasts, and parks on its Web site as well.

Contacts Big Island Visitors Bureau (☎ 808/961–5797, 800/648–2441 for vacation planner and brochures ⊕ www.bigisland.org). **Hawai'i Island Chamber of Commerce** (☎ 808/935–7178 ⊕ www.hicc.biz).

Getting Here and Around

It's a good idea to rent a car with 4-wheel drive, such as a Jeep, on the Big Island. Some of the island's best sights (and most beautiful beaches) are at the end of rough or unpaved roads.

Most agencies make you sign an agreement that you won't drive on the Saddle Road, the path to Mauna Kea and its observatories. Though a good portion of the road is smoothly paved, the Saddle Road is remote, winding, and bumpy in certain areas, unlighted, and bereft of gas stations. Harper's, a local rental company, is the sole exception.

⇨ See Travel Smart Big Island for more information on renting a car and driving.

Island Driving Times

Due to the Big Island's size, it can take quite a bit of time to get from one region of the island to another. Added to that, the island's increasing traffic problems are making driving times even longer, particularly between Kona and the Kohala Coast, and Kona to Kealakekua Bay and Ka'ū.

The state is working on widening Highway 19, which circles the island, and the hope is that the wider highway will cut down on traffic. In the meantime, the following are average driving times between some of the Big Island's most popular sights.

Kailua-Kona to Kealakekua Bay	14 mi./25 min.
Kailua-Kona to Kohala Coast	32 mi./50 min.
Kailua-Kona to Waimea	40 mi./1 hr. 15 min.
Kailua-Kona to Hāmākua Coast	53 mi./1 hr 40 min.
Kailua-Kona to Hilo	75 mi./2 hrs.
Kohala Coast to Waimea	16 mi./ 33 min.
Kohala Coast to Hāmākua Coast	29 mi./ 55 min.
Hilo to Volcano	30 mi./48 min.

Weather-Related Driving Tips

If it's raining, as it tends to quite a bit on the Big Island, there are some alternate routes we recommend. From Kailua-Kona to Volcano: Take the southern route, following Highway 11 through South Kona and Ka'ū around South Point to Volcano (125 mi, just under three hours); Between Kailua-Kona and Hilo: Starting in Kailua-Kona, take Highway 190 east to Highway 19. Follow 19 through Waimea to Hilo (96 mi, two hours or less); From Kohala to Waimea: Take Highway 11 to Waikoloa Road (9 mi south of Hāpuna Beach) and follow it 10 mi to Highway 190. Turn left on 190 and follow it another 11 mi to Waimea (30 mi, 40 minutes).

Dining and Lodging on the Big Island

Hawai'i is a melting pot of cultures, and nowhere is this more apparent than in its cuisine. From lū'au and "plate lunches" to sushi and steak, there's no shortage of interesting flavors and presentations. The same "buy local" trend that is spreading through the rest of the country is really taking hold on the Big Island. This is a giant shift from years past, in which most goods were imported, and it's a happy trend for visitors, who get to taste juicy, flavorful Waimea tomatoes and creamy handmade Hāmākua goat cheese. Whether you're looking for a quick snack or a multicourse meal, *we cover the best eating experiences the island has to offer.*

Consider spending part of your vacation at a resort and part of it at bed-and-breakfasts. The big resorts sit squarely on some of the best beaches on the Island, and they have a lot to offer—spas, golf, and great restaurants for starters. The bed-and-breakfasts, on the other hand, provide a more intimate experience in settings as diverse as an up-country ranch, a jungle tree house, and a Victorian mansion perched on sea cliffs. Several romantic bed-and-breakfasts nestle in the rain forest surrounding Volcanoes National Park—very convenient after a nighttime lava hike.

Will I See Flowing Lava?

The best time to see lava is at night. However, you may or may not see flowing lava. Anyone who tries to tell you they can guarantee it or predict it is lying or trying to sell you something. Your best bet is to call the visitor center at the national park before you head out; even at that you could be pleasantly surprised or utterly disappointed. Keep in mind that the volcano is a pretty amazing sight even if it's not spewing fire.

The hike out to the closest viewing station to the flowing lava requires roughly three to four hours each way—the best way to handle it is to head out in the late afternoon, arrive at the viewing station by nightfall, and then start the trek back when you've had your fill of Pele's fireworks. ■ TIP→ Bring a flashlight and be prepared for some rough going over the lava fields at night.

There are viewing stations along the way as well, so you don't necessarily have to make an eight-hour round-trip journey. In fact, depending on how the lava is flowing, a viewing station farther from the lava could actually afford better views. ⇨ *For more information about visiting Volcanoes National Park, see Chapter 2.*

WHAT IT COSTS

	¢	$	$$	$$$	$$$$
Restaurants	under $10	$10–$17	$18–$26	$27–$35	over $35
Hotels	under $100	$100–$180	$181–$260	$261–$340	over $340

Restaurant prices are for a main course at dinner. Hotel prices are for two people in a standard double room in high season. Condo price categories reflect studio and one-bedroom rates.

TOP BIG ISLAND EXPERIENCES

The Lava Show
(A) Watch as fiery red lava pours, steaming, into the ocean; stare in awe at nighttime lava fireworks; and hike across the floor of a crater at Volcanoes National Park.

Green Sand Beach
(B) It's a hike, but this is the only place in the world to see green sand. And it happens to be surrounded by turquoise waters and dramatic cliffs.

Exploring Waipi'o Valley
(C) Whichever way you choose to get there—on horseback, in a 4WD, or on foot—you'll discover that the "Valley of the Kings" on the Hamakua Coast is full of sky-high waterfalls, lush green cliffs, and a mystical quality that can't quite be described or rivaled.

A Window on the Universe
(D) Teams of astronomers from all over the world come to Mauna Kea for the clearest skies and best conditions anywhere. Head up the mountain in the late afternoon for the prettiest sunset on this island and the best stargazing on this planet.

Play at a Perfect Beach
(E) Whether you follow the paved roads to Hāpuna, Kauna'oa (also known as Mauna Kea), or Kua Bay, or brave the rocky routes to Makalawena, you'll find that the Big Island is full of postcard-perfect beaches.

A Swim Through Coral Gardens
(F) Diving or snorkeling in the crystal clear waters off the coast is like being let loose in your very own ocean-sized aquarium. Bright yellow, purple, and rose-colored coral creates surreal kingdoms ruled by

1

octopi, turtles, rays, dolphins, and fish in every color of the rainbow.

Stunning Waterfalls

(G) Watch rainbows forming in the mist, then take a refreshing dip in the cold, deep pools fed by the powerful waterfalls spilling over the dramatic cliffs of the Hāmākua Coast.

Snooze with a Sea Turtle

(H) Hang out at Punaluʻu Beach, where sea turtles surf the waves and nap on the black sands.

A Healing *Lomilomi* Massage

(I) The *lomilomi* technique uses a combination of arms, elbows, hands, and breath to impart the overall sense of wellbeing associated with this ancient healing tradition.

A Kona Coffee Farm Tour

(J) Spend an hour discovering why it is that Kona coffee commands those high prices. Watch as "cherries" become beans, enjoy the smoky coffee smell of the roasting process, then indulge in the freshest cup of coffee you'll ever have. Did we mention that it's all free? The annual 10-day Kona Coffee Cultural Festival November celebrates coffee with tours, tastings, and special events.

Whale the Day Away

(K) From December to May, you can sit on any beach on the west side of the island and watch the humpback whale migration. The sight of their backs, glistening as they move through the water, or the occasional perfect fluke cutting through the surface, is a matchless experience.

GREAT ITINERARIES

Yes, the Big Island is big, and yes, there's a lot to see. If you're short on time, consider flying into one airport and out of the other. That will give you the opportunity to see both sides of the island without ever having to go backwards. Decide what sort of note you'd rather end on to determine your route—if you'd prefer to spend your last few days sleeping on the beach, go from east to west; if hiking through rain forests and showering in waterfalls sounds like a better way to end the trip, move from west to east. If you're short on time, head straight for Hawai'i Volcanoes National Park and briefly visit Hilo before traveling the Hāmākua Coast route and making your new base in Kailua-Kona.

From exploring the shores of its green- and black-sand beaches to stargazing atop Mauna Kea, there's no shortage of ways to spend the day immersed in nature on the Big Island. Choose a couple or several of our favorite one-day itineraries to suit your interest and length of stay on the island.

Green Hawai'i

Take full advantage of Hawai'i's living classroom. Visit one of the island's botanical gardens in the morning, then head to the Natural Energy Lab for a peek at its desalination plants, sustainable aqua farms, and various natural energy projects.

Finish your day with a farm tour in the afternoon, followed by an evening spent enjoying the delicious products of the Big Island at one of Waimea's top restaurants, such as the island favorite Merriman's Café or its nearby neighbor Daniel Thiebaut's Restaurant.

Black and Green Sand

Check out some of the unusual beaches you'll only find on the Big Island. Start with a hike into Green Sand beach and plan to spend some time sitting on the beach, dipping into the bay's turquoise waters, and marveling at the surreal beauty of this spot.

When you've had your fill, hop back in the car and head south about half an hour to Punalu'u, the island's best-known black-sand beach and favorite resting place of the Hawaiian sea turtle. Although the surf is often too rough to go swimming with the turtles, there are typically at least two or three napping on the beach at any given time of the day.

Sun and Stars

Spend the day lounging on a Kohala Coast beach (Hāpuna, Kauna'oa—also known as Mauna Kea—or Kua Bay), but throw jackets and boots in the car because you'll be catching the sunset from Mauna Kea's summit. Bundle up and stick around after darkness falls for some of the world's best stargazing.

Book a tour or head straight for the visitor center, join their free tour of the summit at 1 PM on Saturday or Sunday, and return to the center to use their telescopes for evening stargazing.

Hike Volcanoes

Devote a full day (at least) to Volcanoes National Park. Head out on the Kīlauea Iki trail—a 4-mi loop at the summit—by late morning. You'll have to leave the park to grab some lunch at nearby restaurants in Volcano Village just a few minutes away, or you can plan ahead and pack your own picnic lunch before you start your morning hike.

After lunch, head down Chain of Craters Road to the coast and the active lava

flows. Bring water, snacks, and a flashlight if you intend to hike out to the end of the road where the lava flows into the ocean.

Start your hike during the day (by 4 PM or earlier) to ensure that you're as close as you can safely be when night falls and to prepare yourself for a spectacular nighttime lava show.

Majestic Waterfalls and Kings' Valleys

Take a day to enjoy the splendors of the Hāmākua Coast—any gorge you see on the road is an indication of a waterfall waiting to be explored. For a sure bet, head to beautiful Waipi'o Valley. Book a horseback, hiking, or 4WD tour or walk on in yourself (just keep in mind that it's an arduous hike back up—25% grade for a little over a mile).

Once in the valley, take your first right to get to the black-sand beach. Take a moment to sit here—the ancient Hawaiians believed this was where souls crossed over to the afterlife. Whether you believe it or not, there's something unmistakably special about this place.

Waterfalls abound in the valley, depending on the amount of recent rainfall. Your best bet is to follow the river from the beach to the back of the valley, where a waterfall and its lovely pool await.

Underwater Day

Explore the colorful reefs populated with tropical fish off the Big Island's coast for one day, and we defy you to stop thinking about the world beneath the waves when you're back on land. Our favorite spots include Two Step (near the City of Refuge), Kealakekua Bay, and the Kapoho Tide Pools.

Early morning is the best time to see the Hawaiian spinner dolphins that frolic off

this coast, but you're likely to see turtles any time of day, along with yellow and white angelfish, spotted moray eels, trumpet fish, and a myriad of other brightly colored varieties.

Volcano Hot Springs and Boiling Pots

Most tourists skip Puna. Venture into this remote area for a morning, and you'll be rewarded with lava tube hikes (Kīlauea Caverns of Fire), volcanically heated pools (Ahalanui Beach Park), and tide pools brimming with colorful coral, fish, and the occasional turtle (Kapoho).

Head to Hilo in the afternoon to catch a glimpse of the Boiling Pots waterfalls, Banyan Drive, and Queen Lili'uokalani Gardens, before dining at one of Hilo's great restaurants.

Pololū and Paniolo Country

North Kohala is a world away from the resorts of the coast. Visit the quaint artists' community of Hāwī, then head to Pololū Valley for amazing views.

A steep-ish ½-mi hike leads to a fantastic black-sand beach surrounded by beautiful sheer green cliffs. Back on the road, head up Highway 250 to Waimea and the pastures of *paniolo* country. Indulge in a memorable meal at one of the fantastic restaurants (we recommend Merriman's, Daniel Thiebaut, or Pakini Grill).

Go Off-Road

Book an ATV tour or take your 4WD for a spin to check out some of the Big Island's isolated beaches. There are green beaches (in addition to *the* Green Sand Beach) waiting in the Ka'ū region and ruggedly beautiful white beaches with perfect turquoise water along the Kohala Coast; deal with the tough, 4WD-only roads into these beaches and you're likely to be rewarded with a pristine tropical beach all to yourself.

THE HAWAIIAN ISLANDS

Oʻahu. The state's capital, Honolulu, is on Oʻahu; this is the center of Hawaiʻi's economy and by far the most populated island in the chain—900,000 residents add up to 71% of the state's population. At 597 square mi, Oʻahu is the third-largest island in the chain; most residents live in or around Honolulu, so the rest of the island still fits neatly into the tropical, untouched vision of Hawaiʻi. Situated southeast of Kauaʻi and northwest of Maui, Oʻahu is a central location for island hopping. Surfing contests on the legendary North Shore, in Pearl Harbor, and on iconic Waikīkī Beach are all here.

Maui. The second-largest island in the chain, Maui is northwest of the Big Island and close enough to be visible from its beaches on a clear day. The island's 729 square mi are home to only 119,000 people but host approximately 2.5 million tourists every year. With its restaurants and lively nightlife, Maui is the only island that competes with Oʻahu in terms of entertainment. Its charm lies in that, although entertainment is available, Maui's towns still feel like island villages compared to the heaving modern city of Honolulu.

Hawaiʻi (The Big Island). The Big Island has the second-largest population of the Islands (167,000) but feels sparsely settled due to its size. It's 4,038 square mi and growing—all the other islands could fit onto the Big Island, and there would still be room left over. The southernmost island in the chain (slightly southeast of Maui), the Big Island is home to Kīlauea, the most active volcano on the planet. It percolates within Volcanoes National Park, which draws 2.5 million visitors every year.

Kauaʻi. The northernmost island in the chain (northwest of Oʻahu), Kauaʻi is, at approximately 550 square mi, the fourth-largest of all the Islands and the least populated of the larger islands, with just under 63,000 residents. Known as the Garden Isle, Kauaʻi claims the title "Wettest Spot on Earth," with an annual average rainfall of about 450 inches. The island is a favorite with honeymooners and others wanting to get away from it all—lush and peaceful, it's the perfect escape from the modern world.

Molokaʻi. North of Lānaʻi and Maui, and east of Oʻahu, Molokaʻi is Hawaiʻi's fifth-largest island, encompassing 260 square mi. On a clear night, the lights of Honolulu are visible from Molokaʻi's western shore. Molokaʻi is sparsely populated, with just under 7,400 residents, the majority of whom are native Hawaiians. Most of the island's 85,000 annual visitors travel from Maui or Oʻahu to spend the day exploring its beaches, cliffs, and former leper colony on Kalaupapa Peninsula.

Lānaʻi. Lying just off Maui's western coast, Lānaʻi looks nothing like its sister islands, with pine trees and deserts in place of palm trees and beaches. Still, the tiny 140-square-mi island is home to nearly 3,000 residents and draws an average of 90,000 visitors each year to two resorts (one in the mountains and one at the shore), both operated by Four Seasons.

Hawaii's Geology

The Hawaiian Islands consist of more than just the islands inhabited and visited by humans. A total of 19 islands and atolls constitute the State of Hawaiʻi, with a total land mass of 6,423.4 square mi.

The Islands are actually exposed peaks of a submersed mountain range called the Hawaiian Ridge-Emperor Seamounts

chain. The range was formed as the Pacific Plate moved very slowly (about 32 mi every million years) over a hot spot in the earth's mantle. Because the plate moved northwestwardly, the Islands in the northwest portion of the archipelago are older, which is also why they're smaller—they have been eroding longer.

The Big Island is the youngest, and thus the largest, island in the chain. It is built from seven different volcanoes, including Mauna Loa, which is the largest shield volcano on the planet. Mauna Loa and Kīlauea are the only Hawaiian volcanoes still erupting with any sort of frequency. Mauna Loa last erupted in 1984. Kīlauea has been continuously erupting since 1983.

Mauna Kea (Big Island), Hualālai (Big Island), and Haleakalā (Maui) are all in what's called the postshield stage of volcanic development—eruptions decrease steadily for up to 250,000 years before ceasing entirely. Kohala (Big Island), Lānaʻi (Lānaʻi), and Waiʻanae (Oʻahu) are considered extinct volcanoes, in the erosional stage of development; Koʻolau (Oʻahu) and West Maui (Maui) volcanoes are extinct volcanoes in the rejuvenation stage—after lying dormant for hundreds of thousands of years, they began erupting again, but only once every several thousand years.

There is currently an active undersea volcano called Loʻihi that has been erupting regularly. If it continues its current pattern, it should breach the ocean's surface in tens of thousands of years.

Hawaiʻi's Flora and Fauna

Hawaiʻi boasts every climate on the planet, excluding the two most extreme: arctic tundra and arid desert. The Islands have wine-growing regions, cactus-speckled ranchlands, icy mountaintops, and the rainiest forests on earth.

More than 90% of Hawaiian plants and animals are endemic, like the koa tree and the yellow hibiscus. Long-dormant volcanic craters are perfect hiding places for rare native plants. The silversword, a rare cousin of the sunflower, grows on Hawaiʻi's three tallest peaks—Haleakalā, Mauna Kea, and Mauna Loa—and nowhere else on Earth. ʻŌhiʻa trees—thought to be the favorite of Pele, the volcano goddess—bury their roots in fields of once-molten lava and sprout ruby pom-pom-like lehua blossoms. The deep yellow petals of ʻilima (once reserved for royalty) are tiny discs, which make the most elegant lei.

But most of the plants you see while walking around aren't Hawaiian at all but came from Tahitian, Samoan, or European visitors. Plumeria creeps over all of the Islands; orchids run rampant on the Big Island; bright orange ʻilima light up the mountains of Oʻahu. These flowers give the Hawaiian lei their color and fragrance.

Hawaiʻi's state bird, the nēnē goose, is making a comeback from its former endangered status. It roams freely in parts of Maui, Kauaʻi, and the Big Island. Rare Hawaiian monk seals breed in the northwestern Islands. With only 1,500 left in the wild, you probably won't catch many lounging on the beaches, though they have been spotted on the shores of Kauaʻi in recent years. Spinner dolphins and sea turtles can be found off the coast of all the Islands; and every year from December to May, the humpback whales migrate past Hawaiʻi in droves.

WHEN TO GO

Long days of sunshine and fairly mild year-round temperatures make Hawai'i an all-season destination. Most resort areas are at sea level, with average afternoon temperatures of 75°F–80°F during the coldest months of December and January; during the hottest months of August and September the temperature often reaches 90°F. Higher "upcountry" elevations typically have cooler and often misty conditions. Only at mountain summits does it reach freezing.

Moist trade winds drop their precipitation on the north and east sides of the Islands, creating tropical climates, while the south and west sides remain hot and dry with desert-like conditions. Rainfall can be high in winter, particularly on those north and east shores.

Most travelers head to the Islands in winter, specifically from mid-December through mid-April. This high season means that fewer travel bargains are available; room rates average 10%–15% higher during this season than the rest of the year.

You can see humpback whales clearly off the western coast of the island from about January until May. The Ironman Triathlon takes place every October in Kailua-Kona. Shortly after the Ironman, the first 10 days of November are devoted to the Kona Coffee Cultural Festival—each day brings numerous caffeinated events including a cooking competition, a picking competition, a barista competition, and of course the cupping competition, which is all about the taste and quality of each coffee. Coffee connoisseurs from all over the world flock to Kona for the festival, and the whole west side of the island goes crazy for coffee.

Hawaiian Holidays

If you happen to be in the Islands on March 26 or June 11, you'll notice light traffic and busy beaches—these are state holidays not celebrated anywhere else. March 26 recognizes the birthday of Prince Jonah Kūhiō Kalaniana'ole, a member of the royal line who served as a delegate to Congress and spearheaded the effort to set aside homelands for Hawaiian people. June 11 honors the first island-wide monarch, Kamehameha I; locals drape his statues with lei and stage elaborate parades.

May 1 isn't an official holiday, but it's the day when schools and civic groups celebrate the quintessential Island gift, the flower lei.

Statehood Day is celebrated on the third Friday in August (admission to the Union was August 21, 1959).

Most Japanese and Chinese holidays are widely observed. On Chinese New Year, homes and businesses sprout bright red good-luck mottoes, lions dance in the streets, and everybody eats *gau* (steamed pudding) and *jai* (vegetarian stew).

Good Friday is a state holiday in spring, a favorite for family picnics.

Climate

The following are average maximum and minimum temperatures for Honolulu; the temperatures throughout the Hawaiian Islands are similar.

HAWAIIAN HISTORY

Hawaiian history is long and complex; a brief survey can put into context the ongoing renaissance of native arts and culture.

The Polynesians

Long before both Christopher Columbus and the Vikings, Polynesian seafarers set out to explore the vast stretches of the open ocean in double-hulled canoes. From western Polynesia, they traveled back and forth between Samoa, Fiji, Tahiti, the Marquesas, and the Society Isles, settling on the outer reaches of the Pacific, Hawai'i, and Easter Island, as early as AD 300. The golden era of Polynesian voyaging peaked around AD 1200, after which the distant Hawaiian Islands were left to develop their own unique cultural practices and subsistence in relative isolation.

The Islands' symbiotic society was deeply intertwined with religion, mythology, science and artistry. Ruled by an *ali'i*, or chief, each settlement was nestled in an *ahupua'a*, a pyramid-like land division from the uplands where the ali'i lived, through the valleys and down to the shores where the commoners resided. Everyone contributed, whether it was by building canoes, catching fish, making tools, or farming land.

A United Kingdom

When the British explorer Captain James Cook arrived in 1778, he was revered as a god upon his arrival and later killed over a stolen boat. With guns and ammunition purchased from Cook, the Big Island chief, Kamehameha, gained a significant advantage over the other ali'i. He united Hawai'i into one kingdom in 1810, bringing an end to the frequent interisland battles that dominated Hawaiian life.

Tragically, the new kingdom was beset with troubles. Native religion was abandoned, and *kapu* (laws and regulations) were eventually abolished. The explorers brought foreign diseases with them, and within a few short years the Hawaiian population was cut in half.

New laws regarding land ownership and religious practices eroded the underpinnings of precontact Hawaii. Each successor to the Hawaiian throne sacrificed more control over the island kingdom. As Westerners permeated Hawaiian culture, Hawaii became more riddled with layers of racial issues, injustice, and social unrest.

Modern Hawai'i

Finally in 1893, the last Hawaiian monarch, Queen Lili'uokalani, was overthrown by a group of Americans and European businessmen and government officials, aided by an armed militia. This led to the creation of the Republic of Hawai'i, and it became a U.S. territory for the next 60 years. The loss of Hawaiian sovereignty and the conditions of annexation have haunted the Hawaiian people since the monarchy was toppled.

Pearl Harbor was attacked in 1941, which engaged the United States immediately into World War II. Tourism, from its beginnings in the early 1900s, flourished after the war and naturally inspired rapid real estate development in Waikīkī. In 1959, Hawai'i officially became the 50th state. Statehood paved the way for Hawaiians and Hawai'i's immigrants to participate in the American democratic process.

HAWAIIAN PEOPLE AND THEIR CULTURE

By July 2009, Hawai'i's population was more than 1.3 million with the majority of residents living on O'ahu. Twenty-five percent are Hawaiian or part Hawaiian, more than 40% are Asian-American, and about 20% Caucasian. More than a fifth of the population list two or more races, making Hawai'i the most diverse state in the United States. Among individuals 18 and older, about 89% finished high school, half attained some college, and a little shy of 30% completed a bachelor's degree or higher.

The Role of Tradition

The kingdom of Hawaii was ruled by a spiritual class system. Although the *ali'i*, or chief, was believed to be the direct descendent of a deity or god, the high priest, known as the *kahuna*, presided over every imaginable life ceremony and *kapu* that strictly governed the commoners. Each part of nature and ritual was connected to a deity—Kane was the highest of all deities, symbolizing sunlight and creation; Ku was the god of war; Lono represented fertility, rainfall, music, and peace; Kanaloa was the god of the underworld or darker spirits; and there is Pele, the goddess of fire. The kapu not only provided social order, they also swayed the people to act with reverence for the environment. Any abuse was met with extreme punishment, often death, as it put the land and people's *mana*, or spiritual power, in peril.

Ancient deities play a huge role in Hawaiian life today—not just in daily rituals, but in the Hawaiians' reverence for their land. Gods and goddesses tend to be associated with particular parts of the land, and most of them are connected with many places, thanks to the body of stories built up around each.

One of the most important ways the ancient Hawaiians showed respect for their gods and goddesses was through the hula. Various forms of the hula were performed as prayers to the gods and as praise to the chiefs. Performances were taken very seriously, as a mistake was thought to invalidate the prayer, or even to offend the god or chief in question. Hula is still performed both as entertainment and as prayer; it is not uncommon for a hula performance to be included in an official government ceremony.

Who Are the Hawaiians Today?

To define the Hawaiians in a page, let alone a paragraph, is nearly impossible. First, there are Hawaiians by residence, similar to Californians, New Yorkers, or Texans. Those considered to be indigenous Hawaiians are descendents of the ancient Polynesians who crossed the vast ocean and settled Hawai'i. According to the government, there are Native Hawaiians or native hawaiians (note the change in capitalization) depending on their blood makeup.

Federal and state agencies apply different methods to determine Hawaiian lineage, from measuring blood percentage to mapping genealogy. This has caused turmoil within the community for the simple fact that it excludes so many. It almost guarantees that, as races intermingle, even those considered Native Hawaiian now will eventually disappear on paper, displacing generations to come.

Modern Hawaiian Culture

Perfect weather aside, Hawai'i might be the warmest place anyone can visit. The Hawai'i experience begins and ends with *aloha*, a word that envelops love, affection, and mercy, and has become a salutation for hello and goodbye. Broken down,

alo means "presence" and *ha* means "breath"—the presence of breath. It's to live with love and respect for self and others with every breath. Past the manicured resorts and tour buses, aloha is a spirit and moral compass that binds all of Hawai'i's people.

Hawaiians have been blessed with some of the most unspoiled natural wonders, and aloha extends to the land, or 'aina. People are raised outdoors and have strong ties to nature. They realize as children that the ocean and land are the delicate source of all life. Even ancient gods were embodied by nature, and this reverence has been passed down to present generations who believe in *kuleana,* their privilege and responsibility.

Hawaiians' diverse cultures unfold in a beautiful montage of customs and arts—including music, to dance, to food. Musical genres range from slack key to *Jawaiian* (Hawaiian reggae) to *hapa-haole* (Hawaiian music with English words). From George Kahumoku's Grammyworthy laid-back strumming, to the late Iz Kamakawiwo'ole's "Somewhere over the Rainbow," to Jack Johnson's more mainstream tunes, contemporary Hawaiian music has definitely carved its ever-evolving niche. The Merrie Monarch Festival is celebrating almost 50 years of worldwide hula competition and education. The fine-dining culinary scene, especially in Honolulu, has a rich tapestry of ethnic influences and talent. But the real gems are the humble hole-in-the-wall eateries that serve authentic cuisines of many ethnic origins in one plate, a deliciously mixed plate indeed.

And perhaps, the most striking quality in today's Hawaiian culture is the sense of family, or *ohana.* Sooner or later, almost everyone you meet becomes an uncle or auntie, and it is not uncommon for near-strangers to be welcomed into a home as a member of the family. Until the late 1950s, the practice of *hanai,* in which a family essentially adopts a child, usually a grandchild, without formalities, was still prevalent. The *hanai,* which means to feed or nourish, still resonates within most families and communities.

How to Act Like a Local

Adopting local customs is a firsthand introduction to the Islands' unique culture. So live in T-shirts and shorts. Wear cheap rubber flip-flops, but call them slippers. Wave people into your lane on the highway, and, when someone lets you in, give them a wave of thanks in return. Never, ever blow your horn, even when the pickup truck in front of you is stopped for a long session of "talk story" right in the middle of the road.

Holoholo means to go out for the fun of it—an aimless stroll, ride, or drive. "Wheah you goin', braddah?" "Oh, holoholo." It's local-speak for Sunday drive, no plan, it's not the destination but the journey. Try setting out without an itinerary. Learn to *shaka*: pinky and thumb extended, middle fingers curled in, waggle sideways. Eat white rice with everything. When someone says, "Aloha!" answer, "Aloha no!" ("And a real big aloha back to you"). And, as the locals say, "No make big body" ("Try not to act like you own the place").

KIDS AND FAMILIES

With dozens of adventures, discoveries, and fun-filled beach days, Hawai'i is a blast with kids. Even better, the things to do here do not appeal only to small fry. The entire family, parents included, will enjoy surfing, discovering a waterfall in the rain forest, and snorkeling with sea turtles. And there are plenty of organized activities for kids that will free parents' time for a few romantic beach strolls.

Choosing a Place to Stay

Resorts: All the big resorts make kids' programs a priority, and it shows. When you are booking your room, ask about "kids eat free" deals and the number of kids' pools at the resort. Also check out the size of the groups in the children's programs, and find out whether the cost of the programs includes lunch, equipment, and activities.

The Hilton is every kid's fantasy vacation come true, with dozens of pool slides, one lagoon for snorkeling and one filled with dolphins, and even a choice between riding a monorail or taking a boat to your room. Not to be outdone, the Four Seasons Hualālai Resort has a fantastic program that will keep your little ones happy and occupied all day, as does the Kona Village Resort, which also offers a kids' dinner and a teens' dinner seating to give parents the option of a solo date night.

Condos: Condo and vacation rentals are a fantastic value for families vacationing in Hawai'i. You can cook your own food, which is cheaper than eating out and sometimes easier (especially if you have a finicky eater in your group), and you'll get twice the space of a hotel room for about a quarter of the price. If you decide to go the condo route, be sure to ask about the size of the complex's pool (some try to pawn off a tiny soaking tub as a pool) and whether barbecues are available. One of the best parts of staying in your own place is having a sunset family barbecue by the pool or overlooking the ocean.

Condos in Kailua-Kona (on or near Ali'i Drive) are the best value on the Big Island. We like Kona Pacific for its pool, barbecues, size of the units, and proximity to town, and Casa de Emdeko for its oceanfront pool and on-site convenience store. On the Kohala Coast, the Vista Waikoloa complex provides extra-large condos and is walking distance to a beautiful, sandy beach (A-Bay). Affordable food is available at restaurants in Kona, if you are looking for a family night out or, even better, for date night.

Ocean Activities

On the Beach: Most people like being in the water, but toddlers and school-age kids tend to be especially enamored of it. The swimming pool at your condo or hotel is always an option, but don't be afraid to hit the beach with a little one in tow. There are several beaches in Hawai'i that are nearly as safe as a pool—completely protected bays with pleasant white-sand beaches. As always, use your judgment, and heed all posted signs and lifeguard warnings.

Calm beaches to try include Kamakahonu Beach and Kahalu'u in Kailua-Kona; Spencer Beach Park, Kauna'oa (aka Mauna Kea Beach), and Hāpuna Beach in Kohala; and Onekahakaha Beach Park in Hilo.

On the Waves: Surf lessons are a great idea for the older kids. Beginner lessons are always on safe and easy waves and tend to last anywhere from two to four hours.

For school-age and older kids, book a four-hour surfing lesson with Ocean Eco Tours

and either join them out on the break or say aloha to a little parents-only time.

The Underwater World: If your kids are ready to try snorkeling, Hawai'i is a great place to introduce them to the underwater world. Even without the mask and snorkel, they'll be able to see colorful fish darting this way and that, and they may also spot turtles and dolphins at many of the island beaches.

Kahalu'u Beach in Kailua-Kona is a great introductory snorkel spot. You can see fish darting just below the surface even before you get into the water, and Hawaiian sea turtles often waddle up on to the rocks or swim around close to the shore.

On the southern tip of the island, Punalu'u provides opportunities to see the sea turtles up close. Though the water can be rough, the sea turtles nest here and there are nearly always one or two napping on the black-sand beach. At nighttime, head to the Sheraton Keauhou or Huggo's on the Rocks in Kailua-Kona to view manta rays; each spot shines a bright spotlight on the water to attract the rays. Anyone, but especially kids, could sit and watch them fly through the ocean in graceful circles for hours. No snorkel required!

Another great option is to book a snorkel cruise or opt to stay dry inside the Atlantis Submarine that operates out of Kailua-Kona. Kids love crawling down into a real-life submarine and viewing the ocean world through its little portholes.

Land Activities

In addition to beach experiences, Hawai'i has rain forests, botanical gardens, numerous aquariums, and even petting zoos and hands-on kids' museums that will keep your kids entertained and out of the sun for a day.

On the Big Island, Volcanoes National Park is a must on a family vacation. Even grumpy teenagers will acknowledge the coolness of lava tubes, steaming earth, and a fiery nighttime lava show.

On the Hilo side, the Pana'ewa Rainforest Zoo is small, but free, and lots of fun for the little ones, with a small petting zoo on Saturdays. Just a few miles north, on the Hāmākua Coast, the Hawai'i Tropical Botanical Garden is beautiful and fun to meander through, checking out huge lily pads and the noisy local frogs.

School-age and older kids will get a kick out of the ATV tours at Kahuā Ranch or the Parker Ranch in Waimea, and horseback rides through Waipi'o Valley with Na'alapa Stables.

After Dark

At nighttime, younger kids get a kick out of lū'au, and many of the shows incorporate young audience members, adding to the fun. The older kids might find it all a bit lame, but there are a handful of new shows in the islands that are more modern, incorporating acrobatics, lively music, and fire dancers. On the Big Island, teens and adults alike are sure to enjoy the music, lighting, acrobatics, fire eating, and overall theatrical quality of Island Breeze Productions' "Firenesia," the story of one man that unites the Hawaiian islands with fire, at the Sheraton Keauhou.

Stargazing from Mauna Kea is another treat. The visitor center has telescopes set up for all visitors to use. If you'd rather leave the planning to someone else, book a tour with Hawai'i Forest and Trail. Their guides are also unbelievably knowledgeable and great at sharing that knowledge in a narrative form that kids—and adults for that matter—enjoy.

TOP 10 HAWAIIAN FOODS TO TRY

Food in Hawai'i reflects the state's diverse cultural makeup and tropical location. Fresh seafood, organic fruits and vegetables, free-range poultry and meat, and locally grown products are the hallmarks of Hawai'i regional cuisine. Its preparations are drawn from across the Pacific Rim, including Japan, the Philippines, Korea, and Thailand—and now, "Hawaiian food" is a cuisine in its own right.

Saimin

The ultimate hangover cure and the perfect comfort food during Hawai'i's mild winters, *saimin* ranks at the top of the list of local favorites. In fact, it's one of the few dishes deemed truly local, having been highlighted in cookbooks since the 1930s. *Saimin* is an Asian-style noodle soup so ubiquitous, it's even on McDonald's menus statewide. In mom-and-pop shops, a large melamine bowl is filled with homemade *dashi* (Japanese soup stock) or chicken broth and wheat-flour noodles and then topped off with strips of omelet, green onions, bright pink fish cake, and *char siu* (Chinese roast pork) and/or canned luncheon meat, such as SPAM. Add *shoyu* (soy sauce) and chili pepper water, lift your chopsticks, and slurp away.

SPAM

Speaking of SPAM, Hawaii's most prevalent grab-and-go snack is SPAM *musubi*. Often displayed next to cash registers at groceries and convenience stores, the glorified rice ball is rectangular, topped with a slice of fried SPAM and wrapped in *nori* (seaweed). Introduced back in the plantation days by Japanese field workers, musubi is a minimeal in itself. But just like sushi, the rice part hardens when refrigerated. So it's best to gobble it up right after purchase.

Hormel Company's SPAM actually deserves its own recognition—way beyond a mere musubi topping. About five million cans are sold per year in Hawaii and the Aloha State even hosts a festival in its honor. One local claims she can stretch a can of SPAM into three separate meals for a family of five. The spiced luncheon meat gained popularity in World War II days, when fish was rationed. Gourmets and those with aversions to salt, high cholesterol, and high blood pressure may cringe at the thought of eating it, but SPAM is here to stay in Hawai'i.

Manapua

Another savory snack is *manapua*, fist-sized dough balls fashioned after Chinese *bao* (bun) and stuffed with fillings such as char siu pork and then steamed. Many mom-and-pop stores sell them in commercial steamer display cases along with pork hash and other dim sum. Modern-day fillings include curry chicken.

Fresh 'Ahi or Tako

There's nothing like fresh 'ahi or *tako* (octopus) *poke* to break the ice at a backyard party, except, of course, the cold beer handed to you from the cooler. The perfect pūpū, *poke* (pronounced poh-kay) is basically raw seafood cut into bite-size chunks and mixed with everything from green onions to roasted and ground kukui nuts. Other variations include round onion, sesame oil, seaweed, and chili pepper water. Shoyu is the constant. These days, grocery stores sell a rainbow of varieties such as kim chee crab and anything goes, from adding mayonnaise to tobiko caviar. Fish lovers who want to take it to the next level order sashimi, the best cuts of 'ahi sliced and dipped in a mixture of shoyu and wasabi.

Tropical Fruits

Tropical fruits such as apple banana and strawberry papaya are plucked from trees in island neighborhoods and eaten for breakfast—plain or with a squeeze of fresh lime. Locals also love to add their own creative touches to exotic fruits. Green mangoes are pickled with Chinese five-spice powder, and Maui Gold pineapples are topped with *li hing mui* (salty dried plum) powder (heck, even margarita glasses are rimmed with it!). Green papaya is tossed in a Vietnamese salad with fish paste and fresh prawns.

Plate Lunch

It would be remiss not to mention the plate lunch as one of the most beloved dishes in Hawai'i. It generally always includes two scoops of white steamed rice; a side of macaroni and/or macaroni-potato salad, heavy on the mayo; and perhaps *kimchee* or *koko* (salted cabbage). There are countless choices of main protein, such as chicken katsu, fried mahimahi, and beef tomato. The king of all plate lunches is the Hawaiian plate. The main item is *laulau* (pork, beef, and fish or chicken with taro leaves wrapped and steamed in ti leaves) or kalua pig and cabbage along with poi, lomilomi salmon, chicken long rice, and steamed white rice.

Bento Box

The bento box gained popularity back in the plantation days, when workers toiled in the sugarcane fields. No one brought sandwiches to work then. Instead it was a lunch box with the ever-present steamed white rice, pickled *ume* (plum) to preserve the rice, and main meats such as fried chicken or fish. In the Hawai'i of today, many stores sell prepackaged bentos, or you may go to an *okazuya* (Japanese tavern) with a hot buffet counter and create your own.

Malasadas

The Portuguese have contributed much to Hawaiian cuisine in the form of sausage, soup, and sweetbread. But their most revered food is *malasadas*, hot, deep-fried doughnuts rolled in sugar. Malasadas are crowd pleasers. Buy them by the dozen, hot from the wok and placed in brown bags to absorb the grease. Or bite into gourmet malasadas at restaurants, filled with vanilla or chocolate cream.

Shave Ice

Much more than just a snow cone, shave ice is what locals crave after a blazing day at the beach or a hot-as-hades game of soccer. If you're lucky, you'll find a neighborhood store that hand-shaves the ice, but it's rare. Either way, the counter person will ask you first if you'd like ice cream and/or adzuki beans scooped into the bottom of the cone or cup. Then they shape the ice into a giant mound and add colorful fruit syrups. First-timers should order the Rainbow, of course.

Crack Seed

There are dozens of varieties of crack seed in dwindling specialty shops and at drugstores. Chinese call the preserved fruits and nuts "see mui" but somehow the pidgin English version is what Hawaiians prefer. Those who like hard candy and salty foods will love li hing mangoes and rock salt plums, and those with an itchy throat will feel relief from the lemon strips. Peruse large glass jars of crack seed sold in bulk or smaller hanging bags—the latter make good gifts for friends back home.

BIG ISLAND'S BEST FARMERS' MARKETS

The Big Island is home to more farmers' markets than most cities, each offering a different range of goods, but all providing at the very least a good place to pick up fresh produce, jarred goods such as jams and salsa, as well as homemade local Hawaiian treats. Not surprisingly, locally grown mango, papaya, pineapple, passion fruit, coconut, and guava are available in abundance at great prices, but you can also find delicious avocados, organic peppers, fantastic goat cheese, and, of course, coffee.

Hawai'i's farmers are experimenting with dozens of varieties of exotic fruits such as poha berries, bilimbi, and mamey sapoy. Because of government restrictions, these fruits generally can't leave the island, so this is your only chance to sample them.

The markets located in Kailua-Kona and Hilo are listed under the corresponding shopping sections; the following markets are scattered about the Big Island. You might happily stumble upon them as you explore the coasts.

On the Kona Side

Hawaiian Homesteaders Association Farmers' Market. Check out the crafts sold here in the Kuhio Hale Building before you head to Waimea's more expensive stores. Produce, flowers, plants, and baked goods are also available. Open 7 am to noon every Saturday.

Ka'ū Farmers' Market. On a trip to the South Point, stock up on local produce and handmade baked goods at this market held at the Na'alehu Theater every Saturday, 8 am to noon.

Under the Banyans Farmers' Market. Fresh produce, seasonal fruit, plants, and craft items are sold at this market way up north in the village of Hāwī. It's open Saturdays from 7:30 am until 1 pm.

On the Hilo Side

Downtown Honok'a Farmers' Market. This good old-fashioned farmers' market in the midst of a charming old plantation town is a good stop during a drive up the Hāmākua Coast. It begins at 8 am on Saturdays.

The following markets are all south of Hilo:

Kea'au Village Farmers' Market. Fresh local farm produce featuring supersweet corn and flowers daily from 7 am to 5 pm; on Fridays, vendors also sell handmade Hawaiian arts and crafts.

Maku'u Farmers' Market. There's food and produce here, but what differentiates it from the rest are the Hawaiian crafts, plants, jewelry, shells, ethnic and recycled clothing, records/CDs, and books. It's along the Kea'au/Pāhoa Highway, Sundays 8 am to noon.

Pāhoa Village Farmers' Market. A great market, held in a large, covered outdoor space with local produce, prepared foods, coffee, clothing, and live music 9 am to 3 pm every Sunday.

Volcano Village Farmers' Market. A favorite on the east side of the island. Local produce, flowers, prepared foods, baked goods, and an occasional clothing swap, in the Cooper Center, every Sunday 8:30–11 am.

HAWAI'I AND THE ENVIRONMENT

Sustainability. It's a word rolling off everyone's tongues these days. In a place known as one of the most remote on Earth (check your globe), Hawai'i is relies heavily on the outside world for food and material goods—estimates put the percentage of food arriving on container ships as high as 90. Like many places, though, efforts are afoot to change that. And you can help.

Shop Local Farms and Markets

From Hilo to Hanalei, farmers' markets are cropping up, providing a place for growers to sell fresh fruits and vegetables. There is no reason to buy imported mangoes, papayas, avocadoes, and bananas at grocery stores, when the ones you'll find at farmers' markets are not only fresher and bigger but tastier, too. Some markets allow the sale of fresh-packaged foods—salsa, say, or smoothies—and the on-site preparation of food—like pork laulau or roasted corn on the cob—so you can make your run to the market a dining experience.

Not only is the locavore movement vibrantly alive at farmers' markets, but Hawai'i's top chefs are sourcing more of their produce—and fish, beef, chicken, and cheese—from local providers as well. You'll notice this movement on restaurant menus, featuring Ki'lauea greens or Hamakua tomatoes or locally caught mahimahi.

And while most people are familiar with Kona coffee farm tours on Big Island, if you're interested in the growing slow-food movement in Hawai'i, you'll be heartened to know many farmers are opening up their operations for tours—as well as sumptuous meals.

Support Hawai'i's Merchants

Food isn't the only sustainable effort in Hawai'i. Buying local goods like art and jewelry, Hawaiian heritage products, crafts, music, and apparel is another way to "green up" the local economy. The County of Kaua'i helps make it easy with their Kaua'i Made program (⊕ *www.kauaimade.net*), which showcases products made on Kaua'i, by Kaua'i people, using Kaua'i materials. The Maui Chamber of Commerce does something similar with its Made in Maui program (⊕ *www.madeinmaui.com*). Think of both as the Good Housekeeping Seal of Approval for locally made goods.

Then there the crafty entrepreneurs who are diverting items from the trash heap by repurposing garbage. Take Muumuu Heaven (⊕ *www.muumuuheaven.com*) on O'ahu. They got their start by reincarnating vintage aloha apparel into hip new fashions. Kini Beach (⊕ *www.Kinibeach.com*) collects discarded grass mats and plastic inflatables from Waikīkī hotels and uses them to make pricey bags and totes.

Choose Green Tour Operators

Conscious decisions when it comes to island activities go a long way to protecting Hawai'i's natural world. The Hawai'i Ecotourism Association (⊕ *www.hawaiiecotourism.org*) recognizes tour operators for, among other things, their environmental stewardship. The Hawai'i Tourism Authority (⊕ *www.hawaiitourismauthority.org*) recognizes outfitters for their cultural sensitivity. Winners of these awards are good choices when it comes to guided tours and activities.

ONLY IN HAWAI'I

Traveling to Hawai'i is as close as an American can get to visiting another country while staying within the United States. There's much to learn and understand about the state's indigenous culture, the hundred years of immigration that resulted in today's blended society, and the tradition of aloha that has welcomed millions of visitors over the years.

Aloha Shirt

To go to Hawai'i without taking an aloha shirt home is almost sacrilege. The first aloha shirts from the 1920s and 1930s were classic canvases of art and tailored for the tourists. Popular culture caught on in the 1950s, and they became a fashion craze. With the 1960s' more subdued designs, the Aloha Friday was born, and the shirt became appropriate clothing for work, play, and formal occasions. Because of its soaring popularity, cheaper and mass-produced versions became available.

Hawaiian Quilt

Although ancient Hawaiians were already known to produce fine *kapa* (bark) cloth, the actual art of quilting originated from the missionaries. Hawaiians have made the designs to reflect their own aesthetic, and bold patterns evolved over time. They can be pricey, but only because the quilts are intricately made by hand and can take years to finish. These masterpieces are considered precious heirlooms that reflect the history and beauty of Hawai'i.

Popular Souvenirs

Souvenir shopping can be intimidating. There's a sea of island-inspired and often kitschy merchandise, so we'd like to give you a breakdown of popular and fun gifts that you might encounter and consider bringing home.

Hula doll. The hula dancer has been immortalized and commodified in many ways, from the classic dashboard bobble hip to the newer hula girl desktop duster.

Grass skirts and coconut bras. Sometimes bought as a set and sometimes as separates, either way this costume will definitely elicit a smile or ten at a lū'au.

Home accessories. Relive your spa treatment at home with Hawaiian bath and body products, or deck out the kitchen in festive lū'au style with bottle openers, pineapple mugs, tiki glasses, shot glasses, slipper and surfboard magnets, and salt-and-pepper shakers.

Lei and shell necklaces. From silk or polyester flower lei to kukui or puka shell necklaces, lei have been traditionally used as a welcome offering to guests (although the artificial ones are more for fun, as real flowers are always preferable).

Lauhala products. Lauhala weaving is a traditional Hawaiian art. The leaves come from the Hala or Pandanus tree and handwoven to create lovely gift boxes, baskets, bags, and picture frames.

Vintage Hawai'i. You can find vintage photos, reproductions of vintage postcards or paintings, heirloom jewelry, and vintage aloha wear in many specialty stores.

Warrior helmets. Traditionally called *makaki'i* or *makini* after ancient Hawaiian warriors, these helmets are miniature masks adorned with feathers. They're popular among a younger crowd and hung on the car's rearview mirror or doorway for protection.

Lū'au

The lū'au's origin is traced back in 1819 when King Kamehameha II broke a great taboo and shared a feast with women and commoners. The name came from

a traditional dish of chicken wrapped in taro leaves and baked in coconut milk. In the olden days, lu'au were enjoyed sitting on the floor where woven lauhala mats were laid and covered with ti leaves and tropical flowers. Platters of *kalua pu'a* (pig baked in the *imu*, or underground oven), salted fish, sweet potatoes and *poi* (pounded taro and a staple in Hawaiian cuisine) were shared in the gathering.

Over time, the hula, fire knife dance and other Polynesian dances became part of the celebration. Today, the lu'au usually commemorates a child's first birthday or graduation. Offered in many elaborate presentations, it remains a Hawaiian experience that most visitors enjoy.

Nose flutes

The nose flute is an instrument used in ancient times to serenade a lover. For the Hawaiians, the nose is romantic, sacred and pure. The Hawaiian word for kiss is *honi*. Similar to an Eskimo's kiss, the noses touch on each side sharing one's spiritual energy or breath. The Hawaiian term, *'ohe hano ihu*, simply translated to "bamboo," with which the instrument is made; "breathe," because one has to gently breathe through it to make soothing music; and "nose," as it is made for the nose and not the mouth.

Slack Key Guitar and the Paniolos

Kiho'alu, or slack key music, evolved in the early 1800s when King Kamehameha III brought in Mexican and Spanish vaqueros to manage the overpopulated cattle that had run wild on the islands. The vaqueros brought their guitars and would play music around the campfire after work. When they left, supposedly leaving their guitars to their new friends, the Hawaiian *paniolos,* or cowboys, began to infuse what they learned from the vaqueros with their native music and chants, and so the art of slack key music was born.

Today, the paniolo culture thrives where ranchers have settled. Slack key music has also enjoyed international recognition and garnered Grammy Awards numerous times for the Hawaiian music genre.

'Ukulele

The 'ukulele or 'uke literally translates to the "the jumping flea" and came to Hawaii in the 1880s by way of the Portuguese and Spanish. Once a fading art form, today it brings international kudos as a solo instrument, thanks to tireless musicians and teachers who have worked hard to keep it by our fingertips.

One such teacher is Roy Sakuma. Founder of four 'ukulele schools and a legend in his own right, Sakuma and his wife Kathy produced O'ahu's first 'Ukulele Festival in 1971. Since then, they've brought the tradition to the Big Island, Kaua'i, and Maui. The free event annually draws thousands of artists and fans all over the globe.

Hula

"Hula is the language of the heart, therefore the heartbeat of the Hawaiian people."— Kalākaua I, the Merrie Monarch. Thousands—from tots to seniors—devote hours each week to hula classes. All these dancers need some place to show off their stuff. The result is a network of hula competitions (generally free or very inexpensive) and free performances in malls and other public spaces. Many resorts offer hula instruction or "hula-cise."

To watch hula, especially in the ancient style, is to understand that this was a sophisticated culture—skilled in many arts, including not only poetry, chant, and dance but also in constructing instruments and fashioning adornments.

TOP 5 BEST OUTDOOR ADVENTURES

Getting out for active adventure is one of the top reason people come to the Big Island.

There are endless options here for spending time outside enjoying the land, the ocean, or the highest points of mountains and volcanoes, but here are a few of our favorites.

Bike Kulani Trails

Stands of 80-foot eucalyptus. Giant tree ferns. The sweet song of honeycreepers overhead. Add single-track of rock and root—no dirt here—and we're talking technical. Did we mention this is a rainforest? That explains the perennial slick coat of slime on every possible surface. Advanced cyclists only.

Snorkel at Kealakekua Bay

Yes, the snorkeling here is tops for Big Island but, to be real, the draw here are the Hawaiian spinner dolphins that rest in the bay during the daytime.

While it's enticing to swim with wild dolphins, doing so can disrupt their sleep patterns and make them susceptible to prey—a.k.a. sharks—so stick to an early morning or late afternoon schedule and give the dolphins their space between 9 and 3.

Search for Lava at Volcanoes National Park

It's not too often that you can witness the creation of rock in action. That's just what happens at Volcanoes National Park. The most dramatic example occurs where lava enters the sea.

Mother Nature rarely gives her itinerary in advance, but if you're lucky, a hike or boat ride may pay off with spectacular views of nature's wonder. Sunrise and sunset makes for the best viewing opportunities.

Word of Mouth: "If you are talking about seeing lava flow into the ocean at Kalapana, then the best time to go is around sunset. If you are talking about seeing Volcanoes National Park and Halemaumau in Kilauea anytime is as good as the next." –wbpiii

Go Horseback Riding in Waipi'o Valley

The Valley of the Kings owes its relative isolation and off-the-grid status to the two-thousand-foot cliffs book-ending the valley. Really, the only way to explore this sacred place is on two legs—or four.

We're partial to the horseback rides that wend deep into the rainforest to a series of waterfalls and pools—the setting for a perfect romantic getaway.

Word of Mouth: "One can spend a few days just in Waipio Valley and not get bored." –fdecarlo

Wade Through Waterfalls on the Hilo Side

The east side of Big Island—also called the Hilo Side (as opposed to the western Kona Side)—is essentially a rainforest, with an average rainfall of 130 inches a year. It's no wonder Hilo is called the "City of Rainbows," and all that rain means tons of waterfalls. Some of our favorites to explore include Pe'epe'e Falls (Boiling Pots) and Rainbow Falls, both easy to access from main roads.

Word of Mouth: "We drove Banyan Drive and went to Coconut Island where you get a lovely view of Hilo. We also went to Rainbow Falls and Boiling Pots. It hadn't been raining very much so Boiling Pots wasn't very boiling, but Rainbow Falls was pretty still." –green33

DID YOU KNOW?

It's only a myth that the Big Island lacks beaches. There are plenty of perfect white sandy beaches on the Big Island; there's just also more island, so getting to the beaches can be slightly less convenient.

WEDDINGS AND HONEYMOONS

There's no question that Hawai'i is one of the country's foremost honeymoon destinations. Romance is in the air here, and the white, sandy beaches and turquoise water and swaying palm trees and balmy tropical breezes and perpetual summer sunshine put people in the mood for love. It's easy to understand why Hawai'i is fast becoming a popular wedding destination as well, especially as the cost of airfare has gone down, and new resorts and hotels entice visitors. A destination wedding is no longer exclusive to celebrities and the superrich. You can plan a traditional ceremony in a place of worship followed by a reception at an elegant resort, or you can go barefoot on the beach and celebrate at a lū'au. There are almost as many wedding planners in the islands as real estate agents, which makes it oh-so-easy to wed in paradise, and then, once the knot is tied, to stay and honeymoon as well.

The Big Day

Choosing the Perfect Place. When choosing a location, remember that you really have two choices to make: the ceremony location and where to have the reception, if you're having one. For the former, there are beaches, bluffs overlooking beaches, gardens, private residences, resort lawns, and, of course, places of worship. It really depends on you. As for the reception, there are these same choices, as well as restaurants and even lū'au. If you decide to go outdoors, remember the seasons— yes, Hawai'i has seasons. If you're planning a winter wedding outdoors, be sure you have a backup plan (such as a tent), in case it rains. Also, if you're planning an outdoor wedding at sunset—which is very popular—be sure you match the time of your ceremony to the time the sun sets at that time of year. If you choose indoors, be sure to ask for pictures of the environs

when you're planning. You don't want to plan a pink wedding, say, and wind up in a room that's predominantly red. Or maybe you do. The point is, it should be your choice.

Finding a Wedding Planner. If you're planning to invite more than a minister and your loved one to your wedding ceremony, seriously consider an on-island wedding planner who can help select a location, help design the floral scheme and recommend a florist as well as a photographer, help plan the menu and choose a restaurant, caterer, or resort, and suggest any Hawaiian traditions to incorporate into your ceremony. And more: Will you need tents, a cake, music? Maybe transportation and lodging? Many planners have relationships with vendors, providing packages—which mean savings.

If you're planning a resort wedding, most have on-site wedding coordinators; however, there are many independents around the island and even those who specialize in certain types of ceremonies—by locale, size, religious affiliation, and so on. A simple "Hawai'i weddings" Google search will reveal dozens. What's important is that you feel comfortable with your coordinator. Ask for references— and call them. Share your budget. Get a proposal—in writing. Ask how long they've been in business, how much they charge, how often you'll meet with them, and how they select vendors. Request a detailed list of the exact services they'll provide. If your idea of your wedding doesn't match their services, try someone else. If you can afford it, you might want to meet the planner in person.

Getting Your License. The good news about marrying in Hawai'i is no waiting period, no residency or citizenship requirements,

and no blood tests or shots are required. However, both the bride and groom must appear together in person before a marriage license agent to apply for a marriage license. You'll need proof of age—the legal age to marry is 18. (If you're 19 or older, a valid driver's license will suffice; if you're 18, a certified birth certificate is required.) Upon approval, a marriage license is immediately issued and costs $60, cash only. After the ceremony, your officiant will mail the marriage license to the state. Approximately 120 days later, you will receive a copy in the mail. (For $10 extra, you can expedite this process. Ask your marriage-license agent when you apply for your license.) For more detailed information, visit ⊕ *www.hawaii.gov* or call ☎ *808/274-3100*.

Also—this is important—the person performing your wedding must be licensed by the Hawai'i Department of Health, even if he or she is a licensed minister. Be sure to ask.

Wedding Attire. In Hawai'i, basically anything goes, from long, formal dresses with trains to white bikinis. Floral sundresses are fine, too. For the men, tuxedos are not the norm; a pair of solid-colored slacks with a nice aloha shirt is. In fact, tradition in Hawai'i for the groom is a plain white aloha shirt (they do exist) with slacks or long shorts and a colored sash around the waist. If you're planning a wedding on the beach, barefoot is the way to go.

If you decide to marry in a formal dress and tuxedo, you're better off making your selections on the mainland and hand-carrying them aboard the plane. Yes, it can be a pain, but ask your wedding-gown retailer to provide a special carrying bag. After all, you don't want to chance losing your wedding dress in a wayward piece of luggage. As for fittings, again, that's something to take care of before you arrive in Hawai'i.

Local customs. When it comes to traditional Hawaiian wedding customs, the most obvious is the lei exchange in which the bride and groom take turns placing a lei around the neck of the other—with a kiss. Bridal lei are usually floral, whereas the groom's is typically made of *maile*, a green leafy garland that drapes around the neck and is open at the ends. Brides often also wear a *haku* lei—a circular floral headpiece. Other Hawaiian customs include the blowing of the conch shell, hula, chanting, and Hawaiian music.

The Honeymoon

Do you want champagne and strawberries delivered to your room each morning? A maze of a swimming pool in which to float? A five-star restaurant in which to dine? Then a resort is the way to go. If, however, you prefer the comforts of a home, try a bed-and-breakfast. A bed-and-breakfast is also good if you're on a tight budget or don't plan to spend much time in your room. On the other hand, maybe you want your own private home in which to romp naked—or just laze around recovering from the wedding planning. Maybe you want your own kitchen in which to whip up a gourmet meal for your loved one. In that case, a private vacation-rental home is the answer. Or maybe a condominium resort. That's another beautiful thing about Hawai'i: The lodging accommodations are almost as plentiful as the beaches, and there's one to match your tastes and your budget.

CRUISING THE ISLANDS

Cruising has become extremely popular in Hawai'i. For first-time visitors, it's an excellent way to get a taste of all the islands; and if you fall in love with one or even two islands, you know how to plan your next trip. It's also a comparatively inexpensive way to see Hawai'i.

The limited amount of time in each port can be an argument against cruising—there's enough to do on any island to keep you busy for a week, so some folks feel shortchanged by cruise itineraries.

Cruising to Hawai'i

Carnival Cruises. They call them "fun ships" for a reason—Carnival is all about keeping you busy and showing you a good time, both onboard and onshore. Great for families, Carnival always plans plenty of kid-friendly activities, and their children's program rates high with the little critics. Carnival offers itineraries starting in Ensenada, Vancouver, and Honolulu. Their ships stop on Maui (Kahului and Lahaina), the Big Island (Kailua-Kona and Hilo), O'ahu, and Kaua'i. ☎ 888/227–6482 ⊕ www.carnival.com.

Holland America. The grande dame of cruise lines, Holland America has a reputation for service and elegance. Holland America's Hawai'i cruises leave and return to San Diego, California, with a brief stop at Ensenada. In Hawai'i, the ship ties up at port in Maui (Lahaina), the Big Island (Kailua-Kona and Hilo), O'ahu, and for half a day on Kaua'i. Holland America also offers longer itineraries (30-plus days) that include Hawai'i, Tahiti, and the Marquesas. ☎ 877/932–4259 ⊕ www.hollandamerica.com.

Princess Cruises. Princess strives to offer affordable luxury. Their prices start out a little higher, but you get more bells and whistles (more affordable balcony rooms, nice decor, more restaurants to choose from, personalized service). They're not fantastic for kids, but they do a great job of keeping teenagers occupied. Princess's Hawaiian cruise is 14 days, round-trip from Los Angeles, with a service call in Ensenada. The *Island Princess* stops in Maui (Lahaina), the Big Island (Hilo and Kailua-Kona), O'ahu, and Kaua'i. For the cruise-goer looking for the epic voyage, Princess Cruises offers a Sydney, Australia, to Los Angeles route, which includes stops in Hawai'i and Tahiti. ☎ 800/774–6237 ⊕ www.princess.com.

Cruising Within Hawai'i

Norwegian Cruise Lines. Norwegian is the only major operator to offer interisland cruises in Hawai'i. Several of their ships cruise the islands. The main one is *Pride of America* (Vintage Americana theme, very new, big family focus with lots of connecting staterooms and suites), which offers seven-day or longer itineraries within the Islands, stopping on Maui, O'ahu, the Big Island, and overnighting in Kaua'i. ☎ 800/327–7030 ⊕ www.ncl.com.

Hawai'i Nautical. Offering a completely different sort of experience, Hawai'i Nautical provides private multiple-day interisland cruises on their catamarans, yachts, and sailboats. Prices are higher, but service is completely personal, right down to the itinerary. ☎ 808/234–7245 ⊕ www.hawaiinautical.com.

Exploring the Big Island

WORD OF MOUTH

"The Big Island has LOTS of things to do! We were there for 10 days and I still didn't get to do all of the things I wanted to do! I liked the Big Island because it was not so commercialized as the other islands."

—ChristieP

Updated by
Bill Harby

Nicknamed "The Big Island," Hawaiʻi the island is a microcosm of Hawaiʻi the state. From long white-sand beaches and crystal clear bays to rain forests, waterfalls, lūʻau, exotic flowers, and birds, all things quintessentially Hawaiian are well represented here.

But an assortment of happy surprises also distinguishes the Big Island from the rest of Hawaiʻi—an active volcano (Kīlauea) oozing red lava and creating new earth every day, the clearest place in the world to view stars in the night sky (Mauna Kea), and some seriously good coffee, from the famous Kona district, of course, and also neighboring Kaʻū.

GEOLOGY

Home to 11 climate zones (missing only tundra), this is the land of fire (thanks to active Kīlauea Volcano) and ice (compliments of not-so-active Mauna Kea, topped with snow and expensive telescopes). At just under a million years old, Hawaiʻi is the youngest of the Hawaiian Islands. The east rift zone on Kīlauea has been spewing lava intermittently since January 3, 1983; an eruption began at Kīlauea's summit caldera in March, 2008, for the first time since 1982. Mauna Loa's explosions caused some changes back in 1984, and it could blow again any minute—or not for years. The third of the island's five volcanoes still considered active is Hualālai. It last erupted in 1801, and geologists say it will probably erupt again within 100 years. Mauna Kea is currently considered dormant, but may very well erupt again. Kohala, which last erupted some 120,000 years ago, is likely dead, but on volatile Hawaiʻi Island, one is never sure.

FLORA AND FAUNA

Sugar was the main agricultural and economic staple of all the Islands, but especially the Big Island. The drive along the Hāmākua Coast from Hilo illustrates recent agricultural developments on the island. Sugarcane stalks have been replaced by orchards of macadamia-nut trees, eucalyptus, and specialty crops (from lettuce to strawberries). Macadamia nuts on the Big Island supply 90% of the state's yield, and coffee continues to be big business, dominating the mountains above Kealakekua Bay. Orchids keep farmers from Honokʻa to Pāhoa afloat, and small organic farms produce meat, fruits, vegetables, and even goat cheese for high-end resort restaurants.

HISTORY

Though no longer home to the capital, the state's history is nonetheless rooted in that of its namesake island, Hawaiʻi. Kamehameha, the greatest king in Hawaiian history and the man credited with uniting the Islands, was born here, raised in Waipiʻo Valley, and died peacefully in Kailua-Kona. The other man who most affected the history of Hawaiʻi, Captain James Cook, spent the bulk of his time in the Hawaiian Islands here, docked in Kealakekua Bay (he landed first on Kauaʻi, but had little contact with the natives there). Thus it was here that Western influence was first felt, and from here that it spread to the rest of the Islands.

KAILUA-KONA

A fun and bustling seaside town, Kailua-Kona has the souvenir shops and open-air restaurants you'd expect in a major tourist hub, with the added bonus of a surprising number of historic sites. Except for the rare deluge, the sun shines year-round. Mornings offer cooler weather, smaller crowds, and more birds singing in the banyan trees; you'll see tourists and locals out running on Ali'i Drive, the town's main drag, by about 5 AM every day. Afternoons sometimes bring clouds and drizzly rain, but evenings are great for cool drinks, brilliant sunsets, and lazy hours spent gazing out over the ocean. Though there are better beaches north of the town on the Kohala Coast, Kailua-Kona is home to a few gems, including a fantastic snorkeling beach (Kahalu'u) and a tranquil bay perfect for kids (Kamakahonu Beach, in front of the King Kamehameha Hotel).

Scattered among the shops, restaurants, and condo complexes of Ali'i Drive are the replica of the homestead where King Kamehameha I spent his last days (he died here in 1819), the last royal palace in the U.S. (Hulihe'e Palace), and a battleground dotted with the graves of ancient Hawaiians who fought for their land and lost. It was also here in Kailua-Kona that Kamehameha's successor, King Liholiho, broke and officially abolished the ancient *kapu* (roughly translated as "forbidden," it was the name for the strict code of conduct islanders were compelled to follow) system by publicly sitting and eating with women. The following year, on April 4, 1820, the first Christian missionaries came ashore here, changing the islands forever. If you want to know more about the village's fascinating past, arrange for a 75-minute guided walking tour with the **Kona Historical Society** (✉ *81-6551 Māmalahoa Hwy. Kealakekua* 📞 *808/323–3222* ⊕ *www.konahistorical.org*).

GETTING HERE AND AROUND

Half a day is plenty of time to explore Kailua-Kona; most of the town's sights are located in or near the downtown area. Still, if you add in a beach trip (Kahalu'u Beach has some of the best and easiest snorkeling on the island), it's easy to while away the bulk of a day. Another option for making a day of it is to tack on a short trip to the charming artists' village of Hōlualoa or to the coffee farms in the mountains just above Kealakekua Bay. There are a few great restaurants here that are far more affordable than those on the Kohala Coast and in Waimea. The town closest to the Kona International Airport (it's about 7 mi away), Kailua-Kona is a convenient home base from which to explore the island.

The easiest place to park your car is at King Kamehameha's Kona Beach Hotel ($15 per day). Some free parking is also available: When you enter Kailua via Palani Road (Hwy. 190), turn left onto Kuakini Highway, drive for a half block, and turn right into the small marked parking lot. Walk *makai* (toward the ocean) on Likana Lane a half block to Ali'i Drive, and you'll be in the heart of Kailua-Kona.

EXPLORING

TOP ATTRACTIONS

Hōlualoa. Hugging the hillside above Kealakekua Bay, the tiny village of Hōlualoa is just up winding Hualālai Road from Kailua-Kona. A charming surprise, it's the kind of place where locals sit on their porches or in front of the stores and "talk story" (pidgin for "shoot the breeze") all day long. It's comprised almost entirely of galleries in which all types of artists, from woodworkers to jewelry makers and more traditional painters, work in their studios in back and sell the finished product up front. Formerly the exclusive domain of coffee plantations, it still has quite a few coffee farms offering free tours and cups of joe.

QUICK BITES

Duck into the cleverly named **Hōluakoa Cafe** (⊠ *76-5900 Mamalahoa Hwy.* ☎ *808/322-2233*) —it refers to the holua (traditional Hawaiian grass sled) made of native koa wood—and grab a cup to sip while you stroll through town. Grab a tasty croissant sandwich and locally made ice cream in tropical flavors, and knock back some of Kona's best coffee at **Kope Lani Coffee** (⊠ *75-5719 Ali'i Dr.* ☎ *808/329-6152*), directly across from the Kona Village Shopping Center. If it's late afternoon, it's time to unwind with one of those umbrella drinks. For cocktails, head to the **Kona Inn Restaurant** (⊠ *75-5744 Ali'i Dr. #135* ☎ *808/329-4455*), a local favorite.

④ Hulihe'e Palace. A lovely rambling old stone home surrounded by jewel-green grass and sweeping ocean views and fronted by an elaborate wrought-iron gate, Hulihe'e Palace is one of only three royal palaces in America (the other two are in Honolulu on O'ahu). The two-story residence was built by Governor John Adams Kuakini in 1838, a year after he completed Moku'aikaua Church. During the 1880s it served as King David Kalākaua's summer palace. It's constructed of local materials, including lava, coral, koa wood, and 'ōhi'a timber. The oversize doors and furniture bear witness to the size of some of the Hawaiian people. On weekday afternoons hula schools rehearse on the grounds. Though severely damaged by the 2006 earthquakes, Hulihe'e Palace underwent a $1.5 million renovation and reopened in September 2009, and now has an expanded gift shop. The palace is operated by the Daughters of Hawai'i, a nonprofit organization focused on maintaining the heritage of the Islands, and its entrance fees, together with donations, are helping to repair the damage. ⊠ *75-5718 Ali'i Dr.* ☎ *808/329–1877* ⊕ *www.daughtersofhawaii.org* ⊠ *$6 for adults, $4 for seniors, $1 for children under 18.* ⊗ *Wed.–Sat. 10–3.*

③ Kailua Pier. Though most fishing boats use Honokōhau Harbor, this pier dating from 1918 is still a hub of ocean activity. Outrigger canoe teams practice and boats shuttle cruise ship passengers to and from Kailua-Kona here, and tour boats depart from these docks most days. Along the seawall children and old-timers cast their lines daily, careful not to hook the pair of sea turtles nesting nearby. For youngsters, a bamboo pole and hook are easy to come by, and plenty of locals are willing to give pointers. Each October close to 1,500 international athletes swim 2.4 mi from the pier to begin the internationally famous Ironman World Championship triathlon competition. ⊠ *Next to King Kamehameha's*

The Big Island of Hawai'i

KOHALA AND WAIMEA

MAUNA KEA AND THE HĀMĀKUA COAST

TO MAU'I

HĀMĀKUA COAST

'UPOLU PT.

'Upolu Airport
Kapa'a Beach Park
Māhukona Beach Park
Hāwī
Kapa'au
Pololū Valley
Pololū Beach

Kohala Forest Reserve

NORTH KOHALA

KOHALA MOUNTAINS

Lapakahi State Historical Park

Māhukona

250

Akoni Pule Hwy.

270

Kawaihae

Pu'ukoholā Heiau National Historic Site, Mailekini Heiau
Spencer Beach Park
Kauna'oa Beach
Hāpuna Beach State Park

Waioka

Kohala Mountain Rd.

Kawaihae Rd.

Waimea (Kamuela)

Waikoloa

Kamuela Airport

SOUTH KOHALA

19

Puakō

'Anaeho'omalu

'Anaeho'omalu Bay

KOHALA COAST

Kīholo Bay

Kekaha Kai State Park

Kona International Airport

Kaloko-Honokōhau National Historical Park

KAILUA-KONA

Kailua Bay

Honokōhau

White Sands Beach Park

Kahalu'u

NORTH KONA

190

Pu'uanahulu

Kalaoa

Hu'ehu'e Ranch

Mount Hualalai 8,271 ft

Mamalahoa Hwy.

Queen Ka'ahumanu Hwy.

Hōlualoa

11

Keauhou

Kealakekua

Hawai'i Belt Rd.

Waiki'i

Saddle Rd.

200

Mauna Kea 13,796 ft

HĀMĀKUA

Hilo Forest Reserve

Waipi'o Valley

WAIPI'O VALLEY OVERLOOK

240

Honoka'a

19

[Māmalahoa Hwy.]

Kalōpā State Rec. Area

Pa'auilo

Kukui'au

O'ōkala

Laupāhoehoe

Pāpa'aloa

Weloka

Ninole

Honohina

Hakalau

Akaka Falls State Park

Honomū

Wailea

Kolekole Beach Park

Kawainui

Wainaku

NORTH HILO

Hawi Belt Rd.

19

Pāpa'ikou

Hilo

Hilo Bay

Reeds Bay Beach Park

LELEIWI POINT

Onekahakaha Beach Park

Hilo International Airport (General Lyman Field)

HILO

SOUTH HILO

Kukuio

Kea'au

130

Kurtistown

Mountain View

11

Kūlani Honor Camp

Ōla'a

Saddle Rd.

200

Mauna Loa Observatory

Stainback Hwy.

Cape Kumukahi

Amalahau

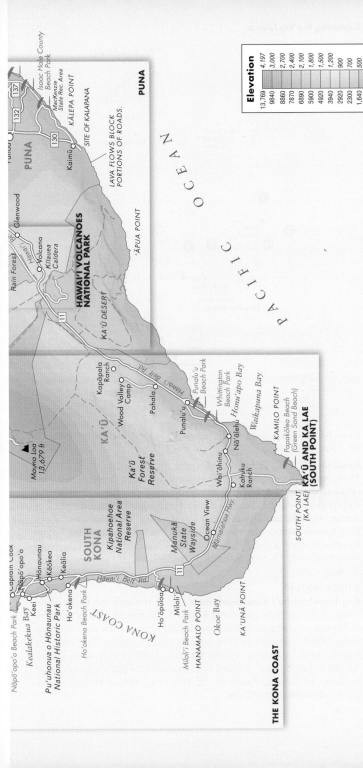

THE KONA COAST

PUNA

PUNA

Isaac Hale County
Beach Park
MacKenzie
State Rec. Area
KĀLEPA POINT

Kaimū

SITE OF KALAPANA

LAVA FLOWS BLOCK
PORTIONS OF ROADS.

132

130

Glenwood

HAWAI'I VOLCANOES
NATIONAL PARK

Rain Forest

Volcano

Kīlauea
Caldera

'APUA POINT

111

KA'Ū DESERT

PACIFIC OCEAN

Mauna Loa
13,679 ft

Kapāpala
Ranch

Wood Valley
Camp

Pahala

Hawai'i Belt Rd.

Punalu'u

Punalu'u
Beach Park

SOUTH KONA

Kīpahoehoe
National Area
Reserve

Ka'ū Forest
Reserve

KA'Ū

Whittington
Beach Park

Honu'apo Bay

Waikapuna Bay

KAMILO POINT

Manukā
State Wayside

Ocean View

Nā'ālehu

Mamalahoa Hwy.

Wai'ōhinu

Kahuku
Ranch

Papakōlea Beach
(Green Sand Beach)

KA'Ū AND KA LAE
(SOUTH POINT)

111

Hawai'i Belt Rd.

Ho'ōpūloa

Miloli'i

Miloli'i Beach Park

HANAMALO POINT

Okoe Bay

KA'UNA POINT

SOUTH POINT
(KA LAE)

KONA COAST

Nāpō'opo'o Beach Park

Keei

Captain Cook

Nāpō'opo'o

Hōnaunau

Kēōkea

Keālia

Kealakekua Bay

Pu'uhonua o Hōnaunau
National Historic Park

Ho'okena

Ho'okena Beach Park

Elevation

feet	meters
13,769	4,197
9840	3,000
8860	2,700
7870	2,400
6890	2,100
5900	1,800
4920	1,500
3940	1,200
2920	900
2300	700
1,640	500
980	300
330	100

0   10 mi

0   10 km

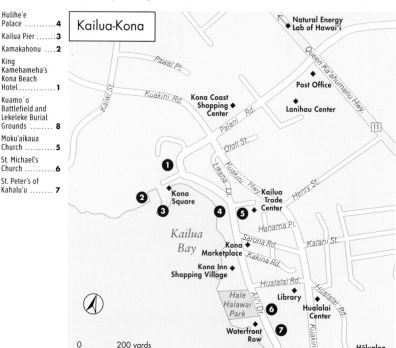

Kona Beach Hotel; seawall is between Kailua Pier and Hulihe'e Palace on Ali'i Dr. ⌖ *$4.*

② **Kamakahonu.** King Kamehameha spent his last years, from 1812 to
★ 1819, near what is now King Kamehameha's Kona Beach Hotel. Part
of what was once a 4-acre homestead complete with several houses
and religious sites has been swallowed by Kailua Pier, but a replica of
the temple, **Ahu'ena Heiau,** keeps history alive. Free tours start from
King Kamehameha's Kona Beach Hotel. Small but pleasant King Kamehameha Beach is a great place to lie in the sun and take an easy swim
after the tour. ✉ *75-5660 Palani Rd.* ☎ *808/329–2911* ⌖ *Free* ☉ *Tours
weekdays at 1:30.*

WORTH NOTING

① **King Kamehameha's Kona Beach Hotel.** Stroll through the high-ceiling
lobby of this recently renovated Kailua-Kona fixture to view displays
of Hawaiian artifacts and mounted marlin from Hawaiian International Billfish tournaments (from when Kailua Pier was still the weigh-in
point). These "granders," marlin weighing 1,000 pounds or more, are
the big attraction here. Classes in Hawaiian arts and crafts are given
regularly. ✉ *75-5660 Palani Rd.* ☎ *808/329–2911 or 800/367–2111*
⊕ *www.konabeachhotel.com.*

8 Kuamo'o Battlefield and Lekeleke Burial Grounds. In 1819 an estimated 300 Hawaiians were killed on this vast, black-lava field, and you can still see their burial mounds there today. After the death of his father, King Kamehameha, King Liholiho was crowned king; shortly thereafter he ate at the table of women, thereby breaking the ancient *kapu* (taboo) system. Chief Kekuaokalani, who held radically different views about religious traditions, unsuccessfully challenged King Liholiho in battle here. ⊠ *South end of Ali'i Dr.*

WORD OF MOUTH

"You need to understand that the Big Island is very laid-back. There are golf courses and a couple of movie theaters. The old town of Kona is pretty funky and simple. It's right on the water and has many open-air restaurants. But nothing super fancy."

—JPJH

5 ★ Moku'aikaua Church. A thatch hut, erected on this site by missionaries in 1820, served as the first Christian church on the Islands. A more permanent structure was built in 1836 with black stone from an abandoned *heiau*. The stone was mortared with white coral and topped by an impressive steeple. Inside, behind a panel of gleaming koa wood, is a model of the brig *Thaddeus*. ⊠ *75-5713 Ali'i Dr.* ☎ *808/329–0655.*

6 St. Michael's Church. The site of Kona's first Catholic church, built in 1840, is marked by a small thatch structure to the left of the present church, which dates from 1850. In front of the church a coral grotto shrine holds 2,500 coral heads, harvested in 1940, when preservation was not yet an issue. ⊠ *75-5769 Ali'i Dr.* ☎ *808/326–7771.*

QUICK BITES

The laid-back **Island Lava Java** (⊠ *75-5799 Ali'i Dr.* ☎ *808/327–2161,* ⊕ *www.islandlavajavakona.com*), in the Ali'i Sunset Plaza, has great coffee, breakfast sandwiches, bagels, and the best and biggest cinnamon rolls on the island. In the afternoon and evening, stop by for fresh fish or *kālua* pig tacos, sandwiches, fruit smoothies, and ice cream. The large outdoor seating area has a bird's-eye view of the ocean. Locals hang out here to read the paper, play board games, or just watch the surf.

7 St. Peter's of Kahalu'u. The definition of "quaint" with its crisp white and blue trim, this tiny old-fashioned steeple church sits on the rocks overlooking the ocean near Kahalu'u Beach. It has appeared on many a Kailua-Kona postcard, and its charm and views bring hundreds of visitors every year. ⊠ *Ali'i Dr., north of mile marker 5.*

THE KONA COAST

South of Kailua-Kona, Highway 11 hugs splendid coastlines, leaving busy streets behind. A detour along the winding narrow roads in the mountains above takes you straight to the heart of coffee country where lush plantations and jaw-dropping views offer a taste of what Hawai'i was like before the resorts took over. Tour one of the coffee farms to find out what the big deal is about Kona coffee, and snag a free sample while you're at it.

A half-hour on the highway from Kailua-Kona will lead you to beautiful Kealakekua Bay, where Captain James Cook arrived in 1778, changing the Islands forever. Hawaiian spinner dolphins frolic in the bay, now a marine preserve nestled alongside high green cliffs more reminiscent of popular images of Ireland than posters of Hawai'i. Snorkeling is superb here, as it is a protected marine reserve, so you may want to bring your gear and spend an hour or so exploring the coral reefs. This is also a nice kayaking spot; the bay is normally extremely calm. ■TIP→ One of our favorite ways to spend a morning is to throw some snorkel gear in a kayak, paddle across the bay, go for a swim and a snorkel, and paddle back, dodging dolphins along the way.

SOUTH KONA AND KEALAKEKUA BAY

The winding road above Kealakekua Bay is home to a quaint little painted church, as well as several reasonably priced bed-and-breakfasts with great views. The communities surrounding the bay (Kainaliu and Captain Cook) are brimming with local and transplanted artists, making them great places to stop for a meal, some unique gifts, or an afternoon stroll.

After a morning of swimming and kayaking, grab your morning coffee for free on a coffee farm tour, then head to one of the great cafés in nearby Kainaliu to refuel (we like the Aloha Angel Cafe in the Aloha Theater for breakfast, and Cafe Nasturtium for lunch).

GETTING HERE AND AROUND

Between the coffee plantations, artsy towns, and Kealakekua Bay, South Kona has plenty of activities to keep you occupied for a day. Bring a swimsuit and snorkel gear, and hit Kealakekua Bay first thing in the morning. You'll have a better chance of a dolphin sighting, and you'll beat the large snorkel cruise groups. Follow the signs off Highway 11 to the bay, then park at Nāpō'opo'o Beach (not much of a beach, but it provides easy access into the water).

EXPLORING

TOP ATTRACTIONS

Captain Cook Monument. No one knows for sure exactly what happened on February 14, 1779, when English explorer Captain James Cook was killed on this spot. He had chosen Kealakekua Bay as a landing place in November 1778. Cook, arriving during the celebration of Makahiki, the harvest season, was welcomed at first. Some Hawaiians saw him as an incarnation of the god Lono.

Cook's party sailed away in February 1779, but a freak storm off the Kona Coast forced his damaged ship back to Kealakekua Bay. Believing that no god could be thwarted by a mere rainstorm, the Hawaiians were not so welcoming this time, and various confrontations arose between them and Cook's sailors. The theft of a longboat brought Cook and an armed party ashore to reclaim it. One thing led to another: shots were fired, daggers and spears were thrown, and Captain Cook fell, mortally wounded.

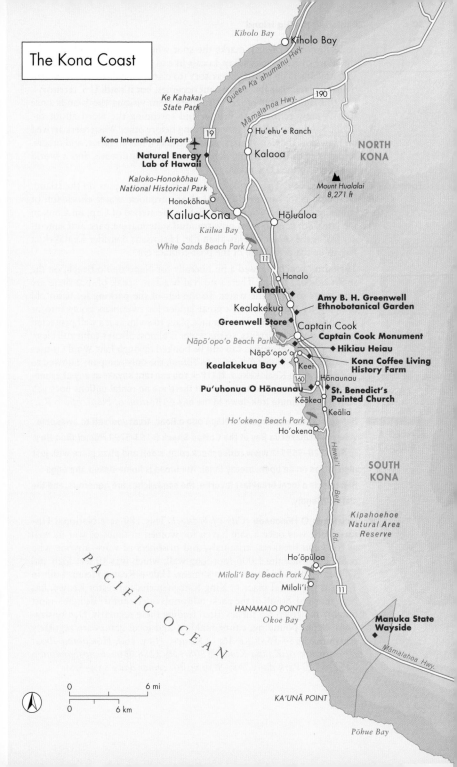

The Kona Coast

Kīholo Bay

Kīholo Bay

Queen Ka'ahumanu Hwy.

190

Māmalahoa Hwy.

Ke Kahakai
State Park

Hu'ehu'e Ranch

NORTH
KONA

Kona International Airport
19

Natural Energy
Lab of Hawaii

Kalaoa

Mount Hualalai
8,271 ft

Kaloko-Honokōhau
National Historical Park

Honokōhau

Kailua-Kona

Hōlualoa

Kailua Bay

White Sands Beach Park

11

Honalo

Kainaliu

Amy B. H. Greenwell
Ethnobotanical Garden

Kealakekua

Greenwell Store

Captain Cook

Captain Cook Monument

Nāpō'opo'o Beach Park

Hikiau Heiau

Nāpō'opo'o

Kona Coffee Living
History Farm

Kealakekua Bay

Keei

Hōnaunau

Pu'uhonua O Hōnaunau

160

St. Benedict's
Painted Church

Keōkea

Keālia

Ho'okena Beach Park

Ho'okena

SOUTH
KONA

Hawai'i

Kipahoehoe
Natural Area
Reserve

Belt

Ho'ōpūloa

Miloli'i Bay Beach Park

Rd.

Miloli'i

11

HANAMALO POINT
Okoe Bay

Manuka State
Wayside

Māmalahoa Hwy.

PACIFIC OCEAN

0   6 mi

0   6 km

KA'UNĀ POINT

Pōhue Bay

A 27-foot-high obelisk marks the spot where Captain Cook died on the shore of Kealakekua Bay. Locals like to point out that the land the monument sits on is British territory (to clarify: the British government owns the land that the monument occupies, but it's still U.S. territory). But this didn't deter other Westerners from visiting the Islands once Cook's crew returned to Britain and spreading the word about the idyllic Sandwich Islands. It wasn't long before other Westerners arrived on Hawai'i's shores: whalers, sailors, traders, missionaries, and others, bringing with them crime, debauchery, alcohol, disease, and a world unknown to the Hawaiians.

Fodor's Choice ★ **Kealakekua Bay.** This is one of the most beautiful spots on the island. Dramatic cliffs surround crystal clear, turquoise water chock-full of stunning coral and tropical fish. Before the arrival of Captain Cook in the late 18th century, this now tranquil state marine park and sanctuary lay at the center of Hawaiian life. Historians consider Kealakekua Bay to be the birthplace of the post-contact era.

The term "beach" is used a bit liberally for **Nāpō'opo'o Beach,** on the south side of the bay. There's no real beach to speak of, but there are easy ways to enter the water. To the left of the parking lot is an old cement pier that serves as a great ladder for swimmers going into or coming out of the bay. This is a nice place to swim as it's well protected from weather or currents, so the water is almost always calm and clear. Excellent snorkel cruises can still be booked through Fair Wind Cruises (*see Chapter 4, Water Activities & Tours*), the only company allowed to drop anchor in Kealakekua. ■TIP→ You can rent kayaks at any of a number of stands along the highway, but there are no rental options once you start the 10-minute trek down to the bay. ⊠ *Bottom of Nāpō'opo'o Rd.*

NEED A BREAK?

Before or after winding down Nāpō'opo'o Road, treat yourself to awesome views of Kealakekua Bay at the **Coffee Shack** (⊠ *83-5799 Māmalahoa Hwy.* ☎ *808/328–9555* ⊕ *www.coffeeshack.com*), a deli and pizza place with just nine tables on an open, breezy lānai. The bread is home-baked, the eggs Benedict is a local breakfast favorite, the sandwiches are generous, and the staff is friendly.

★ **Pu'uhonua O Hōnaunau** (*City of Refuge*). This 180-acre National Historic Park was once a safe haven for women in times of war as well as for *kapu* breakers, criminals, and prisoners of war—anyone who could get inside the 1,000-foot-long wall, which was 10 feet high and 17 feet thick, could avoid punishment. **Hale-o-Keawe Heiau,** built in 1650 as the burial place of King Kamehameha's ancestor Keawe, has been restored. South of the park, tide pools offer another delight—most notably the green sea turtles often feeding there regularly. Demonstrations of poi pounding, canoe making, and local games are regularly scheduled. ⊠ *84-5559 Ke Ala O Keawe, Hwy. 160, Hōnaunau about 20 mi south of Kailua-Kona* ☎ *808/328–2288* ⊕ *www.nps.gov/puho* ⊠ *$3–$5* ☉ *Park daily 7*AM*–8*PM; *visitor center daily 8*AM*–5*PM.

Kealakekua Bay is one of the most beautiful spots on the Big Island.

WORTH NOTING

Amy B. H. Greenwell Ethnobotanical Garden. Easy to drive by on the twisting two-lane highway, this garden offers a wealth of Hawaiian ethnobotanical traditions. On 12 acres grow 250 types of plants that were typical in an early Hawaiian *ahupua'a*, the usually pie-shaped land divisions that ran from the mountains to the sea. Call to find out about guided tours or drop in between 8:30 AM and 5 PM. ⊠ *82-6188 Māalahoa Hwy., Captain Cook* ☎ *808/323–3318* ⊕ *www.bishopmuseum.org/greenwell.*

Greenwell Store. Established in 1850, the homestead of Henry N. Greenwell served as cattle ranch, sheep station, store, post office, and family home all in one. Now, all that remains is the 1875 stone structure, which is listed on the National Register of Historic Places. It houses a fascinating museum that has exhibits on ranching and coffee farming. It's also headquarters for the **Kona Historical Society,** which organizes walking tours of Kailua-Kona. ⊠ *81-6551 Māmalahoa Hwy.Kealakekua* ☎ *808/323–3222* ⊕ *www.konahistorical.org* ⊠ *$7* ☺ *Mon.–Thurs. 9–3.*

Hikiau Heiau. This stone platform was once an impressive temple dedicated to the god Lono. When Captain Cook arrived in 1778, ceremonies in his honor were held here. ⊠ *Bottom of Nāpō'opo'o Rd.*

Kainaliu. Like many of the Big Island's old plantation towns, Kainaliu is experiencing a bit of a renaissance. In addition to a ribbon of funky old stores, many of them traditional Japanese family-operated shops, a handful of new galleries and shops have sprung up in the last few years. Browse around Oshima's, established in 1926, and Kimura's, established in 1927, to find authentic Japanese goods beyond tourist trinkets,

CLOSE UP

Kona Coffee

From the cafés, stores, and restaurants selling Kona coffee, to the farm tours, to the annual Kona Coffee Cultural Festival, coffee is a major part of life on this side of the Big Island. More than 600 farms, most from just three to seven acres in size, grow the delicious—and luxurious, at generally more than $25 per pound—beans. Only coffee from the North and South Kona Districts can be called Kona.

Hawai'i is the only U.S. producer of commercially grown coffee, and it has been growing in Kona since 1828, when Reverend Samuel Ruggles, an American missionary, brought a cutting over from the O'ahu farm of Chief Boki, O'ahu's governor. That coffee plant was a strain of Ethiopian coffee called coffee Arabica, and it is the same coffee still produced today, although a Guatemalan strain of Arabica introduced in the late 1800s is produced in far higher quantities.

In the early 1900s, the large Hawaiian coffee plantations subdivided their lots and began leasing parcels to local tenant farmers, a practice that continues today. Many tenant farmers were Japanese families. In the 1930s, local schools switched summer vacation to "coffee vacation" from August to November so that the kids could help with the coffee harvest, a practice that held until 1969.

Coffee is harvested as "cherries"—the beans are encased in a hard red shell. Kona beans are hand-picked several times each season to guarantee the best product. The cherries are shelled and the beans roasted to a dark brown.

KONA'S COFFEE FESTIVAL

The fun annual **Kona Coffee Cultural Festival** (⊕ www.konacoffeefest. com) runs for 10 days in November and includes parades and concerts, special tours, an art stroll and coffee tasting in Hōlualoa, and the Gevalia Kona Cupping Competition (a judged tasting).

COFFEE-FARM TOURS

Several coffee farms around the Kona coffee-belt area welcome visitors to watch all or part of the coffee process, from harvest to packaging. Some tours are self-guided, and most are free, with the exception of the Kona Coffee Living History Farm.

Greenwell Farms. ⊠ 81-6581 Māmalahoa Hwy., Kealakekua ☎ 808/323–2295 ⊕ www. greenwellfarms.com.

Hōlualoa-Kona Coffee Company. ⊠ 77-6261 Old Māmalahoa Hwy., Hwy. 180, Hōlualoa ☎ 808/322–9937 or 800/334–0348 ⊕ www.konalea.com.

Hula Daddy. ⊠ 74-4944 Māmalahoa Hwy. Hōlualoa ☎ 808/327–9744 or 888/553–2339 ⊕ www.huladaddy. com.

Kona Coffee Living History Farm (D. Uchida Farm). ⊠ 82-6199 Old Māmalahoa Hwy. Captain Cook ☎ 808/323–3222 ⊕ www. konahistorical.org/tours-farm.html.

Royal Kona Coffee Museum & Coffee Mill. ⊠ 83-5427 Māmalahoa Hwy., next to tree house in Hōnaunau ☎ 808/328–2511 ⊕ www. hawaiicoffeeco.com.

Mountain Thunder. ⊠ 79-7469 Hawai'i Belt Rd., Kainaliu ☎ 888/414–5662 ⊕ www.mountainthunder.com

DID YOU KNOW?

Coffee beans are actually the seeds of these cherry-like plants, appropriately named coffee cherries. Be sure to sample some Kona brew while you're in the area.

DID YOU KNOW?

Kealakekua Bay is generally considered the best snorkeling spot on the Big Island, with stunning coral reefs—especially around the Captain Cook Monument—calm waters, and spinner dolphins.

then pop into one of the local cafés for a tasty vegetarian snack. Cross the street to peek into the 1932 Aloha Theatre, where community-theater actors might be practicing a Broadway revue. ⊠ *Hwy. 11, mile markers 112–114.*

Kona Coffee Living History Farm. Known as the D. Uchida Farm, this site is on the National Register of Historic Places. Completely restored by the Kona Historical Society, it includes a 1913 farmhouse surrounded by coffee trees, a Japanese bathhouse, *kuriba* (coffee-processing mill), and *hoshidana* (traditional drying plat-form). Farm tours take place Monday to Thursday from 9 until 2. ⊠ $20. ⊠ *82-6199 Māmalahoa Hwy., Kealakekua* ☎ *808/323–2006* ⊕ *www.konahistorical.org.*

> **FUN THINGS TO DO AROUND KONA**
>
> ■ Hit the beach. Live out your Blue Hawai'i fantasy at Hāpuna or 'Anaeho'omalu (A-Bay).
>
> ■ Tour a coffee farm and taste the best Kona coffee.
>
> ■ Go for a morning snorkel in the clear waters of Kealakekua Bay, then explore ancient Hawaiian culture at the adjacent City of Refuge.
>
> ■ See the artsy side of the Island in Hāwī, Hōlualoa, or Kainaliu.

St. Benedict's Painted Church. The walls, columns, and ceiling of this Roman Catholic church depict colorful biblical scenes through the paintbrush of Belgian-born priest Father Velghe. Mass is still held every weekend. The view of Kealakekua Bay from the entrance is amazing. ⊠ *Painted Church Rd. off Hwy. 160, Hōnaunau* ☎ *808/328–2227.*

NORTH KONA

North of Kona International Airport, along Highway 19, brightly colored bougainvillea stand out in relief against miles of black-lava fields stretching from the mountain to the sea. Most of the lava flows are from the last eruptions of Mt. Hualālai, in 1800 and 1801. You will no doubt notice the miles of white-coral graffiti in the fields. This has been going on for decades, and locals still get a kick out of it, as do tourists. The first thing everyone asks is "where do the white rocks come from?" and the answer is this: they're bits of coral and they come from the ocean. If you want to write a message in the lava, you've got to use the coral that's already out there. This means that no one's message lasts for long, but that's all part of the fun. Some local couples even have a tradition of writing their names in the same spot on the lava fields every year on their anniversary.

GETTING HERE AND AROUND

Head north from Kona International Airport and follow Highway 19 along the coast. Take caution driving at night between the airport and where resorts begin on the Kohala Coast; it's extremely dark and there are few road signs and traffic lights.

EXPLORING

Natural Energy Lab of Hawai'i. Driving south from the Kona International Airport towards Kailua-Kona you'll spot a large mysterious group of buildings with an equally large and mysterious photovoltaic (solar) panel installation just inside its gate. Although it looks like some sort of top-secret military station, this is the site of the Natural

Energy Lab of Hawai'i, NELHA for short, where scientists, researchers, and entrepreneurs are developing and marketing everything from new uses for solar power to energy-efficient air-conditioning systems and environmentally friendly aquaculture techniques. Visitors are welcome at the lab, and there are 1½-hr tours for those interested in learning more about the experiments being conducted. ⊠ 73-4460 Queen Ka'ahumanu Hwy., #101 ☎ 808/329–8073 ⊕ www.nelha.org ✎ Free ☉ Tours Mon.–Thurs. at 10.

THE KOHALA COAST AND WAIMEA

The resorts on the Kohala Coast lay claim to some of the island's finest restaurants and its only destination spas. But the real attraction here is the island's best beaches. On a clear day, you can see Maui from them, and during the winter months, glistening humpback whales cleave the waters just offshore.

Rounding the northern tip of the island, the arid coast shifts rather suddenly to green villages and hillsides, leading to lush Pololū Valley in North Kohala, and the hot sunshine along the coast gives way to cooler temperatures. As you drive north into the mountains, you'll find the quaint towns of Hāwī and Kapa'au.

Just up the hill from Kohala, past Saddle Road (the route to Mauna Kea), Waimea offers a completely different experience from the rest of the island. Rolling green hills, large open pastures, cool evening breezes and morning mists, cattle everywhere, and regular rodeos are just a few of the surprises you'll stumble upon here in *paniolo* (Hawaiian for "cowboy") country.

THE KOHALA COAST

Fodor's Choice ★ If you had only a weekend to spend on the Big Island, this is probably where you'd want to go. The Kohala Coast is a mix of the island's best beaches and swankiest hotels just minutes from ancient valleys and temples, waterfalls, and funky artist enclaves.

In the sugar-plantations-turned-artsy enclaves of Hāwī and Kapa'au, new galleries are interspersed with charming reminders of old Hawai'i—wooden boardwalks, quaint local stores, delicious neighborhood restaurants, friendly locals, and a delightfully slow pace. There's great shopping for everything from designer beachwear to authentic Hawaiian crafts.

GETTING HERE AND AROUND
Two days is sufficient time for experiencing each unique side of Kohala—one day for the resort perks: the beach, the spa, the golf, the restaurants; one day for hiking and admiring the waterfalls and valleys of North Kohala, coupled with a wander around Hāwī and Kapa'au.

Diving and snorkeling are great along this coast, so bring or rent equipment. If you're staying at one of the resorts, they will usually have any equipment you could possibly want. If you're feeling adventurous, get your hands on a four-wheel-drive vehicle and head to one of the unmarked beaches along the Kohala Coast—you may end up with a beach to yourself.

Continued on page 60

BIRTH OF THE ISLANDS

How did the volcanoes of the Hawaiian Islands evolve here, in the middle of the Pacific Ocean? The ancient Hawaiians believed that the volcano goddess Pele's hot temper was the key to the mystery; modern scientists contend that it's all about plate tectonics and one very hot spot.

Plate Tectonics & the Hawaiian Question: The theory of plate tectonics says that the Earth's surface is comprised of plates that float around slowly over the planet's molten interior. The vast majority of earthquakes and volcanic eruptions occur near plate boundaries—the San Francisco earthquakes in 1906 and 1989, for example, were the result of activity along the nearby San Andreas Fault, where the Pacific and North American plates meet. Hawai'i, more than 1,988 miles from the nearest plate boundary, is a giant exception. For years scientists struggled to explain the island chain's existence—if not a fault line, what caused the earthquakes and volcanic eruptions that formed these islands?

What's a hotspot? In 1963, J. Tuzo Wilson, a Canadian geophysicist, argued that the Hawaiian volcanoes must have been created by small concentrated areas of extreme heat beneath the plates. Wilson hypothesized that there is a hotspot beneath the present-day position of the Big Island. Its heat produced a persistent source of magma by partly melting the Pacific Plate above it. The magma, lighter than the surrounding solid rock, rose through the mantle and crust to erupt onto the sea floor, forming an active seamount. Each flow caused the seamount to grow until it finally emerged above sea level as an island volcano. Plausible so far, but why then, is there not one giant Hawaiian island?

HAWAIIAN CREATION MYTH

Holo Mai Pele, often played out in hula, is the Hawaiian creation myth. Pele sends her sister Hi'iaka on an epic quest to fetch her lover Lohi'au. Overcoming many obstacles, Hi'iaka reaches full goddess status and falls in love with Lohi'au herself. When Pele finds out, she destroys everything dear to her sister, killing Lohi'au and burning Hi'iaka's 'ohi'a groves. Each time lava flows from a volcano, 'ohi'a trees sprout shortly after, in a constant cycle of destruction and renewal.

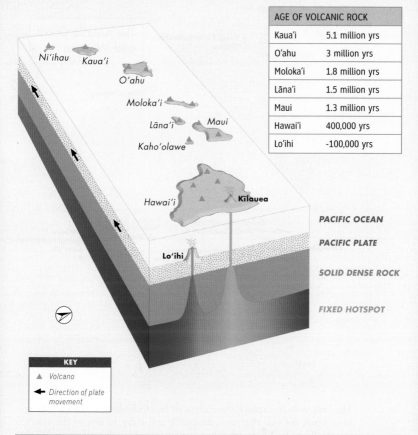

AGE OF VOLCANIC ROCK	
Kaua'i	5.1 million yrs
O'ahu	3 million yrs
Moloka'i	1.8 million yrs
Lāna'i	1.5 million yrs
Maui	1.3 million yrs
Hawai'i	400,000 yrs
Lo'ihi	-100,000 yrs

PACIFIC OCEAN

PACIFIC PLATE

SOLID DENSE ROCK

FIXED HOTSPOT

KEY
▲ Volcano
◀ Direction of plate movement

Volcanoes on the Move: Wilson further suggested that the movement of the Pacific Plate itself eventually carries the island volcano beyond the hotspot. Cut off from its magma source, the island volcano becomes dormant. As the plate slowly moved, one island volcano would become extinct just as another would develop over the hotspot. After several million years, there is a long volcanic trail of islands and seamounts across the ocean floor. The oldest islands are those farthest from the hotspot. The exposed rocks of Kaua'i, for example, are about 5.1 million years old, but those on the Big Island are less than .5 million years old, with new volcanic rock still being formed.

An Island on the Way: Off the coast of the Big Island, the volcano known as Lo'ihi is still submerged but erupting. Scientists long believed it to be a retired seamount volcano, but in the 1970s they discovered both old and new lava on its flanks, and in 1996 it erupted with a vengeance. It is believed that several thousand years from now, Lo'ihi will be the newest addition to the Hawaiian Islands.

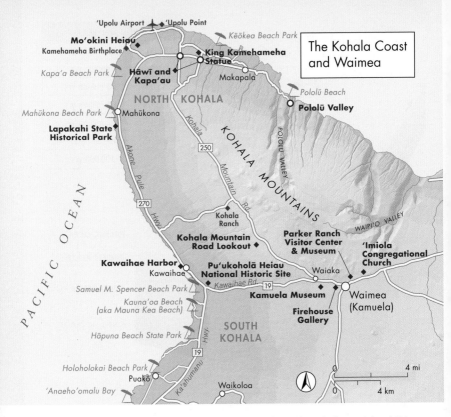

The best way to explore the valleys of North Kohala is with a hiking tour. Look for one that includes lunch and a dip in one of the area's waterfall pools. There are a number of casual lunch options in Hāwī and Kapaʻau (sandwiches, sushi, seafood, local style "plate lunch"), and a few good dinner spots.

EXPLORING

TOP ATTRACTIONS

★ **Hāwī and Kapaʻau.** These two neighboring villages thrived during plantation days. There were hotels, saloons, and theaters—even a railroad. They took a hit when "Big Sugar" left the island, but both towns are blossoming once again today, thanks to strong local communities and an influx of artists keen on honoring the towns' past. Old historic buildings have been restored and now hold shops, galleries, and eateries. In Kapaʻau, browse through the eclectic collection at the Ackerman Gift Gallery (✉ 54-3897 Akoni Pule Hwy. ☎ 808/889–5971 ⊕ www. ackermangalleries.com).

QUICK BITES

If you're looking for something sweet—or savory—**Kohala Coffee Mill & Tropical Dreams** (✉ 55-3412 Akoni Pule Hwy. Hāwī ☎ 808/889–5577) serves great local coffee, breakfast (bagels, espresso-machine steamed eggs) and lunch (hot dogs, vegan soup) plus locally made ice cream that is *ono* (translation: delicious).

Kohala Mountain Road Lookout. The lookout here provides a splendid view of the Kohala Coast and Kawaihae Harbor far below. On clear days, you can see well beyond the resorts. It's one of the most scenic spots on the island and great for a picnic. Often, thick mists drift in, casting an eerie feeling. ⊠ *Kohala Mountain Rd. (Hwy. 250).*

★ **Mo'okini Heiau.** This National Historic Landmark, an isolated *heiau* (ancient place of worship), is so impressive in size it may give you what locals call "chicken skin" (goose bumps)—especially after you learn its history. The heiau's foundations date to about AD 480, but the high priest Pa'ao from Tahiti expanded it several centuries later to offer sacrifices to please his gods. You can still see the lava slab where hundreds of people were killed, which gives this place a truly haunted feel. A nearby sign marks the place where King Kamehameha was born in 1758. The area is now part of the Kohala Historical Sites State Monument. ✛ *Turn off Hwy. 270 at sign for 'Upolu Airport, near Hāwī, and hike or drive in a four-wheel-drive vehicle 1½ mi southwest* ☎ *808/974–6200.*

★ **Pu'ukoholā Heiau National Historic Site.** In 1790 a prophet told King Kamehameha to build a *heiau* on top of Pu'ukoholā (Hill of the Whale) and dedicate it to the war god Kūkā'ilimoku by sacrificing his principal rival, Keōua Kūahu'ula. By doing so, the king would achieve his goal of conquering the Hawaiian Islands. The prophecy came true in 1810. A short walk over arid landscape leads from the impressive, recently renovated visitor center to temples **Pu'ukoholā Heiau** and **Mailekini Heiau.** An even older temple, dedicated to the shark gods, lies submerged just offshore. The center organizes Hawaiian arts-and-crafts programs on a regular basis. Repairs to the *heiau* due to the 2006 earthquakes are nearly complete, and the walkway is still intact, as is the majority of the structure. ⊠ *62-3601 Kawaihae Rd., Kawaihae* ☎ *808/882–7218* ⊕ *www.nps.gov/puhe/index.htm* ⊟ *Free* ☉ *Daily 7:45–5.*

WORTH NOTING

Kawaihae Harbor. This no-frills industrial harbor, where in 1793 the first cattle landed in Hawai'i, is a hub of commercial and community activity. It's especially busy on weekends, when paddlers and local fishing boats float on the waves. Second in size only to Hilo Harbor on the east coast, the harbor is often home to the *Makali'i*, one of three traditional Hawaiian sailing canoes. King Kamehameha and his men launched their canoes from here when they set out to conquer the neighboring islands. ■TIP➡ There are several restaurants with nice sunset views in Kawaihae should you be nearby at dinnertime. ✉ *Kawaihae Harbor Rd. off Hwy. 270.*

King Kamehameha Statue. This is the original of the statue in front of the Judiciary Building on King Street in Honolulu. It was cast in Florence in 1880 but lost at sea when the German ship transporting it sank near the Falkland Islands. A replica was shipped to Honolulu. Two years later an American sea captain found the original in a Port Stanley (Falkland Islands) junkyard and brought it to the Big Island. The legislature voted to erect it near Kamehameha's birthplace. Every year, on King Kamehameha Day (June 11), a magnificent abundance of floral lei adorns the statue of Hawai'i's great king. It's in front of the old Kohala Courthouse next to the highway. ☎ *808/443–2030* ✉ *54-3900 Kapa'au Rd., Kapa'au.*

★ **Lapakahi State Historical Park.** A self-guided, 1-mi walking tour leads through the ruins of the once-prosperous fishing village Koai'e, which dates as far back as the 15th century. Displays illustrate early Hawaiian fishing and farming techniques, salt gathering, games, and legends. A park guide is often on-site to answer questions. Since the shoreline near the state park is an officially designated Marine Life Conservation District, and part of the site itself is considered sacred, swimming is discouraged. For some reason a distinction is made between swimming and snorkeling; the latter is allowed and superb. ✉ *Hwy. 270, mile marker 14 between Kawaihae and Māhukona, North Kohala* ☎ *808/974–6200 or 808/327–4958* ✏ *Free* ◷ *Daily 8–4.*

WAIMEA

In addition to the horses and cattle, Waimea is also where some of the island's top Hawaiian regional cuisine chefs practice their art, which makes it an ideal place to find yourself at dinnertime. In keeping with the recent Big Island restaurant trend toward locally farmed ingredients, a handful of Waimea farms and ranches supply most of the restaurants on the island, and many sell to the public as well. With its galleries, restaurants, and museums, as well as Parker Ranch, Waimea is well worth a stop if you're heading to Hilo or Mauna Kea. ■TIP➡ And the short highway that connects Waimea to North Kohala (Hwy. 170) affords some of our favorite Big Island views.

GETTING HERE AND AROUND

You can see most of what Waimea has to offer in one day, but if you're heading up to Mauna Kea for stargazing (which you should), it could easily be stretched to two. If you stay in Waimea overnight (there are a few bed-and-breakfast options), or just get up really early, you could go for a morning horseback (or ATV) ride around the Parker Ranch, spend the afternoon browsing through town or touring some of the area's fantastic farms and ranches, then indulge in a gourmet dinner—all before heading up Saddle Road for world-renowned stargazing atop Mauna Kea.

A word to the wise—there are no services or gas stations on Saddle Road, the only way to reach the summit of Mauna Kea. Fill up on gas

Mauna Kea's snowcapped summit towers ahead on a drive south from Waimea.

and bring water, snacks and warm clothes with you (there are plenty of gas stations, cafés, and shops in Waimea).

EXPLORING

Firehouse Gallery. Walk across the Parker Ranch Shopping Center parking lot to a historic 79-year-old fire station, now a gallery, to glimpse what the artists in Hāmākua and Kohala are up to. The Waimea Arts Council sponsors free *kaha ki'is* (one-person shows). ⊠ *67-1201 Mamalahoa Hwy., Waimea* ☎ *808/887–1052.* ⊕ *www.waimeaartscouncil.org.*

'Imiola Congregational Church. Stop here to admire the dark koa interior and the unusual wooden calabashes hanging from the ceiling. Be careful not to walk in while a service is in progress, as the front entry of this church, which was established in 1832 and rebuilt in 1857, is behind the pulpit. ⊠ *65-1084 Mamalahoa Hwy., on "Church Row," Waimea* ☎ *808/885–4987.*

Parker Ranch Historic Homes & Garden. The homes chronicle the life of John Palmer Parker (and his descendants), who founded Parker Ranch in 1847. Parker married the granddaughter of King Kamehameha and bought two acres of land from the king for the sum of $10. The original family residence, Mana Hale, is built entirely from native woods such as koa. Puuopelu, added to the estate in 1879, was the residence of Richard Smart, a sixth-generation Parker who expanded the house to make room for his European art collection. Also available are horseback rides, ATV rides, and guided hunting or van tours *(See Cowboys of Hawai'i ATV Rides in Chapter 5, Golf, Hiking & Outdoor Activities).* ⊠ *Parker Ranch Shopping Center, 67-1185 Māmalahoa Hwy., Waimea*

☎ *808/885–5433; 877/885–7999 toll-free* ⊕ *www.parkerranch.com* ✉
homes $10 each, both $14 ⊗ *Homes Tues.–Sat. 10–5.*

QUICK BITES

Stop by **Waimea Coffee Company** (✉ *Parker Sq., 65-1279 Kawaihae Rd.,* *Waimea* ☎ *808/885–8915*) for a steaming latté and a warm pastry. Sit out on their veranda, staring at the manicured lawns and ranch-style building and try to believe you're in Hawai'i.

2

MAUNA KEA

Fodor's Choice ★

Mauna Kea ("white mountain") is the antithesis of the typical island experience. Freezing temperatures and arctic conditions are common at the summit, and snow can fall year-round. You can go even snowboarding up here. Seriously. But just because you can doesn't mean you'll want to. You should be in very good shape and a close-to-expert boarder or skier to get down the slopes near the summit and then up again in the thin air with no lifts. During the winter months, lack of snow is usually not a problem.

But winter sports are the least of the reasons that most people visit this starkly beautiful mountain. From its base below the ocean's surface to its summit, Mauna Kea is the tallest island mountain on the planet. It's also home to little Lake Waiau, one of the highest natural lakes in the world, though the word "pond" is closer to the truth.

Mauna Kea's summit—at 13,796 feet—is reputedly the best place in the world for viewing the night sky. For this reason, the summit is home to the world's largest astronomical observatory. Research teams from eleven different countries operate 13 telescopes on Mauna Kea, several of which are record-holders: the world's largest optical/infrared telescopes (the dual Keck telescopes), the world's largest dedicated infrared telescope (UKIRT), and the largest submillimeter telescope (the JCMT). A still larger thirty-meter telescope has just been cleared for construction, and is slated to open its record-breaking eye to the heavens in 2018.

Mauna Kea is tall, but there are higher mountains in the world, so what makes this spot so superb for astronomy? It has more to do with atmosphere than with elevation. A tropical inversion cloud layer below the summit keeps moisture from the ocean and other atmospheric pollutants down at lower elevations. As a result, the air around the Mauna Kea summit is extremely dry, which helps in the measurement of infrared and submillimeter radiation from stars, planets, and the like. There are also rarely clouds up there; the annual number of clear nights here blows every other place sky high. And, because the mountain is far away from any interfering artificial lights (not a total coincidence—in addition to the fact that the nearest town is nearly 30 mi away, there is an official ordinance limiting light on the island), skies are dark for the astronomers' research. To quote the staff at the observatory, astronomers here are able to "observe the faintest galaxies that lie at the very edge of the observable universe."

Teams from various universities have used the telescopes on Mauna Kea to make major astronomical discoveries, including new satellites around Jupiter and Saturn, new "Trojans" (asteroids that orbit, similar to moons) around Neptune, new moons and rings around Uranus, and new moons around Pluto. Their studies of galaxies are changing the way scientists think about time and the evolution of the universe.

What does all this mean for you? A visit to Mauna Kea is a chance to see more stars than you've likely ever seen before, and an opportunity to learn more about mind-boggling scientific discoveries in the very spot where these discoveries are being made. For you space geeks, a trip to Mauna Kea may just be the highlight of your trip.

If you're in Hilo, be sure to visit the 'Imiola Astronomy Center. It has presentations and planetarium films about the mountain and the science being conducted there, as well as exhibits describing the deep knowledge of the heavens possessed by the ancient Hawaiians.

GETTING HERE AND AROUND

The summit of Mauna Kea is only 34 mi from Hilo and 18 from Waimea, but the drive takes about an hour and a half from Hilo and an hour from Waimea thanks to the steep drive. Between the ride there, sunset on the summit, and stargazing, we recommend allotting at least four hours for your Mauna Kea visit.

To reach the summit, you must drive on Saddle Road, which used to be a narrow, rough, winding highway, but has recently been rerouted and repaved, and is now a beautiful shortcut across the middle of the island (except for that stretch near Waimea). The road to the Visitor Center at Mauna Kea is fine, but the road from there to the summit is a bit more precarious—unpaved and very steep—although most cars can make it up slowly and 4-wheel-drive vehicles won't have any trouble at all. If you're worried about your rental making the drive, you can still head for the summit with one of a handful of tour operators who will take care of everything. If you plan to drive yourself, fill up on gas and bring water and snacks and warm clothes with you, as there is nowhere along the way to stock up.

The second thing, which is extremely important to remember, is the altitude. ■TIP→ **Take the change in altitude seriously—stop at the Visitor Center for at least half an hour, and don't overexert yourself, especially at the top.** Scuba divers must wait at least 24 hours before attempting a trip to the summit to avoid getting the bends. The observatory recommends that children under 16, pregnant women, and those with heart, respiratory, or weight problems not go higher than the Visitor Center.

The last potential obstacle: it's cold, as in freezing. The military personnel stationed in Hawai'i do their cold-weather training atop Mauna Kea. It's difficult to find cold weather clothing in Hawai'i, so, if you plan to visit Mauna Kea, pack your favorite warm things from home.

ONIZUKA VISITOR CENTER

★ **Onizuka Center for International Astronomy Visitor Information Station.** At a 9,300-foot elevation, this is an excellent amateur observation site, with a handful of telescopes and a knowledgeable staff. It hosts nightly stargazing sessions from 6 to 10. This is also where you should stop for a

Mauna Kea's Telescopes

There's a meeting of the minds on the mountaintop, with 13 telescopes operated by astronomers from around the world. Although the telescopes are owned and operated by various countries and organizations, any research team can book time on the equipment.

A U.S.–Japan team comprising astronomers from the University of Hawai'i, University of Tokyo, Tohoku University, and Japan's Institute of Space and Astronautical Science made an important discovery of distant galaxies obscured by cosmic dust, using the JCMT telescope, which is jointly owned and operated by the United Kingdom, Canada, and the Netherlands. Similarly, a team of astronomers from the University of Hawai'i recently used the Keck telescopes (owned/operated by Caltech and the University of California) to discover a distant galaxy that gives astronomers a glimpse of the Dark Ages, when galaxies and stars were first forming in the universe. Here's a list of the telescopes and their owners.

UH 0.6-m telescope University of Hawai'i

UH 2.2-m telescope University of Hawai'i

IRTF (NASA Infrared Telescope Facility) NASA

CFHT (Canada-France-Hawai'i Telescope) Canada/France/University of Hawai'i

UKIRT (United Kingdom Infrared Telescope) United Kingdom

Keck I (W. M. Keck Observatory) Caltech/University of California

Keck II (W. M. Keck Observatory) Caltech/University of California

Subaru (Subaru Telescope) Japan

Gemini (Gemini Northern Telescope) USA/UK/Canada/Argentina/Australia/Brazil/Chile

CSO (Caltech Submillimeter Observatory) Caltech/National Science Foundation (NSF)

JCMT (James Clerk Maxwell Telescope) UK/Canada/Netherlands

SMA (Submillimeter Array) Smithsonian Astrophysical Observatory/Taiwan

VLBA (Very Long Baseline Array) National Radio Astronomers Observatory (NRAO)/Associated Universities, Inc. (AUI)/NSF

---

while to acclimate to the altitude if you're heading for the summit. This is a pleasure to do as you drink hot chocolate and peruse the exhibits on ancient Hawaiian celestial navigation, the ancient history of the mountain as not only a quarry for the best basalt in the Hawaiian Islands, but also as one of its most revered spiritual retreats, and other exhibits on modern astronomy and the unique natural history of the summit. The gift shop is full of great books, posters, and other mementos. On weekends the Onizuka Center offers free escorted summit tours, heading up the mountain in a caravan at 1 PM. To get here from Hilo, which is about 34 mi away, take Highway 200 (Saddle Road), and turn right at mile marker 28 onto John A. Burns Way, which is the only access road to the summit. ☎ *808/961–2180* ⊕ *www.ifa.hawaii.edu/info/vis* ☽ *Daily 9AM–10PM.*

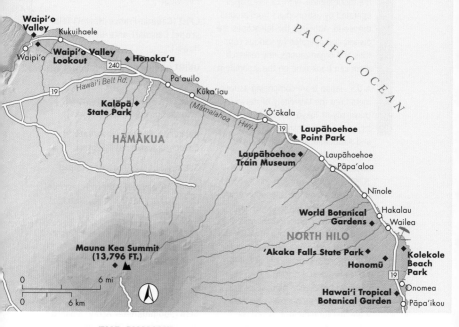

Map labels:
Waipiʻo Valley
Kukuihaele
Waipiʻo Valley Lookout
Waipiʻo
Honokaʻa
240
Paʻauilo
Hawaiʻi Belt Rd.
19
Kūkaʻiau
Kalōpā State Park
(Māmalahoa Hwy.)
ʻŌʻokala
HĀMĀKUA
19
Laupāhoehoe Point Park
Laupāhoehoe Train Museum
Laupāhoehoe
Pāpaʻaloa
Nīnole
Hakalau
World Botanical Gardens
Wailea
NORTH HILO
Mauna Kea Summit (13,796 FT.)
ʻAkaka Falls State Park
Honomū
Kolekole Beach Park
0   6 mi
0   6 km
19
Onomea
Hawaiʻi Tropical Botanical Garden
Pāpaʻikou
PACIFIC OCEAN

THE SUMMIT

Head to the summit before sunset so you're already there to witness the stunning sunset and emerging star show. Only the astronomers are allowed to use the telescopes and equipment up here, but the scenery is free for everybody. So, watch the sun sink into the horizon and then head down to the Visitor Center to warm up and stargaze some more. Or do your stargazing first and then head up here to get a different perspective—if you were blown away by the number of stars crowding the sky over the Visitor Center, this vantage point will really make you speechless. Just take it easy if you're driving back down in the dark— slow and cautious is the name of the game on this steep road.

If you haven't rented a four-wheel-drive vehicle, don't want to deal with driving to the summit, or don't want to wait in line to use the handful of telescopes at the Visitor Center, consider booking a tour. Operators provide transportation to and from the summit, and expert guides; some also provide parkas, gloves, telescopes, dinner, hot beverages, and snacks. Excursion fees range from $90 to $185.

GOING WITH A GUIDE

Arnott's Lodge & Hiking Adventures. A bit cheaper than the others at $90 per person, Arnott's tours leave from Hilo; their tour does not include dinner, they do not bring warm clothing for guests, and they do not have their own telescope. Focusing more on the experience of the mountain than astronomy, Arnott's brings binoculars for each guest and provides an informative lesson on major celestial objects and Polynesian navigational stars. ☎ 808/969–7097 ⊕ *www.arnottslodge.com.*

Hawai'i Forest & Trail. This outfitter stops for dinner along the way at a historic ranch, and brings parkas, gloves, and their own telescope along. Cookies and hot chocolate make cold stargazing more pleasant. The price is $165 per person. ☎ 808/331–8505 or 800/464–1993 ⊕ *www. hawaii-forest.com.*

Jack's Tours. Jack's follows the same itinerary as the other tours—sunset on the summit, followed by stargazing from the Visitor Center. They take larger groups than the other outfitters, and their guides speak English and Japanese. Boxed dinner, hot tea, bottled water, light snack, telescopes, and use of jackets and gloves are included. The price is $165 per person. ☎ 800/442–5557 ⊕ *www.jackstours.com.*

Mauna Kea Summit Adventures. As the first company to specialize in tours to the mountain and the only company to offer only Mauna Kea tours, Mauna Kea Summit Adventures has a bit more cred than the rest of the pack. They use cushy new van coaches for their tours, bring along parkas and gloves, and serve dinner at the Visitor Center before heading up to sunset on the summit. They also bring along their own powerful telescope. The price is $189 per person. ☎ 808/322–2366 ⊕ *www. maunakea.com.*

Onizuka Visitor Center Tours. If you want to charge the summit with a group but don't fancy paying for one of the tours above, consider joining one of the Visitor Center's free summit tours, with multiple departures available from 1 PM to 5 PM every Saturday and Sunday. Reservations are not required, but a 4-wheel-drive vehicle is—visitors follow the center's staff up the summit in their own cars. ☎ 808/961–2180 ⊕ *www. ifa.hawaii.edu/info/vis.*

THE HĀMĀKUA COAST

The spectacular waterfalls, mysterious jungles, emerald fields, and stunning ocean vistas along Highway 19 northwest of Hilo are collectively referred to as the Hilo–Hāmākua Heritage Coast. Brown signs featuring a sugarcane tassel reflect the area's history: thousands of acres of sugarcane are now idle, with no industry to support since "King Sugar" left the island in the early 1990s.

The 45-mi drive winds through little plantation towns, Pāpa'ikou, Laupāhoehoe, and Pa'auilo among them. It's a great place to wander off the main road and see "real" Hawai'i—untouched valleys, overgrown banyan trees, tiny coastal villages. In particular, ■TIP→ The "Heritage Drive," a 4-mi loop just off the main highway, is well worth the detour. Signs mark various sites of historical interest, as well as scenic views along the 40-mi stretch of coastline. Keep an eye out for them and try to stop at the sights mentioned—you won't be disappointed.

Once back on Highway 19, you'll pass the road to Honoka'a, which leads to the end of the road bordering Waipi'o Valley, ancient home to

Hawaiian royalty. The isolated valley floor has maintained the ways of old Hawai'i, with taro patches, wild horses, and a handful of houses.

GETTING HERE AND AROUND

Any turn off along this coast could lead to an incredible view, so take your time and go exploring up and down the side roads. You'll find small communities still hanging on quite nicely, well after the demise of the big sugar plantations that first engendered them. You'll find homey cafés, gift shops and galleries—and a way of life from a time gone by. If you're driving from Kailua-Kona, rather than driving around the northern tip of the island, cut across on the Mamalahoa Highway (190) to Waimea and then catch the 19 to the coast.

If you've stopped to explore the quiet little villages with wooden board-walks and dogs dozing in backyards, or if you've spent several hours in Waipi'o Valley, night will undoubtedly be falling by the time you've had your fill of the Hāmākua Coast. Don't worry: the return to Hilo via Highway 19 only takes about an hour, or you can go the other direction on the same road to stop for dinner in Waimea before heading back to the Kohala Coast resorts (another 25 to 45 minutes). Although you shouldn't have any trouble exploring the Hāmākua coast in a day, a handful of romantic bed-and-breakfasts are available along the coast if you want to spend more time.

EXPLORING

TOP ATTRACTIONS

★ **'Akaka Falls State Park.** A meandering 10-minute loop trail takes you to the best spots to see the two cascades, **'Akaka** and **Kahuna.** The 400-foot Kahuna Falls is on the lower end of the trail. The majestic upper 'Akaka Falls drops more than 442 feet, tumbling far below into a pool drained by Kolekole Stream amid a profusion of fragrant white, yellow, and red torch ginger. ⊠ *4 mi inland off Hwy. 19, near Honomū* ☎ *808/974–6200* ⊡ *Free* ☉ *Daily 7–7.*

Fodor'sChoice   **Waipi'o Valley.** Bounded by 2,000-foot cliffs, the "Valley of the Kings" ★   was once a favorite retreat of Hawaiian royalty. Waterfalls drop 1,200 feet from the Kohala Mountains to the valley floor, and the sheer cliff faces make access difficult. Though completely off the grid today, Waipi'o was once a center of Hawaiian life; somewhere between 4,000 and 20,000 people made it their home between the 13th and 17th centuries. In 1780 Kamehameha I was singled out here as a future ruler by reigning chiefs. In 1791 he fought Kahekili in his first battle at the mouth of the valley. In 1823 the first white visitors found 1,500 people living in this Eden-like environment amid fruit trees, banana groves, taro fields, and fishponds. The 1946 tidal wave drove most residents to higher ground.

Now, as then, waterfalls frame the landscape, but the valley has become one of the most isolated inhabited places in the state. To preserve this pristine part of the island, commercial transportation permits are limited—only four outfits offer organized valley trips—and Sunday the valley rests. A four-wheel-drive road leads down from the **Waipi'o Valley Overlook** (⊠ *Follow Hwy. 240 8 mi northwest of Honoka'a*), but only four-wheel-drive vehicles should attempt the steep road. The walk

DID YOU KNOW?

The dramatic 'Akaka Falls is only one of hundreds of waterfalls on the Hāmākua Coast. Many falls tumble into pristine swimming holes, so bring your swimsuit when you explore this area.

WAIPI'O VALLEY TOURS

A guided tour is the best way to see Waipi'o Valley. You can walk down and up the steep narrow road yourself, but you won't see as much. Costs range from about $50 to $150, depending on the company and the transport mode.

Na'alapa Stables (☎ 808/775–0419 ⊕ www.naalapastables.com) Guided horseback riding trips on the valley floor. Friendly horses, friendly guides.

Waipi'o on Horseback (☎ 808/775–7291, 877/775–7291 ⊕ www.waipioonhorseback.com) The other great outfit offering guided horseback riding trips on the valley floor.

Hawaiian Walkways (☎ 808/775–0372, 800/457–7759 ⊕ www.hawaiianwalkways.com) Their guided Waipi'o Waterfall Hike along the rim above the valley offers stunning views of the vista below.

Waipi'o Valley Shuttle (☎ 808/775–7121) Four-wheel-drive tours.

Waipi'o Valley Wagon Tours (☎ 808/775–9518 ⊕ www.waipiovalleywagontours.com) Muledrawn wagon tours.

down into the valley is less than a mile from here—but keep in mind, the climb back up is strenuous in the hot sun. A crescent of black sand makes it a popular spot for experienced local surfers. ■TIP➔ Continued overuse of the beach area and lack of sanitary facilities have caused serious unhealthy conditions to persist since 2003. Until it's cleaned up, we don't recommend getting into the water. Even then, swimmers need to watch out for rip currents.

WORTH NOTING

★ **Hawai'i Tropical Botanical Garden.** Eight miles north of Hilo, stunning coastline views appear around each curve of the 4-mi scenic jungle drive that accesses the privately owned nature preserve beside Onomea Bay. Paved pathways in the 17-acre botanical garden lead past ponds, waterfalls, and more than 2,000 species of plants and flowers, including palms, bromeliads, ginger, heliconia, orchids, and ornamentals. ✉ 27-717 Old Māmalahoa Hwy., Pāpa'ikou ☎ 808/964–5233 ⊕ www.hawaiigarden.com ☑ $15 ☉ Daily 9–5.

Honoka'a. In 1881 Australian William Purvis planted the first macadamianut trees in Hawai'i near what is now a very friendly, funky little town with a great antique shop, a few interesting galleries, and good cafés. But Honoka'a's true heyday came when sugar was king in the early part of the 20th century. During World War II, this was the place for soldiers stationed around Waimea to cut loose. Today, it's still worth a look at its historic buildings, and a chat with its friendly residents. ✉ Mamane St., Hwy. 240.

QUICK BITES

A quick stop at **Tex Drive-In** (✉ 45-690 Pakalana St. and Hwy. 19 ☎ 808/775–0598) will give you a chance to taste the snack that made it famous: *malasada*, a puffy, doughy Portuguese doughnut without a hole. These deep-fried beauties are best eaten hot. They also come in cream-filled versions, including vanilla, chocolate, and coconut. Or go for the

Hawaiian burger with a fat juicy slice of sweet pineapple on top. There's also a great lunch spot in Laupahoehoe, midway along the coast. Back to the 50's Highway Fountain (✉ *35-2074 Old Mamalahoa Hwy.*☎ *808/962–0808*) serves just what you'd expect, good old-fashioned burgers, fries, onion rings, milk shakes, home-made pies plus lots of other entrées ranging from fish meatloaf to local specialties. The nicely restored old building is packed to the rafters with intriguing rock-and-roll and car culture memorabilia.

Honomū. Its sugar-plantation past is reflected in the wooden boardwalks and tin-roof buildings of this small community. It's fun to poke through old dusty shops such as Glass from the Past, where you'll find an assortment of old bottles. The Woodshop Gallery/Café showcases local artists. ✉ *2 mi inland from Hwy. 19 en route to 'Akaka Falls State Park.*

☺ ★ **Kalōpā State Park.** Past the old plantation town of Pa'auilo, at a cool elevation of 2,000 feet, lies this 100-acre state park. There's a lush forested area with picnic tables and restrooms, and an easy ¾-mi loop trail with additional paths in the adjacent forest reserve. Small signs identify some of the plants. ✉ *12 mi north of Laupāhoehoe and 3 mi inland off Hwy. 19* ☎ *808/775–8852* ✑ *Free* ☽ *Daily 7–7 or by permit.*

Kolekole Beach Park. This rocky beach on the Kolekole River offers an idyllic setting for a barbecue or picnic. A large banyan tree leans over the river, and its rope swing is a hit with local kids during lazy summer days. An old train bridge crosses the river where it empties into the ocean. The surf can be rough, so only experienced swimmers should venture past the river's mouth. Back on the road, a scenic drive takes you from the top of the park through the old town of Wailea back to Highway 19. ✉ *Off Hwy. 19* ☎ *808/961–8311* ✑ *Free* ☽ *Daily 7AM–sunset.*

Laupāhoehoe Point Park. Come here to watch the surf pound the jagged black rocks at the base of the stunning point. This is not a safe place for swimming, however. Still vivid in the minds of longtime area residents is the 1946 tragedy in which 21 schoolchildren and three teachers were swept to sea by a tidal wave. ✉ *On northeast coastline, Hwy. 19, makai side, north of Laupāhoehoe* ☎ *808/961–8311* ✑ *Free* ☽ *Daily 7AM–sunset.*

Laupāhoehoe Train Museum. Behind the stone-loading platform of the once-famous Hilo Railroad, constructed around the turn of the 20th century, the former manager's house is a poignant reminder of the era when sugar was the local cash crop. The railroad, used to transport sugar from the plantations to the port, was one of the most expensive built in its time. It was washed away by the 1946 tsunami. Today one of the vintage switch engines is on display at the museum, and on special occasions even runs a few yards on a short Y-track. ✉ *Hwy. 19, Laupāhoehoe* ☎ *808/962–6300* ⊕ *www.thetrainmuseum.com* ✑ *$3* ☽ *Weekdays 9–4:30, weekends 10–2.*

☺ **World Botanical Gardens.** About 300 acres of former sugarcane land are slowly giving way to a botanical center, which includes native Hawaiian plants such as orchids, palms, ginger, hibiscus, and heliconia. In the 10-acre arboretum children love to wind their way through a maze made of shrubs. From within the gardens you have access to splendid views

of one of the prettiest waterfalls on the isle, triple-tiered **Umauma Falls.**
You may feel a little bit cheated, since it's $8 per person to essentially
drive in, park, get out, and view the falls from a distance, but unfortunately this is the only place to see Umauma without some pretty rigorous
hiking and scrambling. ⊠ *Hwy. 19, from Hilo just past mile marker 16*
☎ *808/963–5427* ⊕ *www.wbgi.com* ✍ *$13* ⊘ *Daily. 9–5:30.*

HILO

When compared to Kailua-Kona, Hilo is often described as "the real
Hawaiʻi." With significantly fewer tourists than residents, more historic
buildings, and a much stronger identity as a long-established community, life does seem more authentic on this side of the island. This quaint,
traditional town stretches from the banks of the Wailuku River to Hilo
Bay, where a few hotels line stately Banyan Drive. The wonderful old
buildings that make up Hilo's downtown have been spruced up as part
of a revitalization effort.

Nearby, the 30-acre Liliʻuokalani Gardens, a formal Japanese garden
with arched bridges and waterways, was created in the early 1900s to
honor the area's Japanese sugar-plantation laborers. It also became a
safety zone after a devastating tidal wave swept away businesses and
homes on May 22, 1960, killing 60 people.

With a population of almost 50,000 in the entire district, Hilo is the
fourth-largest city in the state and home to the University of Hawaiʻi
at Hilo. Although it is the center of government and commerce for the
island, Hilo is clearly a residential town. Mansions with yards of lush
tropical foliage surround older wooden houses with rusty corrugated
roofs. It's a friendly community, populated primarily by descendants of
the contract laborers—Japanese, Chinese, Filipino, Puerto Rican, and
Portuguese—brought in to work the sugarcane fields during the 1800s.

One of the main reasons visitors have tended to steer clear of the east
side of the island is its weather. With an average rainfall of 130 inches
per year, it's easy to see why Hilo's yards are so green, and its buildings
so weather worn. Outside of town, the Hilo District has rain forests
and waterfalls, very unlike the hot and dry white-sand beaches of the
Kohala Coast. But when the sun does shine—usually part of nearly
every day—the town sparkles and, during winter, the snow glistens on
Mauna Kea, 25 mi in the distance. Best of all is when the mists fall and
the sun shines at the same time, leaving behind the colorful arches that
earn Hilo its nickname: the City of Rainbows.

GETTING HERE AND AROUND

Hilo is a great base for exploring the eastern and southern parts of
the island—just be sure to bring an umbrella for sporadic showers. If
you're just passing through town or making a day trip, make the first
right turn into the town off Highway 19 (it comes up fast) and grab a
parking spot in the lot on your left or on any of the surrounding streets.
Downtown Hilo is best experienced on foot. The **Downtown Hilo Improvement Association** (⊠ *329 Kamehameha Ave.* ☎ *808/935–8850* ⊕ *www.
downtownhilo.com* ⊘ *Mon.–Fri. 8:30–4:30*) provides an excellent and

free self-guided walking tour to downtown Hilo. The tour includes historical information, a map, and directions to 18 historic sites. You can download it from their Web site or pick it up in person at their downtown Hilo office.

There are plenty of gas stations and restaurants in the area. Hilo is a good spot to load up on food and supplies—just south of downtown there are several large budget chains. The Merrie Monarch Hula Festival takes place in Hilo every year during the second week of April, and dancers and admirers flock to the city from all over the world. If you're planning a stay in Hilo during this time, be sure to book your room well in advance.

> **FUN THINGS TO DO AROUND HILO**
>
> ■ Enjoy the best shower you've ever had beneath an ancient waterfall.
>
> ■ Watch the world's largest active volcano make the earth beneath your feet.
>
> ■ Take in a starry night on top of Mauna Kea.
>
> ■ Swim with green sea turtles at Punalu'u Black Sand Beach, then hike into Green (yes, green) Sand Beach.
>
> ■ Relax in nature's hot tub—the volcanically heated springs of Puna.

EXPLORING

TOP ATTRACTIONS

Fodor's Choice ★
Hilo Farmers' Market. This abundant and colorful market draws farmers and shoppers from all over the island. Bright orchids, anthuriums, and birds-of-paradise create a feast for the eyes, while exotic vegetables, tropical fruits, and baked goods satisfy the stomach. Craft and jewelry makers and clothing vendors round out the market. Don't dawdle, as it closes in the early afternoon. ⊠ *Mamo and Kamehameha Sts.* ⊙ *Wed. and Sat. "from dawn till it's gone."* ⊕ *www.hilofarmersmarket.com.*

'Imiloa Astronomy Center. Part Hawaiian cultural center, part astronomy museum, the 'Imiloa Astronomy Center provides an educational and cultural complement to the research being conducted atop Mauna Kea. Although visitors are welcome at Mauna Kea, its primary function is as a research center—not observatory, museum, or education center. Those roles have been taken on by 'Imiloa in a big way. With its exhibits, full-dome planetarium shows, and regularly scheduled talks and events, the center is a must-see for anyone interested in the stars, the planets, or Hawaiian culture and history. The center, five minutes from downtown Hilo, also provides an important link between the scientific research being conducted at Mauna Kea and its history as a sacred mountain for the Hawaiian people. ⊠ *600 'Imiloa Pl., at the UH Hilo Science & Technology Park, off Nowelo and Komohana* ☎ *808/969–9700* ⊕ *www.imiloahawaii.org* ⊴ *$17.50* ⊙ *Tues.–Sun. 9–4.*

❷ ★
Lili'uokalani Gardens. Designed to honor Hawai'i's first Japanese immigrants, Lili'uokalani's 30 acres of fish-filled ponds, stone lanterns, half-moon bridges, elegant pagodas, and ceremonial teahouse make it a favorite Sunday destination. The surrounding area used to be a busy residential neighborhood until a tsunami in 1960 swept the buildings

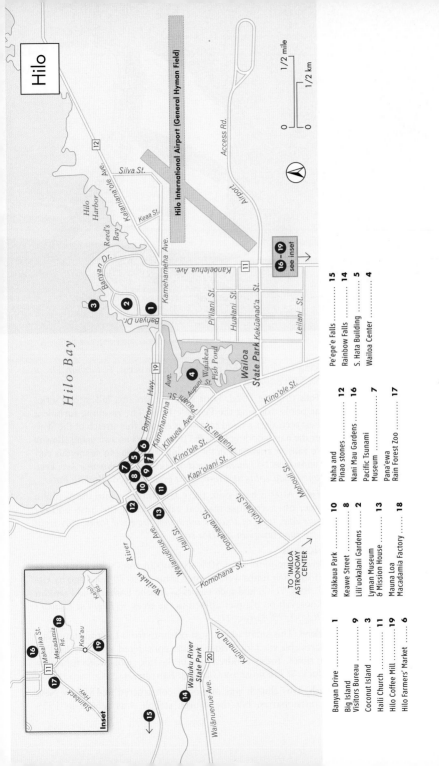

Hilo

Hilo Bay

Hilo Harbor

Reed's Bay

Banyan Dr.

Silva St.

Keaa St.

Hilo International Airport (General Hyman Field)

Access Rd.

Airport

Kalaniana'ole Ave.

Kamehameha Ave.

Kanoelehua Ave.

Pi'ilani St.

Hualani St.

Leilani St.

Kekūanaō'a St.

Wailoa State Park

Aupuni St.

Waiakea Fish Pond

Kino'ole St.

Bayfront Hwy.

Punahoa St.

Kamehameha Ave.

Kīlauea Ave.

Haili St.

Kino'ole St.

Hualalai St.

Kapi'olani St.

Ponahawai St.

Komohana St.

Kinoʻole St.

Kaūmana Dr.

Waiānuenue Ave.

Waiānuenue Ave.

Wailuku River

Waiānuenue Ave.

TO 'IMILOA ASTRONOMY CENTER

Inset

Wailuku River State Park

Makaʻala St.

Macadamia Rd.

Kea'au

Keaʻau

Keaīki Rd.

Stainback Hwy.

1/2 mile

1/2 km

Banyan Drive	**1**
Big Island Visitors Bureau	**9**
Coconut Island	**3**
Haili Church	**11**
Hilo Coffee Mill	**19**
Hilo Farmers' Market	**6**

Kalākaua Park	**10**
Keawe Street	**8**
Lili'uokalani Gardens	**2**
Lyman Museum & Mission House	**13**
Mauna Loa Macadamia Factory	**18**

Naha and Pinao stones	**12**
Nani Mau Gardens	**16**
Pacific Tsunami Museum	**7**
Pana'ewa Rain Forest Zoo	**17**

Pe'epe'e Falls	**15**
Rainbow Falls	**14**
S. Hata Building	**5**
Wailoa Center	**4**

The world's largest optical and infrared telescopes are located at the Keck Observatory on Mauna Kea's summit.

away, taking the lives of 60 people in the process. ⊠ *Banyan Dr. at Lihiwai St.* ☎ *808/961–8311.*

⓯ **Pe'epe'e Falls** *(Boiling Pots)*. Four separate streams fall into a series of circular pools, forming the Pe'epe'e Falls. The resulting turbulent action—best seen after a good rain—has earned this stretch of the Wailuku River the name Boiling Pots. ■ TIP→ **There's no swimming allowed at Pe'epe'e Falls or anywhere in the Wailuku river, due to dangerous currents and undertows.** ⊠ *3 mi northwest of Hilo on Waiānuenue Ave; keep to right when road splits and look for a green sign for Boiling Pots.*

⓮ **Rainbow Falls.** After a hard rain, these falls thunder into the Wailuku
★ River gorge, often creating magical rainbows in the mist. ⊠ *Take Waiānuenue Ave. west of town 1 mi; when the road forks, stay right and look for the Hawaiian warrior sign.*

WORTH NOTING

❶ **Banyan Drive.** The more than 50 leafy banyan trees with aerial roots
★ dangling from their limbs were planted some 60 to 70 years ago by visiting celebrities. You'll find such names as Amelia Earhart and Franklin Delano Roosevelt on plaques affixed to the trees. ✣ *Begin at Hawai'i Naniloa Resort, 93 Banyan Dr.*

❸ **Coconut Island.** This small island, just offshore from Lili'uokalani Gar-
★ dens, is accessible via a footbridge. It was considered a place of healing in ancient times. Today children play in the tide pools while fisherfolk try their luck. ⊠ *Lili'uokalani Gardens, Banyan Dr.*

⓫ **Haili Church.** This church was originally constructed in 1859 by New England missionaries, but the church steeple was rebuilt in 1979

A Walking Tour of Hilo

Put on some comfortable shoes, because Hilo is best explored on foot. All of the downtown destinations are within easy walking distance of each other. Start your excursion in front of the public library, on Waiānuenue Avenue, four blocks from Kamehameha Avenue. Here, you'll find the massive **Naha and Pinao stones,** which legend says King Kamehameha I was able to move as a teenager, thus foretelling that someday he would be a powerful king. Cross the road to walk southeast along Kapi'olani Street, and turn right on Haili Street to visit the historic **Lyman Museum & Mission House.** Back on Haili Street, follow this busy road toward the ocean; on your right you'll pass **Haili Church.**

Soon you'll reach **Keawe Street** with its plantation-style shop fronts. Stop at the **Big Island Visitors Bureau** on the right-hand corner for maps and brochures before taking a left. You'll bump into Kalākaua Street; for a quick respite turn left and rest on the benches in **Kalākaua Park.**

Continue *makai* on Kalākaua Street to visit the **Pacific Tsunami Museum** on the corner of Kalākaua and Kamehameha Avenues. After heading three blocks east, you'll come across the **S. Hata Building,** which has interesting shops and restaurants and the Mokupapapa: Discovery Center for Hawaii's Remote Coral Reefs Museum. Just next door, on either side of Mamo Street, is the **Hilo Farmers' Market.**

---

following a fire. The church is known for its choir, which sings hymns in Hawaiian during services. ✉ *211 Haili St.* ☎ *808/935–4847.*

⑲ Hilo Coffee Mill. With all the buzz about Kona coffee, it's easy to forget that coffee is produced throughout the rest of the island as well. The Hilo Coffee Mill is a pleasant reminder of that fact. In addition to farming their own coffee on-site, the mill has partnered with several local small coffee farmers in East Hawai'i in an effort to put the region on the world's coffee map. You can sample the efforts of the farmers, as well as tour the mill and watch the roasters in action. The shop sells coffee and other locally produced goods. Even if you don't have time for the tour or shopping, the mill's café is a great pit stop on the way to Volcanoes National Park from Hilo. ✉ *17-995 Volcano Rd. (Hwy. 11), between mile markers 12 and 13, Mountain View* ☎ *808/968–1333* ⊕ *www.hilocoffeemill.com* ☞ *Free* ☉ *Mon.–Sat. 7–4.*

⑩ Kalākaua Park. King Kalākaua, who revived the hula, was the inspiration for Hilo's Merrie Monarch Festival. A bronze statue, erected in 1988, depicts the king with a taro leaf in his left hand to signify the Hawaiian peoples' bond with the land. The park also has a huge spreading banyan tree and small fishponds, but no picnic or recreation facilities. In a local tradition, families that have had recent funerals often leave leftover floral displays and funeral wreaths along the fishpond walkway as a way of honoring and celebrating their loved ones. ✉ *Kalākaua and Kino'ole Sts.*

⑧ Keawe Street. Buildings here have been restored to their original 1920s and '30s plantation styles. Although most shopping is along

Kamehameha Avenue, the ambience on Keawe Street offers a nostalgic sampling of Hilo as it might have been 80 years ago.

⑬ Lyman Museum & Mission House. Built in 1839 for David and Sarah Lyman, Congregationalist missionaries, the Lyman House is the oldest frame building on the island. In the adjacent museum, dedicated in 1973, there's a realistic magma chamber and exhibits on the islands' formation. There's also an interesting section on Hawaiian flora and fauna. The gift shop sells Hawaiian books, cards, gifts, and music. ⊠ *276 Haili St.* ☎ *808/935–5021* ⊕ *www.lymanmuseum.org* ⊠ *$10* ⊙ *Mon.–Sat. 10–4:30, Mission House tours, 11–2.*

⑱ Mauna Loa Macadamia Factory. Acres of macadamia trees lead to a giant roasting facility and processing plant with viewing windows. A videotape depicts the harvesting and preparation of the nuts, and there are free samples and plenty of gift boxes with mac nuts in every conceivable form of presentation to buy in the visitor center. Children can run off their energy on the nature trail. ⊠ *Macadamia Rd. off Hwy. 11, 5 mi south of Hilo* ☎ *808/966–8618, 888/628–6256* ⊕ *www.maunaloa.com* ⊙ *Daily 8:30–5.*

⑫ Naha and Pinao stones. These two huge, oblong stones are legendary. The Pinao stone is purportedly an entrance pillar of an ancient temple built near the Wailuku River. King Kamehameha is said to have moved the 5,000-pound Naha stone when he was still in his teens. Legend decreed that he who did so would become king of all the islands. They're in front of the Hilo Public Library. ⊠ *300 Waiānuenue Ave.*

⑯ Nani Mau Gardens. The name means "forever beautiful" in Hawaiian,
★ and that's a good description of this 20-acre botanical garden filled with several varieties of fruit trees and hundreds of varieties of ginger, orchids, anthuriums, and other exotic plants. A botanical museum details the history of Hawaiian flora, and guided tours by tram are available. There are two restaurants, one with a lunch buffet. ⊠ *421 Makalika St., off Hwy. 11* ☎ *808/959–3500* ⊕ *www.nanimau.com* ⊠ *$10, tram tour an additional $7* ⊙ *Daily 8–5.*

❼ Pacific Tsunami Museum. A memorial to all those who lost their lives in
☺ tsunamis that have struck the Big Island, Hawai'i and the world, this small but informative museum offers a poignant history of the devastating waves. In a 1931 C. W. Dickey–designed building—the former home of the First Hawaiian Bank—you'll find an interactive computer center, a science room, a theater, a replica of Old Hilo Town, a children's corner, and a knowledgeable, friendly staff. In the background, a striking quilt tells a silent story. ⊠ *130 Kamehameha Ave.* ☎ *808/935–0926* ⊕ *www.tsunami.org* ⊠ *$8* ⊙ *Mon.–Sat. 9–4.*

⑰ Pana'ewa Rain Forest Zoo. Advertised as "the only natural tropical rain
☺ forest zoo in the United States," this is the home of white Bengal tiger, Namaste. Children enjoy the spider monkeys, the pygmy hippopotamus, and the zoo favorite, Namaste (feedings are every day at 3:30). There is a variety of native Hawaiian species, such as the state bird, the *nēnē* (Hawaiian goose), as well as a small petting zoo every Saturday 1:30–2:30. ⊠ *Left on Mamaki off Hwy. 11, just past the "Kulani 19,*

CLOSE UP

Banyan Drive's Trees

The history of the trees lining Hilo's Banyan Drive is one of the Big Island's most interesting and least-known stories. Banyan Drive was named for these trees, which were planted by VIP visitors to Hilo. Altogether, some 50 or so banyans were planted between 1933 and 1972.

The majority are Chinese banyans, and each one is marked with a sign naming the VIP who planted it and the date on which it was planted. The first trees were planted on October 20, 1933, by a Hollywood group led by director Cecil B. DeMille, who was in Hilo making the film *Four Frightened People*. Soon after, on October 29, 1933, another banyan was planted by the one and only George Herman "Babe" Ruth, who was in town playing exhibition games.

President Franklin D. Roosevelt planted a tree on his visit to Hilo on July 25, 1934. And in 1935, famed aviatrix Amelia Earhart put a banyan in the ground just days before she became the first person to fly solo across the Pacific Ocean.

Trees continued to be planted along Banyan Drive until World War II. The tradition was then revived in 1952 when a young and aspiring U.S. senator, Richard Nixon of California, planted a banyan tree. Nixon's tree was later toppled by a storm and was replanted by his wife, Pat, during a Hilo visit in 1972. On a bright, sunny day, strolling down Banyan Drive is like going through a green, shady tunnel. The banyans form a regal protective canopy over Hilo's own "Walk of Fame."

Stainback Hwy" sign ☎ *808/959–7224* ⊕ *www.hilozoo.com* ✉ *Free* ⊙ *Daily 9–4.*

❺ **S. Hata Building.** Erected as a general store in 1912 by Sadanosuke Hata and his family, this historic structure now houses shops, a restaurant, offices, and a fascinating museum called Mokupapapa: Discovery Center for Hawai'i's Remote Coral Reefs. During World War II Hata family members were interned and the building was confiscated by the U.S. government. When the war was over, a daughter repurchased it for $100,000. A beautiful example of Renaissance-revival architecture, it won an award from the state for the authenticity of its restoration. ✉ *308 Kamehameha Ave., at Mamo St.*

❹ **Wailoa Center.** This circular exhibition center, in Wailoa State Park, features shows by local artists that change monthly. Just in front of the center is a 12-foot-high bronze statue of King Kamehameha I, made in Italy in the late 1980s. Check out his gold Roman sandals. ✉ *200 Pi'opi'o St. off Kamehameha Ave.* ☎ *808/933–0416* ⊙ *Mon., Tues., Thurs., and Fri. 8:30–4:30; Wed. noon–4:30.*

PUNA

The Puna District is wild in every sense of the word. The jagged black coastline is changing all the time; the trees are growing out of control, forming canopies over the few paved roads; the land is dirt-cheap and there are no building codes; and the people, well, there's something about living in an area that could be destroyed by lava at any moment (as Kalapana was in 1990) that makes the laws of modern society seem silly. So it is that Puna has its well-deserved reputation as the "outlaw" region of the Big Island.

That said, it's a unique place that's well worth a detour, especially if you're in this part of the island anyway. There are volcanically heated springs, tide pools bursting with interesting sea life, and some mighty fine people-watching opportunities in Pāhoa, a funky little town that the outlaws call home.

This is also farm country (yes, that kind of farm, but also the legal sort). Local farmers grow everything from orchids and anthuriums to papayas, bananas, and macadamia nuts. Several of the island's larger, rural residential subdivisions are between Kea'au and Pāhoa, including Hawaiian Paradise Park, Orchidland Estates, Hawaiian Acres, Hawaiian Beaches, and others.

When night falls here, the air fills with the high-pitched symphony of hundreds of coqui frogs. Though they look cute on the signs and sound harmless, the coqui frogs are pests both to local crops and to locals, tired of their loud, shrill all-night song.

GETTING HERE AND AROUND

The sprawling Puna District includes part of the Volcano area and stretches northeast down to the coast. If you're staying in Hilo for the night, driving around wild lower Puna is a great way to spend a morning.

The roads connecting Pāhoa to Kapoho and the Kalapana coast form a loop that's about 25 mi long; driving times are from two to three hours, depending on the number of stops you make and the length of time at each stop. There are restaurants, stores, and gas stations in Pāhoa, but services elsewhere in the region are spotty. There are long stretches of the road that may be completely isolated at any given point; this can be a little scary at night but beautiful and tranquil during the day.

Compared to big-city living, it's pretty tame, but there is a bit of a "locals only" vibe in parts of Puna, and a drug problem in Pāhoa, so don't go wandering around at night.

EXPLORING

TOP ATTRACTIONS

Cape Kumukahi Lighthouse. The lighthouse, 1½ mi east of the intersection of highways 132 and 137, was miraculously unharmed during the 1960 volcano eruption here that destroyed the town of Kapoho. The lava flowed directly up to the lighthouse's base but instead of pushing it over, actually flowed around it. Locals say that, Pele, the volcano goddess, protected the Hawaiian fisherfolk by sparing the lighthouse. The lighthouse itself is a simple metal-frame structure with a light on top,

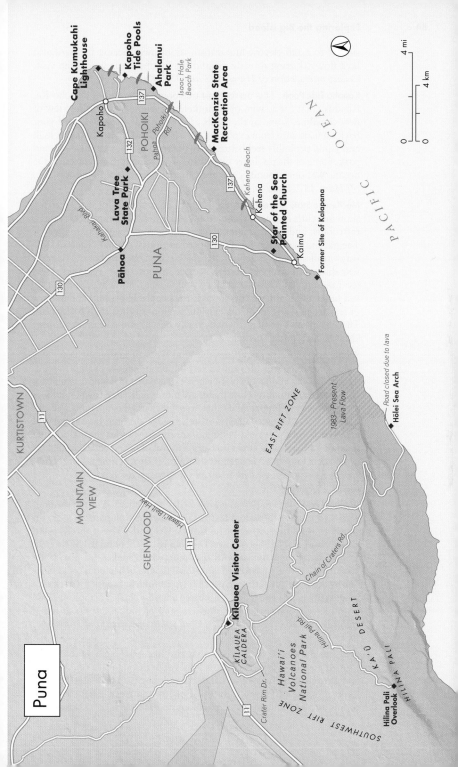

similar to a tall electric-line transmission tower. Seeing the hardened lava flows skirting directly around the lighthouse is worth the visit. ✉ *Past intersection of Hwys. 132 and 137, Kapoho.*

Kapoho Tide Pools. This network of tide pools at the end of Kapoho-Kai Road is great for a swim or a snorkel, or even just a beautiful view of new coastline. Some of the pools are volcanically warmed, so if your back's a little sore from exploring the island, stop for a 10-minute soak and you'll probably feel better. Take the road to the end, turn left, and park. Some of the pools are on private property, but those closest to the ocean, Wai'ōpae (ponds), are open to all. ✉ *End of Kapoho-Kai Rd., off Hwy. 137, Puna District.*

MacKenzie State Recreation Area. This is a coastal park located on rocky shoreline cliffs in a breezy, cool ironwood grove. There are picnic tables, restrooms, and a tent-camping area; bring your own drinking water. The park is significant for the restored section of the old "King's Highway" trail system, which circled the coast in the era before Hawai'i was discovered by the Western world. In those days, regional chiefs used these trails to connect the coastal villages, allowing them to collect taxes and maintain control over the people. Short hikes of an hour or less are possible along the existing sections of the rough rocky trail. There are views of rugged coast, rocky beach, and coastal dry forest. ✉ *Hwy. 137, Puna District.*

Pāhoa. Sort of like a town from the Wild West, this little town even has some wooden boardwalks and rickety buildings—not to mention a reputation as a wild and wooly place where pot growers make up a significant part of the community. Now things are more civilized in town, but there are still plenty of hippies and other colorful characters pursuing alternative lifestyles. The secondhand stores, tie-dye clothing boutiques, and art galleries in quaint old buildings are fun to wander through during the day. Pāhoa's main street boasts a handful of island eateries, the best of which is **Luquin's Mexican Restaurant.** ⊕ *Turn southeast onto Hwy. 130 at Kea'au, drive 11 mi to a right turn marked Pāhoa.*

WORTH NOTING

Ahalanui Park. This park was established with a federal grant in the mid-1990s to replace those lost to the lava flows at Kalapana. It's 2½ mi south of the intersection of highways 132 and 137 on the Kapoho Coast, southeast of Pāhoa town. There's a half-acre pond fed by thermal freshwater springs mixed with seawater, which makes for a relaxing soak. ■TIP→ There have been occasional reports of bacterial contamination by the health department, which is typical with hot springs. Check with on-duty lifeguards and follow any posted advisory signs. Facilities include portable restrooms, outdoor showers, and picnic tables; no drinking water is available. ✉ *Hwy. 137, 2½ mi south of junction of Hwy. 132, Puna District.*

Lava Tree State Park. Tree molds that rise like blackened smokestacks formed here in 1790 when a lava flow swept through the 'ōhi'a forest. Some reach as high as 12 feet. The meandering trail provides close-up looks at some of Hawai'i's tropical plants and trees. There are restrooms and a couple of picnic pavilions and tables. ■TIP→ Mosquitoes live here in abundance, so be sure to bring repellent. ✉ *Hwy. 132, Puna District* ☎ *808/974–6200* 🎫 *Free* ☉ *Daily 30 min. before sunrise–30 min. after sunset.*

Star of the Sea Painted Church. This historic church, now a community center, was moved to its present location in 1990 just ahead of the advancing lava flow that destroyed the Kalapana area. The church, which dates from the 1930s, was built by a Belgian Catholic missionary priest, Father Evarest Gielen, who also did the detailed paintings on the church's interior. Though similar in style, the Star of the Sea and St. Benedict's were actually painted by two different Belgian Catholic missionary priests. Star of the Sea also has several lovely stained-glass windows. ✉ *Hwy. 130, 1 mi north of Kalapana.*

HAWAII VOLCANOES NATIONAL PARK AND VICINITY

Fodor's Choice
★

Few visitors realize that in addition to "the volcano"(Kīlauea)—that mountain oozing new layers of lava onto its flanks—there's also Volcano, the village. Conveniently located next to Hawai'i Volcanoes National Park, Volcano village is a charming little hamlet in the woods that offers a dozen or so excellent inns and bed-and-breakfasts, a decent (although strangely expensive) Thai restaurant, some killer (although strangely expensive) pizza, and a handful of things to see and do that don't include the village's namesake.

For years, writers, artists and meditative types have been coming to the volcano to seek inspiration, and many of them have settled in and around the village. Artist studios (open to the public by appointment) are scattered in the forest.

If you plan to visit the Halema'uma'u summit crater at night (which you absolutely should if it's glowing), or drive down Chain of Craters Road to the coast to see the lava steaming into the sea, spending a night in Volcano village is the ideal way to go about it.

GETTING HERE AND AROUND
There are a handful of dining options, a couple of stores, and gas stations available in Volcano, so most of your needs should be covered. If you can't find what you're looking for, Hilo is about a 35-minute drive away, and the Ke'eau grocery store and fast-food joints are 25 minutes away.

Bring a fleece or a sweater if you plan to stay the night in Volcano; temperatures drop at night and mornings are usually cool and misty. One of the main reasons people choose to stay the night in Volcano is to see the dramatic glow at the summit vent and to drive to the coast to see the lava flow into the sea. ■ TIP→ Make sure you have enough gas to get down to the flow and back up. The entrance to Volcanoes National Park is about one minute from Volcano village, but the drive down is a good 30 minutes. Remember that you'll be coming back around midnight, long after the rangers have gone home.

You may see flowing lava at Kīlauea, the Big Island's youngest and most active volcano.

Speed limits in this area are low for a reason. Paved roads can become unpaved within a few feet; heed the speed limits so that you don't go flying onto a bumpy dirt road at 70 mph. There are also occasionally farm kids riding around on ATVs (and some of them might be going way faster than you're allowed to). It's best to be able to dodge them without ending up crashing into a lava rock.

Fodor's Choice ⭐ **EXPLORING**

Kīlauea Caverns of Fire. Strap on a miner's hat and gloves and get ready to explore the underbelly of the world's largest active volcano. Tours through these fascinating caves and lava tubes underneath the volcano must be arranged in advance, but are well worth a little extra planning. Located off Highway 11 between Hilo and Volcanoes National Park, the caverns are comprised of four main tubes, each 500–700 years old and full of stalactites, stalagmites, and a variety of different-colored flowstone. The largest lava tube in the world is here—40 mi long, it has 80-foot ceilings and is 80 feet wide. Tours can range from safe and easy (safe enough for children five years old and up) to long and adventurous. ✉ *16-1953 7th Rd., Hawaiian Acres, Off Hwy. 11, between Kurtistown and Mountain View* ☎ *808/217–2363* ⊕ *www. kilaueacavernsoffire.com* ✉ *$29 for walking tour, $79 for adventure tour* ☉ *By appointment only.*

See Hawaii Volcanoes National Park highlighted in this chapter.

Volcano Farmers' Market. Local produce, flowers, and food products are on offer every Sunday morning at one of the better farmers' markets on the island. It's best to get there early, before 8 a.m., as vendors tend to sell out of the best stuff quickly. There's also a great bookstore (paperbacks 25 cents, hardbacks 50 cents and magazines 10 cents), and a thrift store with clothes and knickknacks. ■**TIP→** There are also more prepared-food vendors at the Volcano market than Hilo, with such temptations as fresh baked breads and pastries, vegetarian lunch items, and homemade Thai food. ⊠ *Cooper Center, 19-4030 Wright Rd.* ☎ *808/936–9705* ⊕ *www.volcanogallery.com/volcano_farmers.htm* ☉ *Sun. 6:30–9AM.*

QUICK BITES

Lava Rock Cafe (⊠ *19-3972 Old Volcano Hwy., Volcano* ☎ *808/967–8526*) is best for a hearty breakfast. Lunch and dinner plates are passable and service is sometimes slow. But their to-go "seismic sandwiches" are perfect to bring along for a day of hiking around the park or exploring the rest of the area. You can also pick up picnic items and other supplies in their attached convenience store.

Volcano Garden Arts. Located on beautifully landscaped grounds with intriguing sculptures here and there, this charming complex includes an eclectic art gallery and excellent vegetarian café housed in redwood buildings built in 1908. A cute little one-bedroom "artist's cottage" is available for rent on the grounds as well. If you're lucky you'll get to meet the eccentric lord and master of this enclave, the one and only Ira Ono, known for his recycled "trash art," and his friendly hospitality. ⊠ *19-3438 Old Volcano Rd.* ☎ *808/985–8979* ⊕ *www.volcanogardenarts.com* ☞ *Free* ☉ *Tues.–Sat. 10–4.*

Volcano Golf Course and Country Club. Don't let the "country club" bit fool you, this is nothing like the snooty courses on the Kohala coast. First off, the green fees are way lower; second, the course is well maintained but not overly manicured; and third, there are rarely crowds so play is continuous and moves quickly. The course itself is reasonably challenging—an 18-hole, par 72 course—but the real draws are the views and the location. It might be the only course in the world built on an active volcano (Kīlauea), and has views of Mauna Kea and Mauna Loa, as well as frequent hawk, wild turkey, and *nēnē* sightings. The small golf course restaurant also serves a decent (and cheap) breakfast or lunch. ⊠ *99-1621 Pi'i Mauna Dr., across from the entrance to Volcanoes National Park* ☎ *808/967–7331* ⊕ *www.volcanogolfshop.com* ☞ *Green fee $57 including cart* ☉ *Weekdays 8-3, weekends 7:30-3.*

Volcano Winery. Lava rock may not seem like ideal soil for the cultivation of grapes, but that hasn't stopped the Volcano Winery from producing wines, some of which combine grapes with various island ingredients. Their Macadamia Nut Honey wine works well as an after-dinner drink, although it may be a touch too sweet for some. Their white Symphony wines have garnered the most praise from critics and visitors to the winery. The wines here aren't bad, but the primary reason to visit is the novelty of the winery itself—wine produced from an active volcano is undeniably interesting, and the tasting room and gift shop are appealing. And their wine makes for a great, unique (and fairly reasonable) gift to bring home. Staff are friendly and helpful; and their gift store has a selection of local crafts and goods. ⊠ *35 Pi'i Mauna Dr.* ☎ *808/967–7772* ⊕ *www.volcanowinery.com* ☞ *Free tasting* ☉ *Daily 10–5:30.*

Continued on page 94

HAWAI'I VOLCANOES NATIONAL PARK

Exploring the surface of the world's most active volcano—from the moonscape craters at the summit to the red-hot lava flows on the coast to the kīpuka, pockets of vegetation miraculously left untouched—is the ultimate ecotour and one of Hawai'i's must-dos.

The park sprawls over 520 square miles and encompasses Kīlauea and Mauna Loa, two of the five volcanoes that formed the Big Island nearly half a million years ago. Kīlauea, youngest and most rambunctious of the Hawaiian volcanoes, erupted at its summit from the 19th century through 1982. Since then, the top of the volcano had been more or less quiet, frequently shrouded in mist; an eruption in the Halema'uma'u Crater in 2008 ended this period of relative inactivity.

Kilauea's eastern side sprang to life on January 3, 1983, shooting molten lava four stories high. This eruption has been ongoing, and lava flows are generally steady and slow, appearing and disappearing from view. Over 500 acres have been added to Hawai'i's eastern coast since the activity began, and scientists say this eruptive phase is not likely to end anytime soon.

If you're lucky, you'll be able to catch creation at its most elemental—when molten lava meets the ocean, cools, and solidifies into brand-new stretches of coastline. Even if lava-viewing conditions aren't ideal, you can hike 150 miles of trails; camp amid wide expanses of 'a'ā (rough) and *pahoehoe* (smooth) lava; or sip cocktails at Volcano House, a hotel perched on the rim of Kīlauea Caldera. There's nothing quite like it.

- 🏠 P.O. Box 52, Hawai'i Volcanoes National Park, HI 96718
- ☎ 808/985–6000
- 🌐 www.nps.gov/havo
- 💵 $10 per vehicle; $5 for pedestrians and bicyclists. Ask about passes. Admission is good for seven consecutive days.
- 🕐 The park is open daily, 24 hours. Kīlauea Visitor Center: 7:45 am–5 pm. Thomas A. Jaggar Museum: 8:30–5. Volcano Art Center Gallery: 9–5.

(top) Kīlauea Iki Trail
(left) Fuming rim of Pu'u' Ō'ō, source of the current eruption

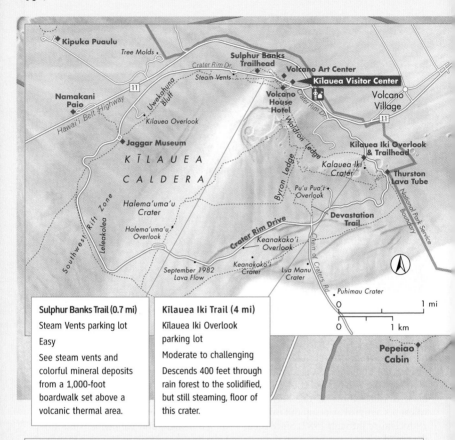

Sulphur Banks Trail (0.7 mi)

Steam Vents parking lot

Easy

See steam vents and colorful mineral deposits from a 1,000-foot boardwalk set above a volcanic thermal area.

Kīlauea Iki Trail (4 mi)

Kīlauea Iki Overlook parking lot

Moderate to challenging

Descends 400 feet through rain forest to the solidified, but still steaming, floor of this crater.

SEEING THE SUMMIT

The best way to explore the summit of Kīlauea is to cruise 11-mile Crater Rim Drive, which encircles the volcano's massive caldera. Volcano House's dining room offers front-row views of this eerie, awe-inspiring spot, which bears an uncanny resemblance to those old Apollo moon photos.

Depending on the number of stops you make, it'll take one to three hours to complete the circuit. Highlights include sulfur and steam vents, a walk-through lava tube, and the southwest rift zone—deep fissures, fractures, and gullies along Kīlauea's flanks.

There's also Halemaʻumaʻu Crater, an awesome depression in Kīlauea Caldera measuring 3,000 feet across and nearly 300 feet deep. When skies are clear, this is a good place to see Mauna Loa and Mauna Kea.

The Thomas A. Jaggar Museum offers breathtaking looks at Halemaʻumaʻu and Kīlauea Caldera, geologic displays, video presentations of volcanic eruptions, and exhibits of seismographs once used by volcanologists at the adjacent Hawaiian Volcano Observatory (not open to the public).

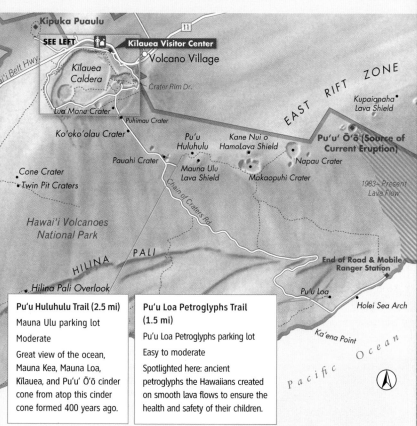

Kipuka Puaulu

SEE LEFT

Kīlauea Visitor Center

Volcano Village

Kīlauea Caldera

Hawai'i Belt Hwy.

Crater Rim Dr.

Lua Manu Crater

Puhimau Crater

Ko'oko'olau Crater

Pu'u Huluhulu

Kane Nui o HamoLava Shield

EAST RIFT ZONE

Kupaianaha Lava Shield

Pu'u' Ō'ō (Source of Current Eruption)

Pauahi Crater

Mauna Ulu Lava Shield

Napau Crater

Cone Crater

Twin Pit Craters

Makaopuhi Crater

1983– Present Lava Flow

Chain of Craters Rd.

Hawai'i Volcanoes National Park

HILINA   PALI

Hilina Pali Overlook

End of Road & Mobile Ranger Station

Pu'u Loa

Holei Sea Arch

Ka'ena Point

Pacific   Ocean

Pu'u Huluhulu Trail (2.5 mi)

Mauna Ulu parking lot

Moderate

Great view of the ocean, Mauna Kea, Mauna Loa, Kīlauea, and Pu'u' Ō'ō cinder cone from atop this cinder cone formed 400 years ago.

Pu'u Loa Petroglyphs Trail (1.5 mi)

Pu'u Loa Petroglyphs parking lot

Easy to moderate

Spotlighted here: ancient petroglyphs the Hawaiians created on smooth lava flows to ensure the health and safety of their children.

SEEING LAVA

Before you head out to find flowing lava, pinpoint the safe viewing spots at the Visitor Center. One of the best places usually is at the end of 19-mile Chain of Craters Road. Magnificent plumes of steam rise where the rivers of liquid fire meet the sea.

There are three guarantees about lava flows in HVNP. First: They constantly change. Second: Because of that, you can't predict when and where you'll be able to see them. Third: New land formed when lava meets the sea is highly unstable and can collapse at any time. Never go into areas that have been closed.

■TIP➔ The view of brilliant red-orange lava flowing from Kīlauea's east rift zone is most dramatic at night.

People watching lava flow at HVNP

PLANNING YOUR TRIP TO HVNP

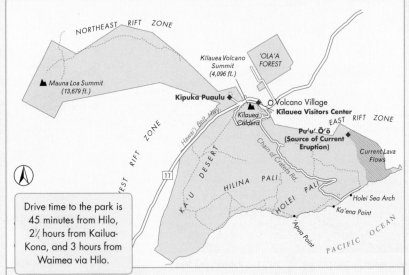

NORTHEAST RIFT ZONE

Kīlauea Volcano Summit (4,096 ft.)

'OLA'A FOREST

▲ Mauna Loa Summit (13,679 ft.)

Kipuka Puaulu ◆

Hawai'i Belt Hwy.

○ Volcano Village
Kīlauea Visitors Center

Kīlauea Caldera

EAST RIFT ZONE

Pu'u 'Ō'ō (Source of Current Eruption) ◆

Current Lava Flows

WEST RIFT ZONE

KA'U DESERT

HILINA PALI

HOLEI PALI

• Holei Sea Arch

Ka'ena Point

Chain of Craters Rd.

• Apua Point

PACIFIC OCEAN

Drive time to the park is 45 minutes from Hilo, 2¼ hours from Kailua-Kona, and 3 hours from Waimea via Hilo.

Lava entering the ocean

WHERE TO START

Begin your visit at the Visitor Center, where you'll find maps, books, and DVDs; information on trails, ranger-led walks, and special events; and current weather, road, and lava-viewing conditions. Free volcano-related film showings, lectures, and other presentations are regularly scheduled.

WEATHER

Weather conditions fluctuate daily, sometimes hourly. It can be rainy and chilly even during the summer; the temperature usually is 14° cooler at the 4,000-foot-high summit of Kīlauea than at sea level.

Expect hot, dry, and windy coastal conditions at the end of Chain of Craters Road. Bring rain gear, and wear layered clothing, sturdy shoes, sunglasses, a hat, and sunscreen.

Photographer on lava table filming lava flow into ocean

FOOD

Volcano House has the only food concessions at HVNP; it's a good idea to bring your own favorite snacks and beverages. Stock up on provisions in Volcano Village, 1½ miles away.

PARK PROGRAMS

Rangers lead daily walks into different areas; check with the Visitor Center for details as times and destinations depend on weather conditions.

Over 60 companies hold permits to lead hikes at HVNP. Good choices are Hawai'i Forest & Trail (www. hawaii-forest.com), Hawaiian Walkways (www.hawaiianwalkways. com), and Native Guide Hawai'i (www.nativeguidehawaii.com).

CAUTION

"Vog" (volcanic smog) can cause headaches; breathing difficulties; lethargy; irritations of the skin, eyes, nose, and throat; and other health problems. Pregnant women, young children, and people with asthma and heart conditions are most susceptible, and should avoid areas such as Halema'uma'u Crater where fumes are thick.

Wear long pants and boots or closed-toe shoes with good tread for hikes on lava. Stay on marked trails and step carefully. Lava is composed of 50% silica (glass) and can cause serious injury if you fall.

Carry at least 2 quarts of water on hikes. Temperatures near lava flows can rise above 100°F, and dehydration, heat exhaustion, and sunstroke are common consequences of extended exposure to intense sunlight and high temperatures.

Remember that these are active volcanoes, and eruptions can cause parts of the park to close at any time. Check the park's Web site or call ahead for last-minute updates before your visit.

Volcanologists inspecting a vent in the East Rift Zone

KAʻŪ AND KA LAE (SOUTH POINT)

The most desolate region of the island, Kaʻū is home to spectacular sights. Mark Twain wrote some of his finest prose here, where macadamia-nut farms, remote green-sand beaches, and tiny communities offer rugged, largely undiscovered beauty. The 50-mi drive from Kailua-Kona to the turn-off for windswept Ka Lae (South Point), where the first Polynesians came ashore as early as AD 750, winds away from the ocean through a surreal moonscape of lava plains and patches of scrub forest. At the end of the 12-mi two-lane to Ka Lae, you can park and hike about an hour to Papakōlea Beach (Green Sand Beach). Back on the highway, the coast passes verdant cattle pastures and sheer cliffs and the village of Naʻalehu on the way to the black-sand beach of Punaluʻu, a common nesting place of the Hawaiian green sea turtle.

GETTING HERE AND AROUND

Kaʻū and Ka Lae are destinations usually combined with a quick trip to the volcano from Kona. This is probably cramming too much into one day, however. The volcano fills up at least a day (two is better), and the sights of this southern end of the island are worth more than a cursory glance.

Our recommendation? Make Green Sand Beach or Punaluʻu your destination for a beach day at some point during your stay, and stop to see some of the other sights on the way there or back. Bring sturdy shoes, water, and a sun hat if Green Sand Beach is your choice (reaching the beach requires a hike). And be careful in the surf here. Don't go in unless you're used to ocean waves. There are no lifeguards at this remote beach. It's decidedly calmer at Punaluʻu. Don't forget your snorkeling gear.

The drive from Kailua-Kona to Ka Lae is a long one (roughly 2½ hours). It's a good idea to fill up on gas and pack a lunch before you leave, as there are few amenities along the way. Or you can eat or get picnic fixings in Naʻalehu. Weather tends to be warm, dry, and windy.

EXPLORING

★ **Ka Lae (South Point).** Windswept Ka Lae is the southernmost point of land in the United States. It's thought that the first Polynesians came ashore here. Check out the old canoe-mooring holes that are carved through the rocks, possibly by settlers from Tahiti as early as AD 750. Some artifacts, thought to have been left by early voyagers who never settled here, date to AD 300. Driving down to the point, you pass rows of giant electricity-producing windmills powered by the nearly constant winds sweeping across this coastal plain. Continue down the road (parts at the end are unpaved, but driveable), bear left when the road forks and park in the lot at the end; walk past the boat hoists toward the little lighthouse. South Point is just past the lighthouse at the southernmost cliff. ∎TIP➔ **Don't leave anything of value in your car, and know that you don't have to pay for parking. It's a free, public park, so anyone trying to charge you is likely running some sort of scam.** ✛ *Turn right past mile marker 70 on Māmalahoa Hwy., then drive 12 mi down South Point Rd.*

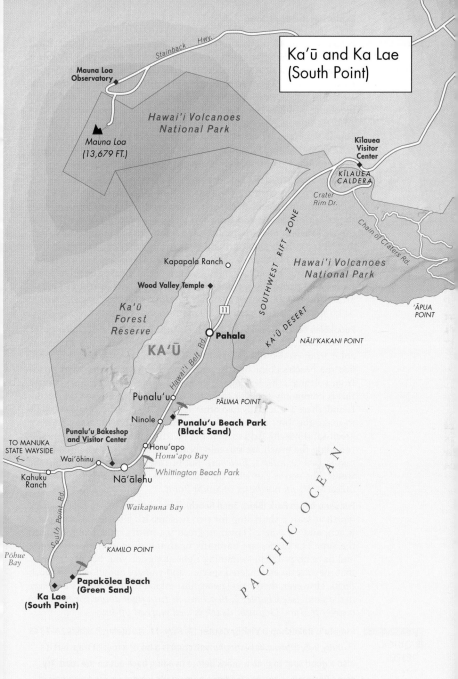

Ka'ū and Ka Lae
(South Point)

Stainback Hwy.

Mauna Loa Observatory

Hawai'i Volcanoes National Park

▲ **Mauna Loa**
(13,679 FT.)

Kīlauea Visitor Center

KĪLAUEA CALDERA

Crater Rim Dr.

Chain of Craters Rd.

Kapapala Ranch ○

SOUTHWEST RIFT ZONE

Hawai'i Volcanoes National Park

'ĀPUA POINT

Wood Valley Temple ◆

Ka'ū Forest Reserve

KA'Ū DESERT

NĀLI'KAKANI POINT

KA'Ū

11 ○ **Pahala**

Hawai'i Belt Rd.

Punalu'u ○

PĀLIMA POINT

Ninole ○ ◆ **Punalu'u Beach Park (Black Sand)**

Punalu'u Bakeshop and Visitor Center

TO MANUKA STATE WAYSIDE ←

Wai'ōhinu ○

○ Honu'apo
Honu'apo Bay

Kahuku Ranch ○

◆ ○ **Nā'ālehu**

Whittington Beach Park

Waikapuna Bay

South Point Rd.

PACIFIC OCEAN

KAMILO POINT

Pōhue Bay

◆ **Papakōlea Beach (Green Sand)**

Ka Lae (South Point)

0 _____ 6 mi
0 _____ 6 km

OFF THE
BEATEN
PATH

Pahala. About 16 mi east of Naʻalehu, beyond Punaluʻu Beach Park, Highway 11 sidesteps this little town. You'll miss it if you blink. Pahala is a perfect example of a sugar-plantation town. Behind it, along a wide cane road, you enter Wood Valley, once a prosperous community, now just a road heavily scented by eucalyptus trees, coffee blossoms, and night-blooming jasmine. Here you'll find Wood Valley Temple (☎ *808/928–8539* ⊕ *www.nechung.org*), a serene and beautiful Tibetan Buddhist temple dedicated by the Dalai Lama during his 1980 visit. Today, you can explore the gardens and the temple, attend a service, or book lodging in the temple's guesthouse for a complete Buddhist retreat.

Manuka State Wayside. This dry, upland forest spreads across several lava flows. A rugged trail follows a 2-mi loop past a pit crater and winds around ancient trees such as *hau* and *kukui*. It's an okay spot to get out of the car and stretch your legs—you can wander through the well-maintained arboretum, snap a few photos of the eerie forest, and let the kids scramble around trees so large they can't get their arms around them. However, we don't recommend spending too much time here, especially if you're planning on driving all the way down to South Point. The pathways are not well maintained, but restrooms, picnic areas, and telephones are available. ⊠ *Hwy. 11, north of mile marker 81* ☎ *808/974–6200* 💲 *Free* ☉ *Daily 7–7.*

Papakōlea Beach (Green Sand Beach). Formed by the spewed cinder of the seaside cone, Puʻu o Mahana, Papakōlea (Green Sand Beach) gets its color from eroded olivine crystals. Wind and heavy surf have intensified the beach's color by stripping away lighter grains of sand (made from volcanic ash), leaving the denser olivine crystals behind. Though this is commonly thought to be the only green-sand beach on the Big Island, there are actually two other remote ones nearby. It takes a while to make the 3-mi coastal trek, but where else are you going to see a green-sand beach? Add to that the fact that the rock formations surrounding the beach are surreally beautiful, and this is a detour worth taking *(see Chapter 3, Beaches)*. But be careful if you venture into the water. The waves can whip up quickly and there are no lifeguards for miles. ⊠ *2½ mi northeast of South Point.*

Punaluʻu Beach Park (Black Sand Beach). This easily accessed beach is well worth at least a short stop for two reasons: it's a beautiful black-sand beach, and it's where Hawaiian green sea turtles often like to bask in the sun. The turtles are naturally unafraid of us nonflippered types, and have no problem swimming right alongside you, but never forget that they are an endangered species, and you are not allowed to touch them. However, there's no law against taking their picture as they nap in the sand. *(see Chapter 3, Beaches).* ⊹ *Turn right down driveway into beach off Hwy. 11 south. Beach is well marked off hwy.*

QUICK
BITES

Punaluʻu Bakeshop & Visitor Center (⊠ *Hwy. 11, Naʻalehu* ☎ *808/929–7343* ☉ *Daily 9–5,* ⊕ *www.bakeshophawaii.com*) is a bit of a tourist trap, but it's also a good spot to grab a snack before heading back out on the road. Try some Portuguese sweet bread or a homemade ice-cream sandwich paired with some local Kaʻū coffee (that's right, not Kona, but equally tasty).

3

Beaches

WORD OF MOUTH

"The Hāpuna beach is great, free of anything but soft sand. If you want a beach, the Hāpuna beach and the Mauna Kea beach are the best swimming beaches in the [Kohala] area."

—sandinmytoes

Updated by
Katie Young
Yamanaka

Don't believe anyone who tells you that the Big Island lacks beaches. It's just one of the myths about Hawai'i's largest island that has no basis in fact. It's not so much that the Big Island has fewer beaches than the other islands, just that there's more island, so getting to the beaches can be slightly less convenient.

That said, there are plenty of those perfect white-sand stretches you think of when you hear "Hawai'i," and the added bonus of black-and green-sand beaches, thanks to the age of the island and its active volcanoes. New beaches appear and disappear regularly, created and destroyed by volcanic activity. In 1989 a black-sand beach, Kamoamoa, formed when molten lava shattered as it hit cold ocean waters; it was closed by new lava flows in 1992. It's part of the ongoing process of the volcano's creation and change dynamic.

The bulk of the island's beaches are on the northwest part of the island, along the Kohala Coast. Black-sand beaches and green-sand beaches are in the southern region, along the coast nearest the volcano. On the eastern side of the island, beaches tend to be of the rocky-coast–surging-surf variety, but there are still a few worth visiting, and this is where the Hawaiian shoreline is at its most picturesque.

KAILUA-KONA

There are a few good sandy beaches in the area near Kailua-Kona town. However, the coastline is generally rugged black lava rock, so don't expect long stretches of wide golden sand. The beaches near Kailua-Kona get lots of use by local residents and visitors will enjoy them, too. Excellent opportunities for snorkeling, scuba diving, swimming, kayaking, and other water sports are easy to find. The beaches here are listed from north to south.

Kaloko–Honokōhau National Historical Park. There are few beaches with as many old Hawaiian archaeological ruins as these two, sheltered in a 1,160-acre park near Honokōhau Harbor, just north of Kailua-Kona town. Both are good for swimming. 'Ai'opio (☞ *Toilets*), **a few yards north of the harbor, is a small beach with calm, protected swimming areas (good for kids) and great snorkeling in the water near the archaeo-logical site of Hale o Mono.** Honokōhau Beach (☞ *No facilities*), a ¾-mi stretch with ruins of ancient fishponds, is also north of the harbor. The park seeks to preserve early Hawaiian archaeological resources includ-ing *heiau* (an ancient Hawaiian place of worship), house platforms, fishponds, petroglyph rock etchings, and more. The park's wetlands provide refuge to a number of waterbirds, including the endemic Hawai-ian stilt and coot. For information about the park, visit its headquarters, a 5- to 10-minute drive away. ✉ *74-425 Kealakehe Pkwy., off Hwy. 19*

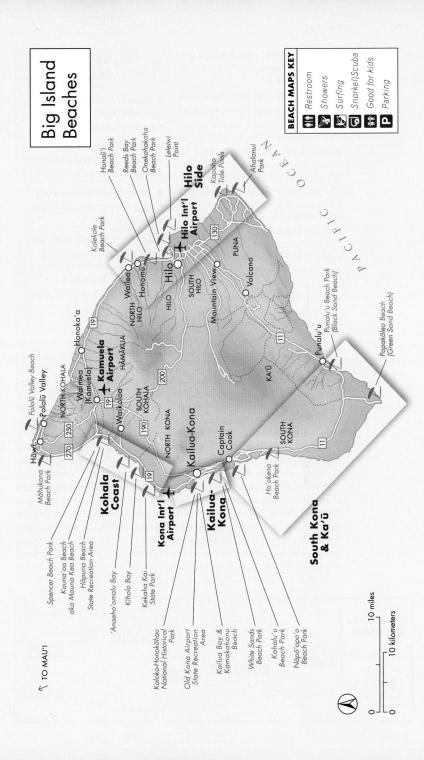

Big Island Beaches

BEACH MAPS KEY

Restroom	
Showers	
Surfing	
Snorkel/Scuba	
Good for kids	
Parking	

↖ TO MAUI

PACIFIC OCEAN

Hilo Side

Honoli'i Beach Park
Reeds Bay Beach Park
Onekahakaha Beach Park
Leleiwi Point
Kapoho Tide Pools
Ahalanui Park

Kolekole Beach Park
Wailea
Honomū
Hilo
Hilo Int'l Airport

130
PUNA
Volcano

NORTH HILO
SOUTH HILO
HILO
HĀMĀKUA
Honoka'a
19
Kamuela Airport
Waimea (Kamuela)
19
Waikoloa
NORTH KOHALA
250
270
Hāwī
Pololū Valley
Māhukona Beach Park
Pololū Valley Beach

Mountain-View
SOUTH KOHALA
200
190
NORTH KONA
Kailua-Kona
Captain Cook
SOUTH KONA
KA'Ū
Punalu'u
11
11

Punalu'u Beach Park (Black Sand Beach)
Papakōlea Beach (Green Sand Beach)

Spencer Beach Park
Kauna'oa Beach aka Mauna Kea Beach
Hāpuna Beach State Recreation Area

Kohala Coast

'Anaeho'omalu Bay
Kīholo Bay
Kekaha Kai State Park
Kaloko-Honokōhau National Historical Park
Old Kona Airport State Recreation Area
Kailua Bay & Kamakahonu Beach
White Sands Beach Park
Kahalu'u Beach Park
Nāpō'opo'o Beach Park

Kailua-Kona
Kona Int'l Airport

Ho'okena Beach Park

South Kona & Ka'ū

0   10 miles
0   10 kilometers

☎ *808/329–6881* ⊕ *www.nps.gov* ⊗ *Park road gate* 8AM*–*5PM ⟲ *Toilets, parking lot.*

Old Kona Airport State Recreation Area. The unused runway—great for jogging—is still visible above this palm-tree-lined beach at Kailua Park, a popular place to picnic, beachcomb, and sunbathe. It's especially busy on weekends. The generally rocky shoreline has a few small pocket coves of white sand with safe entry to the water and tide pools for children, but for adults it's better for snorkeling than swimming. Conditions are best here on calmer days. An offshore surfing break known as Old Airport is popular with local surfers. ⊠ *North end of Kuakini Hwy., Kailua-Kona* ☎ *808/327–4958 or 808/974–6200* ⟲ *Toilets, showers, picnic tables, parking lot.*

BIG ISLAND'S TOP BEACHES

■ Kauna'oa Beach (also known as Mauna Kea Beach) is a beautiful palm-lined golden crescent.

■ Hāpuna Beach is a wide expanse of fine sandy playground and aquamarine water.

■ 'Anaeho'omalu Beach's lovely curving crescent provides lots of water sports options.

■ Kua Bay is a scenic white sand beach with crystal clear water perfect for snorkeling in summer. Punalu'u Beach Park has black sand *and* guaranteed turtle watching.

ᗧ **Kailua Bay and Kamakahonu Beach.** Fronting King Kamehameha's Kona Beach Hotel and next to Kailua Pier, this little crescent of white sand is the only beach in downtown Kailua-Kona. Protected by the harbor, the water here is nice and calm, making this a perfect spot for kids. They can play in the sand, paddle kayaks, take Hawaiian outrigger canoe rides, and splash in the warm water. For adults it's a great place for a swim, some stand-up paddleboarding, or just a lazy beach day. The water is surprisingly clear for being surrounded by an active pier. Snorkeling can be good, especially if you move north of the beach where the water is a little deeper and the coral reef is pristine. There's a kiosk with snorkeling and kayaking equipment rentals. ■**TIP→** **A little family of sea turtles likes to hang out by the swim lane line to feed on the algae that grows there, so keep an eye out.** On a small peninsula protecting the beach is Ahu'ena Heiau, the recognized temple of King Kamehameha the Great, who spent the last years of his life here at Kamakahonu. The area is considered sacred to the Hawaiian people so a high level of respect for nature should be practiced by all visitors. ⊠ *Ali'i Dr.* ⟲ *Toilets available on the adjacent boat pier.*

The calm Kailua Bay is an excellent spot for rowing, snorkeling, and swimming.

White Sands, Magic Sands, or Disappearing Sands Beach. Towering coconut trees provide some shade and lend a touch of tropical beauty to this pretty little beach park, which may well be the Big Island's most intriguing stretch of sand. A migratory beach of sorts, it goes away in winter and returns in summer: winter waves wash away the small white-sand parcel. In summer it re-forms; you'll know you've found it when you see the body- and board surfers. Though not really a great beach, this is a popular summer hangout for young locals. ⊠ *Ali'i Dr., 4½ mi south of Kailua-Kona* ☎ *808/961–8311* ☞ *Lifeguard, toilets, showers, food concession, parking lot.*

Kahalu'u Beach Park. Snorkelers can actually hand-feed the unusually tame reef fish at this spot, although we advise against it—certain human foods may not kill them, but fish fed by humans become dependent on easy feedings and start to lose their survival instincts. Don't even get us started on the folks who think it's okay to feed candy to the fish. Kahalu'u was a favorite of King Kalākaua, whose summer cottage is on the grounds of the neighboring Outrigger Keauhou Beach Resort. The salt-and-pepper beach is a combination of white and black sand mixed with lava and coral pebbles. This is one of the Big Island's most popular swimming and snorkeling sites, thanks to the fringing reef that helps keep the waters calm. But outside the reef there are very strong rip currents, so caution is advised. ■ TIP➔ **Experienced surfers find good waves to ride beyond the reef, and scuba divers like the shore dives—shallow ones inside the breakwater, deeper ones outside.** ⊠ *Ali'i Dr., 5½ mi south of Kailua-Kona* ☎ *808/961–8311* ☞ *Lifeguard, toilets, showers, food concession, picnic tables, parking lot.*

SOUTH KONA AND KA'Ū

You shouldn't expect to find sparkling white-sand beaches on the rugged and rocky coasts of South Kona and Ka'ū, and you won't. What you will find is something a bit more rare and well worth the visit: black- and green-sand beaches. And there's the chance to see the endangered Hawaiian green sea turtles close up. Beaches are listed here from north to south.

Nāpō'opo'o Beach Park. There's no real beach here, but don't let that deter you—this is a great spot and a historically significant one. It's where Captain James Cook landed in late 1778 to refurbish his ships; when he returned in 1779 he was killed in a skirmish with Hawaiians. A monument marks the spot on the north end of the bay. Kealakekua Bay is surrounded by high green cliffs, so the water's usually fairly calm and clear, making it ideal for swimming. Bring a mask along, as the snorkeling in the Kealakekua Bay Underwater Marine Reserve is superb. It's a great place to spot varied marine life, schools of colorful reef fish, corals, and more. This is also a great kayaking spot, and there are several shops in the villages of Honalo, Kainaliu, Kealakekua, and Captain Cook along Highway 11 that rent kayaks, in addition to snorkel gear. You can also take a snorkel, scuba, or glass-bottom boat tour from Keauhou Bay. ⚠ **An earthquake in October 2006 caused rocks and dirt from the surrounding cliffs to fall into the bay. The beach is open, but be aware of the off-limits area (in case of future rockfalls) marked by orange buoys. Do not enter this area.** ⊠ *End of Nāpō'opo'o Rd., off Hwy. 11, Kealakekua Bay* ☎ *808/961–8311* ☞ *Parking lot.*

Ho'okena Beach Park. Driving south on Highway 11 from Kealakekua Bay, you'll see the sign for Ho'okena Beach Park. The road down to the quiet, out-of-the-way beach is narrow and steep, but the views are great. Plus you'll feel like you're venturing off the beaten path. By Hawaiian standards, this is an average beach (the water's nice for swimming, and there's a bit of snorkeling but nothing amazing), but that still makes it great for the rest of us. It's frequented mostly by the people from the nearby village; it's rarely crowded, except on weekends. The smallish beach, blessed with a few shade trees, is composed of black and white sand mixed with lava debris, which gives the sand an overall gray color. The bay is usually calm for swimming, snorkeling, and diving but caution is advised during high surf periods. ⊠ *2-mi drive down road bordered by ruins of stone wall off Hwy. 11, 23 mi south of Kailua-Kona* ☎ *808/961–8311* ☞ *Toilets, showers, picnic tables, parking lot.*

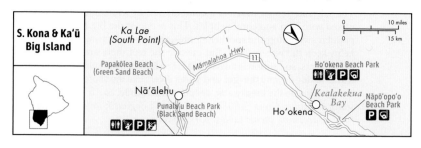

★ **Papakōlea Beach (Green Sand Beach).**
Tired of the same old gold-, white-, or black-sand beach? Then how about a green-sand beach? You'll need good hiking shoes or sneakers at the very least to get to this olive-green crescent, one of the most unusual beaches on the island. It lies at the base of Pu'u o Mahana, at Mahana Bay, where a cinder cone formed during an early eruption of Mauna Loa. The greenish tint is caused by an accumulation of olivine crystals that form in volcanic eruptions. The dry, barren landscape is totally surreal. The surf is often rough and swimming is hazardous due to strong currents, so caution is advised, but a dip in the clear, turquoise water, surrounded by green sand and gray cliffs sculpted into Gaudí-like shapes by the wind, may well be the highlight of your trip. Take the road toward the left at the end of the paved road to Ka Lae (South Point) about 12 mi off Highway 11. Park at the end of the road. △ Anyone trying to charge you for parking is running a scam. To reach the beach, follow the 2-mi coastal trail that ends in a steep and dangerous descent down the cliff side, on an unimproved trail. The hike will take about 2 hours each way so make sure to bring lots of drinking water (4WD vehicles are no longer permitted on the trail). ■TIP→ Though the simple gate blocking the trail is not exactly a huge deterrent, it may be locked for a good reason—dangerous surf, a rock slide— so it's a good idea to check before going around it. ✉ 2½ mi northeast of South Point, off Hwy. 11 ☞ No facilities.

★ **Punalu'u Beach Park (Black Sand Beach).** Endangered Hawaiian green sea turtles nest in the black sand of this beautiful and easily accessible beach. You can see them feeding on the seaweed along the surf break or napping on the sand. You can even swim with the turtles; they're used to people and will swim along right next to you. (Resist the urge to touch them, though.) However, strong shoreward currents make being in the water here a hazard. Don't venture far out, and avoid going past the boat ramp as very strong rip currents are active. ■TIP→ It's quite rocky in the water, even close to shore—you might want to bring a pair of reef shoes if you plan to swim. The beach is a long black-sand crescent backed by low dunes with some rocky outcroppings at the shoreline. It's not usually a tranquil spot, though, since the turtles attract big groups of picture-snapping visitors. At its northern end, near the boat ramp, lie the ruins of Kane'ele'ele Heiau, an old Hawaiian temple. This area used to be a sugar port until the tidal wave of 1946 destroyed the buildings. Inland is a memorial to Henry 'Ōpūkaha'ia. In 1809, when he was 17, 'Ōpūkaha'ia swam out to a fur-trading ship in the harbor and asked to sign up as a cabin boy. When he reached New England, he entered the Foreign Mission School in Connecticut, but he died of typhoid fever in 1818. His dream of bringing Christianity to the Islands inspired the

American Board of Missionaries to send the first Protestant missionaries to Hawai'i in 1820. ⊠ *Hwy. 11, 27 mi south of Hawai'i Volcanoes National Park* ☎ *808/961–8311* ☞ *Toilets, showers, food concession, grills/firepits, parking lot.*

KOHALA COAST

Most of the Big Island's white sandy beaches are found on the Kohala Coast, which is, understandably, home to the majority of the island's first-class resorts. Hawai'i's beaches are public property. The resorts are required to provide public access to the beach, so don't be frightened off by a guard shack and a fancy sign. There is some limited public parking as well. The resort beaches aside, there are some real hidden gems on the Kohala Coast accessible only by boat, four-wheel drive, or a 15- to 20-minute hike. It's well worth the effort to get to at least one of these. ■TIP→ The west side of the island tends to be calmer, but the surf still gets rough in winter. The beaches here are listed in order from north (farthest from Kailua-Kona) to south.

Pololū Valley Beach. On the North Kohala peninsula is one of the Big Island's most scenic black-sand beaches. About 8 mi past Hāwī town, Highway 270 terminates at the overlook of remote Pololū Valley. Beach access is gained by a 15-minute hike down (twice as long back up) a generally steep and rocky trail that can be muddy and slippery. Caution is advised. The beach itself is a nice wide expanse of fine black sand surrounded by sheer green cliffs and backed by high dunes dotted with pine trees. A gurgling stream leads from the beach to the back of the valley. ■TIP→ This is not a particularly safe swimming beach even though locals do swim, body board, and surf here. Dangerous rip currents and usually rough surf pose a real hazard. And because this is a remote, isolated area far from emergency help, extreme caution is advised. The valley leading back from the beach was once farmed with taro patches but is no longer being used. There is very limited parking at the turnaround and along the roadside here. ⊠ *End of Hwy. 270* ☞ *No facilities.*

Māhukona Beach Park. Snorkelers and divers will find excitement in the clear waters of this small beach park. Long ago, when sugar was the economic staple of Kohala, this harbor was busy with boats waiting for overseas shipments. Now it's a great swimming hole and an underwater museum of sorts. Remnants of shipping machinery, train wheels and other parts, and what looks like an old boat are easily visible in the clear water. There's no sandy beach here, but a ladder off the old dock makes getting in the water easy. It's best to venture out only on tranquil days, when the water is calm. A camping area is available. ⊠ *Off Hwy. 270, between mile markers 14 and 15, Māhukona* ☎ *808/961–8311* ☞ *Toilets, showers, picnic tables, grills, parking lot.*

♺ **Spencer Park at 'Ohai'ula Beach.** This smaller beach, gently sloping with white sand and a few pebbles, is popular with local families because of its reef-protected waters. ■TIP→ It's probably the safest beach in west Hawai'i for young children. It's also safe for swimming year-round, which makes it an excellent spot for a lazy day at the beach. Unfortunately, it

does tend to get crowded on weekends, and the beach is often dotted with litter, but the water is crystal clear, although there aren't loads of fish here. The beach park lies just below Pu'ukoholā Heiau National Historic Park, site of the historic temple built by King Kamehameha the Great in 1795. ⊠ *Off Hwy. 270, uphill from Kawaihae Harbor* ☎ *808/961–8311* ☞ *Lifeguard, toilets, showers, picnic tables, grills, parking lot.*

Fodor's Choice
★
Kauna'oa Beach (Mauna Kea Beach). Hands-down one of the most beautiful beaches on the island, Kauna'oa is a long white crescent of sand. The beach, which fronts the Mauna Kea Beach Hotel, slopes very gradually. It's a great place for snorkeling. When conditions permit, there is good body- and board surfing also. Currents can be strong, and powerful winter waves can be dangerous, so be careful. ■ TIP➜ **Public parking at this beach is limited to only 40 spaces, so it's best to arrive before 10 AM. If the lot is full, head to nearby Hāpuna Beach, where a huge parking lot is never full, and try this spot again a different morning. It's worth it!** ⊠ *Off Hwy. 19; entry through gate to Mauna Kea Beach Resort* ☞ *Lifeguard, toilets, showers, parking lot.*

Fodor's Choice
★
Hāpuna Beach State Recreation Area. By any measurement, this is one fine beach. Guidebooks usually say it's a toss-up between Hāpuna and Kauna'oa for "best beach" on the island, but most locals give the prize to Hāpuna. There is ample parking so you don't have to get here at dawn, although the lot can fill up by midday. And while the north end of the beach fronts the Hāpuna Beach Prince Hotel, rest assured that this is a public beach. The beach itself is a long (½-mi), white, perfect crescent, one of the Big Island's largest. The turquoise water is very calm in summer, with just enough rolling waves to make bodysurfing or boogie boarding fun. There's some excellent snorkeling around the jagged rocks that border the beach on either side, but a strong current means it's only for experienced swimmers. In winter, surf can be very rough. Hāpuna tends to get a little windy in the late afternoon; even that can have a benefit, as everyone else leaves just in time to give you a private, perfect sunset. ■ TIP➜ **There are a couple of small protected coves at the north end of the beach with shallow, sandy-bottomed pools ideal for youngsters.** ⊠ *Hwy. 19, near mile marker 69, at Hāpuna Beach Prince Hotel* ☎ *808/974–6200* ☞ *Lifeguard, toilets, showers, picnic tables, grills/firepits, parking lot.*

★
'Anaeho'omalu Beach (A-Bay). This expansive beach of golden sand mixed with black lava grains fronts the Waikoloa Beach Marriott and is perfect for swimming, windsurfing, snorkeling, and diving. It's along a well-

BEACH SAFETY

Hawai'i's world-renown, beautiful beaches can be extremely dangerous at times due to large waves and strong currents—so much so that the state rates wave hazards using three signs: a yellow square (caution), a red stop sign (high hazard), and a black diamond (extreme hazard). Signs are posted and updated three times daily or as conditions change.

Visiting beaches with lifeguards is strongly recommended, and you should only swim when there's a normal caution rating. Never swim alone or dive into unknown water or shallow breaking waves. If you're unable to swim out of a rip current, tread water and wave your arms in the air to signal for help.

Even in calm conditions, there are other dangerous things in the water to be aware of, including razor-sharp coral, jellyfish, eels, and sharks, to name a few.

Jellyfish cause the most ocean injuries, and signs are posted along beaches when they're present. Box jellyfish swarm to Hawai'i's leeward shores 9–10 days after a full moon. Portuguese man-of-wars are usually found when winds blow from the ocean onto land. Reactions to a sting are usually mild (burning sensation, redness, welts); however, in some cases they can be severe (breathing difficulties). If you are stung by a jellyfish, pick off the tentacles, rinse the affected area with water, and apply ice. Seek first aid from a lifeguard if you experience severe reactions.

According to state sources, the chances of getting bitten by a shark in Hawaiian waters are very low; sharks attack swimmers or surfers three or four times per year. Of the 40 species of sharks found near Hawai'i, tiger sharks are considered the most dangerous because of their size and indiscriminate feeding behavior (they eat just about anything at the water's surface). Tiger sharks are easily recognized by their blunt snouts and vertical bars on their sides.

Here are a few tips to reduce your shark-attack risk:

■ Swim, surf, or dive with others at beaches patrolled by lifeguards.

■ Avoid swimming at dawn, dusk, and night, when some shark species may move inshore to feed.

■ Don't enter the water if you have open wounds or are bleeding.

■ Avoid murky waters, harbor entrances, areas near stream mouths (especially after heavy rains), channels, or steep drop-offs.

■ Don't wear high-contrast swimwear or shiny jewelry.

■ Don't swim near dolphins, which are often prey for large sharks.

■ If you spot a shark, leave the water quickly and calmly; never provoke or harass a shark, no matter how small.

The Web site ⊕ *http://oceansafety. soest.hawaii.edu* provides beach hazard maps for O'ahu, Maui, Kaua'i and the Big Island, as well as weather and surf advisories, listings of closed beaches, and safety tips.

protected bay, so even when surf is rough on the rest of the island, it's fairly calm here. Snorkel gear, kayaks, and boogie boards are available for rent at the north end. Graceful coconut palms line the beach and behind it are two old Hawaiian fishponds, Ku'uali'i and Kahapapa, that served the Hawaiian royalty in the old days. A walking trail follows the coastline to the Hilton Waikoloa Village next door, passing by tide pools and ponds. Footwear is recommended for the trail. ✛ *Follow Waikoloa Beach Dr. to Kings' Shops, then turn left; parking lot and beach right-of-way south of Waikoloa Beach Marriott* ☞ *Toilets, showers, food concession, picnic tables, parking lot.*

Kīholo Bay. The brilliant turquoise waters of this bay are a cooling invitation on a warm Kohala day, and a new gravel road to the shoreline makes it an absolute must-see (previously you would have had to hike over lava for 20 minutes). Thanks to Mauna Loa, what was once the site of King Kamehameha's gigantic fishpond is now several freshwater ponds encircling a beautiful little bay. The water's a bit cold and hazy because of the mix of fresh and salty water, but there are tons of green sea turtles in residence year-round here, and the snorkeling is great. If you follow the shoreline southwest toward Kona, just past the big yellow house is another public beach where you'll find some naturally occurring freshwater pools inside a lava tube. This area, called Queen's Bath, is as cool as it sounds. ✉ *Hwy. 19, gravel road between mile markers 82 and 83* ☞ *No facilities.*

Kua Bay. Remoteness does have its merits at this lovely beach, the northernmost beach in the stretch of coast that comprises Kekaha Kai State Park. At one time you had to hike over a few miles of unmarked, rocky trail to get here, which kept many people out. Now, a newly paved road leads to Kua Bay, and while locals are pretty unhappy about it, this beach is still relatively uncrowded compared to others. It's easy to understand why area residents would be so protective. This is one of the most beautiful bays you will ever see—the water is crystal clear, deep aquamarine, and peaceful in summer. Rocky shores on either side keep the beach from getting too windy in the afternoon. The surf here can get very rough in winter. ✉ *Hwy. 19, north of mile marker 88* ☞ *No facilities.*

Kekaha Kai State Park. A 1½-mi narrow, bumpy gravel road leads off Highway 19 to this recently developed beach park. Mahai'ula is to the south while Ka'elehuluhulu is to the north. The wide expanse of good sandy beach provides a lot of space, so it doesn't feel crowded. There are high sand dunes and tidal pools for snorkeling and swimming. The sand is a salt-and-pepper mix of golden and black lava grains and pebbles. ⚠ **Caution is advised for rough surf and strong currents.** You can hike along a historic 4½-mi trail from one beach to the other and, if you're game, work your way to the top of Pu'u Ku'ili, a 342-foot-high cinder cone whose summit offers a fantastic view of the coastline. However, be prepared for the heat and bring lots of drinking water. ✉ *Hwy. 19, sign about 2 mi north of Keāhole–Kona International Airport marks rough road* ☎ *808/327–4958 or 808/974–6200* ☞ *Parking lot at entrance, Mahai'ula: Toilets, picnic area; Ka'elehuluhulu: No facilities.*

Kua Bay is protected from wind by the rocky shores that surround it.

THE HĀMĀKUA COAST AND HILO

There are no real beaches along the jagged cliffs of the Hāmākua Coast, but there are a few surf spots and swimming holes worth an afternoon stop. Hilo isn't exactly known for its beautiful white beaches, but there are a few in the area that provide good swimming and snorkeling opportunities, and most are surrounded by lush rain forest. Puna's few beaches have some unique attributes—swaths of black sand, volcano-heated springs, and a coastline that is beyond dramatic (sheer walls of lava rock dropping into the bluest ocean you've ever seen). Beaches are listed from north to south.

Kolekole Beach Park. This small beach park is a picture postcard of tropical Hawai'i. The Kolekole Stream meets the ocean here between 'Akaka and Umauma Falls, just below a high bridge that crosses the gulch along Highway 19. The beach is composed of large, smooth, waterworn lava rocks. Although the shoreline is rocky, the stream is calm and great for swimming. There's even a rope swing tied to a banyan tree on the opposite side. The stream flows from the lovely 'Akaka Falls Park located about 4 mi upstream. Even though the park is only fair for beach activities, it's surrounded by vegetation and is ideal for a picnic. Local surfers like this spot in the winter. ■TIP→ Where the stream meets the ocean, the surf is rough and the currents strong. Only very experienced swimmers should venture here. ⊠ Off Hwy. 19 ☎ 808/961–8311 ☜ Free ☉ Daily 7AM–sunset ☞ Toilets, showers, picnic tables, grills, parking lot.

Honoli'i Beach Park. There aren't many places along the east Hawai'i coastline to catch the waves when the surf's up, but this is one of the

best. It's popular among the local surf crowd, and it's fun to watch the surfers paddle out to catch the waves. ■TIP➔ **The presence of surfers is not an indication that an area is safe for swimmers.** The sandy beach is minimal here, a mix of sand and coral rubble debris along the mostly rocky coast. There's limited parking beside the narrow roadside. ✉ *1½ mi north of Hilo on Hwy. 19* ☎ *808/961–8311* ☞ *Toilets.*

Reeds Bay Beach Park. Safe swimming, proximity to downtown Hilo, and a freshwater-fed swimming hole, called the Ice Pond, that flows into the backwaters of Hilo Bay are the enticements of this cove. No, there really isn't ice in the swimming hole; it just feels that way on a hot sultry day. The large pond, between Hilo Seaside Hotel and Harrington's Restaurant, is a favorite of local kids who enjoy jumping into and frolicking in the chilly fresh- and saltwater mix. There is no real beach here, however. ✉ *Banyan Dr. and Kalaniana'ole Ave., Hilo* ☎ *808/961–8311* ☞ *No facilities.*

Onekahakaha Beach Park. A white-sand beach with shallow, enclosed tide pools makes this a favorite for Hilo families with small children. The protected pools are great places to look for Hawaiian marine life such as small fish, brittle stars, sea cucumbers, seashells, sea urchins, and more. The water is usually rough beyond the line of large boulders protecting the inner tide pools. Caution is advised in times of heavy surf. ✉ *Kalaniana'ole Ave., 3 mi east of Hilo* ☎ *808/961–8311* ☞ *Lifeguard, toilets, showers, picnic tables, parking lot.*

Leleiwi Beach Park and Richardson Ocean Park. There's hardly any sand here near road's end in Keaukaha, east of Hilo, but these two beaches make up one beautiful spot—laced with bays, inlets, lagoons, and pretty parks. It's a peaceful setting for a lazy day at the beach; the grassy area is ideal for picnics. Rocky outcrops provide shelter for schools of reef fish, and snorkeling can be great, as turtles and dolphins frequent this area. Local kids use the small black-sand pocket beach for body boarding. ✉ *2349 Kalaniana'ole Ave., 4 mi east of Hilo* ☎ *808/961–8311* ☞ *Lifeguard (on weekends), picnic tables, parking lot.*

Kapoho Tide Pools. Snorkelers will find tons of coral and the fish who feed off it in this network of tide pools at the end of Kapoho-Kai Road. This is a great place for getting close-up looks at Hawai'i's interesting marine life and reef fish. Some of the pools have been turned into private swimming pools; those closest to the ocean are open to all. The pools are usually very calm, and some are volcanically heated. It's best to come during the week, as the pools can get crowded on the weekend. Note: there is no real sandy beach here. Take the road to the end, then

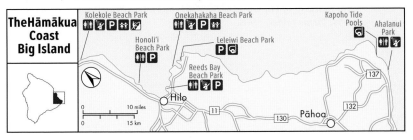

SUN SAFETY

Hawai'i's weather—seemingly never-ending warm, sunny days with gentle trade winds—can be enjoyed year-round with good sun sense. Because of Hawai'i's subtropical location, the length of daylight here changes little throughout the year. The sun is particularly strong, with a daily UV average of 14. Visitors should take extra precaution to avoid sunburns and long-term cancer risks due to sun exposure.

The Hawai'i Dermatological Society recommends these sun safety tips:

■ Plan your beach, golf, hiking, and other outdoor activities for the early morning or late afternoon, avoiding the sun between 10 am and 4 pm when it's the strongest.

■ Apply a broad-spectrum sunscreen with a sun protection factor (SPF) of at least 15. Hawai'i lifeguards use sunscreens with an SPF of 30. Cover areas that are most prone to burning like your nose, shoulders, tops of feet, and ears. And don't forget to use sun protection products on your lips.

■ Apply sunscreen at least 30 minutes before you plan to be outdoors and reapply every two hours, even on cloudy days. Clouds scatter sunlight so you can still burn on an overcast day.

■ Wear light, protective clothing, such as a long-sleeved shirt and pants, broad-brimmed hat, and sunglasses.

■ Stay in the shade whenever possible—especially on the beach—by using an umbrella. Remember that sand and water can reflect up to 85% of the sun's damaging rays.

■ Children need extra protection from the sun. Apply sunscreen frequently and liberally on children over six months of age and minimize their time in the sun. Sunscreen is not recommended for children under six months.

turn left and park. ⊠ *End of Kapoho-Kai Road, off Hwy. 13, about 9 mi southeast of Pāhoa town* ⚲ *No facilities.*

Ahalanui Park. This 3-acre beach park has a ½-acre pond—fresh spring water mixed with seawater—heated by volcanic steam. There's nothing like swimming in this geothermal pool, especially when the nearby ocean is rough. ■TIP→ The pool has had ongoing bacterial contamination problems that are typical of some ocean tidal pools in Hawai'i. Those with skin-lesion problems, or chronic conditions like psoriasis may want to avoid the water here. Others should have no problem. Check with the lifeguard on duty, and heed all posted signs. ⊠ *Hwy. 137, 2½ mi south of junction of Hwy. 132* ☎ *808/961–8311* ⚲ *Lifeguard, toilets, showers, picnic tables, grills.*

Water Activities & Tours

WORD OF MOUTH

"If snorkeling and kayaking are high on your list, go to the Big Island. Have been to Maui and Kona many times and love both equally, but in my opinion the snorkeling is a little better on the Big Island. Don't miss kayaking and snorkeling in Kealakekua Bay."

— sceneisle

Updated by
Bill Harby

The ancient Hawaiians, who took much of their daily sustenance from the ocean, also enjoyed playing in the water. In fact, surfing was the sport of kings. Though it's easy to be lulled into whiling away the day baking in the sun on a white-, gold-, black-, or green-sand beach, getting into and onto the water will be a highlight of your trip to the Big Island.

All of the Hawaiian Islands are surrounded by the Pacific Ocean, making them some of the world's greatest natural playgrounds. But certain experiences are even better on the Big Island: nighttime scuba diving trips to see manta rays; deep-sea fishing in Kona's fabled waters, where dozens of Pacific blue marlin of 1,000 pounds or more have been caught; kayaking among the dolphins in Kealakekua Bay; and sighting humpback whales on a whale-watching cruise. With underwater coral reefs and marine preserves harboring endemic and endangered species, such as the Hawaiian green sea turtle and the Hawaiian monk seal, plus tropical fish in a rainbow of colors, snorkelers are in paradise.

From any point on the Big Island, the ocean is never far away. With the variety of water sports that can be enjoyed—from body boarding and snorkeling to kayaking and surfing—there is something for everyone. For most activities, you can rent gear and go it alone or sign up for a group excursion with an experienced guide who can offer security as well as special insights into Hawaiian marine life and culture. Want to try surfing? You can take lessons as well.

The Kona and Kohala Coasts of west Hawai'i have the largest number of ocean sports outfitters and tour operators. They operate from the small boat harbors and piers in Kailua-Kona, Keauhou, and at the Kohala Coast resorts. There are also several outfitters in the east Hawai'i and Hilo areas.

As a general rule, the waves are gentler here than on the other Islands, but there are a few things to be aware of before heading to the shore. First, don't turn your back on the ocean. It's unlikely, but if conditions are right a wave could come along and push you face-first into the sand or drag you out to sea. Conditions can change quickly, so keep your eyes open. Second, realize that ultimately you must keep yourself safe. We strongly encourage you to obey lifeguards and heed the advice of outfitters from whom you rent equipment. It could save your trip, or even your life.

BODY BOARDING AND BODYSURFING

According to the movies, in the Old West there was always friction between cattle ranchers and sheep ranchers. Sometimes a similar situation exists between surfers and body boarders. That's why they generally

keep to their own separate surfing areas. Often the body boarders stay closer to shore and leave the outside breaks to the board surfers. Or the board surfers may stick to one side of the beach and the body boarders to the other. The truth is, body boarding (often called "boogie boarding" in homage to the first commercial manufacturer of this slick little flexible foam board) is a blast. The only surfers who don't also sometimes carve waves on a body board are hardcore purists, and almost none of that type live on this island.

■TIP➜ Novice body boarders should catch shore-break waves only. Ask lifeguards or locals for the best spots. You'll need a pair of short fins to get out to the bigger waves offshore (not recommended for newbies). As for bodysurfing, just catch a wave and make like Superman going faster than a speeding bullet.

BEST SPOTS

When conditions are right, **Hāpuna Beach State Recreation Area** (⊠ *Hwy. 19, near mile marker 69*)north of Kailua-Kona, is fabulous. The water is very calm in summer, with just enough rolling waves for bodysurfing or body boarding. But this beach isn't known as the "broken-neck capital" for nothing. Ask the lifeguards about conditions before heading into the water, and remember that if almost no one is in the water, there's a good reason for it.

Much of the sand at **White Sands, Magic Sands, or Disappearing Sands Beach Park** (⊠ *Ali'i Dr., 4½ mi south of Kailua-Kona*) washes out to sea and forms a sandbar just offshore. This causes the waves to break in a way that's great for intermediate or advanced body boarding. No wonder the Magic Sands Bodysurfing Contest, which brings out hardcore bodysurfers each winter, is held here. This small beach can get pretty crowded. There can be nasty rip currents at high tide. ■TIP➜ If you're not using fins, wear reef shoes because of the rocks.

North of Hilo, **Honoli'i Cove** (⊠ *Access road off Hwy. 19, just past mile marker 4*) is the best body boarding–surfing spot on the east side of the island. Keep in mind that it is also one of the few good boarding spots in east Hawai'i, and all wave riders need to share the space.

EQUIPMENT

Equipment rental shacks are located at many beaches and boat harbors, along the highway, and at most resorts. Body board rental rates are around $12–$15 per day and around $60 per week. Ask the vendor if he'll throw in a pair of fins—some will for no extra charge.

Honolua Surf Company. This store has a wide selection of men's gear at reasonable prices. There are also several locations statewide. ⊠ *75-5744 Ali'i Dr., Kona Shopping Village, Kailua-Kona* ☎ *808/329–1001* ⊕ *www.honoluasurf.com.*

Orchid Land Surf Shop A solid selection of boards available for a range of prices is the best reason to visit this surf shop. ⊠ *262 Kamehameha Ave., Hilo* ☎ *808/935–1533* ⊕ *www.orchidlandsurf.com.*

Body boarding is popular on the Big Island.

DEEP-SEA FISHING

Along the Kona Coast you can find some of the world's most exciting "blue-water" fishing. Although July, August, and September are peak months, with the best fishing and a number of tournaments, charter fishing goes on year-round. You don't have to compete to experience the thrill of landing a Pacific blue marlin or other big game fish. Some 60 charter boats, averaging 26 to 58 feet, are available for hire, most of them out of **Honokōhau Harbor,** north of Kailua-Kona.

For an exclusive charter, prices generally range from $400 to $750 for a half-day trip (about four hours) and $600 to $1,300 for a full day at sea (about eight hours). For share charters, rates range from about $100 to $140 per person for a half-day and $200 for a full day. If fuel prices continue increasing, expect charter costs to rise. Most boats are licensed to take up to six passengers, in addition to the crew. Tackle, bait, and ice are furnished, but you'll usually have to bring your own lunch. You won't be able to keep your catch, although if you ask, many captains will send you home with a few fillets.

Big fish are weighed in daily at **Honokōhau Harbor's Fuel Dock**. Show up at 11 AM to watch the weigh-in of the day's catch from the morning charters, or 3:30 PM for the afternoon charters. If you're lucky, you'll get to see a "grander" weighing in at 1,000-plus pounds. A surprising number of these are caught just outside Kona Harbor. ■ TIP→ On Kona's Waterfront Row look for the "Grander's Wall" of anglers with their prizes.

THE BIG ISLAND'S TOP THREE WATER ACTIVITIES

Tour company/ Outfitter	Length	AM/ PM	Departure Point	Adult/Kid Price	Kids' Ages	Snack vs. Meal	Alcoholic Beverages Included	Boat Type	Capacity	Worth Noting
Scuba Diving										
Aloha Dive Company	2-tank boat dive	Both	Honokōhau Harbor	$140	10 and up	Snack	No	Small dive boat	6	Locally owned and operated, prefer unusual sites, great for experienced divers
	Manta ray night dive	PM	Honokōhau Harbor	$85	10 and up	Snack	No	Small dive boat	6	
Jack's Diving Locker	2-tank boat dive	AM	Honokōhau Harbor	$125	10 and up	Snack	No	Large dive boat	18	Best for novice and intermediate divers
	Manta ray night dive	PM	Honokōhau Harbor	$145	10 and up	Snack	No	Large dive boat	15	
Torpedo Tours	1-, 2- or 3-tank boat dive	Both	Honokōhau Harbor	$110	10 and up	Meal	No	Medium dive boat	14	Torpedo scooters available
	Manta ray night dive	PM	Honokōhau Harbor	$89	10 and up	Snack	No	Small dive boat	6	
Snorkeling										
Body Glove Cruises	3-4.5 hours	Both	Honokōhau Harbor	$78/ $58	All ages	Meals	No	Large catamaran	149	Good prices; fun for kids
Captain Zodiac	4 hours	Both	Honokōhau Harbor	$93/ $78	4 and up	Snack	No	Pontoon	16	Small size allows access to sea caves and unique sites

Snorkeling cont'd.

	Duration	Time	Location	Price	Ages	Food	Meal incl.	Boat	Capacity	Notes
Fair Winds	3.5-4.5 hours	Both	Keauhou Harbor	$99/$59	All ages	Meal	No	Large catamaran	50	Slide into the water; great for kids
Hula Kai	4-5 hours	Both	Keauhou Harbor	$125-$155	18 and over	Meal	Yes	Large catamaran	45	Elegant boat, full bar, delicious food, great variety of sites
Kona Boys	5.5 hours	Both	Kona Boys shop, just south of mile marker 113 on Hwy 11	$159	10 and up	Meal	No	Kayaks	2 per kayak	Great combo of kayaking and snorkeling

Whale-Watching

	Duration	Time	Location	Price	Ages	Food	Meal incl.	Boat	Capacity	Notes
Blue Sea Cruises	3 hours	PM	Kailua-Kona Pier	$69/$59	All ages	Snacks	No	Large catamaran	75	Glass bottom boat
Body Glove Cruises	3 hours	PM	Honokōhau Harbor	$78/$58	All ages	Snacks	No	Large catamaran	149	Underwater hydrophone
Captain Dan McSweeney's	3 hours	Both	Honokōhau Harbor	$79.50/$69.50	All ages	Snack	No	Large catamaran	42	Specializes in whale-watching and educational cruises

4

BOATS AND CHARTERS

Before you sign up with anyone, think about the kind of trip you want. Looking for a romantic cruise? A rockin' good time with your buddies? Serious fishing in one of the "secret spots"? A family-friendly excursion? Be sure to describe your expectations so your booking agent can match you with a captain and a boat that suits your style.

Charter Locker. This company can provide information on various charter boat fishing trips and make all the arrangements—they can even book you on the luxurious *Blue Hawai'i,* which has air-conditioned staterooms for overnight trips. ⊠ *74-425 Kealakehe Pkwy., Honokōhau Harbor, Kailua-Kona* ☎ *808/326–2553* ⊕ *www.charterlocker.com.*

Charter Services Hawai'i. This booking service represents several Kona fishing boats and can assist with all the details in arranging a charter. ✉ *Box 5234, Kailua-Kona 96745* ☎ *808/334–1881 or 800/567–2650* ⊕ *www.konazone.com.*

Honokōhau Harbor Charter Desk. With about 60 boats on the books, this place can take care of almost anyone. You can make arrangements through your hotel activity desk, but we suggest you go down to the desk at the harbor and look things over for yourself. ⊠ *74-381 Kealakehe Pkwy., Kailua-Kona* ☎ *808/329–5735 or 888/566–2487* ⊕ *www.thecharterdesk.com.*

Humdinger Sportfishing. This game fisher guide has more than three decades of fishing experience in Kona waters. The experienced crew are marlin specialists. The 37-foot *Humdinger* has the latest in electronics and top line rods and reels. Half-day exclusive charters begin at $600, full-day exclusives at $950. ☎ *808/936–3034 or 800/926–2374* ⊕ *www.humdinger-online.com.*

Illusions Sportfishing. Captain Tim Hicks is one of Kona's top fishing tourney producers with several years' experience. The 39-foot *Illusions* is fully equipped with galley, restrooms, an air-conditioned cabin, plus the latest in fishing equipment. Half-day exclusive charters begin at $550, full-day exclusives at $800. ☎ *808/960–7371 (cell); 800/482–3474* ⊕ *www.illusionssportfishing.com.*

Kona Charter Skippers Association. In business since 1956, this company can help arrange half-day and full-day exclusive or share charters on several boats. The *Pamela (below)* is their featured boat. ⊠ *Box 806, 74-857 Iwalani Pl., Kailua-Kona* ☎ *808/329–3600 or 800/762–7546* ⊕ *www.konabiggamefishing.com.*

Pamela Big Game Fishing. This family-operated company has been in the business since 1967. The 38-foot *Pamela* is captained by either Peter Hoogs or his son. They've also got an informative Web site with information on sportfishing. Half-day exclusive charters begin at $550, full-day exclusives at $950. ☎ *808/329–3600 or 800/762–7546* ⊕ *www. konabiggamefishing.com.*

KAYAKING

The leeward west coast areas of the Big Island are protected for the most part from the northeast trade winds, making for ideal near-shore kayaking conditions. There are miles and miles of uncrowded Kona and Kohala coastline to explore, presenting close-up views of stark raw lava rock shores and cliffs, lava tube sea caves, pristine secluded coves, and deserted beaches.

Ocean kayakers can get in close to shore—where the commercial snorkel and dive cruise boats can't reach. This opens up all sorts of possibilities for adventure, such as near-shore snorkeling among the expansive coral reefs and lava rock formations that teem with colorful tropical fish, Hawaiian green sea turtles, and more. You can pull ashore at a quiet cove for a picnic and a plunge into turquoise waters. With a good coastal map and some advice from the kayak vendor, you can explore inland, where you might find ancient battlegrounds, burial sites, bathing ponds for Hawaiian royalty, or old villages.

Kayaking experiences can be enjoyed via a guided tour or on a self-guided paddling excursion. Either way, the kayak outfitter can brief you on recommended routes, manageable currents, and how you can help preserve and protect Hawai'i's ocean resources and coral reef system.

> ## WORD OF MOUTH
>
> "On the main island of Hawaii, even better than taking a snorkel boat to Capt. Cook's Memorial is kayaking there yourself. There are a few local places to rent a kayak pretty cheaply, and they will more often than not strap the kayak to your car for you. Such a fun time, especially considering that the bay is teeming with dolphins."
>
> —kateo

BEST SPOTS

The excellent snorkeling and the likelihood of seeing dolphins makes **Kealakekua Bay** (⊠ *Bottom of Nāpō'opo'o Rd., south of Kailua-Kona*) one of the most popular kayak spots on the Big Island. The bay is usually calm, and the kayaking is not difficult—except during high surf. If you're there in the morning, you may very well see spinner dolphins. Depending on your strength and enthusiasm, you'll cross the bay in 30–60 minutes and put in at the ancient canoe landing about 50 yards to the left of the **Captain Cook Monument.** The monument marks the landfall of Captain James Cook in 1778, the first European to visit Hawai'i. The coral around the monument itself is too fragile to land a kayak, but it makes for fabulous snorkeling.

Ōneo Bay (⊠ *Ali'i Dr., south of Kailua-Kona*) is usually quite a placid place to kayak. It's easy to get to and great for all skill levels. If you can't find a parking spot along Ali'i Drive, there's a parking lot across the street near the farmers' market.

Hilo Bay (⊠ *2349 Kalaniana'ole Ave., about 4 mi east of Hilo*) is a favorite kayak spot. The best place to put in is at **Richardson's Ocean Beach Park.** Most afternoons you can share the bay with local paddling clubs. Stay inside the breakwater unless the ocean is calm (or you're feeling unusually adventurous). Conditions range from extremely calm to quite choppy.

KAYAK SAFETY

- Whether you're a beginner or experienced kayaker, choose appropriate water and weather conditions for your kayak excursion.

- Ask the outfitter about local conditions and hazards, such as tides and currents.

- Beginners should practice getting into and out of the kayak and capsizing in shallow water.

- Before departing, secure the kayak's hatches, etc., to prevent water intake.

- Use a line to attach the paddle to the kayak to avoid losing it.

- Always use a life vest or jacket and slather on plenty of sunblock.

- Wear a helmet if kayaking in and around rough water and rocks.

- Carry appropriate amounts of water and food.

- Don't kayak alone. Create a float plan; tell someone where you're going and when you will return.

EQUIPMENT, LESSONS AND TOURS

There are several rental outfitters on Highway 11 between mile markers 110 and 113. There's also one unofficial stand at the shore, at the house on the corner just across from the parking lot. After you've loaded your kayak onto the roof of your car, follow the 2-mi road down the rather steep hill to the parking lot below. ■ TIP→ There are usually local guys who will set up your kayak and get you into (and out of) the water; tips of between $5 and $10 are encouraged, expected, and appreciated.

Aloha Kayak Co. This Honalo outfitter offers guided Wet-N-Wild Kayak Snorkel/Cave Tours—a four-hour morning tour ($89 per person) and a 2½-hour afternoon version ($65 per person). The morning tour includes a sandwich lunch, snacks, and cold drinks; the afternoon tour includes snacks and drinks. Tours depart from Keauhou Bay. Daily kayak rental rates: single $35, double $60. ■ TIP→ Ask about renting one of their glass kayaks, for a clear and close-up view of the marine life below you. ✉ 79-7248 Mamalahoa Hwy., Honalo ☎ 808/322–2868 or 877/322–1444 ⊕ www.alohakayak.com.

Kona Boys. On the highway above Kealakekua Bay, this full-service outfitter handles kayaks, body boards, and related equipment. Single-seat kayaks are $47 daily (doubles $67), weekly rates are $150 (single) and $275 (double). Dive kayaks with a well for an air tank are also available. The Boys also lead a guided trip to Kealakekua that includes kayaking, snorkeling, and hiking around a lava rock point (half-day starting at $159 per person, includes lunch, snacks, and drinks), a Sunset Kayak & Snorkel Tour for $125 per person, as well as customized overnight camping–kayaking trips to Miloli'i, Pololū, or our favorite, Waipi'o Valley. ✉ 79-7539 Mamalahoa Hwy., Kealakekua ☎ 808/328–1234 ⊕ www.konaboys.com.

Ocean Safari's Kayak Adventures. On the guided 3½-hour morning Sea Cave Tour that begins in Keauhou Bay, you can visit lava tube sea caves along the coast, then swim ashore for a snack. The kayaks are on the beach, so you don't have to hassle with transporting them. The cost is $64 per person. A two-hour Early Riser Dolphin Quest Tour leaves at 7 AM on Tuesdays. It's $35 per person. Kayak daily rental rates are $25 for singles and $40 for doubles. ⊠ *End of Kamehameha III Rd., Kailua-Kona* ☎ *808/326–4699* ⊕ *www.oceansafariskayaks.com.*

PARASAILING

Parasailing, gliding on the winds with a parachute while being pulled behind a power boat, is a relaxing and thrilling experience. If you can handle heights, you'll revel in the experience of being suspended in air while soaring above Kailua Bay. The water is so clear you can almost see the ocean floor. And no swimming is required; takeoffs and landings are from the back of the boat.

EQUIPMENT AND LESSONS

UFO Parasail. This parasailing outfitter runs across Kailua Bay and along the Kona Coast with rides up to 1,200 feet high. They even offer an optional "free fall" that stops short of the water, recreating the rush of a parachute descent. A powerboat and winch provide dry takeoffs and landings; parasailors can "fly" alone or in tandem. Though the flight is short, the boat ride takes about one hour. Rates: standard up to 600 feet, 7 minutes, $60; deluxe up to 1,200 feet, 10 minutes, $70; nonflyers boat ride only, $30. ⊠ *75-5669 Ali'i Dr., Kailua-Kona* ☎ *888/359–4836 or 808/325–5836* ⊕ *www.ufoparasailing.com.*

SAILING

For old salts and novice sailors alike, there's nothing like a cruise on the Kona or Kohala coasts of the Big Island. Calm waters, serene shores, and the superb scenery of Mauna Kea, Mauna Loa, and Hualālai, the Big Island's primary volcanic peaks, make for a great sailing adventure. You can drop a line over the side and try your luck at catching dinner, or grab some snorkel gear and explore when the boat drops anchor in one of the quiet coves and bays. A cruise may well be the most relaxing and adventurous part of a Big Island visit.

BOATS AND CHARTERS

Maile Charters. Ralph Blancato and Kalia Potter offer unique around-the-Islands sailing adventures on the 50-foot GulfStar sloop, Maile. Sails range from half-day excursions to five-day journeys to Maui, Moloka'i, or Lāna'i. Private cabins and hot showers keep you comfortable, and island-style meals keep you satisfied. Fees start at $979 for six passengers for a 5 PM to sunset charter, and go up to $6,797 for five days with a maximum of four adult passengers. Trips are also available for full day and one, two, or three nights. Prices include use of water sports equipment and food can be ordered ahead of time and purchased for an additional fee. ⊠ *Kawaihae Harbor, Kawaihae* ☎ *808/960–9744 or 800/726–7245* ⊕ *www.adventuresailing.com.*

SCUBA DIVING

The Big Island's underwater world is the setting for a dramatic diving experience. With generally calm waters, vibrant coral reefs and rock formations, and plunging underwater drop-offs, the Kona and Kohala coasts provide some great scuba diving. There are also some good dive locations in east Hawai'i, not far from the Hilo area. Divers will find much to occupy their time, including marine reserves teeming with unique Hawaiian reef fish, Hawaiian green sea turtles, an occasional and rare Hawaiian monk seal, and even some playful Hawaiian spinner dolphins. On special night dives to see manta rays, divers descend with bright underwater lights that attract plankton, which in turn attracts these otherworldly creatures. The best spots to dive are listed in order from north to south; all are on the west coast.

BEST SPOTS

Hāpuna Beach State Recreation Area (⊠ *Hwy. 19, near mile marker 69*) in Kohala can be a good shore dive. Just south of the state park is **Puako** (⊠ *Puako Rd., off Hwy. 19*), which offers easy entry to some fine reef diving. Deep chasms, sea caves, rock arches, and more abound with varied marine life.

The water is usually very clear at **Pawai Bay Marine Reserve** (⊠ *Just north of Old Kona Airport Beach Park, at the beginning of Kuakini Hwy.*). This bay near Kailua-Kona has numerous underwater sea caves, arches, and rock formations, plus lots of marine life. It can be busy with snorkel boats but is an easy dive spot. **Plane Wreck Point**, off Keāhole Point, is for expert divers only. Damselfish, fantail, and filefish hover around in the shadows.

One of Kona's best night dive spots is **Manta Village** (⊠ *Off the Sheraton Keauhou Bay Resort at Keauhou[78-6740 Ali'i Dr.], Kailua-Kona*). A booking with a scuba/snorkel night dive operator is required for the short boat ride to the area. If you're a diving or snorkeling fanatic, it's well worth it for the experience of seeing the manta rays.

Dive boats come to **Pu'uhonua O Hōnaunau** (*City of Refuge* ⊠ *Rte. 160, about 20 mi south of Kailua-Kona* ⊕ *www.nps.gov/puho*) for the steep drop-offs and dramatic views. You can also get in the water from the shore on the north end.

EQUIPMENT, LESSONS AND TOURS

There are quite a few good dive shops on the Kona Coast. Most are happy to take on all customers, but a few focus on specific types of trips. Trip prices vary, depending on whether you're already certified and whether you're diving from a boat or from shore. Instruction with PADI, SDI, or TDI certification in three to five days costs $600–$850. Most instructors rent out dive equipment and snorkel gear, as well as underwater cameras. A few organize otherworldly manta ray dives at night or whale-watching cruises in season.

★ **Aloha Dive Company.** Native-born Hawaiian and PADI master dive instructor Mike Nakachi, together with wife Buffy (a registered nurse and PADI dive instructor) and Earl Kam (a videographer and PADI dive master), have been instructing since 1990. Although they'll take

The Kona Coast's relatively calm waters and colorful coral reefs are excellent for scuba diving.

anybody, they're biased in favor of experienced divers who want unique locations and know how to take care of themselves in deep water. Their boat is fast enough to take you places other companies can't reach. They're fun people with great attitudes. Rates begin at $140 for a two-tank boat dive and go up to $250 for a three-tank remote boat dive. ☎ 808/325–5560 or 800/708–5662.

★ **Jack's Diving Locker**. The best place for novice and intermediate divers (certified to 60 feet), Jack's Diving Locker has trained and certified tens of thousands of divers since opening in 1981. The company has two boats that can each take 12 divers. It does a good job looking out for customers and protecting the coral reef. Before each charter the dive master briefs divers on various options and then everyone votes on where to go. Jack's also runs the biggest dive shop on the island and has classrooms and a dive pool for beginning instruction. ■ TIP→ Kona's best dive bargain for newbies is the introductory shore dive from Kailua Pier for $55. ✉ 75-5813 Ali'i Dr., Kailua-Kona ☎ 800/345–4807 or 808/329–7585 ⊕ www.jacksdivinglocker.com.

★ **Torpedo Tours**. Mike and Nikki Milligan specialize in small groups, which means you'll spend more time diving and less time hanging out on the boat waiting to dive. Two-tank morning dives run $110, one-tank manta ray dives are $89, or you can combine the two and do a late afternoon dive plus a manta ray dive for a very reasonable $130. Torpedo Tours will take snorkelers along with divers, and provides its namesake torpedo scooters to both for free. The scooters allow both divers and snorkelers to cover more ground with less kicking, and are a fun novelty to test out. ✉ Honokōhau Harbor, Na Pali Kai II *boat, 74-425 Kealakehe Pkwy., Kailua-Kona* ☎ *808/938–0405* ⊕ *www. torpedotours.com.*

SNORKELING

A favorite pastime on the Big Island, snorkeling is perhaps one of the easiest and most enjoyable water activities for visitors. By floating on the surface, looking through your mask, and breathing through your snorkel, you can see lava rock formations, sea arches, sea caves, and coral reefs teeming with colorful tropical fish. While the Kona and Kohala coasts have more beaches, bays, and quiet coves to snorkel, the east side around Hilo and at Kapoho are also great places to get in the water.

If you don't bring your own equipment, you can easily rent all the gear needed from a beach activities vendor, who will happily provide directions to the best sites for snorkeling in the area. For access to deeper water and assistance from an experienced crew, you can opt for a snorkel cruise. Excursions generally range from two to five hours; be sure you know what equipment and food is included. Kona Boys (*see* Kayaking*)* lead combined kayaking, snorkeling, and hiking tours.

BEST SPOTS

★ **Kealakekua Bay** (⊠ *Bottom of Nāpō'opo'o Rd., south of Kailua-Kona*) is, hands down, the best snorkel spot on the island, with fabulous coral reefs around the Captain Cook monument and generally calm waters. And with any luck, you'll probably get to swim with dolphins. Overland access is difficult, so you can opt for one of several guided snorkel cruises, or kayak across the bay to get to the monument. ■TIP→ Be on the lookout for kayakers who might not notice you swimming beneath them, and stay on the ocean side of the orange buoys near the cliffs.

The snorkeling just north of the boat launch at **Pu'uhonua O Hōnaunau** (*City of Refuge* ⊠ *Rte. 160, about 20 mi south of Kailua-Kona* ⊕ *www. nps.gov/puho*) is really as good as Kealakekua Bay, and it's much easier to reach. It's also a popular scuba diving spot.

White Sands, Magic Sands, or Disappearing Sands Beach Park (⊠ *Ali'i Dr., 4½ mi south of Kailua-Kona*) is a great place for beginning and intermediate snorkelers. In winter it's also a good place to see whales.

Since ancient times, the waters around **Kahalu'u Beach Park** (⊠ *Ali'i Dr., 5½ mi south of Kailua-Kona*) have been a traditional net-fishing area (the water is shallower here than at Kealakekua). The swimming is good, and the snorkeling is even better. You'll see angelfish, parrot fish, needlefish, puffer fish, and a lot more. ■TIP→ Stay inside the breakwater and don't stray too far, as dangerous and unpredictable currents swirl outside the bay.

Kapoho Tide Pools (⊠ *End of Kapoho-Kai Rd., off Hwy. 137*) has the best snorkeling on the Hilo side. Fingers of lava from the 1960 flow (that destroyed the town of Kapoho) jut into the sea to form a network of tide pools. Conditions near the shore are excellent for beginners, and challenging enough farther out for experienced snorkelers.

Continued on page 130

SNORKELING IN HAWAI'I

The waters surrounding the Hawaiian Islands are filled with life—from giant manta rays cruising off the Big Island's Kona Coast to humpback whales giving birth in Maui's Mā'alaea Bay. Dip your head beneath the surface to experience a spectacularly colorful world: pairs of milletseed butterflyfish dart back and forth, red-lipped parrotfish snack on coral algae, and spotted eagle rays flap past like silent spaceships. Sea turtles bask at the surface while tiny wrasses give them the equivalent of a shave and a haircut. The water quality is typically outstanding; many sites afford 30-foot-plus visibility. On snorkel cruises, you can often stare from the boat rail right down to the bottom.

Certainly few destinations are as accommodating to every level of snorkeler as Hawai'i. Beginners can tromp in from sandy beaches while more advanced divers descend to shipwrecks, reefs, craters, and sea arches just offshore. Because of Hawai'i's extreme isolation, the island chain has fewer fish species than Fiji or the Caribbean—but many of the fish that are here exist nowhere else. The Hawaiian waters are home to the highest percentage of endemic fish in the world.

The key to enjoying the underwater world is slowing down. Look carefully. Listen. You might hear the strange crackling sound of shrimp tunneling through coral, or you may hear whales singing to one another during winter. A shy octopus may drift along the ocean's floor beneath you. If you're hooked, pick up a waterproof fishkey from Long's Drugs. You can brag later that you've looked the Hawaiian turkeyfish in the eye.

Picasso Triggerfish	Milletseed Butterflyfish*	Yellow Tang
Moorish Idol	Hawaiian Whitespotted Toby*	Saddleback Wrasse*
Red-lipped Parrotfish	Hawaiian Turkeyfish*	Zebra Moray Eel
Stocky Hawkfish	Green Sea Turtle (Honu)	Spotted Eagle Ray

*endemic to Hawai'i

POLYNESIA'S FIRST CELESTIAL NAVIGATORS: HONU

Honu is the Hawaiian name for two native sea turtles, the hawksbill and the green sea turtle. Little is known about these dinosaur-age marine reptiles, though snorkelers regularly see them foraging for *limu* (seaweed) and the occasional jellyfish in Hawaiian waters. Most female honu nest in the uninhabited Northwestern Hawaiian Islands, but a few sociable ladies nest on Maui and Big Island beaches. Scientists suspect that they navigate the seas via magnetism—sensing the earth's poles. Amazingly, they will journey up to 800 miles to nest—it's believed that they return to their own birth sites. After about 60 days of incubation, nestlings emerge from the sand at night and find their way back to the sea by the light of the stars.

Passengers aboard the Atlantis VII submarine can visit the aquatic world without getting wet.

EQUIPMENT, LESSONS AND TOURS

★ **Body Glove Cruises.** This operator is a good choice for families, particularly if at least one member is a certified diver and the rest want to snorkel. Kids love the waterslide and the high dive platform, and parents appreciate the reasonable prices. The 51-foot catamaran sets off from the Kailua Pier daily for a 4½-hour dive and snorkel cruise, which includes breakfast and a buffet lunch; the three-hour afternoon cruise includes snacks and drinks. Snorkelers pay $78–$120 per adult and $58–$78 per child. Ask about scuba prices. ⊠ 75-5629 Kuakini Hwy., Kailua-Kona ☎ 808/326–7122 or 800/551–8911 ⊕ www.bodyglovehawaii.com.

Captain Zodiac Raft Expedition. The exciting four-hour trip on an inflatable raft offered by this company that started up in 1974 takes you along the Kona Coast to explore gaping lava tube caves, search for dolphins and turtles, and snorkel around Kealakekua Bay; the captain often throws in some Hawaiian folklore and Kona history, too. The morning trip departs at 8:15 AM, the afternoon trip at 1 PM. Adults pay $93 and kids $78. A seasonal (Dec.–Apr.) three-hour whale-watching cruise costs $65 for adults and $59 for kids. ⊠ Honokōhau Harbor, 74-425 Kealakehe Pkwy. Kailua-Kona ☎ 808/329–3199 ⊕ www.captainzodiac.com.

★ **Fair Wind Cruises.** This outfit offers both a 4½-hour morning and ⅛ 3½-hour afternoon snorkeling excursion to Kealakekua Bay, and a luxury cruise *(see Hula Kai below)* that sails into three different secret snorkeling spots a day. Snorkel gear is included (ask about prescription masks), but bring your own towel. On morning cruises you'll get a continental breakfast and a barbecue lunch. These trips are great for families with small kids (lots of pint-size flotation equipment), and they provide underwater viewing devices for those who don't want to use a mask–snorkel setup. Wind staff is fair and flexible; they're very good with people of all ages and swimming and snorkeling ability. Morning cruises cost $119 for adults and $75 for kids; afternoon cruises are cheaper, but you're less likely to see dolphins in the bay. The spring–summer afternoon deluxe cruise includes a late barbecue lunch and snorkel time; adults $99, kids $59. ⊠ *78-7130 Kaleiopapa St., Keauhou Bay, Kailua-Kona* ☎ *808/345–0268 or 800/677–9461* ⊕ *www.fair-wind.com.*

★ **Hula Kai**. Operated by Fair Wind *(see above)*, the Hula Kai is the company's more luxurious, adults-only snorkel cruise—"adults-only" in a peace and quiet, wine and appetizers way, not a clothing-optional way. The swanky hydrofoil boat skims quietly over the island's waters, venturing to areas not easily accessed by the company's other boats, including the southern coast, where snorkeling is fantastic amidst the canyons and reefs. A gourmet breakfast buffet and barbecue lunch is included in the $155/person rate, and whale-watching tours are available in season. The boat also offers scuba diving, which makes it a bonus for couples in groups that have a mix of divers and snorkelers. ⊠ *78-7130 Kaleiopapa St., Keauhou Bay, Kailua-Kona* ☎ *808/345–0268 or 800/677–9461* ⊕ *www.fair-wind.com.*

Snorkel Bob's. You're likely to see his wacky ads in your airline in-flight magazine. The company actually delivers what it promises, and you can make reservations online before beginning your trip. Basic gear package of mask, fins, and snorkel rents for $9–$35 per week; children's equipment and prescription masks are available. ⊠ *75-5831 Kahakai St., Kailua-Kona* ☎ *808/329–0770 or 800/262–7725* ⊕ *www.snorkelbob.com.*

SNUBA

Snuba—a cross between scuba and snorkeling—is a great choice for non-scuba divers who want to go a step beyond snorkeling. You and an instructor dive off a raft attached to a 25-foot hose and regulator; you can dive as deep as 20 feet or so. This is a good way to explore reefs a bit deeper than you can get to by snorkeling. If you get frightened or need a rest, the raft is right there, ready to support you.

LESSONS

Snuba Big Island. Rendezvous with your instructor across from King Kamehameha's Kona Beach Hotel in Kailua-Kona for 30 minutes of instruction and a one-hour dive from the beach ($89 per person). Boat dives lasting three hours leave from Honakahou Harbor ($145 per person). You can also dive in Kealakekua Bay. The minimum age for snuba is eight, but kids four to seven can come along on the Snuba Doo program, which keeps them snorkeling safely on the surface. ☎ *808/324–1650* ⊕ *www.snubabigisland.com.*

SUBMARINE TOURS

☺ **Atlantis VII Submarine.** Want to stay dry while exploring the undersea
Fodor'sChoice world? Climb aboard the 48-foot *Atlantis VII* submarine anchored
★ off Kailua Pier, across from King Kamehameha's Kona Beach Hotel in
Kailua-Kona. A large glass dome in the bow and 13 viewing ports on the
sides allow clear views of the aquatic world more than 100 feet down.
This is a great trip for kids and nonswimmers. Each one-hour voyage costs $99 for adults and $45 for children under 12. The company
also operates on O'ahu and Maui. ☎ *808/329–6626 or 800/548–6262*
⊕ *www.atlantisadventures.com.*

SURFING

The Big Island does not have the variety of great surfing spots found
on O'ahu or Maui, but it does have decent waves and a thriving surf
culture. Local kids and avid surfers frequent a number of places up and
down the Kona and Kohala Coasts of west Hawai'i. Expect high surf
in winter and much calmer activity during summer. The surf scene is
much more active on the Kona side.

BEST SPOTS

Among the best places for experienced surfers to catch the waves is **Pine
Trees** (⊠ *Off Hwy. 11 and south of the Kona Airport and the Natural
Energy Lab of Hawai'i on an unimproved beach road*). Keep in mind
that this is a very popular local surf spot on an island where there
aren't all that many surf spots, so be very respectful. Intermediate surfers brave the rocks to get out to a popular break just slightly north of
Kahalu'u Beach Park (⊠ *Ali'i Dr., 5½ mi south of Kailua-Kona next to
Outrigger Keauhou Beach Hotel*), out past the beach's calm lagoons
and snorkelers. **Banyans** (⊠ *Ali'i Dr. near the Kona Bali Kai condos*) is
another popular spot with local and experienced surfers. There's no
beach here—surfers need to wade in from the rocks and start paddling.
Old Kona Airport State Recreation Area (⊠ *Kuakini Rd. at the old Kona
Airport*) is also a good place for catching wave action. A couple of the
island's outfitters conduct surf lessons here, as the break is far away
from potentially dangerous rocks and reefs. On the east side near Hilo,
try **Honoli'i Cove** (⊠ *Access road off Hwy. 19, just past mile marker 4*).

EQUIPMENT, LESSONS AND TOURS

Hawai'i Lifeguard Surf Instructors. This certified school with experienced
instructors helps novice surfers become wave riders and offers surf tours
that take more experienced riders to Kona's top surfing spots. Though
they offer a one-hour introductory lesson ($75 for a small group, $98
for private instruction), they recommend the two-hour lesson to get you
ready to surf. You can try a two-hour tandem lesson on a board for two.
You can also take a lesson in the latest surfboard sport, paddleboarding.
⊠ *75-5909 Ali'i Dr., Kailua-Kona* ☎ *808/324–0442 or 808/936–7873*
⊕ *www.surflessonshawaii.com.*

Ocean Eco Tours Surf School. This surf school emphasizes the basics of safe
surfing and specializes in beginners. All lessons are taught by certified

Humpback whales are visible off the coast of the Big Island between December and April.

CPR-trained lifeguard instructors, and they guarantee that you will surf! If you're hooked, you can sign up for a three-lesson package for $270. ✉ *Honokōhau Harbor, 74-425 Kealakehe Pkwy., Kailua-Kona* ☎ *808/324–7873* ⊕ *www.oceanecotours.com.*

Orchid Land Surf Shop. The shop has a wide variety of water sports and surf equipment for sale or rent. They stock professional custom surfboards, body boards, and surf apparel, and do repairs. ✉ *262 Kamehameha Ave., Hilo* ☎ *808/935–1533* ⊕ *www.orchidlandsurf.com.*

WHALE WATCHING

Each winter, some two-thirds of the North Pacific humpback whale population (about 4,000–5,000 animals) migrate over 3,500 mi from the icy Alaska waters to the warm Hawaiian ocean to give birth to and nurse their calves. Recent reports indicate that the whale population is on the upswing—a few years ago one even ventured into the mouth of Hilo Harbor, which marine biologists say is quite rare. Humpbacks are spotted here from early December through the end of April, but other species, like sperm, pilot, and beaked whales, can be seen year-round. Most ocean tour companies offer whale outings during the season, but two owner-operators (listed below) do it full time. They are much more familiar with whale behavior and you're more likely to have a quality whale-watching experience. ■ TIP➔ **If you take the morning cruise, you're likely to see dolphins as well.** In addition to the outfitters listed below, **Body Glove Cruises** *(see* Snorkeling*)* offers whale-watching cruises.

TOURS

Blue Sea Cruises Inc. The *Makai,* a 46-foot double-deck catamaran, cruises along the Kona Coast twice a day on two-hour tours. The boat has all the comforts, including a snack bar and restrooms. The narrated tour covers Hawai'i's marine wildlife and the history and culture of the Islands. Sightings include spinner, spotted, and bottlenose dolphins, resident pilot whales, and seasonal humpbacks. Tours depart from Kailua Pier at 8:30 AM and include snacks and cold beverages. The 11 AM tour includes a light lunch. Rates start at $61 per person. ⌂ *Box 2429, Kailua-Kona* ☎ *808/331–8875* ⊕ *www.blueseacruisesinc.com.*

★ **Captain Dan McSweeney's Year-Round Whale Watching Adventures.** This is probably the most experienced small operation on the island. Captain Dan McSweeney offers three-hour trips on his 40-foot boat. In addition to humpbacks in the winter, he'll show you some of the six other whale species that live off the Kona Coast year-round. Three-hour tours cost $70 per adult and $60 for kids under 12 (snacks and juices included). McSweeney guarantees you'll see a whale or he'll take you out again for free. ✉ *Honokōhau Harbor, Kailua-Kona* ☎ *808/322–0028 or 888/942–5376* ⊕ *www.ilovewhales.com.*

> ### WORD OF MOUTH
>
> "From late December to mid- to late April the whales come to Hawai'i, especially the Big Island and Maui. It is one of my favorite times to be there." — Lauricelli

Golf, Hiking, and Outdoor Activities

WORD OF MOUTH

"The black lava was all around us, the volcano was to our right, the ocean was on our left, and the moon was illuminating it all. It was a beautiful night. We could hear the ocean waves hitting the rocks, feel the wind, and see the moon and stars."

—Samsaf

Updated by
Bill Harby

With the Big Island's predictably mild year-round climate, it's no wonder the lifestyle emphasis is on outdoor activities. After all, this is the home of the annual Ironman World Championship triathlon. Whether you are an avid hiker or a beginning bicyclist, a casual golfer or a tennis buff, there are plenty of land-based activities to lure you away from the sun and surf.

You can explore by bike, helicopter, ATV, or horse, or you can put on your hiking boots and use your own horsepower. No matter how you get around, you'll be treated to breathtaking backdrops along the Big Island's 266-mi coastline and within its 4,028 square miles (and still growing!). Aerial tours take in the latest eruption activity and lava flows, as well as the island's gorgeous tropical valleys, gulches, and coastal areas. Trips into the backcountry wilderness explore the rain forest, private ranch lands, coffee farms, and sugar plantation villages that give a glimpse of Hawai'i's earlier days.

Golfers will find acclaimed, championship golf courses at the Kohala coast resorts—Mauna Kea Resort, Hāpuna Beach Prince Hotel, Mauna Lani Resort, Waikoloa Resort, and Four Seasons at Hualālai, among others. And during the winter, if snow conditions allow, you can go skiing on top of Mauna Kea (elevation: 13,796 feet). It's a skiing experience unlike any other.

AERIAL TOURS

There's nothing quite like the aerial view of a waterfall that drops a couple thousand feet into natural pools, or seeing lava flow to the ocean, where clouds of steam billow into the air. You can get this bird's-eye view from a helicopter or a small fixed-wing aircraft. Although there have been a few cases of pilots violating flight paths and altitudes over resident communities in recent years, most operators are reputable and fly with strict adherence to FAA safety rules. How to get the best experience for your money? ■TIP➡ **Before you hire a company, be a savvy traveler and ask the right questions. What kind of aircraft do they fly? Do they have two-way headsets so you can talk with the pilot? What is their safety record?**

Iolani Air. This operator flies fixed-wing two- to six-passenger Gippsland and Cessna aircraft from both the Hilo and Kona airports. Every seat is a window seat with panoramic views. There are four air tours, from a 50-minute Volcano Waterfall tour at $164 per person to a 75-minute Full Circle Island Tour for $317. (Ask about kids' fares.) ☎ 808/329–0018 or 800/538–7590 ⊕ www.iolaniair.com.

Mokulele Airlines. In addition to regular interisland scheduled flights, this commuter line offers a 1½-hour Circle Island Tour in a nine-passenger

Cessna Caravan. The air tour departs Kona Airport and goes over Hawai'i Volcanoes National Park, the Hilo-Hāmākua Coast, and the Kohala Coast. Rates are $279 per person; ask about discounts for seniors, AAA members, and kids. ☎ *808/930–5009* ⊕ *www. mokuleleairlines.com.*

Paradise Helicopters. Paradise flies six-passenger Bell 407 and four-passenger Hughes 500 helicopters. Everyone has a window seat in the four-seaters, and most passengers get a window in the highly maneuverable six-passenger helicopters as well. The friendly and knowledgeable pilots communicate with passengers over two-way headsets. Paradise operates from Kona and Hilo, which is better for volcano viewing. The 50-minute Volcano & Waterfall Adventure (from Hilo) is $226 per person; the top-of-the-line tour is a three-hour Volcanoes & Valley Adventure (from Kona) for $433 per person, including lunch. For an additional thrill and an even better view, you can choose a Doors-Off Experience from Hilo. ⊠ *Hilo Airport, Kona Airport* ☎ *808/969–7392 or 866/876–7422* ⊕ *www.paradisecopters.com.*

Sunshine Helicopters. Ride the six-seater Astar Black Beauties on an exciting air tour that takes in the ocean cliffs and valleys of the Kohala-Hāmākua Coast and the formations and flows of the Kīlauea Volcano. Narrated tours range from 45 minutes ($169–$229 if you book online) to two hours ($405–$520); the longer tour covers both regions, while the shorter tour focuses on the volcano. Afterward, you can buy a DVD of your flight experience. ⊠ *Helipad at Hāpuna Beach Prince Hotel and Hilo Airport* ☎ *808/882–1223 Hāpuna Beach Prince Hotel; 808/969–7501 Hilo; 800/469–3000* ⊕ *www.sunshinehelicopters.com.*

ATV TOURS

A different way to experience the Big Island's rugged coastline and wild ranch lands is through an off-road adventure—a real backcountry experience. At higher elevations, weather can be nippy and rainy, but views can be awesome. Protective gear is provided. Generally, you have to be 16 or older to ride your own ATV, though some outfitters allow children seven and older to be passengers.

ATV Outfitters Hawai'i. These trips take in the scenic beauty of the rugged North Kohala Coast, traveling along coastal cliffs and into the forest in search of waterfalls. The ATV outfitter's three adventures are priced from $129 per person for the 1½-hour Ocean Cliff Adventure to $249 per person for the 22-mi three-hour Deluxe Rainforest & Waterfall Adventure. ATV Outfitters also offers double-seater ATVs for parents traveling with children or adults who don't feel comfortable operating their own ATV. ⊠ *Old Sakamoto Store, Hwy. 270, Kapa'au* ☎ *808/889–6000 or 888/288–7288* ⊕ *www.atvoutfittershawaii.com.*

ATV Ranch Ride. This rugged 2½-hour ATV adventure on a working ranch takes in the Hāmākua Coast and the Waipi'o Valley: dramatic ocean cliffs, quiet forests, and remnants of Hawai'i's once-thriving sugarcane industry. Prices begin at $104 per person. ⊠ *Honoka'a* ☎ *808/775–7291 or 877/775–7291* ⊕ *www.waipioonhorseback.com.*

Cowboys of Hawai'i ATV Rides. Riders cruise Parker Ranch to Holo-holo Hill for an incomparable panorama of the ranch's 175,000 acres and thousands of cattle, or follow the Mana Road in the shadow of towering Mauna Kea. Rates for the two-hour ride begin at $95 per person. ⊠ *Parker Ranch Center, Parker Ranch Shopping Center, 67-1185 Māmalahoa Hwy., Waimea* ☎ *808/885–5006* ⊕ *www. cowboysofhawaii.com.*

Kahuā Ranch ATV Rides. On this working ranch, you can ride the range, from upslope rain forest to midlevel mountain desert. Dramatic cinder cones and backcountry pastures offer scenic views. ■ TIP➔ Ride later in the day, and stay for a ranch barbecue with the family; afterwards, you can stargaze through their powerful telescope and learn how to rope. Rates for the two-hour ride begin at $105 per person (not including dinner). ⊠ *Hwy. 250, 10 mi north of Waimea* ☎ *808/882–7954 or 808/882–4646* ⊕ *www.kahuaranch.com.*

Waipi'o Ride the Rim. On this Waipi'o Valley ride, you'll see expansive black-sand beaches, get to swim in the stream that feeds the 1,200-foot Hi'ilawe Falls, and travel through the lush rain forest surrounding the top edge of the valley. Rates for the three-hour rim tour begin at $159 per person. ⊠ *Waipi'o Valley Artworks Bldg., 48-5416 Kukuihaele Rd., Kukuihaele* ☎ *808/775–1450 or 877/775–1450* ⊕ *www.topofwaipio.com.*

BIKING

The Big Island's biking trails and road routes range from easy to moderate coastal rides to rugged backcountry wilderness treks that will challenge the most serious bikers. En route, bikers can soak up the island's storied scenic vistas and varied geography—from tropical rain forest to rolling ranch country, from high country mountain meadows to dry lava deserts. It's dry, windy, and hot on Kona's and Kohala's coastal trails and cool, wet, and muddy in the upcountry Waimea and Volcano areas, as well as in lower Puna. There are long distances between towns and few services available in the Ka'ū, Puna, South Kona, and Kohala Coast areas, so bikers need to plan accordingly for weather, water, food, and lodging before setting out.

The nonprofit **Hawaii Cycling Club** ☎ *808/326–245* (⌂ *74-5583 Luhia St., Kailua-Kona 96740* ⊕ *www.hawaiicyclingclub.com*) has tons of information on biking the Big Island. For other suggested rides, see the Web site run by **Alternative Hawai'i** (⊕ *www.alternative-hawaii.com/ activity/biecotrb.htm*).

BEST SPOTS

Fodor's Choice
★

Mountain Bike magazine voted **Kulani Trails**, south of Hilo, the best ride in the state—if you're an advanced rider who really wants to get gnarly. To reach the trailhead from the intersection of highways 11 and 19, take Highway 19 south about 4 mi, then turn right onto Stainback Highway and continue on 2½ mi, then turn right at the Waiakea Arboretum. Park near the gate. This technically demanding ride, which passes majestic eucalyptus trees, is for advanced cyclists.

The **Old Puna Trail** (⊠ *Trailhead: From Hwy. 130, about 3 mi south of Keaʻau town, take Kaloli Rd. to Beach Rd.*) is a 10½-mi ride through the subtropical jungle in Puna, one of the island's most isolated areas. You'll start out on a cinder road, which becomes a four-wheel-drive trail. If it's rained recently, you'll have to deal with some puddles—the first few of which you'll gingerly avoid until you give in and go barreling through the rest of them for the sheer fun of it. This is a great ride for all abilities that takes about 90 minutes.

EQUIPMENT

If you want to strike out on your own, there are several rental shops in Kailua-Kona and a couple in Waimea and Hilo. Many resorts rent bicycles that can be used around the properties. Most outfitters listed can provide a bicycle rack for your car. All offer reduced rates for rentals longer than one day.

Bike Works. This branch operation of Hawaiian Pedals *(below)* caters to more advanced bicyclists and Ironman wannabes with its rentals of deluxe road bikes and full-suspension mountain bikes, starting at $40 a day. ⊠ *Hale Hana Centre, 74-5583 Luhia St., Kailua-Kona* ☎ *808/326– 2453* ⊕ *www.bikeworkskona.com.*

Cycle Station. This shop, which has a variety of bikes to rent, from road sport to racing bikes, hybrids to tandems, will also deliver to and pick up at hotels. They have trailers for toddlers. Daily rentals range from $20 for a hybrid to $35 for a road or mountain bike. ⊠ *73-5619 Kauhola St. #105, Kailua-Kona* ☎ *808/327–0087* ⊕ *www. cyclestationhawaii.com.*

Hawaiian Pedals. For those who prefer comfort over speed, Hawaiian Pedals rents seven-speed cruisers, hybrids, and basic mountain bikes starting at $15 for five hours. Full-day rental rates begin at $20. ⊠ *Kona Inn Shopping Village, 75-5744 Aliʻi Dr., Kailua-Kona* ☎ *808/329–2294* ⊕ www.hawaiianpedals.com.

Mid Pacific Wheels. This downtown Hilo bike shop carries a full line of bikes and related accessories. They also rent mountain bikes for exploring the Hilo and east Hawaiʻi area. Rental rates start at $25 per day. They can provide information on the best places to go and what to see, do, and experience on a self-guided bike tour. ⊠ *1133C Manono St., Hilo* ☎ *808/935–6211.* ⊕ www.midpacificwheels.com

GOING WITH A GUIDE

Orchid Isle Bicycling. Geared to cyclists of varying abilities, options range from challenging 3,500-foot climbs up Kohala Mountain to downhill-only rides that end with a swim. Tours, which last from two to five hours and cover 21 to 55 mi, start at $125 per person. The outfitter also runs deluxe seasonal "Tour de Paradise" vacation packages including hotels, some meals, and all gear for $1,895 and up per person for four to six days of cycling. ⊡ *Box 3486, Kailua-Kona 96745* ☎ *808/327–0087 or 800/219–2324* ⊕ *www.orchidislebicycling.com.*

Volcano Bike Tours. Volcano Bike Tours takes visitors on a three- to four-hour bike ride through the rain forests and past the craters of Volcanoes National Park on a mostly downhill route. After cruising through the volcanoes, the tour ends at the Volcano Winery for a tasting at one of the most unique wineries in the country. The $129 tour includes all equipment, an interpretive guide, lunch, beverages, and a support van that drives alongside riders in case anyone tires out early. ⌂ *Box 7474, Hilo 96720* ☎ *888/934–9199, 888/934–9199* ⊕ *http:// bikevolcano.com.*

GOLF

For golfers, the Big Island is a big deal—starting with the Mauna Kea Golf Course, which opened in 1964 and remains one of the state's top courses. Black lava and deep blue sea are the predominant themes on the island. In the roughly 40 mi from the Kona Country Club out to the Mauna Kea Resort, nine courses are carved into sunny seaside lava plains, with four more in the hills above. Indeed, most of the Big Island's best courses are concentrated along the Kona Coast, statistically the sunniest spot in Hawai'i. Vertically speaking, although the majority of courses are seaside or at least near sea level, three are located above 2,000 feet, another one at 4,200 feet. This is significant because in Hawai'i temperatures drop by three degrees for every 1,000 feet of elevation gained.

Green Fees: Green fees listed here are the highest course rates per round on weekdays for U.S. residents. Courses with varying weekend rates are noted in the individual listings. (Some courses charge non–U.S. residents higher prices.) ■ TIP➔ Discounts are often available for resort guests and for those who book tee times on the Web, as well as for those willing to play in the afternoon instead of the morning. Twilight fees are also usually offered; call individual courses for information.

★ **Big Island Country Club.** Set 2,000 feet above sea level on the slopes of Mauna Kea, the Big Island Country Club is rather out of the way but well worth the drive. Pete and Perry Dye (1997) created a gem that plays through an upland woodlands—more than 2,500 trees line the fairways. On the par-5 15th, a giant tree in the middle of the fairway must be avoided with the second shot. Five lakes and a meandering natural mountain stream mean water comes into play on nine holes. The most dramatic is on the par-3 17th, where the Dyes created a knockoff of his infamous 17th at the TPC at Sawgrass. ⊠ *71-1420 Māmalahoa Hwy., Kailua-Kona* ☎ *808/325–5044* ⚐ *18 holes. 7034 yds. Par 72. Green Fee: $85 in the morning, $65 after noon* ⌂ *Facilities: Driving range, putting green, golf carts, rental clubs, pro shop, lessons.*

Hāmākua Country Club. The typical modern 18-hole golf course requires at least 250 acres. The 9-hole, par-33 public Hāmākua course requires just 19. Compact is the word, and with several holes crisscrossing, this is BYO Hard Hat. Holes run up and down a fairly steep slope (a product of Hawai'i's plantation era) overlooking the ocean. There is no clubhouse or other amenities, and the 9th green is square, but for 15 bucks, whaddaya expect? ⊠ *Hwy. 19, 41 mi north of Hilo, Honoka'a* ☎ *808/775–7244* ⚐ *9 holes. 2520 yds. Par 33. Green Fee: $15 for 9 holes, $20 for 18* ⌂ *Facilities: Putting green, golf carts, pull carts.*

TIPS FOR THE GREEN

Golf is golf, and Hawai'i is part of the United States, but island golf nevertheless has its own quirks. Here are a few tips to make your golf experience in the Islands more pleasant.

■ Wear sunscreen, even in December. We recommend a minimum SPF of 30 and that you reapply on the 10th tee.

■ Stay hydrated. Spending four-plus hours in the sun and heat means you'll perspire away considerable fluids and energy.

■ All resort courses and many daily fee courses provide rental clubs. In many cases, they're the latest lines from Titleist, Ping, Callaway, and the like. This is true for both men and women, as well as left-handers, which means you don't have to schlep clubs across the Pacific.

■ Pro shops at most courses are well-stocked with balls, tees, and other accoutrements, so even if you bring your own bag, it needn't weigh a ton.

■ Come spikeless—very few Hawai'i courses permit metal spikes.

■ Resort courses, in particular, offer more than the usual three sets of tees, sometimes four or five. So bite off as much or little challenge as you like. Tee it up from the tips and you'll end up playing a few 600-yard par-5s and see a few 250-yard forced carries.

■ In theory, you can play golf in Hawai'i 365 days a year. But there's a reason the Hawaiian Islands are so green. Better to bring an umbrella and light jacket and not use them than to not bring them and get soaked.

■ Unless you play a muni or certain daily-fee courses, plan on taking a cart. Carts are mandatory at most courses and are included in the green fees.

Hilo Municipal Golf Course. Hilo Muni is living proof that you don't need a single sand bunker to create a challenging course. Trees and several meandering creeks are the danger here. Despite the lack of bunkers, the course, which offers views of Hilo Bay from most holes, has produced many of Hawai'i's top players over the years. Taking a divot reminds you that you're playing on a dormant volcano—the soil is dark black crushed lava. ⊠ *340 Haihai St., Hilo* ☎ *808/959–7711* 🏌 *18 holes. 6325 yds. Par 71. Green Fee: $29 weekdays, $34 weekends* ⚲ *Facilities: Driving range, putting green, golf carts, pull carts, rental clubs, pro shop, lessons, restaurant, bar.*

★ **Hualālai Resort.** Named for the volcanic peak that is the target off the first tee, the Nicklaus Course at Hualālai is semiprivate, open only to guests of the adjacent Four Seasons Resort Hualālai. From the forward and resort tees, this is perhaps Jack Nicklaus's most friendly course in Hawai'i, but the back tees play a full mile longer. The par-3 17th plays across convoluted lava to a seaside green, and the view from the tee is so lovely, you may be tempted to just relax on the koa bench and enjoy the scenery. ⊠ *100 Ka'ūpūlehu Dr., Kohala Coast* ☎ *808/325–8480* ⊕ *www.fourseasons.com/hualalai* 🏌 *18 holes. 7117 yds. Par 72. Green*

Most of the Big Island's top golf courses are located on the sunny Kona Coast.

Fee: $250 for all-day access ☞ *Facilities: Driving range, putting green, golf carts, pull carts, rental clubs, pro shop, lessons, restaurant, bar.*

★ **Kona Country Club.** This venerable country club offers two very different tests with the aptly named Ocean and Ali'i Mountain courses. The Ocean Course (William F. Bell, 1967) is a bit like playing through a coconut plantation, with a few remarkable lava features—such as the "blowhole" in front of the par-4 13th, where seawater propelled through a lava tube erupts like a geyser. The Ali'i Mountain Course (front nine, William F. Bell, 1983; back nine, Robin Nelson and Rodney Wright, 1992) plays a couple of strokes tougher than the Ocean and is the most delightful split personality you may ever encounter. Both nines share breathtaking views of Keauhou Bay, and elevation change is a factor in most shots. The most dramatic view on the front nine is from the tee of the par-3 5th hole, one of the best golf vistas in Hawai'i. The green seems perched on the edge of the earth, with what only seems to be a sheer 500-foot drop just beyond the fringe. The back nine is links-style, with less elevation change—except for the par-3 14th, which drops 100 feet from tee to green, over a lake. The routing, the sight lines and framing of greens, and the risk-reward factors on each hole make this one of the single best nines in Hawai'i. ✉ *78-7000 Ali'i Dr., Kailua-Kona* ☎ *808/322–2595* ⊕ *www.konagolf.com* ⚑ *Ocean Course: 18 holes. 6806 yds. Par 72. Green Fee: $165. Mountain Course: 18 holes. 6673 yds. Par 72. Green Fee: $150* ☞ *Facilities: Driving range, putting green, golf carts, rental clubs, lessons, restaurant, bar.*

Mākālei Country Club. Set on the slopes of Hualālai, at an elevation of 2,900 feet, Mākālei is one of the rare Hawai'i courses with bent-grass putting greens, which means they're quick and without the grain associated with Bermuda greens. Former PGA Tour official Dick Nugent (1994) designed holes that play through thick forest and open to provide wide ocean views. Elevation change is a factor on many holes, especially the par-3 15th, with the tee 80 feet above the green. In addition to fixed natural obstacles, the course is home to a number of wild peacocks and turkeys, which can make for an entertaining game. After noon, green fees dip drastically. ⊠ *72-3890 Hawai'i Belt Rd., Kailua-Kona* ☎ *808/325–6625* ⚐ *18 holes. 7041 yds. Par 72. Green Fee: $99* ⚐ *Facilities: Driving range, putting green, golf carts, rental clubs, pro shop, lessons, restaurant.*

> ### WORD OF MOUTH
>
> "On the Big Island you also have an entire coastline of great golf courses. . . . There are great courses at Mauna Lani (two courses and a good restaurant at the clubhouse). There is also a renowned golf school at Mauna Lani if you want to take a few lessons."
>
> —Leburta

Fodor's Choice ★ **Mauna Lani Resort.** Black lava flows, lush green turf, white sand, and the Pacific's multihues of blue define the 36 holes at Mauna Lani. The South Course includes the par-3 15th across a turquoise bay, one of the most photographed holes in Hawai'i. But it shares "signature hole" honors with the 7th. A long par-3, it plays downhill over convoluted patches of black lava, with the Pacific immediately to the left and a dune to the right. The North Course plays a couple of shots tougher. Its most distinctive hole is the 17th, a par-3 with the green set in a lava pit 50 feet deep. The shot from an elevated tee must carry a pillar of lava that rises from the pit and partially blocks your view of the green. ⊠ *68-1310 Mauna Lani Dr., Kohala Coast* ☎ *808/885–6655* ⊕ *www. maunalani.com* ⚐ *North Course: 18 holes. 6601 yds. Par 72. Green Fee: $260. South Course: 18 holes. 6436 yds. Par 72. Green Fee: $210* ⚐ *Facilities: Driving range, putting green, golf carts, rental clubs, pro shop, lessons, restaurant, bar.*

Volcano Golf & Country Club. Located just outside Volcanoes National Park—and barely a stout drive from Halema'uma'u Crater—Volcano is by far Hawai'i's highest course. At 4,200 feet elevation, shots tend to fly a bit farther than at sea level, even in the often cool, misty air. Because of the elevation and climate, Volcano is one of the few Hawai'i courses with bent-grass putting greens. The course is mostly flat, and holes play through stands of Norfolk pines, flowering *lehua* trees, and multitrunk *hau* trees. The uphill par-4 15th doglegs through a tangle of *hau.* ⊠ *Pi'i Mauna Dr. off Hwy. 11, Volcanoes National Park* ☎ *808/967–7331* ⊕ *www.volcanogolfshop.com* ⚐ *18 holes. 6106 yds. Par 72. Green Fee: $70 mornings, $57 after noon* ⚐ *Facilities: Driving range, putting green, golf carts, rental clubs, restaurant, bar.*

Fodor's Choice ★ **Waikoloa Beach Resort.** Robert Trent Jones Jr. built the Beach Course at Waikoloa (1981) on an old flow of crinkly *'a'ā* lava, which he used to create holes that are as artful as they are challenging. The third tee, for instance, is set at the base of a towering mound of lava. The par-5 12th plays through a chute of black lava to an ocean-side green, the blue sea on the right coming into play on the second and third shots. At the King's Course at Waikoloa (1990), Tom Weiskopf and Jay Morrish built a very links-esque track. It turns out lava's natural humps and declivities remarkably replicate the contours of seaside Scotland. But there are a few island twists—such as seven lakes. This is "option golf" as Weiskopf and Morrish provide different risk-reward tactics on each hole. Beach and King's have separate clubhouses. **Beach Course :** ⊠ *1020 Keana Pl., Waikoloa* ☎ *808/886– 6060* ⊕ *www.waikoloagolf.com* ⚑ *18 holes. 6566 yds. Par 70. Green Fee: $130 for guests, $195 for non-guests* ☞ *Facilities: Driving range, putting green, golf carts, rental clubs, lessons, restaurant, bar.* **Kings' Course :** ⊠ *600 Waikoloa Beach Dr., Waikoloa* ☎ *808/886–7888* ⊕ *www.waikoloagolf.com* ⚑ *18 holes. 6594 yds. Par 72. Green Fee: $195* ☞ *Facilities: Driving range, putting green, golf carts, rental clubs, lessons, restaurant, bar.*

Waikoloa Village Golf Course. Robert Trent Jones Jr., the same designer who created some of the most expensive courses on the Kohala coast, designed this little gem, which is 20 minutes from the coast, in 1972. Though not affiliated with the resorts, the Waikoloa Village course is the site of the annual Waikoloa Open, one of the most prestigious tournaments in Hawai'i. Holes run across rolling hills with sweeping mountain and ocean views. ⊠ *68-1792 Melia St., Waikoloa* ☎ *808/883–9621* ⊕ *www.waikoloa.org/golf* ⚑ *18 holes. 6230 yds. Par 72. Green Fee: $80* ☞ *Facilities: Driving range, putting green, golf carts, rental clubs, lessons, restaurant, bar.*

HIKING

Meteorologists classify the world's weather into 13 climates. Ten are here on the Big Island, and you can experience them all by foot on the many trails that lace the island. The ancient Hawaiians cut trails across the lava plains, through the rain forests, and up along the mountain heights. Many of these paths can still be used today. Part of the King's Trail at 'Anaeho'omalu winds through a field of lava rocks covered with prehistoric carvings called petroglyphs. Many other trails, historic and modern, criss-cross the huge Hawai'i Volcanoes National Park and other parts of the island. Plus, the serenity of remote beaches, such as Papakōlea Beach (Green Sand Beach), is accessible only to hikers.

For information on all Big Island's state parks, contact the **Department of Land and Natural Resources, State Parks Division** (⊠ *75 Aupuni St., Hilo* ☎ *808/974–6200* ⊕ *www.hawaiistateparks.org*).

BEST SPOTS

At **Kekaha Kai (Kona Coast) State Park** (⊠ *Hwy. 19, sign about 2 mi north of Keāhole–Kona International Airport marks rough road*), two 1½-mi-long unpaved roads lead to the Mahaiʻula Beach and Kua Bay sections of the park. Connecting the two is the 4½-mi Ala Kahakai historic coastal trail. Midway, a hike to the summit of Puʻu Kuʻili, a 342-foot-high cinder cone, offers an excellent view of the coastline. It's dry and hot with no drinking water, so be sure to pack sunblock and water.

The **Kealakekua Bay and Captain Cook Monument Trail** (⊠ *Trailhead just off Hwy. 11 at Captain Cook town on Nāpōʻopoʻo Rd. to Kealakekua Bay*) is one of Kona's more popular moderately difficult hikes. About 100 yards from the turnoff, the steep, loose gravel and dirt trail descends several hundred feet across old lava flows. There are some steep switch-backs. Shade along the upper section gives way to sun where the trail opens to lava fields. Nearer to the bay, the trail passes through ancient Hawaiian village ruins and by the Captain Cook Monument, a tall white obelisk on the spot where the famed navigator was killed in 1779 in a dispute with native Hawaiians. The bay is the site of the Kealakekua Underwater Marine Reserve and is popular with divers and snorkelers. The 2½-mi hike is about a three-hour round trip. The hike back up is steep and tiring, so allow plenty of time. Park along the road. Bring sunscreen, a hat, water, and food.

Fodor's Choice ★ **Hawaiʻi Volcanoes National Park** (⊠ *Near Volcano Village, Hwy. 11, 30 mi south of Hilo* ☎ *808/985–6000* ⊕ *www.hawaii.volcanoes.national-park. com*) is perhaps the Big Island's premier area for hikers. The 150 mi of trails provide close-up views of fern and rain forest environments, cinder cones, steam vents, lava fields, rugged coastline, and current lava flow activity. Day hikes range from easy to moderately difficult, and from one or two hours to a full day. For a bigger challenge, consider an overnight or multiday backcountry hike with a stay in a park cabin (available by a remote coast, in a lush forest, or atop frigid Mauna Loa). To do so, you must first obtain a free permit at the Kīlauea Visitor Center. There are also daily guided hikes led by knowledgeable and friendly park rangers. Just outside the park's entrance in Volcano, the Volcano Art Center (⊕ www.volcanoartcenter.org) guides visitors on a free one-hour nature hike of its Naiulani trail every Monday morning at 8:30 AM. The guided walk educates visitors about the flora and fauna of volcanic rain forests, and the cultural and therapeutic uses of various plants, herbs, and flowers in Hawaiian life. *For more on Hawaiʻi Volcanoes National Park, see highlighted feature in the Exploring chapter.*

Muliwai Trail (⊠ *Trailhead is on the west side of Waipiʻo Valley, at the end of Hwy. 240 at the bottom of the valley* ☎ *808/974–4221* ⊕ *http:// hawaiitrails.ehawaii.gov*) begins in the Big Island's most famous valley. On the west side of mystical Waipiʻo, the Muliwai trail leads to the back of the valley, then switchbacks up through a series of gulches, and finally emerges at Eden-like Waimanu Valley. Only very experienced hikers should attempt the full, 18-mile trail, but the first piece of it offers a great peak at Waipiʻo. For those interested in a backcountry adventure, completing the trail can span two to three days of backpack-

Continued on page 150

HAWAI'I'S PLANTS 101

Hawai'i is a bounty of rainbow-colored flowers and plants. The evening air is scented with their fragrance. Just look at the front yard of almost any home, travel any road, or visit any local park and you'll see a spectacular array of colored blossoms and leaves. What most visitors don't know is that the plants they are seeing are not native to Hawai'i; rather, they were introduced during the last two centuries as ornamental plants, or for timber, shade, or fruit.

Hawai'i boasts nearly every climate on the planet, excluding the two most extreme: arctic tundra and arid desert. The Islands have wine-growing regions, cactus-speckled ranchlands, icy mountaintops, and the rainiest forests on earth.

Plants introduced from around the world thrive here. The lush lowland valleys along the windward coasts are predominantly populated by non-native trees including yellow- and red-fruited **guava**, silvery-leafed **kukui**, and orange-flowered **tulip trees**.

The colorful **plumeria flower**, very fragrant and commonly used in lei making, and the giant multicolored **hibiscus flower** are both used by many women as hair adornments, and are two of the most common plants found around homes and hotels. The umbrella-like **monkeypod tree** from Central America provides shade in many of Hawai'i's parks including Kapiolani Park in Honolulu. Hawai'i's largest tree, found in Lahaina, Maui, is a giant **banyan tree**. Its canopy and massive support roots cover about two-thirds of an acre. The native **o'hia tree**, with its brilliant red brush-like flowers, and the **hapu'u**, a giant tree fern, are common in Hawai'i's forests and are also used ornamentally in gardens and around homes.

Bougainvillea

Guava

Monkeypod

Banyan

Ohia Lehua *

Tulip Tree

Plumeria

Pandanus

Hibiscus

Anthurium

Kukui Tree

Hapu'u

*endemic to Hawai'i

DID YOU KNOW?

Over 2,200 plant species are found in the Hawaiian Islands, but only about 1,000 are native. Of these, 282 are so rare, they are endangered. Hawai'i's endemic plants evolved from ancestral seeds arriving on the islands over thousands of years as baggage on birds, floating on ocean currents, or drifting on winds from continents thousands of miles away. Once here, these plants evolved in isolation creating many new species known nowhere else in the world.

Volcanoes National Park's 150 mi of trails offer easy to moderately difficult hikes.

ing and camping, which requires camping permits from the Division of Forestry and Wildlife in Hilo.

Onomea Bay Trail (✛ *Follow signs to 4-mi scenic loop off highway Hwy. 19, turn left onto Old Hawaiian Belt Rd., trail starts just before Botanical Garden* ⊕ *http://hawaiitrails.ehawaii.gov*) is a short but beautiful trail packed with stunning views of the cliffs, bays, and gulches of the Hāmākua coast on the east side of the island. The trail is just under a mile and fairly easy, with access down to the shore if you want to dip your feet in, although we don't recommend trying to swim in the rough waters here. One word of warning: unless you pay the $15 entry fee to the Botanical Garden, entering its gates (which is easy to do even by accident off the trail) will send one of their guards running after you to nicely but firmly point you back to the free trail.

GOING WITH A GUIDE

To get to some of the best trails and places, it's worth going with a skilled guide. Costs range from $95 to $165, and some hikes include picnic meals or refreshments, and gear, such as binoculars, ponchos, and walking sticks. The outfitters mentioned here also offer customized adventure tours.

Hawai'i Forest & Trail. Expert naturalist guides take you to 500-foot Kalopa Falls in North Kohala, through the 4,000-year-old craters at Mount Hualālai, and on bird-watching expeditions throughout the island. In addition to its other expeditions, the company offers tours in Pinzgauers (Austrian all-terrain vehicles) that are perfect for groups, especially those that include off-road junkies. It offers tours into lava tubes and through normally inaccessible areas of Hawai'i Volcanoes

National Park as well, and its two Kohala waterfall tours (one in a Pinzgauer, the other on foot) include cool swims in streams and pools fed by the waterfalls. ☎ 808/331–8505 or 800/464–1993 ⊕ *www.hawaiiforest.com.*

Hawaiian Walkways. Hawaiian Walkways conducts several tours with knowledgeable guides—a Kona Cloud Forest botanical walk, a hike on the "saddle" road between Mauna Kea and Mauna Loa, waterfall hikes, coastal adventures, and jaunts through Hawai'i Volcanoes National Park—as well as custom-designed trips. ☎ 808/775–0372 or 800/457–7759 ⊕ *www.hawaiianwalkways.com.*

HIKING BIG ISLAND TRAILS

■ Trails on the eastern or windward sides of the islands are often wet and muddy, making them slippery and unstable, so wear good hiking shoes or boots.

■ Bring plenty of water, rain protection, a hat, sunblock, and a cell phone, but be aware that service is spotty on the island.

■ Don't eat any unknown fruits or plants.

■ Darkness comes suddenly here, so carry a flashlight if there's a chance you'll be out after sunset.

5

HORSEBACK RIDING

With its *paniolo* (cowboy) heritage and the ranches it spawned, the Big Island is a great place for equestrians. Riders can gallop through green pastures, or saunter through Waipi'o Valley for a taste of old Hawai'i.

GOING WITH A GUIDE

King's Trail Rides. Riders take a four-hour excursion down to Kealakekua Bay for snorkeling and lunch. All your gear is provided, except for fins and reef walkers. Up to four people per trip. $135 per person. ⊠ 81-6420 Mamalahoa Hwy. (Hwy. 11), Kealakekua ☎ 808/323–2388 ⊕ *www.konacowboy.com.*

Na'alapa Stables. This company is a good bet, especially for novice riders. The horses are well trained, and the stable is well run. Rides through Waipi'o Valley cross freshwater streams and pass a black-sand beach. Na'alapa also offers open-range and horse-drawn wagon rides on the historic Kahua Ranch in North Kohala. Rides to Waipi'o depart twice a day, Monday through Saturday, 9:30 AM and 1 PM, from Waipi'o Valley Artworks; Kahua Ranch rides depart twice daily from the ranch at 8:30 AM and 1 PM. Rates for a 2½-hour ride begin at $89 per person for both locations. ⊠ Off Hwy. 240, Kukuihaele ☎ 808/775–0419 ⊕ *www.naalapastables.com.*

Waipi'o Ridge Stables. Two different rides around the rim of Waipi'o Valley are offered—a 2½-hour trek for $85 and a 5-hour hidden-waterfall adventure (with swimming) for $165. Riders meet at Waipi'o Valley Artworks. ⊠ Off Hwy. 240, Kukuihaele ☎ 808/775–1007 or 877/757–1414 ⊕ *www.waipioridgestables.com.*

Waipi'o on Horseback. Not many outfits venture into the green jungle of the Waipi'o Valley. Waipi'o on Horseback takes you to an authentic

Ironman and Friends

Run annually since 1978, the **Iron-man World Championship triathlon** (☎ 808/329–0063 ⊕ http://ironman. com) is the granddaddy of them all. For about a week prior to Race Day (usually the third Saturday of October), Kailua-Kona takes on the air of an Olympic Village as top athletes from across the globe roam the town, carbo-loading and acclimating before competing for glory and $580,000 in prize money at the world's premiere swim/bike/run endurance event. To watch these 1,800 competitors (the max entrants allowed) push them-selves to the ultimate in this grueling event is inspiring; their effort is a testament to the human spirit. The competition starts at Kailua Pier with a 2.4-mi open-water swim, immedi-ately followed by a 112-mi bicycle ride, then a 26.2-mi marathon. The Ironman wouldn't happen without the 7,000 volunteers who donate their time and services. To volunteer, regis-ter online at the Ironman Web site.

The **Honu Half-Ironman Triath-lon** (☎ 808/329–0063 ⊕ www. ironman703hawaii.com) in early June is an Ironman "farm team event." Par-ticipants swim at Hāpuna beach, bike the Ironman course, and run on the Mauna Lani resort grounds.

taro farm. Rides, which depart twice daily, Monday through Saturday, from the Last Chance Store, cost $78. ⊠ *Last Chance Store, off Hwy. 240, Kukuihaele* ☎ *808/775–7291* or *877/775–7291* ⊕ *www.waipio. homestead.com.*

SKIING

Where else but Hawai'i can you surf, snorkel, and snow ski on the same day? In winter, the 13,796-foot Mauna Kea (Hawaiian for "white mountain") usually has snow at higher elevations—and along with that, skiing. No lifts, no manicured slopes, no faux-Alpine lodges, no après-ski nightlife, but the chance to ski some of the most remote (and let's face it, unlikely) runs on Earth. Some people have even been known to use body boards as sleds, but we don't recommend it. As long as you're up there, fill your cooler with the white stuff for a snowball fight on the beach with local kids.

Ski Guides Hawai'i. So you're an experienced skier but didn't pack your gear on a tropical Hawaiian vacation? Christopher Langan of Mauna Kea Ski Corporation is the only licensed outfitter providing transporta-tion, guide services, and ski equipment on Mauna Kea. Snow can fall from Thanksgiving through June, but the most likely months are Feb-ruary and March. This isn't Sun Valley; the runs are fairly short, and hidden lava rocks and other dangers abound. Langan charges $450 per person for a daylong experience that includes refreshments, lunch, ski or snowboard equipment, guide service, transportation from Waimea, and four-wheel-drive shuttle back up the mountain after each ski run. He also offers a $250 mountain ski service without the frills, and ski

DID YOU KNOW?

The Waipio'o Valley is a popular place to go horseback riding. Waipio'o means "curved water;" the valley is named for the Waipio'o River, which flows through it.

or snowboard rentals. ✆ *Box 1954, Kamuela 96743* ☎ *808/885–4188* ⊕ *www.skihawaii.com.*

TENNIS

Many of the island's resorts allow nonguests to play for a fee. They also rent rackets, balls, and shoes. On the Kohala Coast, try the Fairmont Orchid Hawai'i, the Hilton Waikoloa Village, and Waikoloa Beach Marriott. In Kailua-Kona there's the Ohana Keauhou Beach Resort, King Kamehameha's Kona Beach Hotel, and the Royal Kona Resort.

Contact the **County of Hawai'i Department of Parks and Recreation** (⊠ *25 Aupuni St., Hilo* ☎ *808/961–8311* ⊕ *www.hawaii-county.com/directory/ dir_parks.htm*) for information on all public courts.

In Kailua-Kona, you can play for free at the **Kailua Playground** (⊠ *75-5794 Kuakini Hwy., Kailua-Kona* ☎ *808/886–1655*). Tennis courts are available at **Old Kona Airport State Recreation Area** (⊠ *North end of Kuakini Hwy., Kailua-Kona* ☎ *808/327–4958 or 808/974–6200*).

On the Hilo side, there's a small fee to play on the eight courts (three lighted for night play) at **Hilo Tennis Stadium** (⊠ *Ho'olulu County Park, Pi'ilani and Kalanikoa Sts., Hilo* ☎ *808/961–8720*).

Shops and Spas

WORD OF MOUTH

"We spent the day in Hilo and the first stop was the Farmer's Market. We bought a bag with huge strawberry papayas, the biggest avocado I have ever seen, a bag of tomatoes, pineapple, musubi, some sweetened rice covered in taro leaves, and some samosas with a chickpea salad for $15!"

—green33

By Katie
Young
Yamanaka

Residents like to complain that there isn't a lot of great shopping on the Big Island, but unless you're searching for winter coats or high-tech toys, you can find plenty to deplete your pocketbook.

Dozens of shops in Kailua-Kona offer a range of souvenirs from far-flung corners of the globe and plenty of local coffee and foodstuffs to take home to everyone you left behind. Housewares and artworks made from local materials (lava rock, minerals, koa, and milo wood) fill the shelves of small boutiques and galleries throughout the island. Upscale shops in the resorts along the Kohala Coast carry high-quality clothing and accessories, as do a few boutiques scattered around the island. Galleries and gift shops, many showcasing the work of local artists, fill historic buildings in Waimea and North Kohala, and many of the island's former sugar plantation towns have been turned into charming art communities, with local artists selling their wares directly from their studios. Hotel shops generally offer the most attractive and original resort wear but, as with everything else at resorts, the prices run higher than elsewhere on the island.

High prices are entirely too common at the island's resort spas, but a handful of truly unique experiences are worth every penny. Beyond the resorts, the Big Island is also home to independent massage therapists and day spas that offer similar treatments for lower prices, albeit usually in a slightly less luxurious atmosphere. In addition to the obvious relaxation benefits of any spa trip, the Big Island's spas have done a fantastic job incorporating local traditions and ingredients into their menus. Massage artists work with coconut or *kokui* (candlenut) oil, hot stone massages are conducted with lava stones, and ancient healing techniques such as *lomilomi*—a massage technique that combines firm, constant movement and traditional chants—are a staple at every island spa.

SHOPS

In general, stores and shopping centers on the Big Island open at 9 or 10 AM and close by 6 PM. Hilo's Prince Kūhiō Shopping Plaza stays open until 9 PM on weekdays. In Kona, most shops in shopping plazas that are geared to tourists also remain open until 9 PM. Big outlets such as KTA Superstore are open until midnight.

KAILUA-KONA

SHOPPING CENTERS

Coconut Grove Marketplace. Just south of Kona Inn Shopping Village, this meandering labyrinth of airy buildings hides coffee shops, boutiques, ethnic restaurants, and an exquisite gallery. At night locals gather here to watch the outdoor sand volleyball games held in the middle of the

marketplace or grab a couple of beers at the sports bar. ⊠ *75-5795–75-5825 Ali'i Dr.* ☎ *808/326–2555.*

Crossroads Shopping Center. Shopping in Kailua-Kona has begun to go the way of mainland cities—this complex includes both a Safeway and a Wal-Mart. ■TIP→ This is also where you'll find Kona Natural Foods, one of the best whole foods stores on the island, and Manna Korean BBQ, a cheap, fast, and tasty mixed-plate favorite. Borders and Jamba Juice are across the street. ⊠ *75-1000 Henry St.* ☎ *808/329–4822.*

Kaloko Industrial Park. Developed for local consumers, this shopping plaza has outlets such as Costco Warehouse and Home Depot. It can be useful for practical purchases (food from Costco can be a good deal if you're staying in a condo for a week or more) and the occasional surprise gift item (you don't have to tell them you got it at the Hawai'i Costco). ⊠ *Off Hwy. 19 and Hina Lani St., near Kona Airport.*

Keauhou Shopping Center. About 5 mi south of Kailua-Kona, the stores and boutiques here include KTA Superstore, Longs Drugs, and Paradise Found Boutique, along with Kenichi Pacific, a great sushi restaurant; a multiplex movie theater; and Peaberry & Galette, the only hip café on the island. ⊠ *78-6831 Ali'i Dr.* ☎ *808/322–3000* ⊕ *www.keauhoushoppingcenter.com.*

King Kamehameha Shopping Mall. Just around the corner from the King Kamehameha Hotel, this outdoor mall includes a wine market and bar, a couple of quality clothing stores, and a popular Internet café. ⊠ *75-5626 Kuakini Hwy.*

Kona Inn Shopping Village. Originally a hotel, the Kona Inn was built in 1928 to woo a new wave of wealthy travelers. As newer condos and resorts opened along the Kona and Kohala coasts, it lost much of its appeal, and was eventually transformed into a low-rise mall with dozens of clothing boutiques, art galleries, gift shops, and island-style eateries. Broad lawns with coconut trees on the ocean side are lovely for afternoon picnics and the open-air Kona Inn restaurant is a local favorite for evening mai tais. Prior to the construction of the inn, the personal *heiau* (temple) of King Liholiho stood on this shore. ⊠ *75-5744 Ali'i Dr.*

Kona Marketplace. On the *makai* side of Ali'i Drive in the heart of Kailua-Kona, extending for an entire block along Kailua Bay, the village is crammed with boutiques selling bright beach wraps and knickknacks. The marketplace, whose tenants seem to change almost annually, is across the street from Tacos El Unico, one of the few authentic Mexican food joints on the island. ⊠ *75-5744 Ali'i Dr.* ☎ *808/329–6573.*

Makalapua Center. Just north of Kona, off Highway 19, this shopping center attracts islanders for the great bargains at Kmart and island-influenced clothing, jewelry, and housewares at the large Macy's. There's also one of the island's largest movie theaters here. ⊠ *Kamakaeha Ave. at Hwy. 19, south of Kailua-Kona.*

ARTS AND CRAFTS

★ **Antiques and Orchids**. Housed in a great old green building with white trim along Highway 11, this shop lives up to its name, offering shoppers a well-selected collection of antiques and Hawaiiana, interspersed with orchids of assorted colors and varieties. ⊠ *81-6224 Māmalahoa Hwy.Captain Cook* ☎ *808/323–9851.*

Hōlualoa Gallery. In the little coffee town of Hōlualoa, this is one of several excellent galleries that crowd the narrow street. It carries stunning raku (Japanese lead-glazed pottery), original paintings, sculptures, and other collectibles. ⊠ *76-5921 Māmalahoa Hwy., Hōlualoa* ☎ *808/322–8484.*

CLOTHING AND SHOES

★ **Hilo Hattie.** The west coast outlet of this well-known clothier matches his-and-her aloha wear and carries a huge selection of casual clothes, slippers, jewelry, and souvenirs. ■ TIP→ Call for free transportation from nearby hotels. ⊠ *75-5597 Palani Rd., Kopiko Plaza, Kailua-Kona* ☎ *808/329–7200* ⊕ *www.hilohattie.com.*

Honolua Surf Company. Surfer chic, compliments of Roxy, Volcom, and the like is on offer here. This is a great place to look for a bikini or board shorts, or to pick up a cool, casual T-shirt. They have two additional locations in the Kings' Shops in Waikoloa: another branch like this one and one that focuses on women's clothing, with a large assortment of bathing suits and sundresses. ⊠ *Kona Inn Shopping Village* ☎ *808/329–1001* ⊠ *Kings' Shops, 250 Waikoloa Beach Dr., Waikoloa* ☎ *808/886-6422 (surf shop), 808/886-1019 (women's shop)* ⊕ *www.honoluasurf.com.*

★ **Kimura's Lauhala Shop.** Men can pick up an authentic *lau hala* hat here for some stylish sun protection. ⊠ *Māmalahoa Hwy., Hōlualoa* ☎ *808/324–0053.*

Miss M. Kealakekua is home to the first high-end designer boutique on the Big Island, a prayer answered for locals who had been forever complaining that they couldn't find "cool" clothes anywhere. Though the original owner has moved on, and the store has changed its name (it was formerly Sirena), Miss M still carries squeal-worthy contemporary clothing —some made locally—like beautiful printed silk dresses, comfy loungewear, and itsy-bitsy Brazilian bikinis. ⊠ *79-7491 Māmalahoa Hwy., Kealakekua* ☎ *808/322–2260* ⊕ *www.missmboutique.com.*

★ **My Best Friend's Closet.** The airy and modern My Best Friend's Closet seems more like a boutique you'd find in Santa Monica than on the Big Island. The large shop offers the island's widest selection of stylish women's clothing that can't be classified as surfer duds or resort wear. Although there are a handful of other boutiques on the island, this new beauty offers both the best selection *and* the best prices. The shop is in the Kona Marketplace, across the alleyway from Pancho & Lefty's. ⊠ *75-5725 Ali'i Dr., Kailua-Kona* ☎ *808/329–2002.*

Paradise Found. In the Upcountry town of Kainaliu, as well as in two of Kailua-Kona's shopping centers, this reputable spot carries contemporary silk and rayon clothing. ⊠ *Māmalahoa Hwy. 11, Kainaliu* ☎ *808/322–2111* ⊠ *Lanihau Center, 75-5595 Palani Rd., Kailua-Kona* ☎ *808/329–2221* ⊠ *Keauhou Shopping Center, 78-6831 Ali'i Dr., Kailua-Kona* ☎ *808/324–1177.*

FOOD

Kailua Candy Company. The chocolate here is made with locally grown cacao beans from the Original Hawaiian Chocolate Factory, and most truffles and candies incorporate other local ingredients as well (passion fruit truffles—yum). Of course, tasting is part of the fun. Through a glass wall you can watch the chocolate artists at work. ⊠ *In the Koloko Industrial Area, Kamanu and Kauholo Sts., Kailua-Kona* ☎ *808/329–2522* ⊕ *www.kailua-candy.com.*

Kona Coffee & Tea Company. A location 4 mi south of the airport and across from the Honokohau Marina makes this family-owned coffee company's retail outlet a good bet for some easy gourmet gift shopping—or just a coffee or tea stop. The Kona coffee served and sold here won the 2009 Gevalia cupping competition. Try different roasts or a selection of flavored coffees from the coffee bar, and shop for other Hawaiian-made treats from honey and jams to chocolate-covered coffee beans. The shop is behind the Tesoro gas station. ⊠ *74-5035 Queen Ka'ahumanu Hwy., Kailua-Kona* ☎ *808/329–6577* ⊕ *www. konacoffeeandtea.com.*

Kona Wine Market. The new location of this popular wine market carries both local and imported varietals, along with a selection of fine cheeses and other gourmet food products, Hawaiian gifts and products (macadamia nuts, coffee, etc.), and the best selection of cigars and tobacco products on the island. As an added bonus, they'll deliver wine and any of their gourmet food products to your hotel or condo. Their Mixx Bistro Bar, with live music and a happy hour, is still in operation at the store's old location on Kuakina Highway. ⊠ *King Kamehameha Mall, 74-5450 Makala Blvd.* ☎ *808/329–9400* ⊕ *www.konawinemarket.com.*

♺ **Sweet Ohana Candy Factory.** You can spot the bright pink building of this locally owned sweets shop from miles away. Sweet Ohana makes its own delicious taffy and chocolates with no hydrogenated oils or wax. In the tradition of old-fashioned candy stores, it smells absolutely heavenly inside, and it has a 1950s-style soda fountain and café that serves shakes, malts, ice cream sodas, and a limited breakfast and lunch menu. It's a fun stop for kids as well as a wireless hot spot for the laptop-toting crowd. ⊠ *Kuakini Hwy., Kailua-Kona* ☎ *808/329–9676.*

GALLERIES

Kona Arts Center. There's an entire community of artists at work in this complex; feel free to drop in if the doors are open. ⊠ *Māmalahoa Hwy., Hōlualoa.*

Pacific Fine Art. Both the oldest and largest gallery on the island, Pacific Fine Art represents 42 artists from across the globe. They have everything from original paintings to limited editions, sculptures, glass, and raku ceramic pieces. ⊠ *Kona Inn Shopping Village 75-5744 Ali'i Dr., Kailua-Kona* ☎ *808/329–5009.*

MARKETS

Ali'i Gardens Marketplace. More a flea market than a farmers' market, this cluster of about 50 vendor stalls has beautiful tropical flowers, jewelry, clothing, produce, coffee, and even 'ukuleles. It's open Wednesday to Sunday, 9 AM until 5 PM. ⊠ *75-6129 Ali'i Dr., 1½ mi south of*

Kona Inn Shopping Village, Kailua-Kona ☎ *808/334–1381* ⊕ *www. aliigardens.com.*

Keauhou Farmers' Market. Less obvious than the others in its location 5 mi south of Kailua-Kona, this market is packed most Saturdays (8 AM–noon) for good reason: live music, plus local produce (much of it organic, some of it experimental), honey, goat cheese, meat, seafood, flowers, coffee, macadamia nuts, and more. ⊠ *78-6831 Ali'i Dr., Kailua-Kona.*

Kona Inn Farmers' Market. This low-key farmers' market is filled with produce, coffee, and macadamia nuts from around the region. It's held in the parking lot of the Kona Inn Shopping Village from Wednesday through Sunday, 7 AM until 3 PM. ⊠ *75-7544 Ali'i Dr., park at Kona Inn Shopping Village parking lot, Kailua-Kona.*

Kona International Market. The new kid on the block, housed in an open-air facility, has attracted vendors away from a lot of other island markets to sell flowers, local produce, Hawaiian crafts, clothes, and random collectibles. It's open Monday through Sunday, from 9 AM to 5 PM, and includes both farmers' market vendor stalls and proper stores—it's great one-stop shopping for all your souvenirs. There is even a free shuttle to the market from the Kailua pier on days that cruise ships dock. ⊠ *On Luhia St., in Kailua-Kona's Old Industrial Area.*

6

THE KOHALA COAST

SHOPPING CENTERS

Kawaihae Harbor Center. This harborside shopping plaza houses a dive shop, several restaurants, and a few art galleries, including the Harbor Gallery. ⊠ *Hwy. 270, Kamuela.*

King's Shops at Waikoloa Village. Here you can find fine stores such as Under the Koa Tree, with its upscale gift items crafted by artisans, along with high-end outlets such as DFS Galleria and Louis Vuitton. There are also several specialty resort shops and boutiques and, at the other end of the spectrum, a couple of convenience stores, though the prices are stiff. ⊠ *250 Waikoloa Beach Dr., Waikoloa* ☎ *808/886–8811* ⊕ *www. waikoloabeachresort.com.*

The Shops at Mauna Lani. This relatively new complex includes restaurants (Tommy Bahama's Tropical Café, Ruth's Chris Steakhouse, and a new branch of the popular Kenichi sushi restaurant), clothing (Tommy Bahama's and Tori Richard by Quiet Storm), high-end housewares (Oasis), galleries (Lahaina Galleries and the Peter Lik Gallery), jewelry stores, a nail salon, a lingerie shop, and a Foodland Farms market. ⊠ *68-1330 Mauna Lani Dr., Kohala Coast* ☎ *808/885–9501* ⊕ *www. shopsatmaunalani.com.*

Waikoloa Queens' Marketplace. Another large shopping complex on the Kohala Coast, this one houses several clothing shops, a jewelry store, a gallery, gift shops, a few restaurants, and a food court. Its newest anchor tenant is Island Gourmet Markets, a 20,000-square-foot gourmet grocery store. The Marketplace butts up against a new performing arts center and a landscaped network of "Cultural Gardens." ⊠ *201 Waikoloa Beach Dr., Waikoloa* ☎ *877/924–6562* ⊕ *www.waikoloabeachresort.com.*

ARTS AND CRAFTS

Elements Jewelry & Fine Crafts. This shop recently moved out of its old home at Nanbu Hotel and is now located in artsy Hāwī. John Flynn no longer creates his jewelry in the front window for passersby, but he still owns the shop and showcases his exquisite jewelry pieces. Look for the delicate silver leis and gold waterfalls. The shop also carries carefully chosen gifts, including unusual ceramics, paintings, prints, and glass items. ⊠ *55-3413 Akoni Pule Hwy., Hāwī* ☎ *808/889–0760.*

Island Pearls. This store carries a wide selection of fine pearl jewelry, including Tahitian Black Pearls, South Sea white and golden pearls, and Chocolate Tahitian Pearls. Prices are high but you're paying for quality and beauty. ⊠ *201 Waikoloa Beach Dr., Waikoloa* ☎ *808/886–4817* ⊕ *www.waikoloabeachresort.com.*

Gallery at Bamboo. Inside the Bamboo Restaurant, one of the Island's favorite eateries, this gallery seduces visitors with elegant koa wood pieces such as rocking chairs and writing desks. It also has a wealth of gift items such as boxes, jewelry, and Hawaiian wrapping paper. ⊠ *Hwy. 270, Hāwī* ☎ *808/889–1441* ⊕ *www.bamboorestaurant.info/gallery.htm.*

Local Lizard & Friends. Some may find geckos (lizards) to be creepy with their buggy eyes and scaly skin, but not the owners of this store! Local Lizard & Friends rejoices in these pint-size tropical houseguests with a wide variety of gecko-themed clothing, toys, and accessories—the perfect gift for the kids back home. ⊠ *201 Waikoloa Beach Dr., Waikoloa* ☎ *808/886–8900* ⊕ *www.waikoloabeachresort.com*

Hawaiian Quilt Collection. The Hawaiian quilt is a work of art that is prized and passed down through generations. At this store you find everything from hand-quilted purses and bags to wall hangings and blankets. You can even get a take-home kit and make your very own Hawaiian quilt, if you have the time. ⊠ *201 Waikoloa Beach Dr., Waikoloa* ☎ *808/886–0494* ⊕ *www.hawaiianquilts.com.*

CLOTHING AND SHOES

As Hawi Turns. This North Kohala shop, in the historic 1932 Toyama Building, adds a sophisticated touch to resort wear with items made of hand-painted silk. There are vintage and secondhand treasures as well. ⊠ *Akoni Pule Hwy., Hāwī* ☎ *808/889–5023.*

Persimmon. This darling little boutique is stocked with trendy women's clothing from lines such as Three Dots, Trinity, Sky, Michael Stars, Hard Tail, and Zen Knits. They also carry fantastic purses imported from Indonesia as well as locally made jewelry. Other gift items include funky stationery and cards, and island-themed bath and body products. ⊠ *201 Waikoloa Beach Dr., Waikoloa* ☎ *808/886–0303* ⊕ *www.persimmonboutique.com.*

Blue Ginger Family. The Waikoloa branch of this 25-year fashion veteran has really sweet matching aloha outfits for the entire family. ⊠ *201 Waikoloa Beach Dr., Waikoloa* ☎ *808/886–0022* ⊕ *www.blueginger.com.*

Exclusive Designs. This store has everything from the traditional to the contemporary when it comes to Hawaiian-style apparel. They offer casual, resort, evening and swim wear for women, and aloha (or Hawaiian-style) apparel for infants, children, men and women. ⊠ *201 Waikoloa Beach Dr., Waikoloa* ☎ *808/886–0350* ⊕ *www.waikoloabeachresort.com.*

Local Motion. This is one of Hawai'i's favorite local surf shops. Geared towards the younger surfer set, the store carries men's, women's, and children's clothing, plus everything you need for a laid-back day at the beach. Their locally designed license plate frames, slippers, towels, and bags are a great reminder of your trip to the island. ⊠ *201 Waikoloa Beach Dr., Waikoloa* ☎ *808/886–7873* ⊕ *www.localmotionhawaii.com.*

Reyn's. Reyn Spooner aloha shirts are well-known throughout Hawai'i and have been since 1959. The store offers aloha shirts for both men and boys, men's shorts, and some dresses for women and girls. The aloha shirts, by the way, are high-quality—and high-price. ⊠ *201 Waikoloa Beach Dr., Waikoloa* ☎ *808/886–1162* ⊕ *www.reyns.com.*

GALLERIES

Ackerman Fine Art Gallery. Painter Gary Ackerman; his wife, Yesan; and their daughter, Camille, have a fine and varied collection of gifts for sale in their side-by-side gallery and gift shop near the King Kamehameha statue. ⊠ *54-3878 Akoni Pule Hwy., Kapa'au* ☎ *808/889–5971* ⊕ *www.ackermangalleries.com.*

Rankin Gallery. Watercolorist and oil painter Patrick Louis Rankin showcases his own and other local artists' work in his shop in a restored old plantation store (the Wo On Store), next to the Chinese community and social hall, the Tong Wo Society, on the way to Pololū Valley. ⊠ *53-4380 Akoni Pule Hwy., Kapa'au* ☎ *808/889–6849.*

Sue Swerdlow's Gallerie Luna. Sue Swerdlow sells her original paintings and prints in this new location of her gallery. She also carries one-of-a-kind necklaces she designs, as well as various antique pieces and glass works created by local artists. ⊠ *54-3862 Akoni Pule Hwy., Kapa'au* ☎ *808/345–0429.*

WAIMEA

SHOPPING CENTERS

Parker Ranch Center. With a snazzy ranch-style motif, this shopping hub includes a supermarket, coffee shop, natural foods store, and some clothing boutiques. The Parker Ranch Store and Parker Ranch Visitor Center and Museum are also here, and the Kahilu Center next door hosts plays and musical entertainment most nights. ⊠ *67-1185 Māmalahoa Hwy., Waimea* ⊕ *www.parkerranchcenterads.com.*

Parker Square. Browse around boutiques here and in the adjacent **High Country Traders,** where you may find hand-stitched Hawaiian quilts, antiques, or local artworks. ⊠ *65-1279 Kawaihae Rd., Waimea* ☎ *808/331–1000.*

Waimea Center. This standard strip mall has a handful of fast-food restaurants and a grocery store, video store, gift shop, and travel agency. It's highly useful if you're passing through Waimea and need to pick up a few things along the way. ⊠ *65-1158 Māmalahoa Hwy., Waimea.*

ARTS AND CRAFTS

Dan DeLuz's Woods. Master bowl-turner Dan DeLuz creates works of art from 50 types of exotic wood grown on the Big Island. The shop features a variety of items—from picture frames to jewelry boxes—made from koa, monkeypod, mango, *kiawe*, and other fine local hardwoods. Dan's wife, Mary Lou, operates the Koa Shop Kaffee restaurant next door. There's another branch south of Hilo in Kurtistown. ⊠ *64-1013 Māmalahoa Hwy., Waimea* ☏ *808/885–5856* ⊠ *Hwy. 19, Kurtistown* ☏ *808/968–6607.*

Gallery of Great Things. It's not just a cleverly named boutique. At this Parker Square shop, you might fall in love with the Ni'ihau shell lei ranging from $350 to $7,000. More affordable are koa mirrors and other high-quality artifacts from around the Pacific basin. ⊠ *65-1279 Kawaihae Rd., Waimea* ☏ *808/885–7706.*

Harbor Gallery. For fine art, furniture, and decorative pieces made with koa and other native woods, be sure to stop here. Though it also carries some of the usual ocean scene schlock, Harbor has one of the better and more unique selections of art on the island. The gallery is next to Harbor Grill. ⊠ *Kawaihae Shopping Center, Hwy. 270, Kawaihae* ☏ *808/882–1510* ⊕ *www.harborgallery.biz.*

THE HĀMĀKUA COAST

ARTS AND CRAFTS

Glass from the Past. The best place to stop for a quirky gift or just to poke around a truly unique store chock-full of a colorful assortment of old bottles, plus antiques, vintage clothing, and ephemera. ⊠ *28-1672 Old Māmalahoa Hwy., #A, Honomū* ☏ *808/963–6449.*

Kama'aina Woods. A great little shop in charming Honoka'a, and the only place in Hawai'i (possibly in the world) where you can pick up your very own set of "Huli Hands," salad tongs shaped like hula hands and made from koa wood. If the Huli Hands don't catch your eye, the koa-wood bowls surely will. ⊠ *Off Hwy. 19, Honoka'a* ☏ *808/775–7722* ⊕ *www.hulihands.com.*

GALLERIES

Waipi'o Valley Artworks. In this remote gallery you can find finely crafted wooden bowls, koa furniture, paintings, and jewelry—all made by local artists, plus a great little café where you can pick up a sandwich or ice cream before descending into the valley. ⊠ *Off Hwy. 240, Kukuihaele* ☏ *808/775–0958* ⊕ *www.waipiovalleyartworks.com.*

Woodshop Gallery. This pleasant surprise in Honomū, run by local artists Peter and Janette McLaren, showcases their woodwork and photography collections along with beautiful ceramics, woodwork, photography, glass, and fine art from other Big Island artists. The McLarens also serve up plate lunches, shave ice, homemade ice cream, and espresso to hungry tourists in their adjoining café. ⊠ *28-1692 Old Government Rd., Honomū* ☏ *808/963–6363* ⊕ *www.woodshopgallery.com.*

Continued on page 168

ALL ABOUT LEI

Leis brighten every occasion in Hawai'i, from birthdays to bar mitz-vahs to baptisms. Creative artisans weave nature's bounty—flowers, ferns, vines, and seeds—into gorgeous creations that convey an array of heartfelt messages: "Welcome," "Congratulations," "Good luck," "Farewell," "Thank you," "I love you." When it's difficult to find the right words, a lei expresses exactly the right sentiments.

WHERE TO BUY THE BEST LEIS

Florists **Na Pua O Kohala** (54-3760 Akoni Pule Hwy., Kapa'au, 808/885-5541); **Honopua Farm** (Waimea, 808/885-4148); **Hawai'i Tropicals** (71 Banyan Dr., Hilo, 808/961-5575); **Elegant Flowers and Gifts** (68-1845 Waikoloa Rd., Waikoloa Village, 808/883-0225). Lei stands at the Kona and Hilo airports sell a surprisingly nice assortment of leis at reasonable prices. KTA, Safeway, and Costco also sell leis, but they tend to stick to "basics" like plumeria, orchid or tuberose.

LEI ETIQUETTE

■ To wear a closed lei, drape it over your shoulders, half in front and half in back. Open leis are worn around the neck, with the ends draped over the front in equal lengths.

■ Pīkake, ginger, and other sweet, delicate blossoms are "feminine" leis. Men opt for cigar, crown flower, and ti leaf, which are sturdier and don't emit as much fragrance.

■ Leis are always presented with a kiss, a custom that supposedly dates back to World War II when a hula dancer fancied an officer at a U.S.O. show. Taking a dare from members of her troupe, she took off her lei, placed it around his neck, and kissed him on the cheek.

■ You shouldn't wear a lei before you give it to someone else. Hawaiians believe the lei absorbs your *mana* (spirit); if you give your lei away, you'll be giving away part of your essence.

ORCHID

Growing wild on every continent except Antarctica, orchids—which range in color from yellow to green to purple—comprise the largest family of plants in the world. There are more than 20,000 species of orchids, but only three are native to Hawai'i—and they are very rare. The pretty lavender vanda you see hanging by the dozens at local lei stands has probably been imported from Thailand.

MAILE

Maile, an endemic twining vine with a heady aroma, is sacred to Laka, goddess of the hula. In ancient times, dancers wore maile and decorated hula altars with it to honor Laka. Today, "open" maile leis usually are given to men. Instead of ribbon, interwoven lengths of maile are used at dedications of new businesses. The maile is untied, never snipped, for doing so would symbolically "cut" the company's success.

'ILIMA

Designated by Hawai'i's Territorial Legislature in 1923 as the official flower of the island of O'ahu, the golden 'ilima is so delicate it lasts for just a day. Five to seven hundred blossoms are needed to make one garland. Queen Emma, wife of King Kamehameha IV, preferred 'ilima over all other leis, which may have led to the incorrect belief that they were reserved only for royalty.

PLUMERIA

This ubiquitous flower is named after Charles Plumier, the noted French botanist who discovered it in Central America in the late 1600s. Plumeria ranks among the most popular leis in Hawai'i because it's fragrant, hardy, plentiful, inexpensive, and requires very little care. Although yellow is the most common color, you'll also find plumeria leis in shades of pink, red, orange, and "rainbow" blends.

PĪKAKE

Favored for its fragile beauty and sweet scent, pīkake was introduced from India. In lieu of pearls, many brides in Hawai'i adorn themselves with long, multiple strands of white pīkake. Princess Kaiulani enjoyed showing guests her beloved pīkake and peacocks at Āinahau, her Waikīkī home. Interestingly, pīkake is the Hawaiian word for both the bird and the blossom.

KUKUI

The kukui (candlenut) is Hawai'i's state tree. Early Hawaiians strung kukui nuts (which are quite oily) together and burned them for light; mixed burned nuts with oil to make an indelible dye; and mashed roasted nuts to consume as a laxative. Kukui nut leis may not have been made until after Western contact, when the Hawaiians saw black beads from Europe and wanted to imitate them.

HILO

SHOPPING CENTERS

Hilo Shopping Center. This shopping plaza has blossomed with the addition of its newest tenant: Island Naturals Market & Deli. Also look for several trendy boutiques, a store selling everything you need for baby, a salon, a coffee shop, and a few other restaurants. Great cookies, cakes, and baked goodies are at Lanky's Pastries. There's plenty of free parking. ⊠ *Kekuanaoa St. at Kīlauea Ave., Hilo.*

Prince Kūhiō Shopping Plaza. Hilo's most comprehensive mall, Prince Kūhiō Shopping Plaza is where you can find Macy's for fashion, Blockbuster for entertainment, Safeway for food, and Longs Drugs for just about everything else, along with several other shops and boutiques. ⊠ *111 E. Puainako St., at Hwy. 11, Hilo* ☎ *808/959–3555* ⊕ *www.princekuhioplaza.com.*

Waiakea Center. Here you can find a Borders Books & Music, a Ross Dress for Less, an Office Max, and a Wal-Mart. If all the shopping makes you hungry, there's also a food court and one of the island's best restaurants, Hilo Bay Café, tucked away in the corner. ⊠ *Maka'ala St. and Kanoelehua Ave., across from Prince Kūhiō Shopping Plaza, at Hwy. 11, Hilo* ☎ *808/792–7225.*

ARTS AND CRAFTS

Most Irresistible Shop. This place lives up to its name by stocking unique gifts from around the Pacific, be it coconut-flavored butter or whimsical wind chimes. ⊠ *256 Kamehameha Ave.* ☎ *808/935–9644*

The Grove Gallery. If you want a beautiful reminder of the islands, stop by the Grove Gallery where you can get unique, high-quality, locally made items like ceramics, woodwork, Hawaiian quilts, soaps, local photography on canvas, original silk paintings, sarongs, flip-flop drink coasters, pet items, and even a pillow that looks like a piece of *maki* (roll) sushi. ⊠ *302 Kamehameha Ave.* ☎ *808/961–4420 or 866/657–0400* ⊕ *www.thegrovegallery.com.*

BOOKSTORES

Basically Books. This shop stocks one of Hawai'i's largest selections of maps and charts, including topographical and relief maps. It also has Hawaiiana books, with great choices for children. ⊠ *160 Kamehameha Ave., Hilo* ☎ *808/961–0144 or 800/903–6277.*

CLOTHING AND SHOES

★ **Hilo Hattie**. The east coast outlet of the well-known clothier is slightly smaller than its Kailua-Kona cousin, but still offers plenty of the same his-and-her aloha wear, casual clothes, slippers, jewelry, and souvenirs. ⊠ *Prince Kūhiō Shopping Plaza, 111 E. Puainako St., Hilo* ☎ *808/961–3077* ⊕ *www.hilohattie.com.*

★ **Sig Zane Designs**. This acclaimed boutique sells distinctive island wearables with bold colors and motifs. ⊠ *114 Kamehameha Ave., Hilo* ☎ *808/935–7077* ⊕ *www.sigzane.com.*

BIG ISLAND FARMERS' MARKETS

The Big Island is home to more farmers' markets than most cities, each offering a different range of goods, but all providing at the very least a good place to pick up fresh produce, jarred goods such as jams and salsa, as well as homemade local Hawaiian treats. Not surprisingly, locally grown mango, papaya, pineapple, passion fruit, coconut, and guava are available in abundance at great prices, but you can also find delicious avocados, organic peppers, fantastic goat cheese, and, of course, coffee.

Hawai'i's farmers are experimenting with dozens of varieties of exotic fruits such as *poha* berries, *bilimbi*, and *mamey sapoy*. Because of government restrictions, these fruits generally can't leave the island, so this is your only chance to sample them.

The markets located in Kailua-Kona and Hilo are listed under the corresponding shopping sections; the following markets are scattered about the Big Island. You might happily stumble upon them as you explore the coasts.

ON THE KONA SIDE
Hawaiian Homesteaders Association Farmers' Market. Check out the crafts sold here in the Kuhio Hale Building before you head to Waimea's more expensive stores. Produce, flowers, plants, and baked goods are also available. Open 7 AM to noon every Saturday.

Ka'ū Farmers' Market. On a trip to the South Point, stock up on local produce and handmade baked goods at this market held at the Na'alehu Theater every Saturday, 8 AM to noon.

Under the Banyans Farmers' Market. Fresh produce, seasonal fruit, plants, and craft items are sold at this market way up north in the village of Hāwī. It's open Saturdays from 7:30 AM until 1 PM.

ON THE HILO SIDE
Downtown Honok'a Farmers' Market. This good old-fashioned farmers' market in the midst of a charming old plantation town is a good stop during a drive up the Hāmākua Coast. It begins at 8 AM on Saturdays.

The following markets are all south of Hilo:

Kea'au Village Farmers' Market. Fresh local farm produce featuring supersweet corn and flowers daily from 7 AM to 5 PM; on Fridays, vendors also sell handmade Hawaiian arts and crafts.

Maku'u Farmers' Market. There's food and produce here, but what differentiates it from the rest are the Hawaiian crafts, plants, jewelry, shells, ethnic and recycled clothing, records/CDs, and books. It's along the Kea'au/Pāhoa Highway, Sundays 8 AM to noon.

Pāhoa Village Farmers' Market. A great market, held in a large, covered outdoor space with local produce, prepared foods, coffee, clothing, and live music 9 AM to 3 PM every Sunday.

Volcano Village Farmers' Market. A favorite on the east side of the island. Local produce, flowers, prepared foods, baked goods, and an occasional clothing swap, in the Cooper Center, every Sunday 8:30–11 AM.

6

FOOD

★ **Big Island Candies.** This local legend in the cookie- and chocolate-making business is a must-see if you have a sweet tooth. Enjoy a free cookie sample and a cup of Kona coffee as you watch the sweets being made through a big glass window overlooking the factory. Big Island Candies has a long list of interesting and tasty products but they are best known for their chocolate-dipped shortbread cookies. Open 365 days a year, this is a great spot to look for tasty gifts to take home with you. ⊠ *585 Hinano St., Hilo* ☎ *808/935–8890* ⊕ *www.bigislandcandies.com.*

Hilo Coffee Mill. In addition to a fantastic coffee farm tour, the Hilo Coffee Mill sells coffee from a variety of local producers, along with locally made baked goods, candies, artwork, and gifts. ⊠ *17-995 Volcano Road, between mile markers 12 and 13, Mountain View* ☎ *808/968–1333* ⊕ *www.hilocoffeemill.com.*

HOME DECOR

Dragon Mama. Step into this popular downtown Hilo spot to find authentic Japanese fabrics, futons, and antiques, along with a limited but elegant selection of clothing, sleepwear, and slippers for women. ⊠ *266 Kamehameha Ave., Hilo* ☎ *808/934–9081* ⊕ *www.dragonmama.com.*

MARKETS

★ **Hilo Farmers' Market.** The farmers here sell a profusion of tropical flowers, high-quality produce, and macadamia nuts. This colorful, open-air market—the most popular in the state—opens for business Wednesday and Saturday from 6:30 AM to 2:30 PM. ⊠ *Kamehameha Ave. and Mamo St., Hilo.*

★ **Panaewa Hawaiian Homestead Farmers' Market.** The best thing here is the fresh fish, but there are also the usual farmers' market produce vendors 8 AM–5 PM every day on the sidewalk in front of the Hilo Wal-Mart. ⊠ *325 Makaala St., Hilo.*

SPAS

The Big Island's spa directors have done their homework and produced menus full of "only in Hawai'i" treatments well worth a holiday splurge. Local specialties include *lomilomi* massages, hot lava stone massages, and scrubs and wraps that incorporate plenty of coconut, orchids, ginger, and macadamia nuts. Expect to also find Swedish and deep tissue massages and, at some spas, Thai massage. And in romantic Hawai'i, couples can be pampered side by side in a variety of offerings.

■ TIP➔ *Lomilomi massage can be a little too close to deep tissue massage for some, but most kahune (practitioners) are happy to adjust the pressure*

Mauna Lani Spa

to your needs. The only full-service spas on the Big Island are associated with the resorts on the west coast. With the exception of the Four Seasons Spa at Hualālai, the resort spas are open to anyone. In fact, many of the hotels outsource management of their spas, and there is no difference in price for guests and nonguests, although guests have the added bonus of receiving in-room services.

★ **Hale Ho'ola Spa in Volcano.** Those staying in Volcano or Hilo now have quick and easy access to the body treatments, massages, and facials available at the resort spas on the other side of the island—and at far more reasonable prices. Hale Ho'ola's menu includes more local ingredients and traditional Hawaiian treatments than any other spa on the island, including a handful of very traditional Hawaiian massages, such as *lomi hula*, which is *lomilomi* massage choreographed to hula music; *la'au hamo,* which blends *lomilomi* with traditional Hawaiian healing herbs and plant extracts; and *Pō'pōkāpa'i*, which is a divine blend of hot stone massage and *la'au hamo* that incorporates *lomilomi* massage with warm compresses filled with healing herbs. Facials and body scrubs incorporate the usual suspects—ginger, coconut, and macadamia nut—but also some unexpected surprises such as taro, locally grown vanilla, and volcanic clay that works wonders in the form of a facial mask. ⊠ *11-3913 7th St., Mauna Loa Estates, Volcano* ☎ *808/756–2421* ⊕ *www.halehoola.net* ☞ *$75 60-min lomilomi massage, $150 half-day packages. Services: Aromatherapy, body scrubs and wraps, facials, hair removal, makeup, massages, waxing.*

Ho'ola Spa at the Sheraton Keauhou Bay. The Sheraton Keauhou Bay occupies one of the prettier corners of the island, with an unbeatable view from most parts of the hotel. That being the case, it's too bad that the Ho'ola Spa fails to truly take advantage of its location. Although there are plenty of windows with pretty views of the bay, the spa lacks the outdoor treatment areas other island spas are known for. Still, the spa menu includes a variety of locally influenced treatments, and the warm lava-rock massage is a little slice of heaven. There's even a specific massage to nurture and relax mothers-to-be. The packages are an excellent deal, combining several services for far less than you would pay à la carte. For couples, the spa offers an ocean-side massage that takes place on a balcony overlooking the water, followed by a dip in a whirlpool bath. ⊠ *78-128 Ehukai St., Kailua-Kona* ☎ *808/930–4900* ⊕ *www. sheratonkeauhou.com* ☞ *$120 50-min lomilomi massage, $225–$380 half-day packages. Hair salon, hot tub, sauna, steam room. Services: Aromatherapy, body scrubs and wraps, facials, nail treatments, massages, waxing.*

Kalona Salon & Spa at the Outrigger Keauhou Beach Resort. This spa is a great place to get a massage or body treatment for much less than you'd likely pay at the big resorts. Though not quite as nice as the bigger facilities, it's simple and clean, on the ocean, and staffed with well-trained therapists. The spa offers facials using its own line of products made from island ingredients. Be careful if you have sensitive skin. ⊠ *78-6740 Ali'i Dr., Kailua-Kona* ☎ *808/322–3441 or 800/462–6262* ⊕ *www.outrigger.com* ☞ *$95 50-min lomilomi massage, $225 half-day packages. Services: Facials, massage, nail treatments, waxing.*

LOCAL MASSAGE THERAPISTS

Sometimes all you want is a good massage, preferably on the beach—no high prices, herbal tea, or aromatherapy required. Following are a few of our favorite local practitioners. They work by appointment only.

An Ocean Front Therapeutic Massage. Let the marvelous Bea work out your kinks as you listen to the ocean just a few feet away. This is not on the beach, but it is oceanfront, with an ocean view and windows open, so it's pretty darn close. ⊠ *Kona Inn Shopping Village, Suite 250, Kailua-Kona* ☎ *808/329–8912* ☞ *$80 60-min massage.*

Healing Arts Alliance. If you're a deep tissue fan, look no farther than Scott Miller. Specializing in Rolfing and deep tissue massage, Scott is also a licensed acupuncturist with several years' experience. His colleague, Lynn Vrooman, does gentler *lomilomi* massages for those who prefer a gentler touch. ⊠ *103 Kalakaua St., Hilo* ☎ *808/934–7030* ☞ *Scott: $50 60-min deep tissue*

massage. Lynn: $50 90-min lomilomi massage.

Ho'omana Therapies. Two excellent massage therapists operate out of this small but peaceful location across the street from Hilo Bay. Tina Louise Cook specializes in deep tissue massage, structural integration and Zen therapies. Mariposa Blanco specializes in myofacial (deep tissue) and cranial sacral work, rebalancing the nervous system. Both will leave you feeling completely blissful. ⊠ *1266 Kamehameha Ave, suite C., Hilo* ☎ *808/969–7075 for Tina; 808/938–7903 for Mariposa* ☞ *Tina: $65–$120 60- to 90-min deep tissue massage/structural integration. Mariposa: $65 60-min deep tissue massage.*

Pilates and Movement Centre of Kona. Although best paired with a yoga or Pilates session, Laura Crittendon's *lomilomi* is tough to beat. ⊠ *75-5995 Kuakini Hwy., Suite 900, Kailua-Kona* ☎ *808/329–3211* ⊕ *www.konapilates.com* ☞ *$75 60-min massage.*

★ **Kohala Sports Club & Spa at the Hilton Waikoloa Village.** The orchids that run riot in the rain forests of the Big Island suffuse the signature treatments at the Kohala Sports Club & Spa. By the end of the Orchid Isle Wrap, you're completely immersed in the scent and in bone-deep relaxation. The island's volcanic character is also expressed in several treatments, as well as in the design of the lava-rock soaking tubs. Locker rooms are outfitted with private changing rooms for the modest, and a wealth of beauty and bath products. The extensive hair and nail salon could satisfy even Bridezilla with its updo consultations and luxe pedicure stations. The nearby ocean-side cabanas are the perfect venue for a massage on the beach. The fitness center is well-equipped but group classes that roam across the beautifully manicured resort grounds—like the Buddha Point outdoor walk and the Outdoor Circuit Adventure—are much more appealing. ⊠ *Hilton Waikoloa Village, 425 Waikoloa Beach Dr., Kohala Coast* ☎ *808/886–2828 or 800/445–8667* ⊕ *www.kohalaspa.com* ☞ *$160 50-min lomilomi massage, $485–$668 half-day packages. Hair salon, hot tubs (indoor and outdoor), sauna, steam room. Gym with: Cardiovascular machines, free weights, weight-*

training equipment. Services: Acupuncture, aromatherapy, body scrubs and wraps, facials, massage. Classes and programs: Body sculpting, fitness analysis, personal training, Pilates, Spinning, step aerobics, Aqua fit, circuit and abs training, Gyrokinesis, yoga.

★ **Mamalahoa Hot Tubs and Massage.** Tucked into a residential neighborhood above Kealakekua, this little gem is a welcome alternative to the large resort spas. Soaking tubs are made of the finest quality wood, tropical plants and flowers abound, and each tub is enclosed in its own little gazebo, with portholes in the roof for your stargazing pleasure. Tastefully laid out and run, there's no seedy "hot tub party" vibe here, just a pleasant soak followed by, if you like, an hour-long massage. Mamalahoa offers *lomilomi*, Swedish, deep tissue, and a Hawaiian hot stone massage performed with lava rocks collected from around the island. In addition to its secret hideaway ambience, Mamalahoa's prices are lower than any other spa on the island. ⊠ *Kealakekua, south of Kailua-Kona* ☎ *808/323–2288* ⊕ *www.mamalahoa-hottubs.com* ☞ *$30 60-min soak, $95 30-min soak plus 60-min lomilomi, Swedish, or deep tissue massage, $150 30-min soak plus 90-min hot stone massage* ☉ *By appointment only. Open Wed.–Sat. noon–8*PM.

★ **Mandara Spa at the Waikoloa Beach Marriott Resort.** Overlooking the hotel's main pool with a distant view of the ocean, Mandara offers a very complete if not unique spa menu, with more available facial options than you'll find at the island's other spas. Mandara operates spas throughout the world and on a number of cruise lines, and they are managing this one for Marriott, using Elemis and La Therapie products in spa and salon treatments. The spa menu contains the usual suspects—*lomilomi*, a variety of facials, scrubs, and wraps—but they do incorporate local ingredients where appropriate (lemon and ginger in the scrubs, warm coconut milk in the wraps), and the new facilities, designed in a style that combines 20th-century modern American with traditional Asian motifs, are beautiful. ⊠ *69-275 Waikoloa Beach Dr., Kohala Coast* ☎ *808/886–8191* ⊕ *www.mandaraspa.com* ☞ *$145 50-min lomilomi massage, $450–$500 half-day packages. Hair salon, steam room. Gym with: Cardiovascular machines, free weights, weight-training equipment. Services: Aromatherapy, body scrubs and wraps, facials, massage, nail treatments, waxing.*

Fodor's Choice **Mauna Lani Spa.** If you're looking for a one-of-a-kind experience, this is
★ your destination. Most treatments take place in outdoor, bamboo-floor *hales* (houses) surrounded by lava rock. Incredible therapists offer a mix of the old standbys (*lomilomi* massage, moisturizing facials) and innovative treatments, many of which are heavily influenced by ancient traditions and incorporate local products. One exfoliating body treatment is self-administered in one of the outdoor saunas—a great choice for people who aren't too keen on therapists seeing them in their birthday suits. Watsu therapy takes place in an amazing pool filled and heated by the adjacent lava tube, with help from solar panels overhead. Meant to re-create the feeling of being in a womb, the hour-long therapy is essentially an underwater massage. You feel totally weightless, thanks to some artfully applied weights and the buoyancy of the warm salt water. It's a great treatment for people with disabilities that keep them

from enjoying a traditional massage. The aesthetic treatments on the menu incorporate high-end products from Epicuran and Emminence, so a facial will have a real and lasting therapeutic effect on your skin. The spa also offers a full regimen of fitness and yoga classes, as well as more mainland-style procedures like Botox and Restylane injections. ⊠ *Mauna Lani Resort, 68-1400 Mauna Lani Dr., Kohala Coast* ☎ *808/885–6622* ⊕ *www.maunalani.com* ☞ *$159 50-min lomilomi massage, $345–$799 half-day packages. Hair salon, hot tubs (indoor and outdoor), sauna, steam room. Gym with: Cardiovascular machines, free weights, weight-training equipment. Services: Aquatic therapy, baths, body wraps, Botox, facials, massage, Restylane, scrubs, waxing and tinting, nail treatment. Classes and programs: Aerobics, kickboxing, personal training, Pilates, Spinning, weight training, yoga.*

Mauna Kea Spa by Mandara. Mandara Spas blend one-third European, one-third Balinese, and one-third indigenous treatments to create the ultimate spa experience. Things are no different at this newly renovated spa at the Mauna Kea Beach Hotel. Though the facility is on the smaller side, the excellent treatments are up to Mandara Spa standards. Try the Elemis Tri-Enzyme Resurfacing Facial or, even better, the Mandara Four Hand Massage where two therapists work out the kinks simultaneously. *The hotel operates a separate hair salon that offers manicures and pedicures in addition to standard salon services.* ⊠ *69-100 Mauna Kea Beach Drive., Kohala Coast* ☎ *808/882–5630* ⊕ *www.mandaraspa. com* ☞ *$181 50-min lomilomi. Services: Body treatments, facials, massage. Gym with: Cardiovascular and strength training machines. Classes and programs: Yoga.*

Paul Brown Salon & Spa at the Hāpuna Beach Prince Hotel. It's not unusual for locals to drive an hour each way to get their hair cut here. Paul Brown has been in the business for 30 years, and he now has three locations in Hawai'i. Hair is still the specialty, but it's not just a salon. The full-service spa—nicely designed to let in lots of light—has an extensive menu of massages, facials, and body treatments. The most popular massage is the lomilomi (traditional Hawaiian massage) but don't overlook the spa's unique body treatments including the chocolate macadamia nut scrub, the detoxifying volcanic clay treatment, and the Hawaiian salt and aloe exfoliation. This is also the best place for waxing. You can use the gym at the Hāpuna Golf Course's clubhouse, accessible via a free shuttle. ⊠ *62-100 Kauna'oa Dr., Kohala Coast* ☎ *808/880–1111 or 800/882–6060* ⊕ *www.paulbrownhawaii.com* ☞ *$115 50-min lomilomi massage, $338–$410 half-day package; $575 full-day package. Hair salon, sauna, steam room. Services: Acupuncture, body wraps, facials, massage. Classes and programs: Aerobics, yoga.*

The Spa at Hualālai. The Spa at Hualālai is for the exclusive use of Four Seasons Resort guests, so you can sign everything to your room and never have a problem booking a treatment. Though it can feel like a New York spa dropped onto a tropical island, the Spa at Hualālai does include outdoor massage *hales*, which afford more of a Hawaiian experience. The therapists are also top-notch, and a real effort has been made to incorporate local traditions. Apothecary services are available that allow you to customize your treatment with ingredients like

6

honey, kukui nuts, and coconut. ⊠ *72-100 Ka'ūpūlehu Dr., ⫐ Box 1269, Kailua-Kona 96745 Ka'ūpūlehu/Kona96740* ☎ *808/325–8000* ⊕ *www.fourseasons.com* ☞ *$170 50-min massage, $170 body scrub, $170 facials. Hair salon, outdoor hot tubs, sauna, steam room. Gym with: Cardiovascular machines, free weights, weight-training equipment. Services: Body treatments, facials, massage. Classes and programs: Personal training, Pilates, Spinning, tai chi, yoga.*

★ **Spa Without Walls at the Fairmont Orchid Hawai'i.** This is possibly the best massage spa on the island, partially due to its setting—massage tables face either the ocean or a waterfall. Though most people will probably opt for the ocean, both settings are absolutely peaceful. There are other great treatments as well, including caviar facials, fragrant herbal wraps, and coffee and vanilla scrubs, but the massages are the best things going. ⊠ *Fairmont Orchid Hawai'i, 1 N. Kanikū Dr., Kohala Coast* ☎ *808/885–2000* ⊕ *www.fairmont.com* ☞ *$159–179 50-min lomilomi massage. Sauna, steam room. Gym with: Cardiovascular machines, free weights, weight-training equipment. Services: Body treatments, facials, makeup, massage, nail services, scrubs, hair. Classes and programs: Aquaerobics, guided walks, meditation, personal training, yoga.*

Entertainment and Nightlife

WORD OF MOUTH

"The Big Island is about Hawaiian history, culture, etc., an experience which has nothing to do with miniature golf courses and extensive nightlife. Both Kailua-Kona and Hilo fold up their sidewalks precisely at ten (well, nine actually), and people who live there are not seen again."

—fdecarlo

By Katie
Young
Yamanaka

If you're the sort of person who doesn't come alive until after dark, you might be a little lonely on the Big Island. Blame it on the plantation heritage. People did their cane raising in the morning, thus no late-night fun.

Still, there are a few lively bars on the island, a handful of great local playhouses, half a dozen or so movie houses (including those that play foreign and independent films), and plenty of musical entertainment to keep you occupied.

Also, many resorts have bars and late-night activities and events as well, and keep pools and gyms open late so there's something to do after dinner.

And let's not forget the lū'au. These fantastic dance and musical performances are combined with some of the best local food on the island and are plenty of fun for the whole family.

ENTERTAINMENT

DINNER CRUISES AND SHOWS

★ **Evening on the Reef Glass Bottom Dinner Cruise.** Blue Sea Cruises offers a classed-up alternative to the booze cruise, with soothing Hawaiian music, buffet dinner, and tropical juices and cocktails. Its focus is on the sunset and the scenery, with the chance to see spinner dolphins, manta rays (and whales from November to May). Guests also enjoy what's below the surface through the boat's glass bottom. ⊠ *Kailua Pier, Kailua-Kona* ☎ *808/331–8875* ⊕ *www.blueseacruisesinc.com* ⊠ *$88* ⏰ *Mon., Wed., Thurs., Fri. and Sat.*

LŪ'AU AND POLYNESIAN REVUES
KAILUA-KONA

King Kamehameha's Kona Beach Hotel. Witness the royal court procession at the Island Breeze Lū'au, a beachfront event, which includes a 22-item buffet, an open bar, and a show. ⊠ *75-5660 Palani Rd., Kailua-Kona* ☎ *808/326–4969 or 808/329–8111* ⊕ *www.islandbreezeluau.com* ⊠ *$72.86* ⏰ *Tues., Wed., and Sun. 5-8.*

Royal Kona Resort. This resort lights lū'au torches for a full Polynesian show and a Hawaiian-style oceanfront buffet three times a week. ⊠ *75-5852 Ali'i Dr., Kailua-Kona* ☎ *808/329–3111 Ext. 4* ⊕ *www. royalkonaresort.com* ⊠ *$62.50 if you book online, $75 if you book at the hotel* ⏰ *Mon., Wed., and Fri. at 5.*

Sheraton Keauhou Bay. A recent addition to the Big Island's lū'au scene, Island Breeze's production of "Firenesia," tells the story of a young man who journeys through Polynesia and embraces a greater understanding of fire. Get ready for lots of mesmerizing fire dancing in addition to storytelling through traditional hula and Hawaiian language. The open bar doesn't hurt either. ⊠ *75-5852 Ali'i Dr., Kailua-Kona* ☎ *808/930–4900* ⊕ *www.sheratonkeauhou.com* ⊠ *$83.28* ⏰ *Mon.*

THE KOHALA COAST

Fairmont Orchid. The Fairmont's "Gathering of the Kings Polynesian Feast" offers the most entertainment bang for your resort buck. The show is slickly produced and well choreographed, incorporating both traditional and modern dance and choreography as well as beautiful costumes. The meal offers more variety than most, with options representing all the early Hawaiian settlers, including those from New Zealand, Hawaii, Tahiti, and Samoa. ⊠ *1 N. Kaniku Dr., Kohala Coast* ☎ *808/885–2000* ⊕ *www.fairmont.com/orchid* ⊠ *$103* ⊗ *Sat. at 6.*

Hilton Waikoloa Village. The Hilton seats 400 people outdoors at the Kamehameha Court, where the acclaimed Polynesian group Tihati performs a lively show. A buffet dinner provides samplings of Hawaiian food as well as fish, beef, and chicken to appeal to all tastes. ⊠ *425 Waikoloa Beach Dr., Waikoloa* ☎ *808/886–1234* ⊕ *www.hiltonwaikoloavillage.com* ⊠ *$95, includes two cocktails* ⊗ *Tues., Fri., Sun. at 6.*

★ **Kona Village Resort.** In its utter isolation, the lūʻau here is one of the most authentic and traditional on the Islands. As in other lūʻau, activities include the steaming of a whole pig in the *imu* (ground oven). The Wednesday night show focuses solely on Hawaiian traditions and music, while Friday night incorporates Polynesian dancing, music, and traditions as well. The dancing, done on a stage over a lagoon, is magical. On Wednesday, the lūʻau stage gives way to Hawaiian cowboys, or *paniolo*, for cowboy tales and a tasty barbecue. ⊠ *Queen Kaʻahumanu Hwy., 6 mi north of Kona International Airport, Kailua-Kona* ☎ *808/325–5555 or 808/325–4273* ⊕ *www.konavillage.com* ⊠ *$98, includes one cocktail* ⊗ *Wed. and Fri. from 5, imu ceremony at 6, dinner at 6:30, show at 8.*

Mauna Kea Beach Hotel Clambake. A departure from the normal outdoor Hawaiian lūʻau, the Mauna Kea Beach Hotel's weekly clambake is the perfect way to enjoy the bounty of the Pacific Ocean beachside under the stars. There isn't a pig cooked in an underground oven but you will get your fill of fine seafood with an extensive menu that includes oysters on the half shell, ʻahi sashimi, fresh island fish, Manila clams, mussels, Dungeness crab legs and steamed Keāhole lobster. There's even prime rib of beef for meat lovers. The best part of this clambake besides the food is the setting (which can't be beat), and the live Hawaiian music that is often accompanied by a graceful hula dancer. ⊠ *62-100 Mauna Kea Beach Dr., Kohala Coast* ☎ *808/882–5810 or 808/882–7222* ⊕ *www.maunakeabeachhotel.com* ⊠ *$86* ⊗ *Sat. at 6.*

Waikoloa Beach Marriott. At this celebration, entertainment includes a Samoan fire dance as well as songs and dances of various Pacific cultures. Traditional Hawaiian dishes are served alongside more familiar fare. ⊠ *69-275 Waikoloa Beach Dr., Waikoloa* ☎ *808/886–6789* ⊕ *www.marriott.com* ⊠ *$88, including open bar* ⊗ *Wed. and Sun. 5–8:30.*

7

CLOSE UP

Hawaiian Music on Big Island

It's easy to forget that Hawai'i has its own music until you step off a plane onto the Islands—and then there's no escaping it. It's a unique blend of the strings and percussion favored by the early settlers and the chants and rituals of the ancient Hawaiians. Hawaiian music today includes Island-devised variations on acoustic guitar—slack key and steel guitar—along with the 'ukulele (a small, four-string guitar about the size of a violin), and vocals that have evolved from ritual chants to more melodic compositions.

This is one of the few folk music traditions in the United States that is fully embraced by the younger generation, with no prodding from their parents or grandparents. More than half the radio stations on the Big Island play solely Hawaiian music, and concerts performed by Island favorites like Makana are filled with fans of all ages.

The best way to get an introduction to the music is to attend one of the annual festivals: The free **Annual Hawai'i Slack Key Guitar Festival** (July) features a handful of greats performing throughout the day at the Sheraton Keauhou Bay; the **Annual 'Ukulele and Slack Key Guitar Institute** (November) at the Kahilu Theatre in Waimea takes it one step further, providing both a variety of concerts and workshops for those interested in learning to play the instruments; and the **Annual Big Island Hawaiian Music Festival** (July) at the UH Hilo Performing Arts Center is a weekend full of slack key, steel guitar, and 'ukulele madness.

Or, you can catch live performances most nights at one of a handful of local bars and clubs, including **Mixx Bar and Bistro, Huggo's on the Rocks,** or the **Kona Brewing Company** in Kailua-Kona, and **Cronie's Bar and Grill** in Hilo.

FESTIVALS

There is a festival dedicated to just about everything on the Big Island. Some of them are small community affairs, but a handful of film, food, and music festivals provide quality entertainment for visitors and locals alike. The following is a list of our favorites:

Black & White Night. This lovely annual outdoor party is in downtown Hilo. The stores stay open late, the sidewalks are dotted with live jazz bands, and everyone dresses in black and white, some in shorts and tees and others in gowns and tuxes, to enter the "Best Dressed" contest. ☎ 808/933–9772 ⊕ www.poshfestivals.com ⊙ First Friday in Nov.

Chinese New Year. Hilo throws a big free party complete with live music, food, drums, and fireworks downtown to commemorate this holiday every year. There's a smaller celebration along Ali'i Drive in Kona as well. ☎ 808/933–9772 ⊕ www.poshfestivals.com ⊙ Feb.

Kona Brewers Festival. At this great annual party, roughly 30 breweries and 25 restaurants offer samples and live music, fire dancers, and fashion shows. ☎ 808/331–3033 ⊕ www.konabrewersfestival.com ⊙ Early Mar.

Kona Coffee Cultural Festival. The oldest food festival in Hawai'i brings together a variety of events over a 10-day period, but our favorite is the coffee recipe cooking contest. Coffee chili is one of the best things you've never tasted. ⊕ *www.konacoffeefest.com* ☉ *Early Nov.*

★ **Merrie Monarch Festival.** The mother of all Big Island festivals, the Merrie Monarch celebrates all things hula and completely overtakes Hilo for one fantastic weekend a year. The largest event of its kind in the world honors the legacy of King David Kalākaua, Hawai'i's last king and the man responsible for reviving a lot of the fading Hawaiian traditions including the hula (of which he was a big fan). The festival is staged at the spacious Edith Kanaka'ole Stadium during the first week following Easter Sunday. Hula *hālau* (schools) compete in various classes of ancient and modern dance styles. ■TIP➔ **You need to reserve accommodations and tickets up to a year in advance.** If you're planning on being in Hilo during this time of year but not attending the festival, know that most accommodations will be booked about a year out and plan accordingly. ☏ *808/935–9168* ⊕ *www.merriemonarchfestival.org* ☉ *Apr.*

A Taste of the Hawaiian Range Food and Agricultural Festival. Since 1995, this culinary event has been giving locals and visitors a taste of what the Island's best chefs and farms have to offer, from grass-fed beef and bison to organic produce, cheese, chocolates, and coffee. ☏ *808/981–5199* ⊕ *www.ctahr.hawaii.edu/taste* ☉ *Sept. or Oct.*

FILM

FESTIVALS

Aloha Spirit Film Festival. This independent film festival, held in mid-September, screens cutting-edge documentaries, shorts, and feature films from throughout the islands. Screenings and festivities are held at the Aloha Theatre in Kainaliu. ☏ *808/326–2099.*

Louis Vuitton Hawai'i International Film Festival. Showing throughout the Islands and in Hilo (Palace Theater) and Kainaliu (Aloha Theatre) on the Big Island, this festival has been blazing trails in the exhibition of Asian and Pacific feature films since 1981. It runs for about 10 days in late October. ⊕ *www.hiff.org.*

KAILUA-KONA

Keauhou 7 Cinemas. This is a splendid seven-theater complex, and there are several pre- or post-movie food options in the center. ⊠ *Keauhou Shopping Center, 78-6831 Ali'i Dr.* ☏ *808/324–7200.*

Makalapua Stadium Cinemas. The 10-screen theater has stadium seating and digital surround sound. ⊠ *Makalapua Ave., next to Kmart* ☏ *808/327–0444.*

HILO

First-run films are shown on the nine screens of the **Prince Kūhiō Stadium Cinemas** (⊠ *Prince Kūhiō Plaza, 111 E. Puainako St.* ☏ *808/961–3456*). **Kress Cinemas** (⊠ *174 Kamehameha Ave.* ☏ *808/961–0066*) shows critically acclaimed films and the occasional art-house flick on four screens in a pretty Art Deco building. Since the movies shown here are not-so-recently released, the price is right at $1–$1.50 per person depending on what day and time you go. You can even get a hot dog for $1.50 and free refills on large popcorns and sodas. **Honoka'a People's Theater**

Continued on page 186

MORE THAN A FOLK DANCE

Hula has been called "the heartbeat of the Hawaiian people" and also "the world's best-known, most misunderstood dance." Both are true. Hula isn't just dance. It is storytelling. No words, no hula.

Chanter Edith McKinzie calls it "an extension of a piece of poetry." In its adornments, implements, and customs, hula integrates every important Hawaiian cultural practice: poetry, history, genealogy, craft, plant cultivation, martial arts, religion, protocol. So when 19th century Christian missionaries sought to eradicate a practice they considered depraved, they threatened more than just a folk dance.

With public performance outlawed and private hula practice discouraged, hula went underground for a generation, to rural villages. The fragile verbal link by which culture was transmitted from teacher to student hung by a thread. Even increasing literacy did not help because hula's practitioners were a secretive and protected circle.

As if that weren't bad enough, vaudeville, Broadway, and Hollywood got hold of the hula, giving it the glitz treatment in an unbroken line from "Oh, How She Could Wicky Wacky Woo" to "Rock-A-Hula Baby." Hula became shorthand for paradise: fragrant flowers, lazy hours. Ironically, this development assured that hundreds of Hawaiians could make a living performing and teaching hula. Many danced ʻauana (modern form) in performance; but taught kahiko (traditional), quietly, at home or in hula schools.

Today, 30 years after the cultural revival known as the Hawaiian Renaissance, language immersion programs have assured a new generation of proficient—and even eloquent—chanters, songwriters, and translators. Visitors can see more, and more authentic, traditional hula than at any other time in the last 200 years.

Like the culture of which it is the beating heart, hula has survived.

Lei *po'o*. Head lei. In kahiko, greenery only. In 'auana, flowers.

Face emotes appropriate expression. Dancer should not be a smiling automaton.

Shoulders remain relaxed and still, never hunched, even with arms raised. No bouncing.

Eyes always follow leading hand.

Lei. Hula is rarely performed without a shoulder lei.

Arms and hands remain loose, relaxed, below shoulder level—except as required by interpretive movements.

Traditional hula skirt is loose fabric, smocked and gathered at the waist.

Hip is canted over weight-bearing foot.

Knees are always slightly bent, accentuating hip sway.

Kupe'e. Ankle bracelet of flowers, shells, or—traditionally—noise-making dog teeth.

In kahiko, feet are flat. In 'auana, they may be more arched, but not tiptoes or bouncing.

BASIC MOTIONS

Speak or Sing

Moon or Sun

Grass Shack or House

Mountains or Heights

Love or Caress

At backyard parties, hula is performed in bare feet and street clothes, but in performance, adornments play a key role, as do rhythm-keeping implements.

In hula kahiko (traditional style), the usual dress is multiple layers of stiff fabric (often with a pellom lining, which most closely resembles *kapa*, the paperlike bark cloth of the Hawaiians). These wrap tightly around the bosom but flare below the waist to form a skirt. In pre-contact times, dancers wore only kapa skirts. Monarchy-period hula is performed in voluminous Mother Hubbard mu'umu'u or high-necked muslin blouses and gathered skirts. Men wear loincloths or, for monarchy period, white or gingham shirts and black pants—sometimes with red sashes.

In hula 'auana (modern), dress for women can range from grass skirts and strapless tops to contemporary tea-length dresses. Men generally wear aloha shirts, but sometimes grass skirts over pants or even everyday gear. (One group at a recent competition wore wetsuits to do a surfing song!)

SURPRISING HULA FACTS

■ Grass skirts are not traditional; workers from Kiribati (the Gilbert Islands) brought this custom to Hawai'i.

■ In olden-day Hawai'i, *mele* (songs) for hula were composed for every occasion—name songs for babies, dirges for funerals, welcome songs for visitors, celebrations of favorite pursuits.

■ Hula *ma'i* is a traditional hula form in praise of a noble's genitals; the power of the *ali'i* (royalty) to procreate gave *mana* (spiritual power) to the entire culture.

■ Hula students in old Hawai'i adhered to high standards: scrupulous cleanliness, no sex, daily cleansing rituals, certain food prohibitions, and no contact with the dead. They were fined if they broke the rules.

WHERE TO WATCH

■ **Brown's Beach House** at the Fairmont Orchid. Hula dancers perform nightly on a moonlit grassy knoll.

■ **Kamaha'o "The Wondrous Myths of Hawai'i."** The island's most talented dancers perform in this weekly lū'au production at the Sheraton Keauhou.

■ **Merrie Monarch Festival.** The king of all hula festivals, held annually the first Thursday after Easter Sunday in Hilo. Tickets are hard to get so book as early as possible.

■ **Volcano Center & Volcanoes National Park Na Mea Hawai'i Hula Kahiko.** A series of free public performances takes place outdoors facing Halema'uma'u crater, the sacred home of the volcano goddess Pele.

(✉ *Mamane St., Honoka'a* ☏ *808/775–0000*) screens selected art films during the week and more mainstream films on weekends.

Palace Theatre. After decades of being closed, the 1925 theater has been beautifully restored and now showcases everything from old movies to musical productions to holiday concerts and even youth plays. ✉ *38 Haili St., Hilo* ☏ *808/934–7010.*

THEATER

Aloha Angel Performing Arts Center. Local talent stages musicals and Broadway plays at this charming old plantation center near Kailua-Kona. ✉ *Aloha Angel Theatre Café, 79-7384 Māmalahoa Hwy., Kainaliu* ☏ *808/322–2122.*

★ **Kahilu Theatre.** For legitimate theater, the little town of Waimea is your best bet. The Kahilu Theater hosts regular internationally acclaimed performances, interspersed with a variety of top-notch music acts. In a recent season, Chick Corea, Laurie Anderson, and Pink Martini shared the calendar with modern dance performances, plays, and traditional Hawaiian dance shows. ✉ *Parker Ranch Center, 67-1185 Māmalahoa Hwy., Waimea* ☏ *808/885–6868* ⊕ *www.kahilutheatre.org.*

University of Hawai'i at Hilo Theater. A full concert series of varied performances, acts, musical groups, and plays is held from September through May each year. ✉ *200 W. Kawili St., Hilo* ☏ *808/974–7310.*

★ **Volcano Art Center.** Annual and special performances of Hawaiian music and dance, as well as theatre performances, are hosted by this local art center. People drive here from all over the island for some of their Hawaiian music concerts. ✉ *P.O. Box 129* ☏ *808/967–8222* ⊕ *www. volcanoartcenter.org.*

NIGHTLIFE

KAILUA-KONA

BARS

Kona Brewing Company. Still very popular, the Kona Brewery has been a local favorite practically since it opened. Good food, good local beer (go for the sampler and try them all), and an outdoor patio with live music on Sunday nights make sure it stays that way. ✉ *75-5629 Kuakini Hwy.* ☏ *808/334–2739* ⊕ *www.konabrewingco.com.*

Mixx Bar and Bistro. Kailua-Kona's first and only wine bar, Mixx, is also the only air-conditioned bar in Kona, but it's got a few other things going for it as well—namely good food, stiff and inventive cocktails, and live music nightly on their outdoor patio. ✉ *King Kamehameha Mall, 75-5626 Kuakini Hwy.* ☏ *808/329–7334* ⊕ *www. konawinemarket.com.*

Oceans Sports Bar & Grill. A popular gathering place, this sports bar in the back of the Coconut Grove Marketplace has a pool table and an outdoor patio, along with the dozens of TVs you'd expect at a sports bar. This place really gets hopping on the weekends and on its weekly

BEST BETS FOR SUNSET MAI TAIS

There's nothing quite like kicking back with a mai tai while watching the sun set over the Pacific. Here are some of our favorite places to try:

Crystal Blue at the Sheraton Keauhou (Kailua-Kona). Fantastic sunset views from plush lounge chairs, followed by spotlighted glimpses of nearby manta rays.

Huggo's on the Rocks (Kailua-Kona). Literally on the rocks with a sand-floored bar, strong drinks, and live music Friday and Saturday.

Kawaihae Harbor Grill (Kohala). Views off the deck of the upstairs Seafood Bar, great food in the restaurant next door, and well-poured drinks.

Kona Inn (Kailua-Kona). Wide, unobstructed view, in the middle of downtown, best mai tais on the island.

Wai'oli Lounge in the Hilo Hawaiian Hotel (Hilo). A nice view of Coconut Island, live music Friday and Saturday nights.

karaoke nights. ⊠ *Coconut Grove Marketplace, 75-5811 Ali'i Dr., Kailua-Kona* ☎ *808/327–9494.*

CLUBS

Huggo's on the Rocks. Jazz, country, and even rock bands perform at this popular restaurant, so call ahead to find out what's on. Outside, people often dance in the sand to Hawaiian songs. The crowd skews to slightly older and better behaved than Lulu's across the street. ⊠ *75-5828 Kahakai Rd., at Ali'i Dr., Kailua-Kona* ☎ *808/329–1493* ⊕ *www.huggos.com.*

Lulu's. On weekends, the young crowd gyrates until late in the evening to hot dance music—hip-hop, R&B, and rock—spun by a professional DJ. ⊠ *75-5819 Ali'i Dr., Kailua-Kona* ☎ *808/331–2633.*

THE KOHALA COAST

BARS

Malolo Lounge. A favorite after-work spot for employees from the surrounding hotels, this lounge in the Hilton Waikoloa Village offers decent live music (usually jazz), friendly bartenders, and a pool table. ⊠ *425 Waikoloa Beach Dr., Waikoloa* ☎ *808/886–1234* ⊕ *www.hiltonwaikoloavillage.com.*

Luana Terrace. This wood-paneled watering hole in the Fairmont Orchid Hawai'i has a huge lānai and a great view. Bartenders are great, and service is impeccable. The crowd's not rowdy, so it's a great place for an early evening cocktail or an after-dinner port. ⊠ *1 N. Kanikū Dr., Kohala Coast* ☎ *808/885–2000* ⊕ *www.fairmont.com/orchid.*

HILO

BARS

Cronie's Bar & Grill. A sports bar and hamburger joint by day, Cronie's is a local favorite when the lights go down, with a packed bar and a steady schedule of live local bands. ✉ *11 Waianuenue Ave, Hilo* ☎ *808/961–9666.*

Shooter's Bar & Grill. Another sports bar-turned-nightclub: Come for the game, stay for the late-night live music and drunken karaoke. ✉ *121 Banyan Dr., Hilo* ☎ *808/969–7069.*

Where to Eat

WORD OF MOUTH

"Are you planning to go to Volcanoes National Park? If so, have dinner at the Thai restaurant in Volcano. The best Thai I think I've ever had. Nothing fancy, but the owners bring their own spices from 'home.' Delish. Make reservations."

—starrs

WHERE TO EAT PLANNER

Eating-Out Strategy

Where should we eat? With dozens of island eateries competing for your attention, it may seem like a daunting question. But our expert writers and editors have done most of the legwork—the 80-plus selections here represent the best eating experience this island has to offer. Search "Best Bets" for top recommendations by price, cuisine, and experience.

Reservations

Though it's rare to find a restaurant completely booked on the Big Island, a select few are sticklers about reservations. If you're booking a special occasion dinner, call ahead just in case, or check with your hotel concierge.

What to Wear

There isn't a single place on the Big Island that requires formal attire. The general rule is anything goes, although there are a handful of restaurants (Pahui'a at the Four Seasons, the CanoeHouse at the Mauna Lani, and Manta & Pavilion Wine Bar at Mauna Kea) where you might feel out of place in your beach clothes.

With Kids

Little ones are welcome almost everywhere on the kid-friendly Big Island; the exceptions are a small handful of fine-dining restaurants that cater to adults. The majority of restaurants feature a kid's menu, and many have toys and gimmicks, from coloring kits to spotlights on local marine life, to keep kids entertained.

Smoking

Smoking is prohibited in all Hawai'i restaurants and bars.

Hours and Prices

Though it might seem at first glance like the Big Island's dining scene consists of either very high-end restaurants or divey holes-in-the-wall, there is in fact a fairly large middle ground of quality restaurants that cater both to local and visiting families, and new places are cropping up all the time. Prices are generally higher than on the mainland, mostly because the cost of living is higher here in general, and because restaurants have to import a good portion of their raw materials, though there is an increasing emphasis on locally sourced food.

Tipping is similar here to elsewhere in the country: 15%–20% of the bill or $1 per drink at a bar. Bills for large parties generally include an 18% tip, as do bills at some resort restaurants, so be sure to check your bill before leaving extra.

WHAT IT COSTS				
	¢	$	$$	$$$	$$$$
AT DINNER	under $10	$10–$17	$18–$26	$27–$35	over $35

Restaurant prices are for a main course at dinner, excluding 4.7% excise tax.

BEST BETS FOR BIG ISLAND DINING

Where can I find the best food the island has to offer? Fodor's writers and editors have selected their favorite restaurants by price, cuisine, and experience in the lists below. In the first column, the Fodor's Choice properties represent the "best of the best" across price categories. You can also search by area for excellent eats—just peruse our complete reviews on the following pages.

Fodor's Choice ★

Bamboo, $$, p. 202
Brown's Beach House, $$$$, p. 203
Ke'ei Café, $$, p. 201
Manta & Pavilion Wine Bar, $$$$, p. 205
Merriman's, $$$, p. 205
Pahui'a, $$$$, p. 206

By Price

¢

Ba-Le, p. 193
Big Island Grill, p. 193
Aloha Luigi, p. 218
U-Top-It, p. 199

$

The Coffee Shack, p. 201
Kona Brewing Company, p. 196
Sombat's Fresh Thai Cuisine, p. 221
Merriman's Market Café, p. 205
Lilikoi Café, p. 208

$$

Café Pesto, p. 219
Hilo Bay Café, p. 220
Jackie Rey's Ohana Grill, p. 195
Kiawe Kitchen, p. 216
Pau, p. 215

$$$

Beach Tree at the Four Seasons Resort Hualālai, p. 202
Kilauea Lodge, p. 216
Fujimamas, p. 208
Huggo's, p. 195
Kenichi Pacific, p. 196

$$$$

Daniel Thiebaut's Restaurant, p. 208
Manta & Pavilion Wine Bar, p. 205
Hale Samoa at Kona Village Resort, p. 204
KPC (Kamuela Provision Company), p. 204

By Cuisine

HAWAIIAN

Pakini Grill, $$, p. 215
Hilo Bay Café, $$, p. 220
Jackie Rey's Ohana Grill, $$, p. 195
Manago Hotel, $, p. 201
Pahui'a, $$$$, p. 206

PLATE LUNCH

Ba-Le, p. 193
Blane's Drive-In, p. 219
Big Island Grill, p. 193
Café 100, p. 219
Kona Mix Plate, p. 196

SUSHI

Kenichi Pacific, $$$ p. 196
Norio's Sushi Bar, $$$ p. 205
Sansei Seafood Restaurant & Sushi Bar, $$-$$$, p. 206

Sushi Rock, $$, p. 207
Wasabi's, $$, p. 199

By Experience

MOST KID-FRIENDLY

Bubba Gump Shrimp Company, $, p. 193
Ken's House of Pancakes, $, p. 220
Beach Tree, $$-$$$, p. 202
The Seaside Restaurant, $$, p. 221
U-Top-It, ¢, p. 199

MOST ROMANTIC

Hale Samoa, $$$$, p. 204
Manta & Pavilion Wine Bar, $$$$, p. 205
Huggo's, $$$, p. 195
Ke'ei Café, $$, p. 201
Pahui'a, $$$$, p. 206

BEST VIEW

Brown's Beach House, $$$$, p. 203
Bubba Gump Shrimp Company, $, p. 193
Island Lava Java, $, p. 195
Huggo's, $$$, p. 195

8

By Katie
Young
Yamanaka

Between star chefs and an influx of quality local farms, the Big Island restaurant scene has been heating up in the last couple of years. In the past it used to be a pleasant surprise for visitors to discover a gourmet meal on the island; now food writers from national magazines are praising the chefs of the Big Island for their ability to turn the local bounty into inventive blends of the island's cultural heritage. The Big Island has become a destination for vacationing foodies who are drawn by rave reviews and the reputations of some world-renowned chefs.

Hotels along the Kohala Coast have long invested in celebrated chefs who know how to make a meal memorable, from inventive entrées to spot-on wine pairings. But great food on the Big Island doesn't begin and end with the resorts. A handful of cutting-edge chefs have retired from the fast-paced hotel world and opened up their own small bistros closer to the farms in upcountry Waimea. And, as the old plantation towns transform into youthful arts communities, unique and wonderful restaurants have cropped up in Hāwī, Kainaliu, and on the east side of the island in Hilo. Though the larger, gourmet restaurants (especially those at the resorts) tend to be very pricey, there are still *ono grindz* (Hawaiian slang for tasty local food) to be found at budget prices throughout the island, from greasy plate lunch specials to reasonably priced organic fare at a number of cafés and health food markets. Less populated areas like Kaʻū, the Hāmākua Coast, and Puna offer limited choices for dinner, but usually at least one or two spots that do a decent plate lunch, and a handful of excellent bakeries.

In addition to the individual restaurants, events such as the Great Waikoloa Food, Wine & Music Fest at the Hilton Waikoloa Village, the Kona Coffee Cultural Festival at the Outrigger Keauhou, and Cuisines of the Sun at the Mauna Lani Bay Hotel draw hundreds of guests to starlit open-air dinners celebrating the bounty of the isle's land and waters. Island tourism bureaus have also made an effort as of late to promote agritourism, and it has turned into a booming new business. Farm tours afford visitors the opportunity to meet with and learn from the local farmers and tour a variety of organic farms. Some tours conclude with a meal comprised of items sourced from the same farms. From goat farms churning creamy, pungent goat cheese to Waimea farms planting row after row of bright tomatoes to small aquaculture operations, visitors can see exactly where their next meal will come from and taste the difference that local, fresh, and organic production can make.

KAILUA-KONA

¢ ✕ **Ba-Le**. Comparable to Kona Mix Plate in terms of prices, food qual-
VIETNAMESE ity, and street cred, Ba-Le serves a great plate lunch. It also has tasty
Vietnamese-influenced food, such as their popular croissant sandwiches
stuffed with mint, lemongrass, sprouts, and your choice from a variety
of Vietnamese-style meats. *Pho* (Vietnamese noodle soup) is another
great option, especially if you have the misfortune of catching an island
cold. Ba-Le has 20 other locations throughout the state, but the business
is locally owned and operated, so it doesn't feel like a chain. ✉ *Kona
Coast Shopping Center, 74-5588 Palani Rd., Kailua-Kona* ☎ *808/327–
1212* ▭ *MC, V.*

$ ✕ **Bangkok House Thai Restaurant**. It may not look like much, with its
THAI small, dark interior and tired carpets, but Bangkok House is the local
go-to for good Thai food. One of few Thai restaurants on the island
to add enough spice to their sauces, Bangkok serves up tasty curries,
satays, and soups, along with a random assortment of Chinese entrées.
The huge menu can actually be a bit overwhelming (there are over 100
options) but the Rainbow salad, panang curry, and spring rolls are all
standouts. Make sure to save room for homemade lychee ice cream.
✉ *75-5626 Kuakini Hwy., in the King Kamehameha Mall* ☎ *808/329–
7764* ▭ *MC, V* ☉ *Closed Sun.*

¢–$ ✕ **Big Island Grill**. This typical, local Hawaiian restaurant looks like an
HAWAIIAN old coffee shop or a Denny's—it's dark and nondescript inside, with
booths along the walls and basic tables with bingo hall chairs in the
middle of the room. Local families love it for the huge portions of pork
chops, chicken *katsu*, and an assortment of grilled or pan-seared fish
specialties at very reasonable prices. It has been popular with locals
since it opened a few years back and there's sometimes a wait for a table.
"Biggie's" also serves a great breakfast—the prices and portions make
this a good place to take large groups or families. ✉ *75-5702 Kuakini
Hwy.* ☎ *808/326–1153* ▭ *AE, MC, V* ☉ *Closed Sun.*

$ ✕ **Boston Basil's**. This tiny traditional trattoria serves solid, family-style
ITALIAN Italian food and great pizzas at very good prices. The atmosphere is
similar to hundreds of Italian restaurants in the U.S.—the tablecloths
are checkered, the candles are in Chianti bottles, there's spaghetti on
the menu, and it always feels a little hot and greasy inside. That said,
you can't beat the location on Ali'i Drive in downtown Kailua-Kona,
right across the street from the ocean. ✉ *75-5707 Ali'i Dr., Kailua-Kona*
☎ *808/326–7836* ⊕ *www.bostonbasils.com* ▭ *MC, V.*

$ ✕ **Bubba Gump Shrimp Company**. Okay, it's a chain, and a chain that
AMERICAN centers around a Tom Hanks movie, no less. Get over it. For starters,
it has one of the largest oceanfront patios on the island. And the food's
not bad, once you get past the silly names. Anything with popcorn
shrimp in it is good, and the "Run Chicken Run" salad (a combination
of chicken, Gorgonzola cheese, walnuts, and cranberries) is the perfect
size for lunch. Too bad they're no longer doing breakfast—they used
to be one of the best in town for it. ✉ *75-5776 Ali'i Dr., Kailua-Kona*
☎ *808/331–8442* ⊕ *www.bubbagump.com* ▭ *MC, V.*

8

The Plate Lunch Tradition

To experience island history first-hand, take a seat at one of Hawai'i's ubiquitous "plate lunch" eateries, and order a segmented Styrofoam plate piled with rice, macaroni salad, and maybe some fiery pickled vegetable condiment. On the sugar plantations, native Hawaiians and immigrant workers from many different countries ate together in the fields, sharing food from their *kaukau* kits, the utilitarian version of the Japanese *bento* lunchbox. From this melting pot came the vibrant language of pidgin and its equivalent in food: the plate lunch.

At beaches and events, you can probably see a few tiny kitchens-on-wheels, another excellent venue for sampling plate lunch. These portable

restaurants are descendants of lunch wagons that began selling food to plantation workers in the 1930s. Try the deep-fried chicken *katsu* (rolled in Japanese panko flour and spices). The marinated beef teriyaki is another good choice, as is miso butterfish. The noodle soup, *saimin*, with its Japanese fish stock and Chinese red-tinted barbecue pork, is a distinctly local medley. Koreans have contributed spicy barbecue *kal-bi* ribs, often served with chili-laden kimchee (pickled cabbage). Portuguese bean soup and tangy Filipino adobo stew are also favorites. The most popular Hawaiian contribution to the plate lunch is the *laulau*, a mix of meat and fish and young taro leaves, wrapped in more taro leaves and steamed.

$$
PACIFIC RIM

✕ **Don the Beachcomber at the Royal Kona Resort.** The "original home of the mai tai," Don the Beachcomber also offers a great oceanfront breakfast buffet and has recently become a popular local spot for lunch, thanks to delicious 'ahi sandwiches and addictive sweet-potato fries. Though dinners may seem a bit pricey for this hotel, the location and surprising quality of the food are worth the markup. Try any of the nightly seafood specials or the Huli Huli Chicken, and save room for the Molten Lava Cake. ✉ *75-5852 Ali'i Dr., in the Royal Kona Resort* ☎ *808/329–3111* ▭ *AE, D, MC, V.*

$$–$$$
PACIFIC RIM

✕ **Fish Hopper.** The Hawai'i location of the popular Monterey, California, restaurant has an expansive menu, with inventive fresh fish specials alongside the fish-and-chips and clam chowder the original restaurant is known for. The owners spent serious time and money renovating the old and funky Ocean View Inn, and the restaurant itself is lovely—lots of koa wood, Hawaiian art, and an open-air floor plan that takes advantage of the ocean view. The food is decent, but may not feel worth the price. However, they do have a two-course, early-bird dinner and different lunch and dinner specials daily. The wine list is outstanding, and there are frequent bottle specials, so this is a great spot for wine and appetizers with a view. Don't forget to ask your greeter for a card that will get you a free appetizer or small discount off your meal. ✉ *75-5683 Ali'i Dr.* ☎ *808/326–2002* ⊕ *www.fishhopper.com* ▭ *AE, D, MC, V.*

¢
SEAFOOD

✕ **Harbor House.** This open-air restaurant on the docks at Kona's busy harbor is one of the best spots on the island for fresh fish, and a fun place to grab a beer and a bite after a long day fishing, surfing, or diving. The fish is probably a few hours off the boat—if that. The place is nothing fancy—an old wooden bar, and dozens of plastic tables and chairs scattered about the covered patio—but Harbor House is a local favorite for fresh fish sandwiches and a variety of fried fish-and-chip combos. The icy schooners of Kona Brewing Company ale don't hurt, either. ⊠ *74-425 Kealakehe Pkwy., Ste. 4, Honokōhau Harbor* 🕾 *808/326–4166* 🖃 *AE, MC, V.*

$$$ ✕ **Huggo's.** This is the only restaurant in town with prices and atmo-
PACIFIC RIM sphere comparable to the splurge restaurants at the Kohala-coast resorts. Open windows extend out over the rocks at the ocean's edge, and at night you can almost touch the manta rays drawn to the spotlights. Relax with a cocktail for two and feast on fresh local seafood; the catch changes daily, and the nightly chef's special is always a good bet. **Huggo's on the Rocks,** next door, is a great outdoor bar with a floor of sand; it's become Kailua-Kona's hot spot for drinks and live music on Friday nights. ⊠ *75-5828 Kahakai Rd., off Ali'i Dr., Kailua-Kona* 🕾 *808/329–1493* ⊕ *www.huggos.com* 🖃 *AE, D, DC, MC, V.*

$ ✕ **Island Lava Java.** This place is packed to the gills, especially on week-
AMERICAN ends. Order your food at the counter then sit outside at one of the
BISTRO/GRILL wooden, umbrella-shaded tables where you can sip 100% Kona coffee and take in the ocean view. The delicious eats on offer include island-style pancakes for breakfast, fresh fish tacos for lunch, and butternut squash lasagna for dinner. There are also pizzas, salads, sandwiches, and plenty of choices for both vegetarians and meat eaters. The giant cinnamon rolls are hugely popular. Portions are large and most everything on the menu is fresh, local, and organic. You get free Wi-Fi with purchase. Even better, you can order your meal online for pick-up or get your lunch or dinner delivered right to your hotel — free! ⊠ *75-5799 Ali'i Dr., Kailua-Kona* 🕾 *808/327–2161* ⊕ *www.islandlavajava. com* 🖃 *AE, D, MC, V.*

$$ ✕ **Jackie Rey's Ohana Grill.** Uphill from downtown Kailua-Kona, this
MODERN bright green open-air restaurant is a popular lunch destination, and
HAWAIIAN increasingly crowded for dinner as well, thanks to the chef's fantastic *poke*, perfectly prepared local seafood dishes, and a few juicy meat standouts, including Korean-style short ribs and a delicious blackened prime rib. At lunchtime, the fresh fish sandwiches with wasabi mayo and the chicken sandwich with avocado and Swiss are both excellent combinations of flavors, and the fries are crisped to perfection. On the lighter side, inventive salads like the Angie salad, with candied walnuts, papaya, Maui onions, dried cranberries, and blue cheese, keep it healthy but flavorful. ⊠ *Pottery Terrace, 75-5995 Kuakini Hwy., Kailua-Kona* 🕾 *808/327–0209* ⊕ *www.jackiereys.com* 🖃 *AE, D, MC, V.*

$$–$$$ ✕ **Kai at the Sheraton Keauhou Bay.** Aside from the lobby, this restaurant
PACIFIC RIM is the best-looking part of the Sheraton Keauhou Bay, with a prime view facing the bay. The enormous windows are left open most of the time, making it feel almost like an outdoor restaurant. The menu is limited, but each entrée is good, from the sweet chili-glazed ono to the award-winning Kona coffee–crusted lamb chops. Everything is prepared with that fusion of Pacific Rim and Continental that makes up Hawaiian cuisine. The seared 'ahi appetizer is not to be missed. Breakfast is a

good bet as well; very reasonable, great buffet, and the view during the daytime is just about perfect. ✉ *78-128 Ehukai St., Kailua-Kona* ☎ *808/930–4900* ⊕ *www.sheratonkeauhou.com* ▭ *AE, MC, V.*

$ ✕**Kanaka Kava.** A popular local hangout, and not just because da kava
HAWAIIAN makes you mellow. Their *pūpū* (appetizers) rock! Fresh *poke*, bowls of smoky, tender pulled kālua pork, and healthy sautéed veggies are available in fairly large portions for less than you'll pay anywhere else on the island. Seating is at a premium, but don't be afraid to share a table and make friends. ✉ *75-5803 Ali'i Dr., Space B6, in the Coconut Grove Market Pl.* ☎ *808/883–6260* ▭ *MC, V.*

$$$ ✕**Kenichi Pacific.** With its black-lacquer tables and lipstick-red ban-
JAPANESE quettes, Kenichi's seems a little out of place in this small strip mall. The location keeps many tourists from finding it, even though it's been open for several years now. This is where everyone in Kailua-Kona goes when they feel like splurging on top-notch sushi. It's a little on the pricey side, but it's worth it. The sashimi is so fresh it melts in your mouth, and the signature rolls are inventive and tasty. For vegetarians, the Austin roll—asparagus tempura—is fish-free and delicious. ✉ *Keauhou Shopping Center, 78-6831 Ali'i Dr., Kailua-Kona* ☎ *808/322–6400* ⊕ *www.kenichirestaurants.com* ▭ *No credit cards.*

$ ✕**Kona Brewing Company & Brewpub.** This large and cheery spot with
AMERICAN a huge outdoor patio features an excellent and varied menu including pulled-pork quesadillas, gourmet pizzas, and a killer spinach salad with Gorgonzola cheese, macadamia nuts, and strawberries. Go for the beer tasting menu—your choice of four of their eight available microbrews in miniature glasses that add up to about two regular-size mugs for the price of one. ✉ *75-5629 Kuakini Hwy., just past Palani intersection on right, Kailua-Kona* ☎ *808/329–2739* ⊕ *www.konabrewingco.com* ▭ *MC, V.*

$$–$$$ ✕**Kona Inn Restaurant.** This historic open-air restaurant offers some of
AMERICAN the best, unobstructed ocean views on the island. It's a great place to have a mai tai and some appetizers while watching the sunset, or to enjoy a tasty calamari or ono sandwich and a salad at lunch. Dinner is also available, but the entrées are less than stellar and for the prices there are better options once the sun disappears. ✉ *75-5744 Ali'i Dr., Kailua-Kona* ☎ *808/329–4455* ⊕ *www.windandsearestaurants.com* ▭ *AE, MC, V.*

¢ ✕**Kona Mix Plate.** Don't be surprised if you find yourself rubbing elbows
HAWAIIAN with lots of hungry locals at this inconspicuous Kona lunch spot. The antithesis of a tourist trap, this casual island favorite with fluorescent lighting and wooden tables is all about the food. Try the teriyaki chicken, shrimp tempura, or *katsu*—a chicken breast fried with bread crumbs and served with a sweet sauce. ✉ *341 Palani St., Kailua-Kona* ☎ *808/329–8104* ▭ *No credit cards* ⊘ *Closed Wed.*

$$$ ✕**La Bourgogne.** A genial husband-and-wife team owns this relax-
FRENCH ing, country-style bistro with dark-wood walls and private, romantic booths. The traditional French menu has classics such as escargots, beef with a cabernet sauvignon sauce, rack of lamb with roasted garlic and rosemary, and a less traditional venison dish with a pomegranate glaze. Call well in advance for reservations. ✉ *77-6400 Nālani St., Kailua-*

BEST BETS FOR ROMANCE

Hale Samoa at Kona Village Resort (Kohala). Enjoy your five-course meal under the stars as you listen to gentle waves lap the shore.

Huggo's (Kohala). Savor delicious cuisine while looking out over the ocean as manta rays dance in the waters below you.

Ke'ei Cafe (Kainaliu). Tropical breezes waft into a beautiful koa-wood dining room through huge open windows. Diners enjoy views of the treetops and a blend of local

fish and meats and Asian and South American influences.

Manta & Pavilion Wine Bar at Mauna Kea Beach Hotel (Kohala). A lovely glass of wine, a spectacular meal, and a view that will make your trip one to remember.

Pahui'a at the Four Seasons Hualālai (Kohala). Perfect food meets its match in a stunning view from an intimate, well-designed space.

Kona ☎ 808/329–6711 ⌁ Reservations essential ▭ AE, D, DC, MC, V ⊘ Closed Sun. and Mon. No lunch.

¢ ✕ **Los Habaneros.** A surprising find in the corner of this shopping mall,
MEXICAN next to the movie theater, Habaneros serves up tasty, fresh, and fast Mexican food for low, low prices. Our favorites are usually the day's specials, which can be anything from enchilada plates to homemade sopes and chiles rellenos. Their giant burritos are also a solid pick, stuffed with meat, beans, cheese, and all the fixings. ⊠ Phase II, Keauhou Shopping Center ☎ 808/324–4688 ▭ No credit cards ⊘ Closed Sun.

$ ✕ **Mahina Pizza.** Locals were ecstatic to see Mahina's, a favorite pizza
ITALIAN joint in town from a few years back, reopen in the Kona Inn Shopping Village. Upstairs, above the shops, Mahina's serves up some of the tastiest pies on the island (from the usual pepperoni, sausage, and mushroom combos to a great "Garden of Eden" vegetarian option) accompanied by cool ocean breezes and pleasant "downtown" Kona views. It is not uncommon for the owner to close up shop to go paddling, so call ahead to make sure they're open. ⊠ 75-5744 Ali'i Dr., in the Kona Inn Shopping Village ☎ 808/326–1577 ▭ No credit cards ⊘ Closed Sun

$ ✕ **Mixx Bistro.** Kona never knew it needed a wine bar until it got Mixx,
CAFE but now the town would seem strange without it. In addition to their fantastic wine and cheese delivery service, Mixx serves up a tasty menu of bistro-inspired pūpū (appetizers) ranging from super healthy plates of sautéed veggies and tofu to what they claim are "the Island's best fries." They also offer a handful of entrée options, including steak frites and a whole crab or lobster served with drawn butter. And then of course there's the cheese plate. And the wine. Sigh. Live music keeps the patio lively most nights and Sunday afternoons. ⊠ 75-5626 Kuakini Hwy., in the King Kamehameha Center ☎ 808/329–7334 ⊕ www.konawinemarket.com ▭ MC, V.

$ ✕ **Pancho & Lefty's.** Across the street from the Kona Village Shopping
MEXICAN Center, Pancho & Lefty's is a typical Tex-Mex place—great for nachos and margaritas (watch out, they pour 'em strong) on a lazy afternoon.

8

Some of the items on the menu are expensive, and some of the combos are described exactly the same way in other sections of the menu for less, so read carefully. ✉ *75-5719 Ali'i Dr., Kailua-Kona* ☎ *808/326–2171* ▭ *MC, V.*

$ ✕ **Peaberry & Galette**. This little creperie is a welcome addition to the
CAFE   neighborhood. It serves Illy espresso, excellent sweet and savory crepes, and rich desserts like lemon cheesecake and chocolate mousse that are made fresh daily. It's got a cool, urban-café vibe, and is a nice place to hang for a bit if you're waiting for a film at the theater next door, or just feel like taking a break from paradise to sip a decent espresso and flip through the latest *W* magazine. ✉ *Keauhou Shopping Center, 78-6740 Makolea St., Kailua-Kona* ☎ *808/322–6020* ⊕ *www.peaberryandgalette.com* ▭ *MC, V.*

$ ✕ **Pine Tree Café**. Located next to Matsuyama's market in the Kohanaiki
HAWAIIAN   business park along Highway 11, north of Kona, Pine Tree is filling the giant void left by Sam Choy's closing up shop. The menu is on a dry erase board on the wall and consists of local classics such as Huli Huli Chicken and Loco Moco alongside new inventions like the shrimp curry bisque with corn bread. The fresh fish plate is always great, and all meals are served with fries or rice and that macaroni, potato, and tuna salad concoction that you only get in Hawaii. Portions are huge and prices are low, which keeps locals coming back. ✉ *Kohanaiki Plaza, 73-4354 Māmalahoa Hwy. (Hwy. 11)* ☎ *808/327–1234* ▭ *AE, D, MC, V.*

¢ ✕ **Quinn's Almost By the Sea**. Okay, Quinn's is a bit of a dive. That said,
AMERICAN   it does have a few things going for it—some of the best ono sandwiches on the island, for example. It's open until 11 PM, later than any other restaurant in Kailua-Kona (except Denny's). If time gets away from you on a drive to South Point, Quinn's is awaiting your return with a cheap beer and a basket of excellent calamari. You can also have a beer at the funky bar filled with fishermen. ✉ *75-5655A Palani Rd., Kailua-Kona* ☎ *808/329–3822* ▭ *D, MC, V.*

$–$$ ✕ **Restaurant Hayama**. Tucked into Kopiko Plaza, just below Long's,
JAPANESE   this local favorite for quality Japanese fare goes beyond sushi. Hayama serves traditional Japanese specialties like tempura, unagi, broiled fish, teriyaki, and *udon* noodles, all made from quality local ingredients. Sushi is available as well, but only traditional *nigiri*, slices of raw fish layered with wasabi and rice, and sashimi. Lunch specials are a great deal, and dinner specials provide a three-course dinner for two for $40. Despite its strip mall location, Hayama manages to pull off a Zen vibe that matches the quiet and attentive, albeit slow, service. ✉ *75-5660 Kopiko St., D1* ☎ *808/331–8888* ▭ *D, MC, V.*

¢ ✕ **Tacos El Unico**. Choose from an array of authentic soft-taco choices
MEXICAN   (beef and chicken, among others), burritos, quesadillas, and great home-made tamales. Order at the counter, take a seat outside at one of a dozen yellow tables with blue umbrellas, and enjoy all the good flavors served up in those red plastic baskets. ✉ *Kona Marketplace, 75-5729 Ali'i Dr., Kailua-Kona* ☎ *808/326–4033* ▭ *No credit cards.*

$ ✕ **Thai Rin Restaurant**. The Thai owner at this old-timer in Ali'i Sunset
THAI   Plaza is likely to take your order, cook it, and bring it to your table himself. The restaurant is small, with about 10 tables total, but bright and

BEST BETS FOR KEIKI (KIDS)

Beach Tree at the Four Seasons Hualālai (Kohala). Plenty of room for kids to run and play on the sand, and fun gadgets to keep them entertained at the table.

Bubba Gump's (Kailua-Kona). A quirky theme with a great kids' menu and virgin umbrella drinks.

Ken's House of Pancakes (Hilo). What kid doesn't want to eat pancakes for dinner?

Seaside (Hilo). What's not kid-friendly about a restaurant perched above aquaculture ponds surrounded by egrets?

U-Top-It (Kailua-Kona). The taro cake is healthy for kids without them realizing it.

clean, with plenty of windows, white tablecloths, light blue walls, and various bits of Thai artwork and knickknacks spread throughout. The menu includes five curries, a green papaya salad, and a popular platter that combines spring rolls, satay, beef salad, and *tom yum* (lemongrass soup). ⊠ *75-5799 Aliʻi Dr., Kailua-Kona* ☎ *808/329–2929* ▭ *AE, D, DC, MC, V.*

¢ ╳ **U-Top-It.** Tucked behind the shops and cafés of the Coconut Grove
AMERICAN Marketplace, U-Top-It is a local favorite breakfast joint. Opened by a former Kona Village resort chef, all dishes at U-Top-It are built upon the restaurant's terrific taro pan crepes, which guests can choose to top with any combination of over 100 different toppings ranging from straightforward fruit or egg combinations to more unusual choices. At lunchtime, try pairing one of the crepes with beef or chicken teriyaki. ⊠ *75-5799 Aliʻi Dr., Coconut Grove Market Pl.* ☎ *808/329–0092* ▭ *MC, V* ☺ *Closed Mon.*

$$ ╳ **Wasabi's.** A tiny little place tucked into the back of the Coconut
JAPANESE Plaza on Aliʻi, Wasabi's five little tables tend to be occupied by the west side's Japanese population who come for some of the best sashimi on the island. Prices may seem steep, but the fish is of the highest quality. Fans of Americanized sushi rolls will find the familiar California and spicy tuna rolls here, along with a few unique inventions. And for those who will never be hip to the raw fish thing, teriyaki, *udon,* and sukiyaki options abound. ⊠ *75-5803 Aliʻi Dr., Coconut Grove Market Pl.* ☎ *808/326–2352* ▭ *MC, V.*

THE KONA COAST

¢ ╳ **Adriana's.** A tiny little hole in the wall housed in a small shopping
MEXICAN center, Adriana's is easy to miss if you don't happen to catch their homemade sign down on the highway pointing the way. It's worth keeping an eye out. The restaurant's owner and namesake serves up home-cooked El Salvadoran food—generally very similar to Mexican food, except

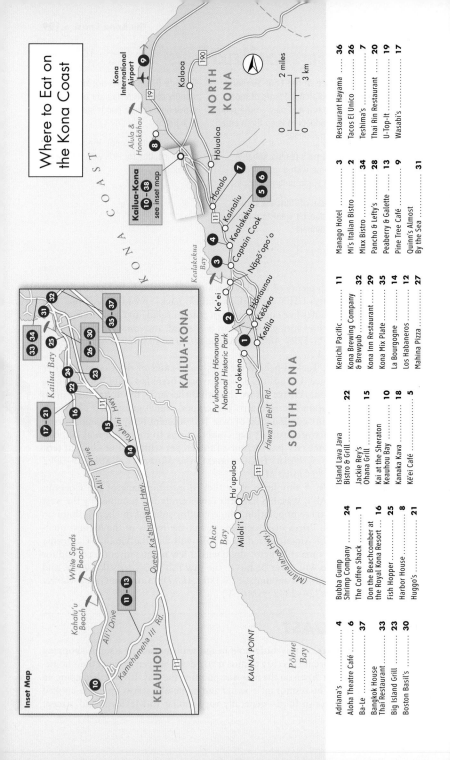

Where to Eat on the Kona Coast

Inset Map

Kahalu'u Beach
White Sands Beach
Ali'i Drive
Kamehameha III Rd.
Queen Ka'ahumanu Hwy
Kuakini Hwy
Ali'i Drive
Kailua Bay

KEAUHOU

KAILUA-KONA

Ho'okena
Ke'ei
Kealakekua Bay
Napo'opo'o
Honaunau
Ke'okea
Keauhou Bay
Kealia
Pu'uhonua o Honaunau National Historic Park

SOUTH KONA

Okoe Bay
Hu'upuloa
Miloli'i
Mamalahoa Hwy
Hawai'i Belt Rd.

KAUNĀ POINT

Pōhue Bay

KONA COAST

NORTH KONA

Kona International Airport
Kalaoa
Hōlualoa
Alula & Honokōhau
Honalo
Kainaliu
Kealakekua
Captain Cook
Māmalahoa Hwy

Kailua-Kona 10-38
see inset map

0   2 miles
0   3 km

Adriana's	4
Aloha Theatre Café	6
Ba-le	37
Bangkok House Thai Restaurant	33
Big Island Grill	23
Boston Basil's	30
Bubba Gump Shrimp Company	24
The Coffee Shack	1
Don the Beachcomber at the Royal Kona Resort	16
Fish Hopper	25
Harbor House	8
Huggo's	21
Island Lava Java Bistro & Grill	22
Jackie Rey's Ohana Grill	15
Kai at the Sheraton Keauhou Bay	10
Kanaka Kava	18
Kē'ei Café	5
Kenichi Pacific	11
Kona Brewing Company & Brewpub	32
Kona Inn Restaurant	29
Kona Mix Plate	35
La Bourgogne	14
Los Habaneros	12
Mahina Pizza	27
Manago Hotel	3
Mi's Italian Bistro	34
Mixx Bistro	28
Pancho & Lefty's	13
Peaberry & Galette	9
Pine Tree Café	27
Quinn's Almost By the Sea	31
Restaurant Hayama	36
Tacos El Unico	26
Teshima's	7
Thai Rin Restaurant	20
U-Top-It	19
Wasabi's	17

with slightly fewer chilies. Adriana's handmade tamales are incredible, and no other spot on the island has a salsa bar to compete with this one. ⊠ *Kealakekua Ranch Center* ☎ *808/217–7405* ▭ *No credit cards* ⊗ *Closed weekends. No dinner.*

$ ╳ **Aloha Theatre Cafe.** With an emphasis on healthy, organic fare,
AMERICAN this friendly café adjacent to the Aloha Theatre serves tasty, mostly good-for-you options on a lānai overlooking Kealakekua Bay and the orchards above it. Choose from an assortment of egg dishes and pastries in the morning; burgers, fish sandwiches, and salads for lunch; and pasta, grilled fish, or steak for dinner, all at very reasonable prices. For dessert, try one of the selections from the café's killer pastry case. The only problem here is that service is glacially slow—even the locals complain, so you know it's bad; plan on chilling out on their veranda and taking in the views for awhile. Dinner is only served on nights when there is an event at the theatre. ⊠ *79-7384 Māmalahoa Hwy., Kainaliu* ☎ *808/322–3383* ⊕ *www.alohatheatrecafe.com* ▭ *MC, D, V.*

$ ╳ **The Coffee Shack.** There's really no flaw to this place. The view is
AMERICAN stunning, the service is excellent even when it's busy (which is most of the time), and the eggs Benedict and hot Reuben sandwich are the best on the island. Breads and pastries are all homemade, and the coffee is strong and tasty. On your way to nowhere in particular, stop by for a Hawaiian smoothie, an iced honey mocha latte, or homemade lū'au bread—all worth a detour. In the evening, enjoy gourmet pizza and an amazing sunset view. ⊠ *83-5799 Māmalahoa Hwy.* ☎ *808/328–9555* ▭ *MC, V.*

$$ ╳ **Ke'ei Café.** This beautiful restaurant is in a plantation-style building
ECLECTIC 15 minutes south of Kona. Delicious dinners with Brazilian, Asian, and
Fodor's Choice European flavors utilize fresh ingredients provided by local farmers. Try
★ the Thai red curry or wok-seared 'ahi accompanied by a selection from the extensive wine list. The owners are Brazilian, so the *caipirinhas* are outstanding if you're tired of mai tais. ⊠ *Hwy. 11, ½ mi south of Kainaliu, Hōnaunau* ☎ *808/322–9992* ⌂ *Reservations essential* ▭ *MC, V* ⊗ *Closed Sun. and Mon.*

$ ╳ **Manago Hotel.** About 20 minutes south of Kailua-Kona, Manago is
HAWAIIAN a time-warp experience. A vintage neon sign identifies the hotel, and Formica tables, ceiling fans, and venetian blinds add to the flavor of this film-noir spot. The T-shirts (which are great souvenirs for friends at home) brag that the hotel has the best pork chops in town, and it's not false advertising. The fresh fish is excellent as well, especially the ono and butterfish. Unless you request otherwise, the fish is all sautéed with a tasty house butter-soy sauce concoction. Meals come with rice for the table and an assortment of side dishes that changes from time to time, but usually includes a macaroni, potato, and tuna salad, and some sort of braised tofu and sautéed veggie dish. ⊠ *82-6155 Māmalahoa Hwy., Captain Cook* ☎ *808/323–2642* ▭ *D, DC, MC, V* ⊗ *Closed Mon.*

$$ ╳ **Mi's Italian Bistro.** A fairly recent addition to the Kainaliu dining
ITALIAN scene, Mi's is a classed-up, white tablecloth establishment in a tiny strip mall on the mountain (*mauka*) side of Highway 11. The restaurant's husband-and-wife owners prepare homemade pastas and focaccia daily. Daily specials are always delicious and usually include a lasagna,

8

focaccia, and risotto option. The homemade herb-cheese ravioli are rich and delicious, and even the salad options are a notch above, with ingredients such as candied macadamia nuts, roasted beets, and sautéed haricots verts. Homemade desserts are worth saving room for, particularly the banana rum flambé. ⊠ *81-6372 Māmalahoa Hwy., Kainaliu* ☎ *808/323–3880* ⊕ *www.misitalianbistro.com* ⊟ *D, MC, V.*

$ ✕ **Teshima's.** Come here for the most authentic Japanese cuisine on the
JAPANESE   island. Locals show up at this small, neighborhood restaurant whenever they're in the mood for fresh sashimi, puffy shrimp tempura, or *hekka* (beef and vegetables cooked in an iron pot) at a reasonable price. Teshima's doesn't look like much, inside or out, but it's been crowded since 1929 for a reason. You might also want to try a *teishoku* (set meal) of assorted Japanese delicacies, or the popular bento box lunch. The service is laid-back and friendly. The restaurant is 15 minutes south of Kailua-Kona. ⊠ *Māmalahoa Hwy., Honalo* ☎ *808/322–9140* ⊟ *No credit cards.*

THE KOHALA COAST

$$ ✕ **Bamboo Restaurant.** It's out of the way, but the food at this spot in the
PACIFIC RIM   heart of Hāwī is good and the service and ambience have a Hawaiian–
Fodor'sChoice   country flair. Creative entrées feature fresh island fish prepared several
★   ways. The Thai-style fish, for example, combines lemongrass, Kaffir lime leaves, and coconut milk; it's best washed down with a passion fruit margarita or passion fruit iced tea. Bamboo accents, bold local artwork, and an old unfinished wooden floor make the restaurant cozy. Local musicians entertain on Friday and Saturday nights. ⊠ *Hwy. 270, Hāwī* ☎ *808/889–5555* ⊕ *www.bamboorestaurant.info* ⊟ *MC, V* ☉ *Closed Mon. No dinner Sun.*

$$–$$$ ✕ **Beach Tree at the Four Seasons Resort.** True oceanside dining is one of
AMERICAN   the main attractions at Beach Tree, the Four Seasons Resort Hualālai's newest restaurant that sits right on the sand. The beautifully designed restaurant with vaulted ceilings and custom wood furnishings has expansive outdoor seating and a casual, relaxed feel. Chef de Cuisine Nick Mastrascusa is a transplant from New York who brings Californian cuisine with Italian influence to Beach Tree's new menu. The braised short ribs with carrot puree literally slide off the bone and the gnocchi in oxtail ragout are fluffy little pillows that melt in your mouth. Dishes are elegant but not pretentious. Save room for dessert like the Batik Room Bon Bons that arrive in a cute metal pail, cushioned by a ti leaf that appears to be on fire thanks to a piece of dry ice. Kids will love it here. There's a great children's menu and activities to keep them busy, like a fun rotating pasta fork and ice cream cone spinner. The entire family can enjoy the live Hawaiian music played nightly. ⊠ *72-100 Ka'ūpūlehu*

Dr. ☎ *Box 1269, Kohala 96745 96740* ☎ *808/325–8000* ⊕ *www.fourseasons.com/hualalai* ⊟ *AE, D, DC, MC, V.*

$$$$
MODERN
HAWAIIAN
Fodor'sChoice
★

✕ **Brown's Beach House at the Fairmont Orchid Hawai'i.** This waterfront wonder is well worth the splurge—the menu is inventive (but not too inventive), and the wine list is excellent. Though you can order steak here, the seafood is really where it's happening. Their crab-crusted mahimahi is a little piece of heaven, sitting on clouds of Waimea sweet corn mashed potatoes. Leave room for dessert; the sweets change regularly, but they're always worth the indulgence. Local musicians play nightly on the grassy knoll outside. ✉ *Fairmont Orchid Hawai'i, 1 N. Kanikū Dr., Kohala Coast* ☎ *808/885–2000* ⊕ *www.fairmont.com/orchid* ⊟ *AE, D, DC, MC, V* ☽ *No lunch.*

$$
ITALIAN

✕ **Café Pesto.** This branch of Café Pesto, in the quaint harbor town of Kawaihae, is just as popular as its sibling in Hilo. Exotic pizzas (with chili-grilled shrimp, shiitake mushrooms, and cilantro crème fraîche, for example), Asian-inspired pastas and risottos, and fresh seafood reflect the ethnic diversity of the island. Local microbrews and a full-service bar make this a good place to end the evening, and the lounge-y bar area with sofas and comfy chairs is a great place to grab a drink while you're waiting for a table. ✉ *Kawaihae Harbor Center, Hwy. 270, Kawaihae* ☎ *808/882–1071* ⊕ *www.cafepesto.com* ⊟ *AE, D, DC, MC, V.*

$$$$
PACIFIC RIM

✕ **CanoeHouse at the Mauna Lani Bay Hotel & Bungalows.** Although the open-air, beachfront setting is stunning, the CanoeHouse is starting to lose some ground to other resort restaurants in the food department. It was among the first on the island to offer Pacific Rim fusion, and it still does it well, but the menu seems unoriginal now that fusion is a mainstay at most resort restaurants—it focuses on meat or seafood paired with internationally inspired sauces and made with local fruits and vegetables. Choose from appetizers such as 'ahi tuna napoleon with a tomato basil shooter or house-cured corned beef with horseradish royale. The selection of entrees might include tamari-glazed *moi* with Rougié foie gras or organic chicken "grande mere" with melted leeks. The wine list is great, and the location makes the price tag worth it on clear evenings, even with better restaurants a few miles away. ✉ *Mauna Lani Bay Hotel & Bungalows, 68-1400 Mauna Lani Dr., Kohala Coast* ☎ *808/885–6622* ⊕ *www.maunalani.com* ⊟ *AE, D, DC, MC, V.*

8

$$ ╳ **Coast Grille at Hāpuna Beach Prince Hotel**. This is a beautiful spot, with
MODERN high ceilings and a lānai overlooking the ocean. American Bistro-style
HAWAIIAN dishes showcase what the Big Island has to offer, using sustainable,
organic, and wild ingredients whenever possible. Try the Kona lobster
bisque, the grass-fed Big Island burger with Maui onion marmalade,
or the pan-roasted mahimahi with Waipo'o warabi fern. Coast Grille
also has an early-bird selection of three-course prix-fixe meals (before
6:30 PM). If you're in the mood for an early supper this is a great deal.
✉ *Hāpuna Beach Prince Hotel, 62-100 Kauna'oa Dr., Kohala Coast*
☎ *808/880–3192* ⊕ *www.princeresortshawaii.com* ▭ *AE, D, DC, MC,*
V ☉ *No lunch.*

╳ **Hakone Steakhouse & Sushi Bar at the Hāpuna Beach Prince Hotel**. It's
hard not to start whispering in this tranquil and graceful restaurant.
Choose from exquisite Japanese sukiyaki, *shabu shabu* (thin slices of
beef cooked in broth), and the selections at the elaborate sushi bar.
The broad selection of sake (try a sakitini, a martini made with sake)
is guaranteed to enliven your meal. The best time to visit is on a Friday
or Saturday night when the restaurant serves a great dinner buffet.
✉ *Hāpuna Beach Prince Hotel, 62-100 Kauna'oa Dr., Kohala Coast*
☎ *808/880–3192* ⊕ *www.princeresortshawaii.com* ▭ *AE, D, DC, MC,*
V ☉ *No lunch.*

$$$$ ╳ **Hale Samoa at Kona Village Resort**. Formal and romantic, this Kona
MODERN Village restaurant has a magical atmosphere, especially at sunset. Sit
HAWAIIAN beneath the stars and feast on five-course prix-fixe dinners that change
nightly. Specialties may include sautéed abalone from a local aqua-farm,
papaya-and-coconut bisque, duck stuffed with andouille sausage, or
wok-charred prime strip loin. Reservations can be made only on the day
you dine. ✉ *Kona Village Resort, Hwy. 19, 12 mi north of Kailua-Kona,*
North Kona Coast ☎ *808/325–5555* ⌕ *Reservations essential* ⊕ *www.*
konavillage.com ▭ *AE, DC, MC, V* ☉ *Closed Tues. and Wed.*

$$$$ ╳ **KPC (Kamuela Provision Company) at the Hilton Waikoloa Village**. Quiet
MODERN guitar music, tables set along a breezy lānai, and a sweeping view of the
HAWAIIAN Kohala coast are the perfect accompaniments to the elegant yet down-
to-earth Hawaiian regional cuisine. The lānai offers the best seats in the
house—get there by 5:30 if you want to score a seat for the sunset. Pop-
ular are the macadamia nut–crusted *opakapaka* (Pacific red snapper),
the ginger-steamed Kona *kampachi*, and the "new wave *mauka* and
makai" (a grilled beef tenderloin and tempura lobster). Great appetiz-
ers include the roasted Kamuela tomato soup and the Maui onion ring
tower with spicy aioli. ✉ *Hilton Waikoloa Village, 425 Waikoloa Beach*
Dr., Kohala Coast ☎ *808/886–1234* ⊕ *www.hiltonwaikoloavillage.com*
▭ *AE, D, DC, MC, V* ☉ *No lunch.*

$$ ╳ **Kawaihae Harbor Grill & Seafood Bar**. This little restaurant is always
SEAFOOD packed—there's something about the crisp green-and-white 1850s
building, along with the scent of fresh local seafood being sautéed with
garlic, that draws people in. The food downstairs at the Harbor Grill
costs a bit more than some want to pay for basics like grilled mahimahi
and fish-and-chips, but the Seafood Bar, upstairs in a separate structure
that also dates from the 1850s, serves a dynamite and fairly well-priced
bar menu with sandwiches and *pūpū* (appetizers), and a good lunch as

well. The upstairs area is also a bit more fun and casual than downstairs; it's been a hot spot since it opened in 2003. ✉ *Kawaihae Harbor, Hwy. 270, Kawaihae* ☎ *808/882–1368* ⊕ *www.kawaihae-restaurants. com* ▭ *MC, V.*

$$$$
MODERN
HAWAIIAN
Fodor's Choice
★

× **Manta & Pavilion Wine Bar at the Mauna Kea Beach Hotel.** The Mauna Kea Beach Hotel has long been known for excellence in dining and the newly renovated Manta & Pavilion Wine Bar is no exception. Perched on the edge of a bluff overlooking the sparkling waters of Mauna Kea Beach, this is an amazing spot for a romantic meal at sunset, especially at one of the outside tables. The restaurant's Enomatic wine system (one of only two in the state) allows guests to sample 48 different wines by the glass in 1-, 2-, or 5-ounce pours. Dinner here is beyond fantastic. Chef George Gomes, Jr. has really outdone himself with a menu that shines from start to finish. The crispy pork belly appetizer with Kona baby abalone is not to be missed. Even if you don't love beets, you should try the roasted baby beet salad. The kobacha squash soup with kālua pig, 'ohelo berries, and truffled marshmallow is warm, sweet, and satisfying. Main dishes include a macadamia nut–crusted lamb, a Big Island butterfish, Ka'ū coffee beef filet, a butter poached Keāhole lobster, and a perfectly prepared seared 'ahi with Moloka'i sweet potato puree and foie gras spring roll. This is also the spot for a spectacular Sunday brunch with an impressive spread that includes an omelet station, prime rib, smoked salmon, tempura, lobster bisque, and a build-your-own-sundae bar. ✉ *62-100 Mauna Kea Beach Dr.Kohala Coast* ☎ *808/882–5810* ⊕ *www. princeresortshawaii.com* ▭ *AE, D, DC, MC, V.* ⊘ *No lunch.*

$–$$
MEDITERRANEAN

× **Merriman's Market Café.** From Peter Merriman, one of Hawai'i's star chefs, comes a more affordable alternative to his upscale Waimea and Maui restaurants. The simple but delicious Mediterranean-influenced menu includes a variety of pasta dishes, tasty appetizers, and some of the island's best salads. Its huge patio has quickly become a favorite for locals and visitors alike, which means you could have a bit of a wait for a table. ✉ *King's Shops at Waikoloa Village, 250 Waikoloa Beach Dr., Kohala Coast* ☎ *808/886–1700* ▭ *AE, MC, V.*

$$$–$$$$
JAPANESE

× **Norio's Sushi Bar & Restaurant.** Norio's is great, but it's very pricey for sushi and there are less expensive sushi restaurants of equal or higher caliber down the road at The Shops at Mauna Lani (Kenichi Pacific), or north of Kohala in Hāwī (Sushi Rock). Still, Norio's is a solid choice. Sashimi and sushi are lovingly prepared with the freshest possible fish (both from the ocean and from the numerous aqua-farms on the island). The flounder, 'ahi, and abalone are not to be missed. Some equally delicious hot dishes include baked sea scallops and miso butterfish. The assortment of tropical drinks is tasty, as is the sinfully good chocolate fondue, served with an assortment of tropical fruits. ✉ *Fairmont Orchid Hawai'i, 1 N. Kaniku Dr., Kohala Coast* ☎ *808/885–2000* ⊕ *www. fairmont.com/orchid* ▭ *AE, D, DC, MC, V* ⊘ *Closed Wed. No lunch.*

$
AMERICAN

× **Number 3 at the Mauna Kea Beach Hotel.** Though it sits right on the edge of the hotel's golf course, this is not just a restaurant for golf enthusiasts. A short walk from the main entrance to the hotel, the newly renovated, spacious dining room has seating both inside and out, and service is

8

quick and on-point. Number 3 serves up a great lunch menu with dishes such as 'ahi sashimi, a kālua pig quesadilla, and beer-battered fresh-fish tacos. The best item has to be their signature #3 burger— a Kahuā Ranch American Wagyu beef burger with caramelized onion, Waimea tomatoes, Maytag blue aioli, and sweet onion fries. For the kids and kids-at-heart, order the "loaded" banana split (with banana bread, ice cream, sorbet, crème fraiche, and toasted macadamia nuts). Then lay down for a well-deserved nap. ✉ *62-100 Mauna Kea Beach Dr., Kohala Coast* 🕾 *808/882–5810* ⊕ *www.princeresortshawaii.com* 🖃 *AE, D, DC, MC, V* ⊘ *No dinner.*

$$$–$$$$

MODERN HAWAIIAN

Fodor'sChoice ★

✕ **Pahui'a at the Four Seasons Resort Hualālai.** *Pahui'a* means aquarium, so it's fitting that a 9- by 4-foot aquarium in the entrance casts a dreamy light through this exquisite restaurant. Presentation is paramount, and the food tastes as good as it looks. Asian-influenced dishes stand out for their layers of flavor. Don't miss the three sashimi and three caviar appetizers, or the crispy whole *moi* served with Asian slaw, black beans, and sweet chili–lime vinaigrette. In keeping with the island-wide trend, the restaurant is featuring special prix-fixe dinner menus that change seasonally and focus on local produce, meats, and fish. Breakfasts are superb; the lemon ricotta pancakes are so good they should be illegal. Reserve a table on the patio and you may be able to spot whales while dining. ✉ *72-100 Ka'ūpūlehu Dr.* ⌂ *Box 1269, Kailua-Kona 96745 96740* 🕾 *808/325–8000* ⊕ *www.fourseasons.com/hualalai* 🖃 *AE, D, DC, MC, V* ⊘ *No lunch.*

$$$

MODERN HAWAIIAN

✕ **Roy's Waikoloa Bar & Grill.** Roy's is part of a chain, and it's located in a strip mall. If either of those things turns you off immediately, skip it—there are as good or better meals to be had elsewhere on the island. If, however, you're looking for consistently decent food and you're staying nearby, you could do worse. And if you're looking for a light meal, you can easily fill up on the enormous selection of great appetizers, and the extensive wine-by-the-glass list offers good pairing options. Roy's changes its menu frequently based on what local items are in season but mainstays include Roy's signature short ribs and his macadamia nut-crusted fish. Both are quite tasty. ✉ *King's Shops at Waikoloa Village, 250 Waikoloa Beach Dr., Kohala Coast* 🕾 *808/886–4321* ⊕ *www.roysrestaurant.com* 🖃 *AE, D, DC, MC, V.*

$$$$

STEAK

✕ **Ruth's Chris Steakhouse.** Located in the Shops at Mauna Lani complex, the Hawai'i location of the popular Louisiana steak-house chain serves the same sizzling steaks and heaping sides the restaurant is known for throughout the country. Ask about early evening "Prime Time" specials that include a salad, entrée, side, and dessert for a fraction of the price. They claim to have vegetarian options, but Ruth's Chris is a true steak house in every way and as such is best suited to meat lovers. Steaks come sizzling; tasty, unhealthy classic sides, which are á la carte, include creamed spinach, broccoli with cheddar cheese, and potatoes au gratin. ✉ *68-1330 Mauna Lani Dr., Kohala Coast* 🕾 *808/887–0800* ⊕ *www.ruthschris.com* 🖃 *AE, D, MC, V* ⊘ *No lunch.*

$$–$$$

SEAFOOD

✕ **Sansei Seafood Restaurant & Sushi Bar.** This restaurant serves heavenly interpretations of sushi and contemporary Asian cuisine. More than a few dishes have won awards including the shrimp dynamite in a creamy garlic masago aioli and unagi glaze, and the Dungeness crab ramen with Asian truffle broth. There are tried-and-true favorites that are mainstays, however, the menu is consistently updated to include new and exciting options such as the Hawaiian *moi* sashimi rolls and the torched Kona kampachi. You can certainly make a meal out of the appetizers and sushi rolls, or try some of Sansei's great entrees from both land and sea. Anyone who loves sushi knows that multiple rolls can get pricey so a good tip is to go for an early dinner on Sunday or Monday when everything is 50% off until 6 PM. Or opt for a late-night meal on Friday or Saturday when a good section of the menu is 50% off from 10 PM until 1 AM (you just have to put up with the karaoke singers). ✉ *201 Waikoloa Beach Dr., Waikoloa* ☎ *808/886–6286* ⊕ *www.sanseihawaii. com* ⊟ *AE, D, MC, V.*

$–$$
JAPANESE

✕ **Sushi Rock.** In Hāwī's funky Without Boundaries, Sushi Rock isn't big on ambience—its narrow dining room is brightly painted and casually decorated with various Hawaiian and Japanese knickknacks—but hungry locals and visiting couples flock here not for the decor but for some of the island's freshest raw fish. The restaurant prides itself on using fresh local ingredients like goat cheese, macadamia nuts, and mango in their island-inspired sushi rolls but also serves up a variety of cooked seafood, chicken, noodle dishes, and salads for lunch and dinner. Everything is plated beautifully and served either at the sushi bar, at one of the handful of indoor tables in the restaurant's narrow dining room, or on the covered back patio. There's also a full bar. ✉ *55-3435 Akoni Pule Hwy., Hāwī* ☎ *808/889–5900* ⊕ *sushirock.gokohala.com* ⊟ *AE, DC, MC, V* ☉ *Closed Wed.*

$$$–$$$$
MODERN
HAWAIIAN

✕ **Tommy Bahama's Tropical Café.** It's funny that a chain known for its "Hawaiian-ness" would start in California and then one day end up in Hawai'i, but that is Tommy Bahama's story. Located in the Shops at Mauna Lani, in an open-air space above the Tommy Bahama store, the restaurant does a good job of making guests forget they're in a shopping center. And the food is decent, although derivative of other menus on the island. The macadamia-crusted *opakapaka* (Pacific red snapper) is a standout. Some of the best items, and best values, on the menu are actually in the appetizer section—the *poke* is outstanding—and salad list, which includes a fresh take on a roasted beet and arugula salad with hearts of palm and a *liliko'i* (passion fruit)–infused dressing. Desserts are decadent and great for sharing. ✉ *68-1330 Mauna Lani Dr., #102* ☎ *808/881–8686* ⊕ *www.tommybahama.com* ⊟ *AE, D, MC, V.*

$
SOUTHWESTERN

✕ **Tres Hombres Beach Grill.** The food is decent, if a bit pricey, but what you come here for are the marvelous margaritas. They're in all sorts of tropical flavors, including *liliko'i* (passion fruit). Lunch is the usual Mexican combination platters (tacos, enchiladas, chiles rellenos) as well as burgers and sandwiches. Dinner entrées include fresh fish, killer fajitas, bean-and-rice combinations, and steaks. ✉ *Kawaihae Harbor Center, Hwy. 270, Kawaihae* ☎ *808/882–1031* ⊟ *MC, V.*

8

WAIMEA

$$$–$$$$
MODERN
HAWAIIAN

✕ **Daniel Thiebaut's Restaurant.** This restaurant features the creations of respected local chef Daniel Thiebaut in a quaint little yellow building that once housed the historic Chock In Store, which catered to the ranching community beginning in 1900. Collectibles abound, such as antique porcelain pieces. The French-Asian menu includes an amazing appetizer of sweet-corn

crab cake with a lemongrass, coconut, and lobster sauce. Other signature dishes include Hunan-style rack of lamb served with eggplant compote, and Big Island goat cheese. The restaurant has reopened for lunch during the week with a buffet on Sundays. Good lunch choices are the local grass-fed beef burger or the braised short ribs. ⊠ *65-1259 Kawaihae Rd., Waimea* ☎ *808/887–2200* ▭ *MC, V.*

$$–$$$
PACIFIC RIM

✕ **Fujimamas.** This popular Kona restaurant has relocated to upcountry Waimea in the space formerly occupied by Edelweiss restaurant. They specialize in tasty Asian fusion food like shiitake sirloin with kimchee mashed potatoes, corn-crusted daily catch on stir-fried greens, and a positively addictive "Thai Caesar salad" with crispy calamari croutons that is big enough to share. Fujimamas has a full sushi bar as well. Don't miss the "Four Towers" roll with shrimp, 'ahi, crab, avocado, and cucumber that is tempura-battered and deep-fried. Then wash it all down with a crisp saketini. ⊠ *65-1299 Kawaihae Rd., Waimea* ☎ *808/327–2125* ⊕ *www.fujimamas.com* ▭ *AE, D, MC, V* ☉ *Closed Sun.*

$
MODERN
HAWAIIAN

✕ **Huli Sue's BBQ and Grill.** Owned and operated by the same folks that run the fantastic and popular Fujimamas restaurant in Waimea, Huli Sue's serves large portions of updated Hawaiian classics in a casual little restaurant along the highway between Waimea and Honoka'a. The barbecue menu, which includes your choice of meat (classics like ribs, pork roast, brisket) with one of four sauces, is melt-in-your-mouth delicious. The menu includes many other options, including a baked potato stuffed with your choice of meat, cilantro sour cream, and Fontina cheese, a variety of curry dishes, and a handful of fantastic appetizers such as the chicken sausage cakes with cilantro pesto and the quesadilla with crab, smoked pepper, onion, and Fontina. Salads, with produce from a nearby farm, are great, too. ⊠ *64-957 Māmalahoa Hwy. (Hwy. 11)* ☎ *808/885–6268* ▭ *MC, V.*

$
CONTINENTAL

✕ **Lilikoi Cafe.** This gem of a café is tucked away in the back of the Parker Ranch Shopping Center. Locals love that it's hard to find because they want to keep Lilikoi Café's delicious breakfast crepes, freshly made soups, and croissants Waimea's best-kept secret. Owner and chef John Lorda puts out an impressive display of salad choices daily, including chicken curry, beet, fava bean, chicken pesto, and Mediterranean pasta. The Israeli couscous with tomato, red onion, cranberry, and basil is a hit, as is the half avocado stuffed with tuna salad. Order the combo and get your choice of one, two, or three of his healthy salad options.

Continued on page 215

LŪ'AU: A TASTE OF HAWAI'I

The best place to sample Hawaiian food is at a backyard lū'au. Aunts and uncles are cooking, the pig is from a cousin's farm, and the fish is from a brother's boat.

But even locals have to angle for invitations to those rare occasions. So your choice is most likely between a commercial lū'au and a Hawaiian restaurant.

Most commercial lū'au will offer you little of the authentic diet; they're more about umbrella drinks, laughs, spectacle, and fun. Expect to spend some time and no small amount of cash.

For greater authenticity, folksy experiences, and rock-bottom prices, visit a Hawaiian restaurant (most are in anonymous storefronts in residential neighborhoods). Expect rough edges and some effort negotiating the menu.

In either case, much of what is known today as Hawaiian food would be as foreign to a 16th-century Hawaiian as risotto or chow mien. The pre-contact diet was simple and healthy–mainly raw and steamed seafood and vegetables. Early Hawaiians used earth ovens and heated stones to cook seafood, taro, sweet potatoes, and breadfruit and seasoned their food with sea salt and ground kukui nuts. Seaweed, fern shoots, sweet potato vines, coconut, banana, sugarcane, and select greens and roots rounded out the diet.

Successive waves of immigrants added their favorites to the ti leaf-lined table. So it is that foods as disparate as salt salmon and chicken long rice are now Hawaiian—even though there is no salmon in Hawaiian waters and long rice (cellophane noodles) is Chinese.

AT THE LŪʻAU: KĀLUA PORK

The heart of any lūʻau is the *imu*, the earth oven in which a whole pig is roasted. The preparation of an imu is an arduous affair for most families, who tackle it only for special occasions or at Thanksgiving, when many Islanders prefer to imu their turkeys. Commercial lūʻau operations have it down to a science, however.

THE ART OF THE STONE

The key to a proper imu is the *pohaku*, the stones. Imu cook by means of long, slow, moist heat released by special stones which can withstand a hot fire without exploding. Many Hawaiian families treasure their imu stones, keeping them in a pile in the back yard and passing them on through generations.

PIT COOKING

The imu makers first dig a pit about the size of a refrigerator, then lay down *kiawe* (mesquite) wood and stones, and build a white-hot fire that is allowed to burn itself out. The ashes are raked away, and the hot stones covered with banana and ti leaves. Well-wrapped in leaves and a net of chicken wire, the pig is lowered onto the leaf-covered stones. *Laulau* may also be placed inside. The whole is topped with more leaves, wet burlap sacks, and a canvas tarp, and left to steam for the better part of a day.

OPENING THE IMU

This is the moment everyone waits for: The imu is unwrapped like a giant present and the imu keepers gingerly wrestle out the steaming pig. When it's unwrapped, the meat falls moist and smoky-flavored from the bone, looking and tasting just like Southern-style pulled pork, but without the barbecue sauce.

WHICH LŪʻAU?

Fairmont Orchid. Blends modern and traditional music with stories of the kings of Hawaiʻi, Tahiti, Samoa, and New Zealand. Foods from all four cultures are served.

Sheraton Keauhou. Fantastic show blends modern lighting and aesthetic with traditional myths and dances. Open bar and full buffet are bonuses.

Kona Village. The imu ceremony and tradional show make this a long-time island favorite. In addition to the pig, they put fresh fish in the imu—delicious.

MEA 'AI 'ONO.
GOOD THINGS TO EAT.

LAULAU
Steamed meats, fish, and taro leaf in ti-leaf bundles: fork-tender, a medley of flavors; the taro resembles spinach.

LOMI LOMI SALMON
Salt salmon in a piquant salad or relish with onions, tomatoes.

POI (DON'T CALL IT LIBRARY PASTE.)
Islanders are beyond tired of jokes about poi, a paste made of pounded taro root.

Consider: The Hawaiian Adam is descended from *kalo* (taro). Young taro plants are called "keiki"—children. Poi is the first food after mother's milk for many Islanders. 'Ai, the word for food, is synonymous with poi in many contexts.

Not only that, we like it. "There is no meat that doesn't taste good with poi," the old Hawaiians said.

But you have to know how to eat it: with something rich or powerfully flavored. "It is salt that makes the poi go in," is another adage. When you're served poi, try it with a mouthful of smoky kālua pork or salty lomi lomi salmon. Its slightly sour blandness cleanses the palate. And if you don't like it, smile and say something polite. (And slide that bowl over to a local.)

Laulau

Lomi Lomi Salmon

Poi

E HELE MAI 'AI! COME AND EAT!

Hawaiian restaurants tend to be inconveniently located in well-worn storefronts with little or no parking, outfitted with battered tables and clattering Melmac dishes, open odd (and usually limited) hours and days, and often so crowded you have to wait. But they personify aloha, invariably run by local families who welcome tourists who take the trouble to find them.

Many are cash-only operations and combination plates are a standard feature: one or two entrées, a side such as chicken long rice, choice of poi or steamed rice and—if the place is really old-style—a tiny portion of coarse Hawaiian salt and some raw onions for relish.

Most serve some foods that aren't, strictly speaking, Hawaiian, but are beloved of kama'āina, such as salt meat with watercress (preserved meat in a tasty broth), or *akubone* (skipjack tuna fried in a vinegar sauce).

Our two favorites: **Kanaka-Kava and Kūhiō Grille.**

MENU GUIDE

Much of the Hawaiian language encountered during a stay in the Islands will appear on restaurant menus and lists of lū'au fare. Here's a quick primer.

'ahi: *yellowfin tuna.*

aku: *skipjack, bonito tuna.*

'ama'ama: *mullet; it's hard to get but tasty.*

bento: *a box lunch.*

chicken lū'au: *a stew made from chicken, taro leaves, and coconut milk.*

haupia: *a light, pudding-like sweet made from coconut.*

imu: *the underground ovens in which pigs are roasted for lū'au.*

kālua: *to bake underground.*

kaukau: *food. The word comes from Chinese but is used in the Islands.*

kimchee: *Korean dish of pickled cabbage made with garlic and hot peppers.*

Kona coffee: *coffee grown in the Kona district of the Big Island.*

laulau: *literally, a bundle. Laulau are morsels of pork, chicken, butterfish, or other ingredients wrapped with young taro leaves and then bundled in ti leaves for steaming.*

liliko'i: *passion fruit, a tart, seedy yellow fruit that makes delicious desserts, juice, and jellies.*

lomi lomi: *to rub or massage; also a massage. Lomi lomi salmon is fish that has been rubbed with onions and herbs; commonly served with minced onions and tomatoes.*

lū'au: *a Hawaiian feast; also the leaf of the taro plant used in preparing such a feast.*

lū'au leaves: *cooked taro tops with a taste similar to spinach.*

mahimahi: *mild-flavored dolphinfish, not the marine mammal.*

mai tai: *potent rum drink with orange and lime juice, from the Tahitian word for "good."*

malasada: *a Portuguese deep-fried doughnut without a hole, dipped in sugar.*

manapua: *dough wrapped around diced pork or other fillings.*

manō: *shark.*

niu: *coconut.*

'ōkolehao: *a liqueur distilled from the ti root.*

onaga: *pink or red snapper.*

ono: *a long, slender mackerel-like fish; also called wahoo.*

'ono: *delicious; also hungry.*

'opihi: *a tiny shellfish, or mollusk, found on rocks; also called limpets.*

pāpio: *a young ulua or jack fish.*

pohā: *Cape gooseberry. Tasting a bit like honey, the pohā berry is often used in jams and desserts.*

poi: *a paste made from pounded taro root, a staple of the Hawaiian diet.*

poke: *chopped, pickled raw tuna or other fish, tossed with herbs and seasonings.*

pūpū: *Hawaiian hors d'oeuvre.*

saimin: *long thin noodles and vegetables in broth, often garnished with small pieces of fish cake, scrambled egg, luncheon meat, and green onion.*

sashimi: *raw fish thinly sliced and usually eaten with soy sauce.*

tī leaves: *a member of the agave family. The fragrant leaves are used to wrap food while cooking and removed before eating.*

uku: *deep-sea snapper.*

ulua: *a member of the jack family that also includes pompano and amberjack. Also called crevalle, jack fish, and jack crevalle.*

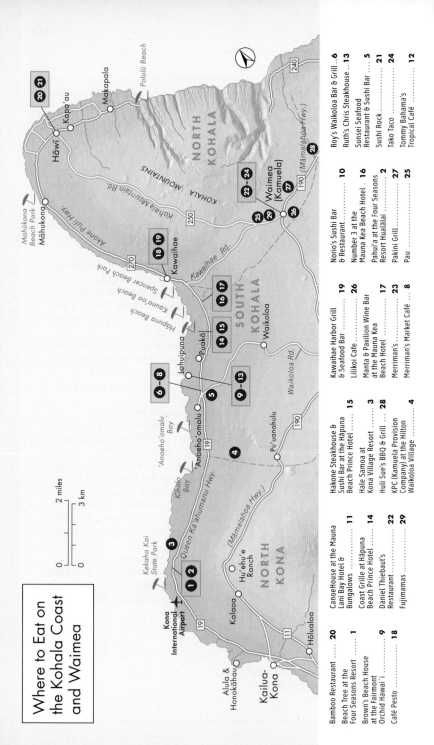

Where to Eat on the Kohala Coast and Waimea

There are also sandwiches and hot entrees. The food is fresh, many of the ingredients are organic, and everything is homemade, including the rice pudding and fruit cobblers created by John's wife, Frances. This earth-conscious eatery even uses 100% compostable tableware like forks made out of corn and cups created from sugar. (Don't worry, you won't be able to tell the difference.) ⊠ *67-1185 Māmalahoa Hwy. (Hwy. 11), Waimea* ☎ *808/887–1400* ⊟ *AE, D, MC, V* ☽ *Closed Sun. No dinner.*

$$$–$$$$
MODERN
HAWAIIAN
Fodor'sChoice
★

✕**Merriman's.** By far one of the best restaurants in Waimea, this is the signature restaurant of Peter Merriman, one of the pioneers of Hawaiian regional cuisine. is the home of the original wok-charred ʻahi, usually served with buttery Wainaku corn. If you prefer meat, try the Kahuā Ranch lamb, raised to the restaurant's specifications, or the prime Kansas City Cut steak, grilled to order. The wine list includes 22 selections poured by the glass, and the staff is refreshingly knowledgeable. For true foodies, Merriman's now offers a farmers' market tour—four hours spent browsing around local ranches and food stands, culminating in a fantastic five-course meal using produce and meat bought throughout the day. ⊠ *ʻOpelo Plaza, 65-1227 ʻOpelo Rd., Waimea* ☎ *808/885–6822* ⋈ *Reservations essential* ⊕ *www.merrimanshawaii. com* ⊟ *AE, MC, V.*

$$
MODERN
HAWAIIAN

✕**Pakini Grill.** Four lifetime friends from Honokaʻa have created a fresh and modern grill in Waimea that's perfect for families. Kids have space to roam around and mom and dad can watch the game on one of the two big-screen TVs at the bar. With lots of tables, a few booths, and plenty of bar seats, you're bound to find a comfy spot to enjoy your meal. Try their signature hoisin-ginger-braised short ribs or potato nest *opakapaka* (Pacific red snapper). Good lunch options include the smoked beef brisket sandwich, Korean chicken, or the Big Saimin (perfect for Waimea's chilly climate). The restaurant also has a full bar and live entertainment in the evenings (Wed. through Sun.), and offers a limited kid's menu. ⊠ *65-1144 Māmalahoa Hwy. (Hwy. 11), Waimea* ☎ *808/885–3333* ⊕ *www.pakinigrill.com* ⊟ *AE, D, MC, V.*

$–$$
ITALIAN

✕**Pau.** The name here is the Hawaiian word for "done," which we're guessing alludes to the restaurant's quick service and possibly how eagerly you will gobble up their sensational pizzas. You order at the counter and find your own seat in the small but neat inside dining area. The big draw is the wide selection of appetizers, salads, sandwiches, and pizzas loaded with lots of local, fresh ingredients. Try the Pau soba noodle salad; "Superfood" salad with quinoa, brown rice, edamame, grapes, and spiced nuts; or the warm and gooey focaccia cheesy bread. When it comes to the pizzas, anything goes: order one of Pau's signature pies or create your own. The restaurant is a little tricky to find, but it's right next to the Merriman's in Waimea. ⊠ *65-1227 Opelo Rd., Waimea* ☎ *808/885–6325* ⊕ *www.paupizza.com* ⊟ *AE, MC, V* ☽ *Closed Sun.*

$
MEXICAN

✕**Tako Taco.** Everyone in Waimea and beyond loves Tako Taco, one of the best Mexican restaurants on the island. Housed in a small, brightly painted hut, Tako Taco feels more like a mainland burrito joint than an island Mexican food restaurant. Its authentic food makes it hugely popular with both locals, who line up for to-go orders, and visitors

8

Big Island Farm Tours

As local ingredients continue to play a more prominent role on Big Island menus, chefs and farmers are working together to support a burgeoning agritourism industry in Hawai'i. Several local farms have cropped up over the past few years to make specialty items that cater to the island's gourmet restaurants. The **Hawai'i Island Goat Dairy** produces specialty cheese; lone beekeeper Richard Spiegel of **Volcano Island Honey Co.** produces a rare and delicious honey now available not only in local restaurants but on the shelves of high-end stores like Neiman Marcus; and the **Hāmākua Heritage Farm** has turned mowed-down koa forests into a safe haven for gourmet mushrooms. While a handful of farms—like **Mountain Thunder**, which produces 100% organic Kona coffee, and **Hawaiian Vanilla Vineyards**, which is cultivating vanilla from orchids growing wild on the Hāmākua Coast—are open to the public and offer free tours, others have opted instead to offer limited tours through group operators. The **Big Island Farm Bureau** has also tried to encourage local farming and agritourism through the creation of **Hawai'i AgVentures**, an organization that schedules farm visits (to either single or multiple farms) for interested parties (see ⊕ *www.hawaiiagventures. com* for more information).

who snag one of the plastic booths and eat in. With a focus on fresh ingredients, Tako Taco whips up awesome tacos, burritos, Mexican salads, enchiladas, rellenos, and seriously *ono* (Hawaiian slang for "tasty") quesadillas fresh to order. The tomatillo pineapple salsa is the bee's knees, and they also serve top-shelf margaritas, both classic and flavored—strawberry, mango, or *liliko'i* (passion fruit)—along with local beers and wine. ⊠ *64-1066A Mamalahoa Hwy.* ☎ *808/887–1717* ☰ *MC, V.*

VOLCANO

$$
ITALIAN
✕ **Kiawe Kitchen.** Everyone around here says the same thing: "Kiawe has awesome pizza, but it's a little expensive for pizza." And it's true—the wood-fired pizza at this warm and pretty Italian eatery, with red walls and wood floors, has a perfect thin crust and an authentic Italian taste, but you have to be prepared to spend around $15 on a typical pie. Food options are limited in this area, though. Go for it. ⊠ *19-4005 Old Volcano Rd., Volcano* ☎ *808/967–7711* ☰ *MC, V.*

$$–$$$
CONTINENTAL
✕ **Kīlauea Lodge.** Chef Albert Jeyte combines contemporary trends with traditional cooking styles from the mainland, France, and his native Hamburg, Germany. Entrées include venison, duck à l'orange with an apricot-mustard glaze, and authentic *hasenpfeffer* (braised rabbit) served with Jeyte's signature sauerbraten. The coconut-crusted brie appetizer is huge, melty, and absolutely delicious, as are Jeyte's made-from-scratch soups and breads. Built in 1937 as a YMCA camp, the restaurant still has the original "Friendship Fireplace" made from stones from around the world. The roaring fire, koa-wood tables, and warm lighting make the sunny main building feel like a lodge. ⊠ *19-3948*

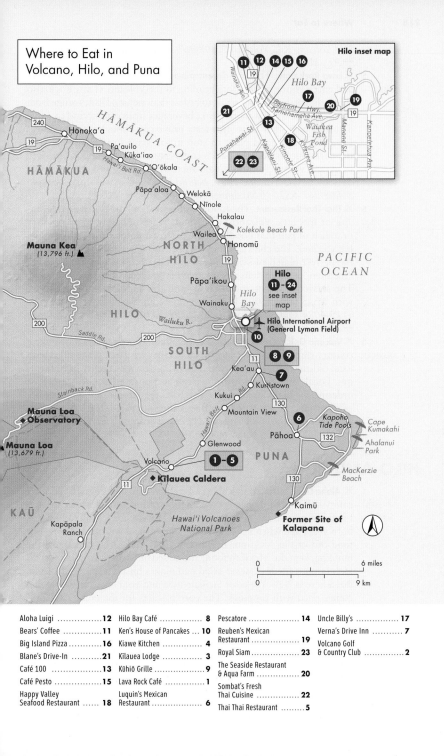

Where to Eat in Volcano, Hilo, and Puna

Hilo inset map

Hilo Bay

Waianuku Ave.

19

Bayfront Hwy.
Kamehameha Ave.

19

Waiakea
Fish
Pond

19

Ponahawai St.

Kapiolani St.

Kilauea Ave.

Kinoole St.

Manono St.

Kanoelehua Ave.

HĀMĀKUA COAST

240

Honoka'a

19

19

Pa'auilo
Kūka'iao

Hawai'i Belt Rd.

O'ōkala

HĀMĀKUA

Pāpa'aloa

Welokā

Nīnole

Hakalau

Wailea

Kolekole Beach Park

Mauna Kea
(13,796 ft.)

NORTH
HILO

Honomū

PACIFIC
OCEAN

19

Pāpa'ikou

Hilo
Bay

Hilo
11 - 24
see inset map

200

HILO

Wailuku R.

Wainaku

Saddle Rd.

200

Hilo International Airport
(General Lyman Field)

200

SOUTH
HILO

10

Mauna Loa
Observatory

Stainback Rd.

Kea'au

8 9

7

Kurtistown

Mauna Loa
(13,679 ft.)

Hawai'i Belt Rd.

Kukui

130

Mountain View

6

Kapoho
Tide Pools

Cape
Kumakahi

Glenwood

Pāhoa

132

Ahalanui
Park

Volcano

1 - 5

PUNA

Kīlauea Caldera

130

MacKerzie
Beach

11

KAŪ

Kapāpala
Ranch

Hawai'i Volcanoes
National Park

Kaimū

Former Site of
Kalapana

0   6 miles

0   9 km

Old Volcano Rd., Volcano ☎ *808/967–7366* ⊕ *www.kilauealodge.com* ⊟ *AE, MC, V.*

$ ✕ **Lava Rock Café.** This is a decent place to grab a sandwich or a coffee AMERICAN and check your e-mail before heading to the Volcano. (Lava Rock also serves dinner, but service tends to be less than stellar.) Dishes range from chicken salad to New York steak, beverages from cappuccino to wine. Saturday night they serve up a tasty prime rib. Though it's not perfect, Lava Rock is a good place to stop if you want to take a picnic into the park: once inside, the park's concessionaires sell bland, overpriced food, and within Volcano Village there are no other fast and tasty deli options. ⊠ *Old Volcano Hwy., behind Kīlauea General Store, Volcano* ☎ *808/967–8526* ☉ *No dinner Sun. and Mon.* ⊟ *MC, V.*

$ ✕ **Thai Thai Restaurant.** The food is authentic, and the prices are reason-THAI able at this little Volcano Village find. A steaming hot plate of curry or a dish of pad thai noodles is the perfect antidote to a chilly day on the volcano. The chicken satay is excellent—the peanut dipping sauce the perfect match of sweet and spicy. Be careful when you order, as "medium" is more than spicy enough even for hard-core chili addicts. The service is warm and friendly, and the dining room is pleasant, with white tablecloths, Thai art, and a couple of silk wall hangings. ⊠ *19-4084 Old Volcano Rd., Volcano* ☎ *808/967–7969* ☉ *No lunch* ⊟ *MC, V.*

$ ✕ **Volcano Golf & Country Club.** This restaurant does not feel much like a AMERICAN country club—it's simple and not at all fancy with oak tables filled with local old-timers talking story and chowing down on greasy local favorites. Locals love this spot for its large portions and classic breakfasts: ordering the breakfast burger (with fried egg, cheese, and your choice of meat) and a cup of local coffee is the way to go. If it's lunchtime, you can't beat the hamburgers. ⊠ *Pi'i Mauna Dr., off Hwy. 11, Volcano* ☎ *808/967–8228* ☉ *No dinner* ⊟ *MC, V.*

HILO AND PUNA

¢ ✕ **Aloha Luigi.** Situated in a cheery, bright yellow building, this popular ITALIAN/ eatery serves up a delicious combination of Italian and Mexican fare. MEXICAN Luigi has been in the restaurant business for decades. Aloha Luigi was born years ago when he was helping out a friend who served Mexican food out of this location. Eventually Luigi took over, remodeled the building, kept the Mexican food, and added his signature Italian dishes. He's famous for his Caesar salad and makes his own special dressing. Pizza here is New York– or Sicilian-style and your slice (or whole pie) comes piled with toppings. The corn tortillas for the tacos are hand-made and the giant burritos (like the mahimahi and the carnitas) are the best around. Luigi also makes a mean coconut macaroon and will soon be serving his very own ice cream that he creates on-site. There's also pasta, hot baked subs, and a brunch menu served all day. Order a refreshing Rainforest Treasure iced tea, grab a seat outside in the beautiful garden area, and enjoy your little slice of heaven in downtown Hilo. ⊠ *264 Keawe St., Hilo* ☎ *808/934–9112* ⊟ *D, MC, V* ☉ *Closed Sun.*

$ ✕**Bears' Coffee.** A favorite Hilo breakfast spot, much loved for their
DINER fresh-fruit waffles and tasty morning coffee. Service can be a little slow,
Ⓒ but where are you running off to anyway? For lunch they serve up huge
deli sandwiches and decent entrée-size salads. In keeping with its name,
the little diner is full of stuffed bears, ceramic bears, even bear wallpa-
per. ✉ *106 Keawe St.* ☎ *808/935–0708* ▭ *No credit cards.*

$ ✕**Big Island Pizza.** If spending a twenty on a large pizza is something
ITALIAN you just can't come to grips with, steer clear of Big Island Pizza. If, on
the other hand, you can rationalize paying more for a pie that's topped
with things like Black Tiger shrimp or smoked salmon, then order up
and get ready for a little slice of heaven. They also serve sandwiches,
wraps, pastas, and salads. There are only a handful of tables for eating
in, but they do a brisk take-out business and also deliver to the eastern side of the island. ✉ *760 Kilauea Ave.* ☎ *808/934–8000* ⊕ *www.
bigislandpizza.com* ▭ *AE, D, MC, V.*

¢ ✕**Blane's Drive-In.** With a vast menu second only to Ken's House of
HAWAIIAN Pancakes, Blane's serves up everything from standard hamburgers to
chicken *katsu.* There's a mean plate lunch with tons of fresh fish for
only $7. The slow-cooked homemade chili and sticky white rice is a
meal in itself, and costs less than $3. At one point it was a real drive-in,
with car service. Now, customers park, order at the window and then
eat either at one of the few picnic tables provided or in their cars, or
take their food to go. ✉ *217 Wainuenue Ave., Hilo* ☎ *808/969–9494*
▭ *No credit cards.*

¢ ✕**Café 100.** This popular restaurant is famous for its tasty *loco moco* (a
HAWAIIAN local staple that is traditionally made by topping rice with a hamburger
patty, gravy, and a fried egg), prepared in more than a dozen unique
ways. They also have dirt-cheap breakfast specials. (You can stuff yourself for $3 if you order right.) However, if you're looking for a salad,
keep walking. The word restaurant, or even café, is used liberally here—
you order at a window and eat your plate lunch on one of the outdoor
benches provided—but you come here for the food and prices, not the
ambience. ✉ *969 Kīlauea Ave., Hilo* ☎ *808/935–8683* ▭ *MC, V.*

$$ ✕**Café Pesto.** One of the better restaurants in Hilo for the price, Café
ITALIAN Pesto offers exotic pizzas (with fresh Hāmākua mushrooms, artichokes,
and rosemary gorgonzola sauce, for example), Asian-inspired pastas
and risottos, fresh seafood, delicious salads, and appetizers that you
could make a meal of. Try the shrimp "half moon" nachos, Asian Pacific
crab cake salad, coconut-crusted calamari, smoked salmon pizzette,
or the sesame-crusted Big Island goat cheese. All are dynamite. Prod-
ucts from local farmers feature heavily on the menu here—everything
from the Kulana free-range beef to the Kawamata Farms tomatoes to
the Kapoho Farms Lehua blossom honey is made on the island. Right
in downtown Hilo and across from the bay, this is an excellent place
to end your evening with friends. Live local musicians provide enter-
tainment at dinner on the weekends. ✉ *308 Kamehameha Ave., Hilo*
☎ *808/969–6640* ⊕ *www.cafepesto.com* ▭ *AE, D, DC, MC, V.*

$$ ✕**Happy Valley Seafood Restaurant.** Don't let the name fool you. Though
CHINESE Hilo's best Chinese restaurant does specialize in seafood (the salt-and-
pepper prawns are fantastic), they also offer a wide range of other

8

Cantonese treats, including a sizzling lamb platter, salt-and-pepper pork, Mongolian beef or chicken, and vegetarian specialties like garlic eggplant and crispy green beans. The food is good, portions are large, and the price is right, but don't come here expecting any ambience—this is a funky and cheap Chinese restaurant, with a few random pieces of artwork tacked up here and there. ✉ *1263 Kilauea Ave., Ste. 320* ☎ *808/933–1083* ▭ *MC, V.*

$–$$
AMERICAN

✕ **Hilo Bay Café**. What this eatery lacks in setting—it's in a strip mall that contains Office Max and Wal-Mart—it makes up for with modern decor and fantastic food. It's a popular restaurant among locals for "special" occasions like birthdays and anniversaries due to the high quality of food, but truth be told, the prices are reasonable enough you can come just to celebrate a Tuesday. Highly recommended are the roasted eggplant-parmesan custard and the crab-mascarpone stuffed calamari with shaved coppa and beurre blanc. The vegan offerings, which range from garlic fries to potpie, are good enough to seduce meat-eaters. Daily specials always include a vegetarian, meat, and fish choice, and the menu changes twice a year to keep things fresh. The chef tries to use organic and local products wherever possible. Don't forget to order a drink from the restaurant's well-stocked bar—the mojitos are made with freshly squeezed lime juice. ✉ *315 Makaala St., Hilo* ☎ *808/935–4939* ⊕ *www.hilobaycafe.com* ▭ *AE, DC, MC, V.*

$
DINER

✕ **Ken's House of Pancakes**. For years this 24-hour coffee shop between the airport and the hotels along Banyan Drive has been a gathering place for both Hilo residents and travelers. As its name implies, Ken's serves good pancakes, but there are about 180 other tasty local specialties and American diner–inspired items from which to choose. Sunday is all-you-can-eat spaghetti night, Tuesday is all-you-can-eat tacos, and Wednesday is prime rib night. ✉ *1730 Kamehameha Ave., Hilo* ☎ *808/935–8711* ⊕ *www.kenshouseofpancakes-hilohi.com* ▭ *AE, D, DC, MC, V.*

$
HAWAIIAN

✕ **Kūhiō Grille**. There's no ambience to speak of, and water is served in unbreakable plastic, but if you're searching for local fare—that eclectic and indefinable fusion of ethnic cuisines—Kūhiō Grille is a must. Sam Araki serves a 1-pound *laulau* (a steamed bundle of taro leaves and pork) that is worth the trip. The fried rice is also out-of-this-world. This diner at the edge of Hilo's largest mall opens at 6 AM. ✉ *Prince Kūhiō Shopping Plaza, 111 E. Puainako St., at Hwy. 11* ☎ *808/959–2336* ▭ *AE, MC, V.*

$
MEXICAN

✕ **Luquin's Mexican Restaurant**. Long an island favorite for tasty, albeit greasy, Mexican grub, Luquin's is still going strong in the funky town of Pāhoa. Tacos are great here (go for crispy), especially when stuffed with grilled, seasoned local fish. Chips are warm and salty, the salsa's got some kick, and the beans are thick with lard and topped with melted cheese. This is not the place to eat right before going for a swim, but it's perfect after a long day of exploring. ✉ *Main St., Pahoa* ☎ *808/965–9990* ▭ *MC, V.*

$$
ITALIAN

✕ **Pescatore**. With dim lights, stately high-back chairs, and dark-wood paneling, Pescatore conjures up an Italian trattoria. The food is good, but not amazing, with plenty of Italian basics such as lasagna, chicken marsala, and chicken or veal parmigiana. Lunch consists of Italian-style sandwiches; breakfast, served on weekends only, features omelets and crepes. Families love the simple pastas made to please choosy children. ✉ *235 Keawe St., at Haili St., Hilo* ☎ *808/969–9090* ☐ *AE, D, DC, MC, V.*

$ ✕ **Reuben's Mexican Restaurant.** It's
MEXICAN not the best Mexican food you've ever had, but if you're in Hilo and you're jonesing for some carne asada or chicken flautas, Reuben's has got you pretty well covered. You could make a meal out of their warm chips and salsa alone, and they're known for pouring a stiff margarita in all sorts of interesting flavors like *likoʻi* (passion fruit), guava, mango, coconut, and watermelon. Since the restaurant has been completely remodeled with new tables, a new bar, and air conditioning, this is a lively place to spend your afternoon or evening. ✉ *336 Kamehameha Ave., Hilo* ☎ *808/961–2552* ⊕ *www. reubensmexican.com* ☐ *AE, D, MC, V.*

$ ✕ **Royal Siam.** A downtown Hilo fixture, this authentic Thai eatery offers
THAI little ambience. But you don't need a dramatic view when you can choose from a menu that includes five kinds of curries and plenty of stir-fried meals. The tangy stir-fried garlic shrimp with coconut milk and wild mushrooms is particularly good. ✉ *70 Mamo St., Hilo* ☎ *808/961– 6100* ☐ *AE, D, DC, MC, V.*

$$ ✕ **The Seaside Restaurant and Aqua Farm.** The Nakagawa family has been
SEAFOOD running this eatery since the early 1920s. The latest son to manage the restaurant has transformed both the menu and the decor, and that, paired with the setting (the restaurant sits on a 30-acre natural brackish water fish pond) makes this one of the most romantic and interesting places to eat in Hilo. You can't get fish fresher than this. Islanders travel great distances for the fried *āholehole* (young Hawaiian flagtail) that's raised on the aqua-farm. Other great dishes from the sea include the steamed Kona *kampachi*, *furikake* salmon, and macadamia nut–crusted mahimahi. Of course, it's not all fish. The Pacific Rim menu includes plenty of selections for landlubbers too. Arrive before sunset and request a table by the window for a view of the egrets roosting around the fish ponds. ✉ *1790 Kalanianaʻole Ave., Hilo* ☎ *808/935– 8825* ⊕ *www.seasiderestaurant.com* ☐ *AE, DC, MC, V* ☻ *Closed Mon. No lunch.*

$ ✕ **Sombat's Fresh Thai Cuisine.** The name says it all. Sombat Parente uses
THAI only the freshest local ingredients (many of the herbs come from her own garden) to prepare authentic and tasty Thai treats like coconut curries, fresh basil rolls, eggplant stir-fry, and green papaya salad. You can have most dishes prepared with your choice of tofu, pork, beef, chicken, or fish. The weekday lunch plate special is a steal ($6–$8). And if you can't leave the island without it, Sombat's famous pad thai sauce is available to take home in jars. ✉ *88 Kanoelehue Ave., Waiakea Kai Plaza* ☎ *808/969–9336* ⊕ *www.sombats.com* ☐ *MC, V* ☻ *Closed Sun.*

8

$$ ✕ **Uncle Billy's.** Uncle Billy's is pure Hawaiian kitsch—right out of 1930s
HAWAIIAN   Hollywood—but the thatch roofs, tinkling capiz-shell wind chimes, and
Tahitian-print curtains add to the fun, as does a free nightly hula show.
The show and the ambience are the reasons to visit; the food is so-so.
Choose from mahimahi meunière, teriyaki chicken, and local special-
ties. ⊠ *Hilo Bay Hotel, 87 Banyan Dr., Hilo* ☎ *808/935–0861* ⊟ *AE,
D, DC, MC, V* ☽ *No lunch.*

¢   ✕ **Verna's Drive-In.** Verna's is a favorite among locals who come for the
HAWAIIAN   moist homemade burgers and filling plate lunches. The price is right
with a burger combo that includes fries and a drink for just $5. If you're
hungry for more, try the traditional Hawaiian plate with *laulau*, beef
stew, chicken long rice, *lomi* salmon, rice, and macaroni salad; or the
smoked meat plate (a local specialty) smothered in onions and served
with rice and macaroni salad. Whatever you choose, you won't leave
hungry. Late-night revelers take note: Verna's is one of the only joints
in Hilo that's open 24 hours on the weekend. ⊠ *1765 Kamehameha
Ave., Hilo* ☎ *808/935–2776* ⊟ *MC, V.*

Where to Stay

WORD OF MOUTH

"The Big Island—due to its size, small population, and geological diversity—is often recommended to the more adventurous types, but it is also great for relaxing at the wonderful Kohala Coast Resorts."

–kailani

WHERE TO STAY PLANNER

Hotels and Resorts

The resorts—all clustered on the Kohala Coast—are expensive, there are no two ways about it. That said, many offer free nights with longer stays (fifth or seventh night free) and often team up with airlines or consolidators to offer great package deals that may include a rental car, meals, spa treatments, golf, and other activities. Children under 17 can sometimes stay for free. Ask about specials when you book, and check their Web site as well—many resorts have Internet-only deals.

B&Bs and Inns

Bed-and-breakfasts and locally run inns are a nice halfway point between the resorts and condos, offering a bit more privacy than a resort, as well as some of the perks of hotels (breakfast and maid service), but without the extras that drive up rates at resorts.

Be sure to check the association Web sites as well as property Web sites and call to ask questions. There is still a few "B&Bs" that are really just dumpy rooms in someone's house, and you don't want to end up there.

Condos and Vacation Rentals

Condos and vacation homes are the best deal going on the island. There are hundreds to choose from in and around Kailua-Kona, dozens more dotted around the island, and more being built every day, which keeps driving rates down. You can get more space and save some money by eating in (although groceries aren't cheap on the island).

Reservations

You'll almost always be able to find a room on the Big Island, but you might not get your first choice if you wait until the last minute. Make reservations six months to a year in advance if you're visiting during the winter season (December 15 through April 15). During the week after Easter Sunday, when the Merrie Monarch Festival is in full swing, all of Hilo's rooms are booked. Kailua-Kona is packed in mid-October during the Ironman World Triathlon Championship.

Prices

Generally, the farther you are from the beach, the less you'll pay. If you're willing to drive 10 to 30 minutes to get to the beach, you can find great deals. At the beach, garden view rooms are less expensive than those with an ocean view. High season is usually considered December to February and June to August.

Keep in mind that most of the resorts now charge "resort fees" for things like parking, daily newspaper service, and activities, and some condos and vacation rentals charge an additional cleaning fee. Always ask about extra fees as well as specials and discounts when you book.

WHAT IT COSTS

	¢	$	$$	$$$	$$$$
For Two People	under $100	$100–$180	$181–$260	$261–$340	over $340

Hotel prices are for two people in a standard double room in high season. Condo price categories reflect studio and one-bedroom rates.

BEST BETS FOR BIG ISLAND LODGING

Fodor's writers and editors have selected their favorite hotels, resorts, condos, vacation rentals, and bed-and-breakfasts by price and experience. Fodor's Choice properties represent the "best of the best" across price categories. You can also search by area for excellent places to stay—check out our complete reviews on the following pages.

9

By Katie
Young
Yamanaka

Even among locals, there is an ongoing debate about which side of the Big Island is "better," so don't worry if you're having a tough time deciding where to stay. Our recommendation? Do both. Each side of the island offers a totally different range of accommodations, restaurants, and activities.

Consider staying at one of the resorts along the Kohala Coast or in a condo in Kailua-Kona for half of your trip. Then, shift gears and check into a romantic bed-and-breakfast on the Hāmākua Coast or near the volcano. If you've got children in tow, opt for a vacation home or one of Hilo's family-friendly hotels. On the west coast, lounge on the pristine beaches and try some of the fine-dining restaurants; on the east, hike through rain forests, frolic in waterfalls, and go for a plate lunch.

Some locals like to say that the east is "more Hawaiian," but we argue that King Kamehameha himself made the west his last resting place, and Hawaiians have always loved the beach. Another reason to try a bit of both: your budget. You can justify splurging on a west coast resort for a few nights because you'll spend the rest of your time paying one-third that rate in the east. And although food at the resorts is very expensive (except for Kona Village, which is all-inclusive), you don't have to eat every meal there. Condos and vacation homes can be ideal for a family trip or for a group of friends looking to save money and live like locals for a week or two. Many of the homes also have private pools and/or hot tubs, lānai, ocean views, and more; you can go as budget or as high-end as you like.

If you choose a bed-and-breakfast, inn, or an out-of-the-way hotel, explain your expectations fully and ask plenty of questions before booking. Be clear about your travel and location needs. Some places require stays of two or three days. When booking, ask about car-rental arrangements, as many bed-and-breakfast networks offer discounted rates. No matter where you stay, you'll want to rent a car—preferably one with four-wheel drive. This is imperative for getting to some of the best beaches and really seeing the island. However, some rental car companies do have restrictions about taking their vehicles to certain Big Island scenic spots, so make sure to ask about rules before you book.

Members of the Big Island–based **Hawai'i Island Bed & Breakfast Association** ⊕ *www.stayhawaii.com* are listed with phone numbers and rates in a comprehensive online brochure. In order to join this network, bed-and-breakfasts must be evaluated and meet fairly stringent minimum requirements, including a yearly walk-through by association officers, to maintain their membership.

Other bed-and-breakfast associations include **Hawai'i's Best Bed & Breakfasts** (☎ 808/985–7488 or 800/262–9912 ⊕ *www.bestbnb.com*).

For information on camping at county parks, including Spencer Beach Park, contact the **Department of Parks and Recreation** (⊠ *25 Aupuni St., Hilo* ☎ *808/961–8311* ⊕ *www.hawaii-county.com*).

KAILUA-KONA

Kailua-Kona, a bustling little village full of restaurants, shops, and entertainment options, has a zillion lodging options. In addition to half a dozen hotels, oceanfront Ali'i Drive is crammed with condo complexes and homes on both sides of the street, and there are several grocery stores for those who choose to go the condo or vacation home route. Kailua-Kona has three beaches, White Sands, Kahalu'u, and King Kamehameha, and each has its selling point: Kahalu'u is renowned for its snorkeling, White Sands is a local favorite that's great for bodysurfing (but the beach is small), and King Kamehameha is a small beach next to a calm marina, which makes it nice for kids. The downside to staying here is that you'll have to drive 30–45 minutes up the road to the Kohala Coast to get Hawai'i's signature long white-sand beaches. However, you'll also pay about half what you would at any of the beachfront resorts, and Kailua-Kona has a bit more local charm.

$$$–$$$$
RENTAL

🏠 **Aston Kona by the Sea Resort.** Complete modern kitchens, tile lānai, and washer-dryer units can be found in every suite of this comfortable oceanfront condo complex. Despite being near the bustling town of Kailua-Kona, this four-story place is quiet and relaxing. The nearest sandy beach is 2 mi away, but the pool is next to the ocean and many of the rooms have ocean views. Guests are lulled to sleep by the ocean nightly. Be sure to check the Web site for specials: they usually offer a fourth or fifth night free and often advertise deals only on their own Web site. **Pros:** oceanfront, quiet and peaceful. **Cons:** no beach, not many kid-friendly features. ✉ 75-6106 Ali'i Dr., Kailua-Kona ☎ 808/327–2300 or 800/922–7866 ⊕ www.astonhotels.com 🛏 72 units ⚿ In-room: A/C, kitchen. In-hotel: pool, spa ▭ AE, D, DC, MC, V.

¢–$
☺
RENTAL

🏠 **Casa de Emdeko.** A large and pretty complex on the *makai* (oceanfront) side of Ali'i Drive, Casa de Emdeko offers a few more amenities than most condo complexes, including an on-site convenience store that makes great sandwiches, a sandy oceanfront area for sunbathing, and both fresh and saltwater pools. As with any complex, the decor and maintenance of units varies depending on the owner, so be sure to view photos of the specific unit you're renting. All units have lānai, with either garden or ocean views (ocean view is a bit more expensive). **Pros:** oceanfront fresh- and saltwater pools, on-site convenience store. **Cons:** quality can be hit or miss depending on owner, some units are located close to high-traffic road. ✉ 75-6082 Ali'i Dr., Kailua-Kona ☎ 808/329–2160 ⊕ casadeemdeko.org 🛏 106 units ⚿ In-room: A/C, kitchen. In-hotel: pools ▭ AE, MC, V.

$
B&B/INN

🏠 **Hale Hualālai.** Perfect for couples, Hale Hualālai has two suites with exposed beams, whirlpool bathtubs, and private lānai. Perhaps the most memorable aspect of Hale Hualālai is the food—owner Lonn Armour was a professional chef for 20 years, and cooks up a breakfast that puts other bed-and-breakfast offerings to shame. His creations reflect individual guest preferences and options include everything from blueberry coffee cake to frittatas to sweet bread French toast. The inn is near the artsy village of Hōlualoa. **Pros:** gourmet breakfast with Kona coffee, new and tastefully decorated house, whirlpool tubs. **Cons:** not kid-friendly, removed from local beaches and restaurants. ✉ 74-4968 Māmalahoa

9

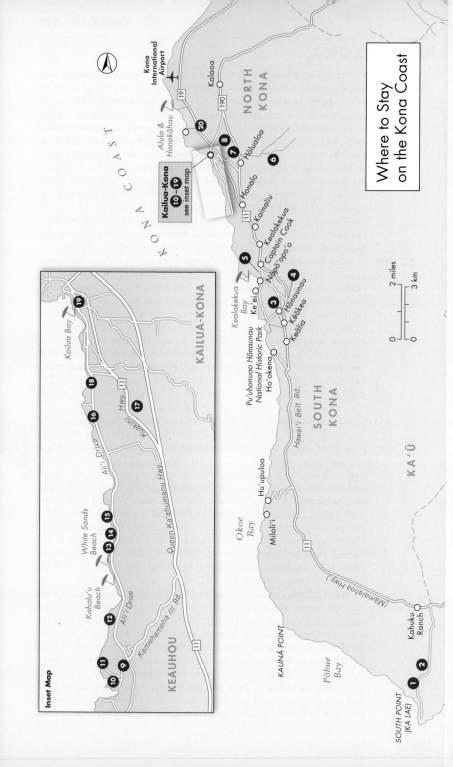

Where to Stay on the Kona Coast

Kona International Airport

Kalaoa

NORTH KONA

19
190

20

Alula & Honokōhau

8
7
Hōlualoa

6

Kailua-Kona
10 – 19
see inset map

Honalo

Kainaliu

11

Kealakekua

Captain Cook

Nāpoʻopoʻo

5

Keʻei

Kealakekua Bay

4

3

Hōnaunau

Keōkea

Kealia

Puʻuhonua o Hōnaunau National Historic Park

Hoʻokena

Hawaiʻi Belt Rd.

SOUTH KONA

Huʻupuloa

Okoe Bay

Miloliʻi

11

KAUNĀ POINT

11

(Mamalahoa Hwy.)

Kahuku Ranch

1
2

SOUTH POINT (KA LAE)

Pōhue Bay

KAʻŪ

0   2 miles
0   3 km

KONA COAST

Inset Map

Kailua Bay

19

Kailua Bay

18

16

17

11
Hwy.

Kuakini

Aliʻi Drive

White Sands Beach

15

13 14

Kahaluʻu Beach

12

Aliʻi Drive

Queen Kaʻahumanu Hwy.

Kamehameha III Rd.

11

KEAUHOU

11

9

10

KAILUA-KONA

WHERE TO STAY ON THE KONA COAST

Hotels & Resorts

	Property Name	Worth Noting	Cost $	Pools	Beach	Golf Course	Tennis Courts	Gym	Spa	Children's Programs	Rooms	Restaurants	Other	Location
12	Keauhou Beach Resort	Close to Kahulu'u Beach	$$$-$$$$	1	yes		6	yes			317	1		Kailua-Kona
18	Kona Tiki Hotel	Oceanfront lānai	$	1							15		no A/C	Kailua-Kona
5	Manago Hotel		$								106	1	no A/C	Captian Cook
19	Royal Kona Resort	Good rates for oceanfront	$$	1	yes		4	yes	yes		460	1		Kailua-Kona
9	Sheraton Keauhou Bay	Cool pool with slide	$$$	1	yes		2	yes	yes		521	1		Kailua-Kona

Condos & Vacation Rentals

	Property Name	Worth Noting	Cost $	Pools	Beach	Golf Course	Tennis Courts	Gym	Spa	Children's Programs	Rooms	Restaurants	Other	Location
14	Aston Kona by the Sea Resort	Oceanfront pool	$$$-$$$$	1					yes		78		kitchens	Kailua-Kona
15	Casa de Emdeko	Oceanfront saltwater pool	$	2							85		kitchens	Kailua-Kona
11	Keauhou Kona Surf & Racquet Club	Tennis courts, big pool	$$-$$$	1			3				188		kitchens	Kailua-Kona
13	Kona Magic Sands	Ocean view from all units	$	1							37	1	kitchens	Kailua-Kona
16	Kona Nalu	Huge lānai, ocean views	$$	1	yes						15		kitchens	Kailua-Kona
17	Kona Pacific	Ocean view from pool, BBQ	$	1							80		kitchens	Kailua-Kona
10	Outrigger Kanaloa at Kona	Oceanfront restaurant	$$-$$$	3			2				166		kitchens	Kailua-Kona
20	Silver Oaks Guest Ranch	Working ranch	$-$$	1							2		no A/C	Kailua-Kona
1	South Point Banyan	Deck with hot tub	$$	14							1		no A/C	Ka'u

BBs & Inns

	Property Name	Worth Noting	Cost $	Pools	Beach	Golf Course	Tennis Courts	Gym	Spa	Children's Programs	Rooms	Restaurants	Other	Location
3	Aloha Guesthouse	Eco-conscious	$-$$								5			South Kona
4	Dragonfly Ranch: Healing Arts Center	Exotic island treehouse	$-$$					yes	yes		6			South Kona
8	Hale Hualalai	Outstanding breakfast	$								6		no A/C	Hōlualoa
7	Hōlualoa Inn	Beautiful interior	$$$-$$$$	1							6		no A/C	Hōlualoa
2	Kalaekilohana	Hot breakfast, cozy linens	$$								4		no A/C	Ka'u
6	Nancy's Hideaway	Lots of privacy	$								6		no A/C	Kailua-Kona

Hwy., Hōlualoa ☎ 808/326–2909
⊕ *www.hale-hualalai.com* ⤳ 2
suites ♿ *In-room: no A/C, Wi-Fi,
no room phones, refrigerators* ▭
MC, V.

$$$–$$$$
B&B/INN
▦ **Hōlualoa Inn.** Six spacious rooms
are available in this beautiful cedar
home on a 30-acre coffee-country
estate, 4 mi above Kailua Bay and
steps away from the artists' town of
Hōlualoa. The Gardenia suite, one
of the nicest here, has wraparound
windows with stunning views. A
lavish breakfast includes estate-
grown coffee as well as breakfast
treats like Punalu'u sweet bread
French toast stuffed with *liliko'i*
(passion fruit) cream cheese. There
are rooftop gazebos, a dedicated
massage pavilion, a labyrinth, and
an old donkey trail dotted with his-
toric sites if you feel like taking a stroll. **Pros:** within walking distance to
small village, well appointed with wood floors and lots of windows, pan-
oramic views. **Cons:** a bit far away from beaches and restaurants, expen-
sive for location, not kid-friendly. ✉ 76-5932 *Māmalahoa Hwy. Box
222, Hōlualoa* ☎ 808/324–1121 *or* 800/392–1812 ⊕ *www.holualoainn.
com* ⤳ 6 *rooms* ♿ *In-room: no A/C, no room TVs. In-hotel: pool* ▭ *AE,
D, DC, MC, V.*

$$$–$$$$
RESORT
▦ **Keauhou Beach Resort.** Recent renovations at this resort have gone
a long way in rejuvenating the property. The lobby and restaurant
have both gotten a face-lift and all guest rooms now have new car-
pet, furniture, and artwork. The hotel still preserves a unique part of
Hawaiian history (the grounds include a *heiau*, a sacred fishpond, and
a replica of the summer home of King David Kalākaua) and is adjacent
to Kahalu'u, one of the best snorkeling beaches on the island. There is
a complimentary trolley service into downtown Kailua-Kona, Magic
Sands Beach, Keauhou Bay, and several shopping destinations from
7:30 AM to 8 PM daily and a free, full breakfast buffet is available to
guests every morning. **Pros:** large rooms, free full breakfast daily, next
to one of the island's best snorkeling beaches. **Cons:** big price increase
since renovations, not within walking distance of downtown shops
and restaurants. ✉ 78-6740 *Ali'i Dr., Kailua-Kona* ☎ 808/322–3441
or 800/462–6262 ⊕ *www.outrigger.com* ⤳ 306 *rooms, 3 suites* ♿ *In-
room: A/C, Internet, in-room safes, refrigerators. In-hotel: restaurant,
bar, tennis courts, pool, gym, beachfront, laundry facilities, laundry
service* ▭ *AE, D, DC, MC, V.*

$$–$$$
RENTAL
▦ **Keauhou Kona Surf & Racquet Club.** This large, gated complex sits right
along the ocean, offering prime views from oceanfront units and the
pool. Condos are large, comfortable, and very well maintained. Unlike
many other complexes, Keauhou Kona has tennis courts and a very large
pool. The two-story town houses are ideal for larger groups, although

---

HAWAII ON A BUDGET

Kona Tiki Hotel (Kailua-Kona).
Oceanfront, 1950s Hawai'i motif,
all rooms have ocean views, walk-
ing distance to downtown.

Manago Hotel (South Kona).
Historic, Japanese theme, clean,
some oceanfront rooms, super
reasonable, excellent restaurant.

Nāmakani Paio Cabins (Volcano
Village). Close to the volcano,
cheap, clean, recently renovated.

Royal Kona Resort (Kailua-Kona).
Old-school Hawai'i, oceanfront,
great bar, good package deals,
close to downtown Kailua-Kona.

these are a bit more dated than the rest of the complex. **Pros:** oceanfront complex with many ocean-view units, close to harbor and golf course, tennis courts and large pool in complex. **Cons:** removed location requires drive to local restaurants, no a/c in some units. ✉ *78-6800 Ali'i Dr., Kailua-Kona* ☎ *800/799–5662 or 808/322–6696* ⊕ *www.kksrc.com* ➥ *188 units* ⚿ *In-room: A/C in some rooms, kitchen. In-hotel: tennis courts, pool, laundry facilities* ▭ *MC, V.*

$
RENTAL
⬚**Kona Magic Sands.** Cradled between two small beaches, this condo complex is great for swimmers and sunbathers in summer (the sand at Magic Sands Beach washes away in winter). Units vary because they're individually owned, but all the studios are oceanfront, spacious, and light. Some units have enclosed lānai, and all have an ocean view. **Pros:** next door to popular beach, ocean view from all units. **Cons:** studios only, some units are very dated. ✉ *77-6452 Ali'i Dr., Kailua-Kona* ☎ *808/329–9393 or 800/622–5348* ⊕ *www.konahawaii.com/ms.htm* ➥ *37 units* ⚿ *In-room: A/C in some rooms, kitchen. In-hotel: pool* ▭ *D, MC, V.*

$$
RENTAL
⬚**Kona Nalu.** One of the nicest complexes on the ocean side of Ali'i, Kona Nalu units are large and beautifully furnished with supersized lānai, and ocean views from all units. The pool is tiny, but they have a small sandy beach for lying in the sun, and the complex itself is small so you won't be fighting for pool room. **Pros:** extra-large units, ocean views. **Cons:** not within walking distance of stores or restaurants, sandy beach doesn't provide safe ocean entry. ✉ *76-6212 Ali'i Dr., Kailua-Kona* ☎ *808/329–6438* ⊕ *www.sunquest-hawaii.com* ➥ *15 units* ⚿ *In-room: A/C in some rooms, kitchen. In-hotel: pool, beachfront, laundry facilities* ▭ *MC, V.*

$
RENTAL
⬚**Kona Pacific.** Once a hotel, the Kona Pacific gives you plenty of space. The one-bedroom units, which comfortably sleep four, are the size of two large hotel rooms, with a full kitchen and usually two bathrooms. There are ocean views from the lānai of most units and the pool. This large and well-maintained complex is just at the edge of Kailua-Kona, within walking distance of shops and restaurants. If you don't feel like cooking or barbecuing by the pool, there is a Hawaiian grill serving fresh seafood and awesome 'ahi sandwiches across the street behind the complex. Note that the acceptance of credit cards varies with the unit owners. **Pros:** very large units, some with two lānai, ocean-view pool, well-maintained complex. **Cons:** some units in better shape than others, some units get noise from nearby highway. ✉ *75-5865 Walua*

KONA CONDO COMFORTS

Crossroads Shopping Center. The **Safeway** here is the cleanest, largest, and best-stocked store on the island. It's right next to **Kona Natural Foods,** so you can supplement with local organic produce, and **Coldstone Creamery.** ✉ *75-1000 Henry St., Kailua-Kona.*

Blockbuster. ✉ *Kona Coast Shopping Center, 74-5588 Palani Rd., Kailua-Kona* ☎ *808/326–7694.*

Pizza-wise, **Kona Brewing Company** ✉ *75-5629 Kuakini Hwy., just past Palani intersection on right, Kailua-Kona* ☎ *808/329–2739* is best if you can pick it up.

9

Rd., Kailua-Kona ☎ *808/329–6140* ⊕ *www.konacoastvacations.com* ⇌ *25 units* ♿ *In-room: A/C in some rooms, kitchen. In-hotel: pool.*

$

HOTEL

🛏 **Kona Tiki Hotel.** The best thing about this three-story walk-up budget hotel, about a mile south of Kailua-Kona, is that all the units have lānai right next to the ocean. The rooms are modest but pleasantly decorated. You can sunbathe by the seaside pool, where a complimentary Continental breakfast is

served. Some would call this place old-fashioned; others would say it's local, has a certain kitschy charm, and is the best deal in town, with glorious sunsets no different from those at the resorts. **Pros:** very low price, oceanfront lānai and pool, convenient location. **Cons:** older hotel in need of update, no beach, doesn't accept credit cards. ✉ *75-5968 Ali'i Dr., Kailua-Kona* ☎ *808/329–1425* ⊕ *www.konatiki.com* ⇌ *15 rooms* ♿ *In-room: no A/C, Wi-Fi, no room phones, no room TVs, refrigerators. In-hotel: pool* 🚫 *No credit cards.*

$

B&B/INN

🛏 **Nancy's Hideaway.** A few miles up the hill from Kailua-Kona, this charming cottage and studio offer modern comforts and ocean views. Each has its own entrance, a lānai, and a wet bar. The cottage stands alone; the studio is attached to the main house, but is very private. Breakfast is served in the rooms to give guests their privacy. This place is ideal for couples, but not for families with kids. **Pros:** plenty of privacy, ocean views. **Cons:** slightly inconvenient location, not kid-friendly. ✉ *73-1530 Uanani Pl., Kailua-Kona* ☎ *808/325–3132 or 866/325–3132* ⊕ *www.nancyshideaway.com* ⇌ *2 rooms* ♿ *In-room: no A/C.* 🚫 *D, MC, V.*

$$–$$$

RENTAL

🛏 **Outrigger Kanaloa at Kona.** The 16-acre grounds provide a peaceful and verdant background for this low-rise condominium complex bordering the Keauhou-Kona Country Club. It's walking distance from the golf course and within a five-minute drive of the nearest beaches (Kahalu'u and White Sands). Large one-, two-, and three-bedroom apartments have koa-wood cabinetwork and washer-dryers; oceanfront villas have private hot tubs. **Pros:** across the street from acclaimed golf course, three pools with hot tubs. **Cons:** not within walking distance of grocery store or beach, no restaurant on property. ✉ *78-261 Manukai St., Kailua-Kona* ☎ *808/322–9625, 808/322–2272, or 800/688–7444* ⊕ *www.outrigger.com* ⇌ *166 units* ♿ *In-room: A/C in some rooms, in-room safes, kitchen. In-hotel: tennis courts, pools, laundry facilities* 🚫 *AE, D, DC, MC, V.*

$$

RESORT

🛏 **Royal Kona Resort.** This is a great option if you're on a budget. The location is great, the lobby, pool, and restaurant are right on the water, and most of the hotel's large, lānai-front rooms have been recently updated from Hawaiian kitsch to a more toned-down modern take that includes neutral-tone walls, classic Hawaiian art, and bamboo headboards. The hotel is within walking distance of Kailua-Kona and across the street from numerous shops and restaurants. The weekly lū'au with Polynesian entertainment (on Monday, Wednesday, and Friday) is fun and quite popular. Make sure to book online, where the rates can be as much as 50% less than the rack rates, and select rooms in the Ali'i or Lagoon tower if you'd like a recently renovated room. **Pros:** convenient location, waterfront pool, low prices. **Cons:** oceanfront lagoon is often closed, staff are sometimes grumpy. ☒ *75-5852 Ali'i Dr., KailuaKona* ☎ *808/329–3111 or 800/222–5642* ⊕ *www.royalkona. com* ➭ *436 rooms, 8 suites* ♻ *In-room: A/C, Internet, in-room safes, refrigerators. In-hotel: restaurant, bar, tennis courts, pool, gym, spa, beachfront, laundry facilities, Internet Room* ▭ *AE, D, DC, MC, V.*

$$$
RESORT
♻ 🛏 **Sheraton Keauhou Bay Resort & Spa.** For the big-resort style of the Kohala Coast at a less astronomical price, the Sheraton is a good bet. Longtime Big Island visitors might remember it as the old Kona Surf. Sheraton took over about six years ago and went to great lengths to restore it to its former glory. The lobby, with floor-to-ceiling windows and carved marble architectural elements, is particularly stunning, and the well-designed restaurant, Kai, serves a limited but excellent menu. The only remnants of the old hotel in the bright and modern Sheraton rooms are the small and unimpressive bathrooms. On the upside, 80 % of the rooms have full ocean views and large lānai. The big selling point for those traveling with kids is the pool, which can only be described as massive and one of the coolest on the island, boasting the longest slide in the state, waterfalls, a kids area with sand, pool volleyball and basketball, and an ocean view. The resort also has a full-service, oceanfront spa (Ho'ola), a highly acclaimed new lū'au, an oceanfront wedding area, and the Manta Ray Experience, which allows guests to view manta rays nearly every night (provided the rays cooperate). **Pros:** fantastic pool, manta rays on view nightly, resort style at lower price. **Cons:** no beach, only one restaurant. ☒ *78-128 Ehukai St., Kailua-Kona* ☎ *808/930–4900* ⊕ *www.sheratonkeauhou. com* ➭ *510 rooms, 11 suites* ♻ *In-room: A/C, Internet, Wi-Fi, in-room safes, refrigerators. In-hotel: restaurant, bar, tennis courts, pool, gym, spa, water sports* ▭ *AE, D, DC, MC, V.*

$–$$
RENTAL
🛏 **Silver Oaks Guest Ranch.** These two private cottages set on a 10-acre working ranch are one of the best deals going on the west side of the island. Five miles from the airport and from Kailua-Kona, the cottages afford total privacy, with a few more amenities than a vacation house or condo. Owners Mark and Amy drop off a welcome basket with breakfast goodies your first day, and there's a washer and dryer in each unit,

---

BEST BETS FOR ROMANCE

Palms Cliff House Inn (Hāmākua Coast). Stunning views, private in-room hot tubs.

Kona Village Resort (Kohala Coast). Beautiful setting, completely private *hales*.

South Point Banyan Treehouse (Ka'ū). Tucked into a banyan tree with a hot tub on the deck.

Volcano Teapot Cottage (Volcano). Unbelievably charming, from the fireplace to the antiques to the hot tub in the back.

Waianuhea (Hāmākua Coast). Gorgeous house, hot tub, and a great wine-andhors d'oeuvres hour.

9

BIG ISLAND LODGING ALTERNATIVES

HOME EXCHANGES

If you would like to exchange your home for someone else's, join a home-exchange organization, which will send you its updated listings of available exchanges for a year and will include your own listing in at least one of them. It's up to you to make specific arrangements.

Exchange Clubs HomeLink USA (✉ 2937 NW 9th Terrace, Wilton Manors, FL ☎ 954/566–2687 or 800/638–3841 ⊕ www.homelink.org; $75 yearly for a listing and online access; an additional $45 to receive directories. **Intervac U.S** (✉ 30 Corte San Fernando, Tiburon, CA ☎ 800/756–4663 ⊕ www.intervacus. com) ;$128 yearly for a listing, online access, and a catalog; $68 without catalog.

HOSTELS

No matter what your age, you can save on lodging costs by staying at hostels. In some 4,500 locations in more than 70 countries around the world, Hostelling International (HI), the umbrella group for a number of national youth-hostel associations, offers single-sex, dorm-style beds and, at many hostels, rooms for couples and family accommodations. Membership in any HI national hostel association, open to travelers of all ages, allows you to stay in HI-affiliated hostels at member rates; one-year membership is about $28 for adults (C$35 for a two-year minimum membership in Canada, 15 in the U.K., A$52 in Australia, and NZ$40 in New Zealand); hostels charge about $10–$30 per night. Members have priority if the hostel is full; they're also eligible for discounts around the world, even on rail and bus travel in some countries.

Organizations Hostelling International–USA (✉ 8401 Colesville Rd., Suite 600, Silver Spring, MD ☎ 301/495–1240 ⊕ www.hiusa.org).

Local Resources Hilo Bay Hostel (✉ 101 Waianuenue Ave., Hilo ☎ 808/933–2771 ⊕ www. hawaiihostel.net). **Holo Holo Inn** (✉ 19-4036 Kalani Honua Rd., Volcano Village ☎ 808/967–7950 ⊕ www.enable.org/holoholo). **Koa Wood Hale Inn** (✉ 75-184 Ala Ona Ona St., Kailua-Kona ☎ 808/329–9663 ⊕ www.alternative-hawaii. com/affordable/kona.htm).

an outdoor pool and hot tub, great ocean views from your private deck, and the ranch is like a little petting zoo with horses, goats, and chickens throughout. Each cottage is stocked with a library of books and videos, various beach toys, backpacks, coolers, beach towels, binoculars, robes, hair dryers, and even snorkeling equipment. **Pros:** very private, deck with ocean views. **Cons:** five-night minimum stay, not within walking distance of stores or restaurants, dated decor. ✉ 73-4570 Māmalahoa Hwy., just north of Kaloko Dr., Kailua-Kona ☎ 877/325–2300 or 808/325–2000 ⊕ www.silveroaksranch.com ⬅2 cottages ⌂ In-room: no A/C, Wi-Fi, kitchen. In-hotel: pool, laundry facilities ☰ MC, V.

SOUTH KONA AND KA'Ū

There are no resorts in this area, but there are plenty of fantastic bed-and-breakfasts and inns around Kealakekua Bay and some great deals to be had on vacation condos and homes in the hills above the bay. The main attraction here *is* the bay, where kayaking and snorkeling are superb. The towns of Captain Cook and Kainaliu provide some excellent dining and shopping options, and there are dozens of coffee farms open for tours as well. You can get to the volcano in about an hour. It's a nice place to stay if you want to be out of the fray, but the drawback is that there are no beaches in this area. The "beach" by Kealakekua Bay is all rocks, although the bay is great for a swim; Kailua-Kona area beaches are a 15- to 30-minute drive, and the sandy Kohala Coast is an hour or more away.

$–$$
B&B/INN

Aloha Guesthouse. In the hills above Kealakekua Bay, Aloha Guesthouse offers quiet elegance, complete privacy, and ocean views from every room. With a focus on nature, the house is furnished in earth tones. The bath products are 100% organic, and the yummy full breakfasts are as close to organic as they can muster. Common areas include a kitchenette for guests who want to cook their own meals, as well as a DVD library and a computer with high-speed Internet. **Pros:** eco-conscious, full breakfast, views of Kealakekua Bay. **Cons:** remote location, no grocery stores or restaurants within walking distance. ⊠ *Old Tobacco Rd., off Hwy. 11 near mile marker 104, Captain Cook 96704* ☎ *808/328–8955* ⊕ *www.alohaguesthouse.com* 🛏 *5 rooms* ⚴ *In-room: A/C, Wi-Fi, refrigerators, in-room DVD players. In-hotel: Internet Room* ⊟ *AE, MC, V.*

$–$$
B&B/INN

Dragonfly Ranch: Healing Arts Center. A unique, slightly hippie-ish hideaway built into the trees of Hōnaunau (about 10 mi south of Kealakekua Bay), the Dragonfly is not for everyone, but for some it is paradise. Dubbed as a green eco-spa, this remarkable jungle tree house brings the outside in, with screened walls and sliding glass mirrored doors everywhere, lots of open-air sitting areas, and plants and flowers galore. The ranch doubles as a Healing Arts Center, and food is prepared from the ranch's organic garden. A labyrinth walk, far-infrared sauna, and *lomilomi* massages are available, as are other spa amenities and dolphin swims (they take you to the bay to "commune respectfully with dolphins"). There's even a variety of musical instruments in the front room for anyone to play. **Pros:** unique in every way, emphasis on health, dolphin swims. **Cons:** can be a little New Agey, prices are high for location and vibe. ✆ *Box 675, Honaunau off Hwy. 160, Captain Cook 96726* ☎ *808/328–2159* ⊕ *www.dragonflyranch.com* 🛏 *2 rooms, 3 suites, 1 3-bedroom cottage* ⚴ *In-room: A/C, Wi-Fi* ⊟ *MC, V.*

$$
B&B/INN

Kalaekilohana. You wouldn't really expect to find a top-notch bed-and-breakfast in Ka'ū, but just up the road from South Point, this charming yellow house offers large, comfortable private suites with beautifully restored hardwood floors, private lānai with ocean and mountain views, and big, comfy beds decked out with high-thread-count sheets and fluffy down comforters. Choose between a full hot breakfast or a Continental breakfast of local fruits and baked goods—both come with plenty of

9

award-winning local Ka'ū estate coffee. For those who want to explore the area's green- and black-sand beaches, or hike the south side of Volcanoes National Park (the newly opened south entrance is less than 2 mi away), hosts Kenny Joyce and Kilohana Domingo are happy to share their knowledge of the area. The bed-and-breakfast prides itself on its programs and work surrounding Hawaiian cultural arts, and guests are welcome to take part in lei-making workshops and other lessons in traditional Hawaiian handicrafts. **Pros:** luxurious beds, beautifully restored house, delicious breakfast. **Cons:** not for children under 10, no pool. ⊠ *94-2152 South Point Rd., Na'alehu* ☎ *808/939–8052* ⊕ *www. kau-hawaii.com* ⬧ *4 rooms* ⚷ *In-room: no A/C, Internet. In-hotel: laundry facilities* ▭ *MC, V.*

¢ 🏠 **Manago Hotel.** This historic hotel is a good option if you want to escape the touristy thing but still be close to everything on the island. Don't let the front TV room creep you out—you have not checked into an old folks' home. The place has an authentic Hawai'i vibe, and the restaurant is one of the best on the island. Dwight Manago—whose grandparents, Kinzo and Osame Manago, built the main building in 1917—has maintained one Japanese-style room with tatami mats and a *furo*, a traditional Japanese bath, and this is the room to book. The other rooms are nothing special, but they're clean, and those in the newer wing have great views high above the Kona Coast. **Pros:** local color, rock-bottom prices, terrific on-site restaurant. **Cons:** a bit run-down, not the best sound insulation between rooms. ⊠ *81-6155 Māmalahoa Hwy. Box 145, Captain Cook* ☎ *808/323–2642* ⊕ *www. managohotel.com* ⬧ *64 rooms, 42 with bath* ⚷ *In-room: no A/C, no in-room phones, no room TVs. In-hotel: restaurant* ▭ *D, MC, V.*

HOTEL

$$ 🏠 **South Point Banyan Tree House.** Ideal for romance, this charming little tree cottage is built into a Chinese banyan tree. The partially transparent roof is the world's greatest skylight, letting in lots of light and offering views of the beautiful tree canopy above. A wraparound deck with a hot tub provides one of the best places on the island to watch the sunset. Ask about special rates when booking. **Pros:** secluded and romantic, interesting architecture, hot tub with a view. **Cons:** remote location, not within walking distance to grocery store or restaurants, no pool or beach. ⊠ *Hwy. 11 at Pinao St., Waiohinu (near South Point)* ☎ *715/212–9946 or 808/217–2504* ⊕ *www.southpointbth.com* ⬧ *1 cottage* ⚷ *In-room: no A/C, kitchen. In-hotel: laundry facilities* ▭ *MC, V.*

RENTAL

KOHALA

The Kohala Coast is home to all of the Big Island's megaresorts. One after the other, manicured lawns and golf courses, luxurious hotels, and white-sand beaches break up the long expanse of black lava rock along the northwest coast. Many visitors to the Big Island check in here and rarely leave, except to try the restaurants, spas, or golf courses at neighboring resorts. If you're looking to be pampered (for a price!) and lounge on the beach or by the pool all day with an umbrella drink in hand, this is where you need to be. That's not to say that staying in Kohala makes it difficult to see the rest of the island. On the contrary,

CONDOS AND VACATION RENTALS

Renting a condo or vacation house gives you much more room than the average hotel, the chance to meet more people (neighbors are usually friendly, kids always hang together at the pool), lower nightly rates, and the option of cooking or barbecuing some nights rather than eating out. When booking, remember that most are individually owned, and most owners outsource the rental process to property management companies. A handful of property management and rental agencies handle the bulk of condo and vacation home rentals on the Big Island, and their Web sites are the best places to look for rentals. Following is a list of our favorites for various lodging types throughout the island. Be sure to call and ask questions before booking, even if the pictures online are *real purdy.*

Abbey Vacation Rentals (⊕ *www. waikoloarentals.com*) has luxury condos on the Kohala Coast.

Big Island Villas (⊕ *www. bigislandvillas.com*) lists a variety of condos attached to the Four Seasons Hualālai, Mauna Kea, and Mauna Lani resorts.

CJ Kimberly Realty (⊕ *www. cjkimberly.com*) offers fantastic deals on some oceanfront homes and condos.

Hawaiian Beach Rentals (⊕ *www. hawaiianbeachrentals.com*) and **Tropical Villa Vacations** (⊕ *www. tropicalvillavacations.com*) are excellent for high-end, ocean- or beachfront homes.

Hawai'i Vacation Rentals (⊕ *www. vacationbigisland.com*) lists several properties on the beach in Puako, a sleepy beach settlement just up the road from the Kohala coast resorts.

Keauhou Property Management (⊕ *www.konacondo.net*) has condos along the Kona coast, just south of Kailua-Kona around Keauhou Bay.

Kolea Vacations (⊕ *www. koleavacations.com*) lists dozens of condos at the Kolea at Waikoloa complex as well as a stunning oceanfront home on Ali'i in Kailua-Kona.

Kona Coast Vacations (⊕ *www. konacoastvacations.com*) offers a large variety of condos on the west side of the island and wins high marks for good service.

Kona Hawai'i Vacation Rentals (⊕ *www.konahawaii.com*) offers very affordable condos in Kailua-Kona.

Knutson and Associates (⊕ *www. konahawaiirentals.com*) handles rentals for a wide variety of Kailua-Kona condos and oceanfront vacation homes.

Property Network (☎ 808/329–7977 ⊕ *www.hawaii-kona.com*) lists and manages dozens of condo rentals in and around Kailua-Kona.

Rent Hawai'i Home (⊕ *www. renthawaiihome.com*) offers several affordable cottage and beach house rentals, ideal for those who are staying for a while and want some room/privacy, but don't want to spend half a year's salary on a beachfront palace.

South Kohala Management (⊕ *www.southkohala.com*) lists a wide variety of luxury Kohala Coast condos.

Vacation Rental By Owner (⊕ *www.vrbo.com*) has homes and condos for rent all over the island.

9

Four Seasons Resort Hualālai

most of the hiking and adventure tour companies on the island offer pickups at the Kohala resorts, and many of the hotels have deals with various rental car agencies so you can be as active or lazy as you like.

Along the Kohala Coast, most of the available condos are associated with the resorts and can be booked through the resorts' reservations desks. There are, however, a couple of nearby housing developments that have vacation homes for rent. Most owners let a local property management company do the work, but some prefer to handle it themselves, through Web sites like Vacation Rental By Owner ⊕ *www.vrbo. com*. Nothing in this area will be bad in terms of proximity to the beach, restaurants, airport, and good weather, but double-check that the home is located on the coast and not in North Kohala (North Kohala is beautiful, but wetter and more rain forest–like than the coast). Be sure to ask about things like parking, pools, and cleaning deposits.

$$$$
RESORT
Fairmont Orchid Hawai'i. The Fairmont is a megaresort in every sense of the word—huge, crowded, expensive, and with grand staircases, domed ceilings, chandeliers, and marble everywhere. If you're looking for a unique, intimate experience, this is not your hotel, but with its antiques and 32 acres of beachfront gardens, the Orchid provides the perfect old-school hotel experience for some. Its restaurants are also among the best on the island, with a large variety of options ranging from sushi to modern Hawaiian cuisine to an upscale steak house. A one-time $65 per adult/$50 per child activity-pass, good for your entire stay, gets you access to all sorts of classes, equipment rentals, and various other amenities. The resort also offers hour-long Beach Boy outrigger canoe adventures or, if you're looking for a workout with a view, try the stand-up paddleboarding. The "Gold Floor" of the hotel includes free breakfast and a daily wine-and-hors d'oeuvres hour, a deal that is useful if you can't start your day without a big breakfast. **Pros:** oceanfront location, great restaurants. **Cons:** mammoth resort lacks personal feel, outdated room decor. ⊠ *1 N. Kanikū Dr., Kohala Coast* ☎ *808/885–2000 or 800/845–9905* ⊕ *www.fairmont.com* ⇘ *486 rooms, 54 suites* ⚐ *In-room: A/C, Wi-Fi, in-room safes. In-hotel: 4 restaurants, bars, golf courses, tennis courts, pool, gym, spa, beachfront, water sports, children's programs (ages 5–12)* ☐ *AE, D, DC, MC, V.*

$$$$
Fodor's Choice
★
RESORT
Four Seasons Resort Hualālai. Beautiful views everywhere, polished wood floors, brand-new furnishings and linens in warm earth and cool white tones, and Hawaiian artwork make Hualālai a peaceful retreat. Ground-level rooms have outdoor garden showers. Bungalows are large and cozy, with down comforters and spacious slate-floor bathrooms. One of the five pools, called King's Pond, is a brackish pond with loads of fish and two manta rays that guests have the opportunity to feed daily. The main infinity pool looks like something out of an ad for an expensive liquor—it's long and peaceful, surrounded by cabanas and palm trees with a clear view to the ocean beyond. The on-site Hawaiian Cultural Center honors the grounds' spiritual heritage, and the sports club and spa offer top-rate health and fitness options. Hualālai's golf course hosts the Senior PGA Tournament of Champions. Despite its quiet luxury, the resort is also super kid-friendly, with a great activities program, and a few pool options for families. The property is beautiful,

9

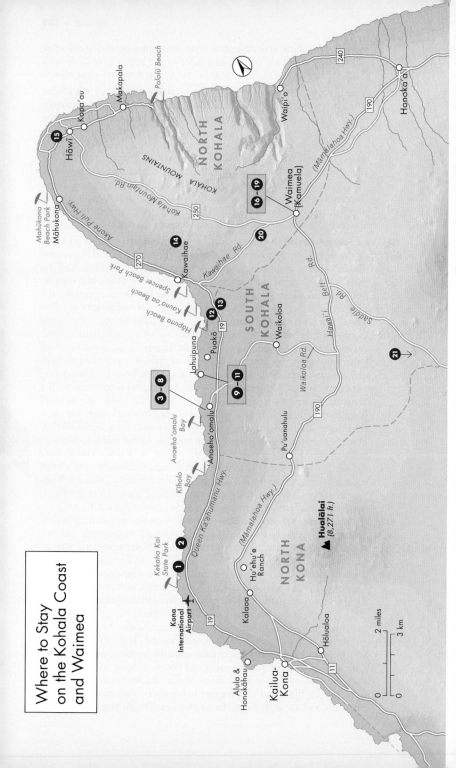

Where to Stay
on the Kohala Coast
and Waimea

WHERE TO STAY ON THE KOHALA COAST AND WAIMEA

Hotels & Resorts

	Property Name	Worth Noting	Cost $	Pools	Beach	Golf Course	Tennis Courts	Gym	Spa	Children's Programs	Rooms	Restaurants	Other	Location
9	Fairmont Orchid Hawai'i	Massages on the beach	$$$$	1	yes	yes	10	yes	yes	5-12	540	4	shops	South Kohala
1 ★	Four Seasons Hualālai	King's Pond snorkeling	$$$$	5	yes	yes	8	yes	yes	5-12	274	3		North Kona
12	Hāpuna Beach Prince	Fantastic beach	$$$$	1	yes	yes	13	yes	yes	5-12	350	5		South Kohala
3	Hilton Waikoloa Village	Dolphin Quest program	$$$-$$$$	3	yes	yes	8	yes	yes	5-12	1297	10	shops	Waikoloa
2 ★★	Kona Village Resort	2 lū'au options	$$$$	2	yes	yes	3	yes	yes	6-17	125	2	no A/C	North Kona
13	Mauna Kea Beach Hotel	Amazing design; fantastic beach	$$$$	1	yes	yes	11	yes	yes	5-12	258	3	shops	South Kohala
10	Mauna Lani Bay Hotel	Renowned golf & spa	$$$$	1	yes	yes	16	yes	yes	5-12	350	8		South Kohala
4	Waikoloa Beach Marriott	Great deal for location	$$$-$$$$	1	yes	yes	6	yes	yes	5-12	545	1		Waikoloa
18	Waimea Country Lodge	Includes breakfast	$								21		no A/C	Waimea

Condos & Vacation Rentals

	Property Name	Worth Noting	Cost $	Pools	Beach	Golf Course	Tennis Courts	Gym	Spa	Children's Programs	Rooms	Restaurants	Other	Location
19	Aloha Vacation Cottages	Private, close to beach	$		yes						2		no A/C	Waimea
11	Mauna Lani Point, Islands	Waterfall pool	$$$$	1		priv.					61		kitchens	South Kohala
5	Outrigger Fairway Villas	Infinity pool, gym	$$$-$$$$	1				yes			80		kitchens	Waikoloa
6	Outrigger Kolea at Waikoloa	Infinity pool, kids pool	$$$$	2				yes			70		kitchens	Waikoloa
7	ResortQuest Shores at Waikoloa	Great package deals	$$$-$$$$	1			2	yes			75		kitchens	Waikoloa
8	Vista Waikoloa	2 lānai per unit	$$$	1			1	yes			70		kitchens	Waikoloa
	Waimea Gardens Cottage	Mountainside stream	$								3		kitchens	Waimea

B&Bs & Inns

	Property Name	Worth Noting	Cost $	Pools	Beach	Golf Course	Tennis Courts	Gym	Spa	Children's Programs	Rooms	Restaurants	Other	Location
20	Aaah, The Views!	Streamside, those views	$								4		kitchens	Waimea
14	Hale Ho'onanea	Great deal	$								3		no A/C	Kawaihae
17	Jacaranda Inn	Good breakfast, big rooms	$$-$$$								9		no A/C	Waimea
15	Hawaii Island Retreat at Ahu Pohaku Ho'omaluhia	Eco-resort	$$$-$$$$								9		no A/C, no phone, no TV	Waimea

the restaurants are fantastic (the new Beach Tree has the ultimate al fresco dining and Pahui'a serves up the best beachfront Sunday brunch on the island), the rooms are more than comfortable, and the service is definitely of Four Seasons quality. **Pros:** beautiful location, island's best restaurants. **Cons:** can be noisy poolside, pricey. ⊠ *72-100 Ka'ūpūlehu Dr.* 🏠 *Box 1269, Kailua-Kona 96745* ☎ *808/325–8000, 800/819–5053, or 888/340–5662* ⊕ *www.fourseasons.com/hualalai* ⤴ *243 rooms, 51 suites* 🔥 *In-room: A/C, Internet, Wi-Fi, in-room safes, in-room DVD players. In-hotel: 3 restaurants, room service, bars, golf course, tennis courts, pools, gym, spa, beachfront, children's programs (ages 5–12), laundry service* ⊟ *AE, DC, D, MC, V.*

$

B&B/INN

🏠 **Hale Ho'onanea.** A comfortable home with three detached guest suites, this 3-acre property in the Kohala Estates lives up to the English translation of its name, "House of Relaxation." From its bluff above the ocean, you can watch the sun rise over Mauna Kea and set over the Pacific, and view the sparkling beauty of Hawai'i's night sky. It's minutes away from dining and shopping at Waimea and the attractions of the Kohala Coast. The rooms are comfortable and spacious and the price is a steal at less than half the nightly rate of the Kohala Coast resorts. Continental breakfast is included. There's a two-night minimum if you book less than a week in advance; a $25 fee applies to single-night bookings made within seven days of arrival. **Pros:** detached suites for maximum privacy, panoramic ocean views from private lānai, good price for the neighborhood. **Cons:** not within walking distance to restaurants, no pool. ⊠ *Kohala Estates, 59-513 Ala Kahua Dr., Kawaihae* ☎ *808/882–1653 or 877/882–1653* ⊕ *www.houseofrelaxation.com* ⤴ *3 suites* 🔥 *In-room: no A/C, kitchen* ⊟ *MC, V.*

$$$$

🕐

RESORT

🏠 **Hāpuna Beach Prince Hotel.** Often more reasonably priced than its neighbors, thanks to a variety of ongoing discount options, the Hāpuna Beach Prince is no less luxurious and happens to be sitting on a corner of one of the best beaches on the island. Initially designed with business travelers in mind, rooms at the Hāpuna Prince are spacious, with large marble bathrooms and plenty of in-room amenities. However, the generous rooms and beachfront location have turned the hotel into more of a family vacation destination than a business hotel, which means that couples seeking a romantic getaway might be disappointed by the number of kids playing Marco Polo at the pool. Still, the place is large enough to escape from other guests if you so desire, and the staff is exceedingly helpful. The golf course, designed by Arnold Palmer and Ed Seay, has topped many a "best courses" list and was recently named one of the most women-friendly courses in the world (what that means, we're still trying to figure out). A hiking trail and a frequent shuttle connect Hāpuna with its sister hotel, the Mauna Kea Beach Hotel, with access to yet another great beach. After a day in the sun, get pampered with a massage or facial at the Paul Brown Salon and Spa. **Pros:** extra-large rooms, full or partial ocean views from most rooms, direct access to one of island's best beaches. **Cons:** tons of kids around the pool can make it noisy, restaurant standards have been slipping lately. ⊠ *62-100 Kauna'oa Dr., Kohala Coast* ☎ *808/880–1111 or 800/882–6060* ⊕ *www.princeresortshawaii.com* ⤴ *314 rooms, 36 suites* 🔥 *In-room: A/C, Internet, refrigerators.*

In-hotel: 5 restaurants, bars, golf course, tennis courts, pool, gym, spa, beachfront, children's programs (ages 5–12) ☐ AE, D, DC, MC, V.

$$$–$$$$
Fodor's Choice
★
B&B/INN

🖼 **Hawaii Island Retreat at Ahu Pohaku Hoʻomaluhia.** Ahu Pohaku is set above the cliffs of North Kohala near Pololū valley. The retreat generates its own solar power, uses a water catchment tank, and grows almost all of its own food. Beautiful hardwood floors are built from sustainably harvested woods, and rooms take advantage of natural light and ventilation to keep energy usage low. Surrounded by 60 acres, 20 of which are a dedicated conservation area, the retreat feels both luxurious and completely hidden from the world. Rooms are large and bright, with ocean views and brightly colored walls. Most have private balconies, and all are equipped with large bathrooms that include both soaking tubs and showers. Sustainability meets luxury here without sacrificing comfort. The owners added seven luxury yurts during a recent renovation and a full-service spa in 2008. A van shuttles guests to and from the airport, into nearby Kapaʻau or Hāwī, or out to the beaches. Three meals a day are prepared from the retreat's garden supply, augmented by additions from local farms. Ahu Pohaku's owners even make their own creamy and delicious goat cheese. **Pros:** stunning location, new and beautiful construction with no expense spared, eco-friendly. **Cons:** not within walking distance of restaurants, no pool, off the beaten path. ⊠ *Follow signs off Hwy. 270 in Kapaʻau, North Kohala* ☎ *808/889–6336* ⊕ *www.hawaii-island-retreat.com* 🛏 *9 rooms* ⟁ *In-room: no A/C, no phone, no room TVs. In-hotel: restaurant* ☐ *AE, MC, V.*

$$$–$$$$
♻
RESORT

🖼 **Hilton Waikoloa Village.** Dolphins chirp in the lagoon; a pint-size daredevil zooms down the 175-foot waterslide; a bride poses on the grand staircase; a fire-bearing runner lights the torches along the seaside path at sunset—these are some of the scenes that may greet you at this 62-acre playground of a resort. Shaded pathways lined with a multimillion-dollar Pacific Island art collection connect the three tall buildings; Swiss-made trams and Disney-engineered boats shuttle those weary of the long hallways and meandering paths. In another nod to Disney, employees access the various areas of the resort via underground tunnels. **The stars of Dolphin Quest** (⊠ *800/248–3316* ⊕ *www.dolphinquest.org*) **are the resort's pride and joy; reserve in advance for an interactive learning session.** Though there's no ocean beach, there is a seaside trail to ʻAnaehoʻomalu Bay, aka A-Bay, one of the island's most pleasant beaches. A man-made sand beach borders the 4-acre resort lagoon. Modern rooms in neutral

KOHALA CONDO COMFORTS

There are fewer stores and take-out options on the Kohala Coast than elsewhere on the island, but, as the condos are all associated with resorts, most of your needs will be met. If you require anything not provided by the management, both the **Kings' Shops** (⊠ *250 Waikoloa Beach Dr., Waikoloa* ☎ *808/886–8811*) and the **Queens' Marketplace** (⊠ *201 Waikoloa Beach Dr., Waikoloa* ☎ *808/886–8822*) in the Waikoloa Beach Resort are good places to go. There is a small grocery store, a liquor store, and a couple of decent takeout options at the Kings' Shops.

9

tones have private lānai and are large enough to accommodate the families that flock here. In addition to the resort's assortment of restaurants, the nearby Kings' Shops and Queens' Marketplace offer further options, plus there's a small grocery store for picnic provisions. Be sure to leave your room with plenty of time before any appointment, or you'll learn to appreciate the size of this place as you sprint past the tram. ■TIP→ Brides-to-be, take note: this is one-stop shopping, as the resort has a wedding-planning office, cakes, flowers, photography, and even fireworks and a "Just Married" boat ride. **Pros:** a kid's idea of paradise, lots of restaurant and activity options. **Cons:** gigantic, crowded, and often noisy; restaurants are pricey. ⊠ *425 Waikoloa Beach Dr., Waikoloa* ☎ *808/886–1234 or 800/445–8667* ⊕ *www.hiltonwaikoloavillage.com* ❧ *1,182 rooms, 58 suites* ⚑ *In-room: A/C, Internet, in-room safes, refrigerators. In-hotel: 10 restaurants, room service, bars, golf courses, tennis courts, pools, gym, spa, beachfront, water sports, children's programs (ages 2-9), laundry facilities, laundry service* ▭ *AE, D, DC, MC, V.*

$$$$
Fodor's Choice
★
RESORT

🖼 **Kona Village Resort.** The most Hawaiian of the Kohala Coast resorts, Kona Village was one of the first, and it makes a real effort to keep modern life at bay. Without phones, televisions, or radios, the Kona Village is in a time warp—the perfect place for couples or families to get away from it all in their own thatch-roof *hale* (house) near the resort's sandy beach. Built on the grounds of an ancient Hawaiian village, the bungalows reflect styles of South Seas cultures—Tahitian, Samoan, Maori, Fijian, or Hawaiian. Most oceanfront *hale* have private hot tubs. Some of the bungalows are oceanfront, some are nestled around the ancient Hawaiian fishing lagoon, and no matter where your *hale* is and how crowded the resort is, you'll feel as if this is your own little hideaway. The other bonus about Kona Village that sets it apart from many of the other resorts is that it tends to attract repeat customers for decades, and it retains its staff for equally as long, which breeds a very comfortable vibe around the resort. The beach here is small, but idyllic, with sea turtles nesting in the sand around a calm, turquoise bay. Rates include all meals, an authentic Polynesian Wednesday- or Friday-night lū'au, grounds tours, tennis, and sports activities. The resort's ocean program has recently been expanded to include sea kayaking, outrigger canoe paddling, stand-up paddleboarding, scuba diving on a new boat that can accommodate up to six divers, and snorkeling excursions. ■TIP→ Children's programs are not available in portions of May or September, which are designated "adults-only" months, so if you're planning a honeymoon to Hawai'i and want to stay at Kona Village, May or September is a good choice. **Pros:** detached bungalows afford ultimate privacy, sea

Kona Village Resort

Hawaii Island Retreat at Ahu Pohaku Ho'omaluhia

turtles nest on the resort's private beach, all meals and many activities included. **Cons:** somewhat isolated location, no phones in rooms. ✉ *Queen Ka'ahumanu Hwy., Box 1299, Kailua-Kona* ☎ *808/325–5555 or 800/367–5290* ⊕ *www.konavillage.com* ⇆ *125 bungalows* ⌂ *Inroom: no A/C, no room phones, no room TVs. In-hotel: 2 restaurants, bars, tennis courts, pools, gym, spa, beachfront, children's programs (ages 5–12).* ☰ *AE, D, MC, V.*

$$$$
Fodor's Choice
★

Mauna Kea Beach Hotel. The grande dame of Kohala Coast, the Mauna Kea Beach Hotel was designed by Laurance S. Rockefeller in the early 1960s and opened in 1965. It has long been regarded as one of the world's premier vacation resort hotels, and it borders one of the island's finest white-sand beaches, Kauna'oa. The Mauna Kea was damaged in the earthquake of October 2006, but $150 million in renovations not only restored the property to its original glory, it also increased the hotel's luxury status tenfold. Many guest rooms have almost doubled in size and include allnew furnishings and artwork, as well as a built-in entertainment center with a large flat-screen TV. The bathrooms are large and luxurious and come with L'Occitane bath amenities you won't want to leave behind. You might never want to rise from your plush bed, but you should because Mauna Kea Beach Hotel has much to offer, including an 18-hole championship golf course, the Seaside Tennis Club, and a fitness center with daily classes. If all you want to do is relax, there's the first-rate Mandara spa, a freshwater swimming pool, and lots of comfy lounge chairs on the beach, which, incidentally, is a perfect crescent of sand and sea that will wash all your cares away. Despite the amenities, however, this place is far from formal and stuffy. More appropriately, it's casually elegant. You will have to stay a few nights to really appreciate all the property has to offer, including its signature Manta & Pavilion Wine Bar, which showcases Kohala regional cuisine paired with an Enomatic wine system that dispenses 48 different wines by the glass. There's also a lavish brunch, a weekly lū'au, and a popular clambake under the stars. The hotel has two wings: the Main and the Plumeria Beach. The latter is great for families because ground-floor units allow children to wake up and run right out to the beach. **Pros:** beachfront, extra-large updated rooms, excellent restaurants. **Cons:** no supermarkets or shopping centers within walking distance, no nightlife nearby. *808/880–3112* ✉ *62-100 Mauna Kea Beach Dr., Kohala Coast* ☎ *808/882–7222 or 800/882–6060* ⊕ *www.princeresortshawaii.com* ⇆ *258 rooms, 10 suites* ⌂ *In-room: A/C, Internet, in-room safes, refrigerators. In-hotel: 4 restaurants, bars, golf courses, tennis courts, pool, gym, spa, beachfront, water sports, children's programs (ages 5–12), laundry service* ☰ *AE, D, DC, MC, V.*

$$$$
RESORT

Mauna Lani Bay Hotel & Bungalows. A Kohala Coast classic, popular with honeymooners and anniversary couples for decades, the elegant Mauna Lani is still one of the most beautiful resorts on the island. The open-air lobby has ceilings near the stratosphere, ocean views, and a constant, pleasant breeze. The vast majority of the large, recently renovated rooms have ocean views, and all have a large lānai. The resort is known for its two spectacular golf courses and award-winning spa. The award-winning, on-site Canoe House restaurant has been highly acclaimed for years and makes for a beautiful dining experience (open-air, right on the beach, tons of beautiful koa wood and candlelight), but the other restaurants in the resort are just so-so. **Pros:** beautiful design, award-winning spa, each room has a large private lānai. **Cons:** some so-so restaurants, lacks kid-friendly features. ⊠ *68-1400 Mauna Lani Dr., Kohala Coast* ☎ *808/885–6622 or 800/367–2323* ⊕ *www.maunalani. com* ⬮ *324 rooms, 14 suites, 5 bungalows* ⬦ *In-room: A/C, Wi-Fi, in-room safes, refrigerators, in-room DVD players. In-hotel: 3 restaurants, bars, golf courses, tennis courts, pool, gym, spa, beachfront, children's programs (ages 5–12), Internet Room* ⊟ *AE, D, DC, MC, V.*

\$\$\$\$
RENTAL
▦ **Mauna Lani Point Villas and The Islands of Mauna Lani Condominiums.** Surrounded by the emerald greens of a world-class ocean-side golf course, the spacious two-story suites at Islands of Mauna Lani offer a private, independent home away from home. The privately owned units, individually decorated according to the owners' tastes, have European cabinets and oversize soaking tubs in the main bedrooms. The pool has a little waterfall. The Mauna Lani Point villas are closer to the beach, which means they're priced a little higher, but an ocean view from the lānai of most units may be worth it. A number of celebrities have booked vacations here to escape the media glare. Whether you choose to stay closer to the golf course at Mauna Lani Point, or to the beach at Mauna Lani Terrace, you're just a short distance from The Shops at Mauna Lani where you can shop, dine, or stock up your kitchen with gourmet groceries from Foodland Farms. **Pros:** privacy, soaking tubs, extra-large units. **Cons:** can get very pricey, no access to nearby resort amenities. ⊠ *68-1050 Mauna Lani Point Dr., Kohala Coast* ☎ *808/885–5022 or 800/642–6284* ⊕ *www.classicresorts.com* ⬮ *61 units* ⬦ *In-room: A/C, kitchen. In-hotel: pool* ⊟ *AE, MC, V.*

\$\$\$–\$\$\$\$
RENTAL
▦ **Outrigger Fairway Villas at Waikoloa.** These large and comfy town houses just off the fairway of the Waikoloa golf course are a short walk from ʻAnaehoʻomalu Bay. The Fairway Villas, designed in the style of plantation-era homes, are decorated with rattan furniture and cozy earth tones. Unlike most of the other condominium complexes there is a uniformity to the Fairway Villas—units are individually owned, but all are managed by Outrigger, which means they are all decorated and laid out similarly. The villas have their own infinity pool, a lava-rock whirlpool spa, and a small gym right next to the pool. Guests do not have access to the fitness or pool facilities at the neighboring Hilton Waikoloa Village, but they are welcome at the spa, restaurants, shops, and grounds. **Pros:** good location for beach and golf, infinity pool, kid-friendly. **Cons:** don't have complete use of resort facilities, no 1-bedroom units. ⊠ *Waikoloa Beach Resort, 69-200 Pohakulana Pl., Waikoloa* ☎ *808/886–0036* ⊕ *www.outrigger.com* ⬮ *80 units* ⬦ *In-room: A/C, kitchen. In-hotel: pool, gym, laundry facilities, Internet Room* ⊟ *AE, D, DC, MC, V.*

\$\$\$\$
RENTAL
▦ **Outrigger Kolea at Waikoloa.** One of the latest upscale condo developments to join the Waikoloa Beach Resort, Kolea is aiming to capture the very high-end crowd typically associated with the Mauna Lani and Four Seasons. These fairly new condos are impeccably furnished and turned out, views from each unit's lānai are spectacular, and the complex is

9

closer to the beach than any of the others in this area. Kolea also offers far more amenities than the average condo complex, with both an infinity pool and a kids' pool at their ocean-side Beach Club, a fitness center, and a lava-rock hot tub. **Pros:** high design, close to beach and activities, resort amenities. **Cons:** pricey, no on-property restaurants. ⊠ *Waikoloa Beach Resort, 69-289 Waikoloa Beach Dr., Waikoloa* ☎ *808/886–0036* ⊕ *www.outrigger.com* ↻ *70 units* ⚹ *In-room: A/C, in-room DVD players, kitchen. In-hotel: pools, gym* ☰ *AE, D, DC, MC, V.*

$$$–$$$$ 🏠 **ResortQuest Shores at Waikoloa.** Villas with red-tile roofs are set amid
RENTAL   landscaped lagoons and waterfalls at the edge of the championship Waikoloa Village Golf Course. The spacious villas and condo units—the ground floor and upper floor are available separately—are privately owned, so furnishings vary from unit to unit. Sliding glass doors open onto large lānai. Picture windows look out onto rolling green fairways. All units have complete kitchens with washer-dryers, and come with maid service. Check the Web site for deals; separate rates are quoted for online booking, and they often advertise specials exclusively on their Web site. ResortQuest also offers a variety of air-inclusive packages, which can be a great deal. You'll pay more for a room with a view of the golf course. **Pros:** good prices, great location, fully self-sufficient condos with maid service. **Cons:** no access to resort amenities, fee for Internet access. ⊠ *69-1035 Keana Pl., Waikoloa* ☎ *808/886–5001 or 800/922–7866* ⊕ *www.resortquesthawaii.com* ↻ *80 units* ⚹ *In-room: A/C, Internet, kitchen. In-hotel: tennis courts, pool, gym, laundry facilities* ☰ *AE, D, DC, MC, V.*

$$$ 🏠 **Vista Waikoloa.** Older and more reasonably priced than most of
RENTAL   the condo complexes along the Kohala Coast, the two-bedroom, two-bath Vista condos offer ocean views and a great value for this part of the island. All are large and well-appointed, with two lānai per unit, plus they are within walking distance to A-Bay, the Kings' Shops and Queens' Marketplace at Waikoloa, and the restaurants and amenities of the Hilton Waikoloa, and within short driving distance of the airport, other resorts, and a variety of Big Island sights. **Pros:** centrally located, reasonably priced, very large units, newly renovated 75-foot lap pool. **Cons:** hit-or-miss on decor because each unit is individually owned, some owners charge (refundable) security deposits. ⊠ *Waikoloa Beach Resort, 69-1010 Keana Pl., Waikoloa* ☎ *808/886–3594* ⊕ *www. waikoloarentals.com* ↻ *122 units* ⚹ *In-room: A/C, kitchen. In-hotel: pool, gym, laundry facilities, Internet Room* ☰ *AE, MC, V.*

$$$–$$$$ 🏠 **Waikoloa Beach Marriott.** The most affordable resort on the Kohala
RESORT   Coast, the Waikoloa Beach Marriott covers 15 acres and encompasses ancient fishponds, historic trails, and petroglyph fields. All the Marriott's rooms have low-slung, sleek modern beds, bright white linens, Hawaiian art, and private lānai. The new pool area has three separate pools—a heated infinity pool, a pool with a partial sand bottom for kids, and one with a waterslide for the young and young-at-heart. Dining is not the hotel's strong suit but its Hawaii Calls Restaurant & Lounge has weekly food specials including entrée discounts on specified nights. In addition, there are tons of restaurants within walking distance at the Kings' Shops and Queens' Marketplace. The hotel's Mandara

Spa offers a full range of treatments in a spacious new wellness center. Bordering the white-sand beach of 'Anaeho'omalu Bay, the hotel has a range of ocean activities, including stand-up paddleboards, hydro-bikes, kayaks, and wedding-vow renewals on a catamaran. **Pros:** great location at a great price, brand-new hotel, well-designed interiors. **Cons:** no standout restaurants, nothing particularly Hawaiian about it. ⊠ 69-275 Waikoloa Beach Dr., Waikoloa ☎ 808/886–6789 or 800/688–7444 ⊕ www.marriott.com ⤴ 523 rooms, 22 suites ♿ In-room: A/C, Internet, refrigerators. In-hotel: restaurant, bars, golf courses, tennis courts, pool, gym, spa, beachfront, children's programs (ages 5–12), laundry facilities ⊟ AE, D, DC, MC, V.

WAIMEA

Though it seems a world away, Waimea is only about a 15- to 20-minute drive from the Kohala Coast resorts, which means it takes roughly the same amount of time to get to the Island's best beaches from Waimea as it does from Kailua-Kona. Yet, few visitors think to book lodging in this pleasant upcountry village, where cool mornings and evenings are enjoyable after a day spent bathing in the sun. To the delight of residents and visitors, a few retired resort chefs have opened up their own little projects in Waimea. Sightseeing is easy from here, too: Mauna Kea is a short drive away, and Hilo and Kailua-Kona can be reached in about an hour. Because Waimea doesn't attract as many visitors as the coasts, you won't find as many condos and hotels, but the bed-and-breakfasts in the area are superb. They also offer some of the island's best lodging deals, especially when you consider that their vantage point up in the hills affords some pretty spectacular views.

$
B&B/INN

Aaah, The Views! This tranquil and pretty stream-side mountain home in upcountry Waimea is lovingly tended by owners Erika and Derek Stuart. Rooms are clean and bright, with lots of windows to enjoy the views. The Dream Room is actually an apartment, with a full kitchen, private deck, and hot tub. The house has a sauna and a yoga room (private lessons available), and an in-house massage therapist as well. This is a popular spot with couples and is not well-suited to families with young children. **Pros:** away from it all, beautiful countryside views, on-site yoga and massage. **Cons:** not kid-friendly, no pool, must drive to area restaurants and attractions. ⊠ 66-1773 Alaneo St., off Akulani, just past mile marker 60 on Hwy. 19, Waimea ☎ 808/885–3455 ⊕ www.aaahtheviews.com ⤴ 4 rooms ♿ In-room: A/C, Wi-Fi, refrigerators, kitchen (some). In-hotel: Wi-Fi ⊟ No credit cards.

$
RENTAL

Aloha Vacation Cottages. Set on several acres of North Kohala property, these two rental cottages don't look like much from the outside, but inside they are clean, comfortable, and well stocked with beach toys, towels and mats, books, cable TV, videos, you name it. The price is right, and they are just a 10-minute drive from the Kohala Coast. There is a minimum stay of five nights, though this rule is sometimes waived, depending on availability. The owners give generous discounts for extended stays, so check the Web site. **Pros:** each cottage equipped with gas grill, free Wi-Fi, 10-minute drive from great beaches. **Cons:**

9

somewhat remote location, can't walk to restaurants or stores, no pool. ☐ *Box 1395, Waimea 96743* ☎ *877/875–1722 or 808/885–6535* ⊕ *www.alohacottages.net* ⤳ *2 units* ☐ *In-room: no A/C, Wi-Fi, in-room DVD players, kitchen* ☐ *MC, V.*

$$–$$$
B&B/INN

☐ **Jacaranda Inn.** Charming inside and out, the lavender Jacaranda Inn can be spotted from miles away. Built in 1897, the sprawling estate was once the home of the manager of Parker Ranch; it's been redecorated in hues of raspberry and lavender, with lots of koa-wood accents. Most of the rooms have hot tubs. A separate nearby cottage that sleeps six has been renovated with new hardwood floors, a stone fireplace, and a large outdoor hot tub. This place is a great deal, and the rooms are very comfortable. **Pros:** country charm, hot tubs in most rooms, walking distance to Waimea restaurants. **Cons:** no pool, lots of purple. ☐ *65-1444 Kawaihae Rd., Waimea* ☎ *808/885–8813* ⊕ *www.jacarandainn.com* ⤳ *8 suites, 1 cottage* ☐ *In-room: no A/C, no room phones, no TV in some rooms. In-hotel: Wi-Fi, no-smoking rooms* ☐ *MC, V.*

$
HOTEL

☐ **Waimea Country Lodge.** In the heart of cowboy country, this modest ranch house–style lodge offers views of the green, rolling slopes of Mauna Kea. It's so quiet you forget you're close to busy Waimea. The rooms are large and clean, with Hawaiian quilt prints lending an authentic touch. You can even charge meals at Merriman's and Paniolo Country Inn to your room. A handful of studios with recently remodeled kitchenettes are also available, and there are plenty of grocery stores in Waimea to stock up on provisions. **Pros:** affordable, large rooms equipped with kitchenettes; charge meals to your room at one of the island's best restaurants (Merriman's). **Cons:** rooms could use additional updating, no pool. ☐ *65-1210 Lindsey Rd., Waimea* ☐ *Box 2559, Kamuela 96743* ☎ *808/885–4100 or 800/367–5004* ⊕ *www. castleresorts.com* ⤳ *21 rooms* ☐ *In-room: no A/C, Internet, kitchen (some).* ☐ *AE, D, DC, MC, V.*

$
RENTAL

☐ **Waimea Gardens Cottage.** These charming stream-side cottages in Waimea's upcountry are surrounded by flowering private gardens and contain surprisingly luxe suites that look like they just leapt out of a glossy magazine. One (Kohala) includes a full kitchen and the others (Waimea and the Garden Studio) a kitchenette, and all are stocked with provisions for a self-serve Continental breakfast. All have their own private gardens and beautiful hardwood floors. The Kohala cottage has a luxury bath with whirlpool soaking tub and the Garden Studio is

BEST BETS FOR BED AND BREAKFASTS

Hōlualoa Inn (Kailua-Kona). Gorgeous wood floors, quiet location, beautiful coffee-country views, close to the quaint artists' community of Hōlualoa.

Jacaranda Inn (Waimea). Charming, country-style, Jacuzzis, walking distance to all the best restaurants in Waimea.

Shipman House Bed & Breakfast (Hilo). Historic mansion with antique koa pieces, tropical breakfast spread, lei making and hula lessons.

Waianuhea (Hāmākua Coast). Stunning views, hot tub, delicious hors d'oeuvres-and-wine tasting.

equipped with a rain-head shower. The grounds are full of birds and plant life that will make you want to move in for good. Inquire for seasonal specials. **Pros:** no detail left out, beautiful self-contained cottages, gardens, complete privacy. **Cons:** pricey for the area, requires payment in full six weeks prior to arrival. 🔲 *Box 520, Kamuela 96743* 🕿 *808/885–8550* ⊕ *www.waimeagardens.com* 🖙 *2 cottages, 1 studio* 🖒 *In-room: A/C, Wi-Fi, in-room DVD players, kitchen* 🖃 *No credit cards.*

HĀMĀKUA COAST

One of the most beautiful stretches of coastline in the world, the Hāmākua Coast is an ideal spot for those seeking peace, tranquility, and beautiful views, which is why it tends to be a favorite with honeymooners. A half dozen or so über-romantic bed-and-breakfasts dot the coast, each with its own personality and views. As with Hilo, the beaches are an hour's drive away or more, so most visitors spend a few nights here and a few closer to the beaches on the west coast. A handful of vacation homes provide an extra level of privacy for couples, groups, or families, but the nearest grocery store is 15 mi up the road in either Hilo or Waimea.

$$$
B&B/INN

🖼 **The Palms Cliff House Inn.** This handsome Victorian-style mansion, 15 mi north of Hilo, is perched on the sea cliffs 150 feet above the crashing surf of the tropical Hāmākua Coast. You can pick tropical fruit and macadamia nuts from the gardens of the 3½-acre estate. Individually decorated rooms have private lānai. Suites include double hot tubs (the one in Room 8 is by the window with a stunning view of the coast), but there's also a communal hot tub in the garden. A husband-and-wife team serves breakfast with pride on the veranda overlooking the cliffs; meals generally include fresh-baked muffins, locally grown fruit, a warm egg or meat dish (they always ask about food allergies or dietary restrictions ahead of time), and, of course, fantastic local coffee. They can help you plan activities, including hula lessons. **Pros:** stunning views, terrific breakfast, comfortable rooms with every amenity. **Cons:** no pool, no lunch or dinner on-site, remote location means you have to drive to Hilo town for restaurants and shopping. 🖂 *28-3514 Māmalahoa Hwy., Honomū* 🕿 *866/963–6076 or 808/963–6076* ⊕ *www.palmscliffhouse.com* 🖙 *4 rooms, 4 suites* 🖒 *In-room: A/C in some rooms, Internet, Wi-Fi, in-room safes, in-room DVD players* 🖃 *AE, D, DC, MC, V.*

$$–$$$
Fodor'sChoice
★
B&B/INN

🖼 **Waianuhea.** Waianuhea defines Hawaiian country elegance. Fully self-contained, this gorgeous country home sits in a forested area on the Hāmākua Coast. The four guest rooms and large suite have tasteful color schemes and lavish furnishings, complete with extra pillows, fluffy down comforters, and soaking tubs, and there is contemporary artwork throughout. The large common room with its stunning ocean views and lava-rock fireplace is a big attraction, especially at the wine tasting and hors d'oeuvres hour each evening. Stroll the flower garden and fruit orchards. The house has solar-electric power. **Pros:** eco-friendly hotel, hot and healthy three-course breakfast, beautiful views. **Cons:** very remote location, unreliable phone and Internet access. 🖂 *45-3503*

9

Kahana Dr., Honoka'a ☎ *888/775–2577 or 808/775–1118* ⊕ *www. waianuhea.com* ⤴ *4 rooms, 1 suite* ⚬ *In-room: no A/C, in-room DVD players. In-hotel: Wi-Fi, Internet Room* ▭ *AE, D, MC, V.*

$
B&B/INN

▦ **Waipi'o Wayside.** Nestled amid the avocado, mango, and kukui trees of a plantation estate, this serene inn provides a retreat close to the Waipi'o Valley. Jacqueline Horne has given each room its own character with, for example, rare Chinese antiques or patchwork quilts. A sprawling garden has an orchid-covered deck, and a little gazebo has hammocks to help you indulge your lazy side. Many of the rooms have ocean views and some also have skylights. Breakfast includes fresh organically grown fruit from the estate, organic coffee, granola, yogurt, and muffins. **Pros:** close to Waipi'o, authentic Hawaiian feel, hammocks with views. **Cons:** remote location, no hot breakfast. ⊠ *Waipi'o Valley Rd., Hwy. 240, Honoka'a* ☎ *808/775–0275 or 800/833–8849* ⊕ *www. waipiowayside.com* ⤴ *5 rooms* ⚬ *In-room: no A/C, Wi-Fi, no in-room phones, no TVs in rooms* ▭ *MC, V.*

HILO

Hilo is the wetter, more lush eastern side of the Big Island, which means if you stay here you'll be close to waterfalls and rain-forest hikes, but not to a warm, dry, white-sand beach. Though Hilo had the wind knocked out of its sails a bit when sugar left the islands over a decade ago, it has gotten back on its feet in the last couple of years and is experiencing something of a revival. Locals, driven farther and farther east by development in the west, have taken a greater interest in Hilo; signs of that interest are showing in new restaurants, restored buildings, and a handful of clean and pleasant parks. Hilo has a few decent hotels, but none of the high-end resorts that are the domain of the west. So, get into the groove at one of Hilo's fantastic bed-and-breakfasts. Most have taken over lovely historic homes and serve breakfast comprised of ingredients from their backyard gardens. The volcano is only a 30- to 40-minute drive, as are the sights of the Puna region. The beaches, unfortunately, are at least an hour's drive.

$
B&B/INN

▦ **The Bay House.** Overlooking Hilo Bay and just steps away from the "Singing Bridge" into Hilo's historic downtown area, this small, quiet bed-and-breakfast is pleasantly decorated, with comfy beds and private lānai. An outdoor hot tub on the cliff offers excellent views of the bay below. A Continental breakfast buffet is provided with fresh fruits, breads, and coffee from the area—guests are invited to take what they want from the buffet back to their lānai for a more private breakfast. **Pros:** cliffside hot tub, Hilo Bay views. **Cons:** no hot breakfast, books up fast. ⊠ *42 Pukihae St., Hilo* ☎ *888/235–8195 or 808/961–6311* ⊕ *www.bayhousehawaii.com* ⤴ *3 rooms* ⚬ *In-room: no A/C, Wi-Fi* ▭ *AE, MC, V.*

$
⟳
HOTEL

▦ **Dolphin Bay Hotel.** A glowing lava flow sign marks the office and bespeaks owner John Alexander's passion for the volcano. Stunning lava pictures adorn the common area, and Alexander is a great source of information for visiting the park and for exploring the back roads of Hilo. Units in the 1950s-style motor lodge are modest, but they are clean

Waianuhea

and inexpensive. Recently remodeled bathrooms include custom-built corner bathtubs with seats. Coffee and fresh fruit are offered daily. Four blocks from Hilo Bay, in a residential area called Pu'ue'o, the hotel borders a verdant 2-acre Hawaiian garden with jungle trails and shady places to rest. Guests of the hotel return repeatedly, and it's ideal for families who seek a home base. **Pros:** great value, extremely helpful and pleasant staff, rates go down the longer you stay. **Cons:** located along a busy road; basic, motel-style rooms. ✉ *333 'Iliahi St., Hilo* ☎ *808/935–1466* ⊕ *www. dolphinbayhotel.com* ⤳ *18 rooms, 13 studios, 4 1-bedroom units, 1 2-bedroom unit* ♿ *In-room: no phone, no A/C, kitchen, Wi-Fi* ▭ *MC, V.*

> ### BEST BETS FOR KIDS
>
> **Casa de Emdeko** (Kailua-Kona). Two large pools, one of salt water and perched at the ocean's edge.
>
> **Dolphin Bay Hotel** (Hilo). Adjacent to a huge, clean, safe park, walking distance to downtown Hilo, very reasonable prices.
>
> **Hilton Waikoloa Village** (Kohala Coast). Disneyland meets Polynesia, with plenty of entertainment options for teens and adults, too.
>
> **Nāmakani Paio Cabins** (Volcano). Camping in a birdhouse cabin next to an active volcanic crater. It doesn't get much better.

$ **Hale Kai.** On a bluff above Hilo Bay, this 5,400-square-foot modern
B&B/INN home is 2 mi from downtown Hilo. Four impeccable rooms with lānai have been freshly painted and spruced up by new owners Maria Macias and Ricardo Zepeda. All rooms have grand ocean views and are within earshot of lapping waves. Fresh flowers add a warm, European touch. Maria and Ricardo serve a full hot breakfast every morning on an outdoor deck or in the kitchen's bay-window dining area. **Pros:** delicious hot breakfast, panoramic views, privacy. **Cons:** removed from town, no kids under 13. ✉ *111 Honoli'i Place, Hilo* ☎ *808/935–6330* ⊕ *www. halekaihawaii.com* ⤳ *3 rooms, 1 suite* ♿ *In-room: A/C. In-hotel: pool, no kids under 13* ▭ *MC, V.*

$–$$ **Hilo Hawaiian Hotel.** Though it does show its age and some of the
HOTEL rooms are in dire need of a refresh (at this writing, rooms were scheduled to be refurbished soon), this older hotel, with large bay-front rooms offering spectacular views of Mauna Kea and Coconut Island, is one of the most pleasant lodgings on Hilo Bay. Street-side rooms overlook the golf course. Most accommodations have private lānai, and kitchenettes are available in some one-bedroom suites. Views of the bay are showcased in the Queen's Court dining room, and the Wai'oli Lounge— where you can get a grab-and-go lunch or cocktails and appetizers— has entertainment Thursday through Saturday. **Pros:** Hilo Bay views, private lānai in most rooms, large rooms. **Cons:** not many options for lunch at the hotel, prices high for quality of rooms. ✉ *71 Banyan Dr., Hilo* ☎ *808/935–9361; 800/367–5004 from mainland; 800/272–5275 interisland* ⊕ *www.castleresorts.com* ⤳ *264 rooms, 21 suites* ♿ *In-room: A/C, Internet, Wi-Fi (some), kitchen (some), refrigerators. In-hotel: restaurant, bar, pool, laundry facilities* ▭ *AE, D, DC, MC, V.*

$–$$

B&B/INN

Hilo Honu Inn. A charming old Craftsman home lovingly restored by a friendly and hospitable couple from North Carolina, the Hilo Honu offers quite a bit of variety. Its three rooms range from the small and reasonably priced Honu's Nest to the large and luxurious Samurai Suite. The Honu's Nest provides fantastic views of the sunrise over Hilo Bay from the comforts of a large, cozy bed. The larger Bali Hai Suite has a sitting room and a window seat that looks out on tree ferns, orchids, and anthuriums. Upstairs, the entire second floor is the Samurai Suite, furnished with traditional tatami mats and beautiful antiques imported from Japan. The suite also includes a large stone soaking tub for two and a beautiful sun porch that looks out over all of Hilo and the bay beyond. Breakfast is delicious and usually includes a variety of home-made baked goods. **Pros:** beautifully restored home, spectacular Hilo Bay views, delicious breakfast. **Cons:** only three rooms, not walking distance to downtown Hilo. ⊠ *465 Haili St., Hilo* ☎ *808/935–4325* ⊕ *www.hilohonu.com* ↪ *3 rooms* ⚲ *In-room: no A/C, Wi-Fi, in-room DVD players, refrigerators. In-hotel: no kids under 6* ▭ *AE, MC, V.*

$

B&B/INN

The Inn at Kulaniapia Falls. The Inn at Kulaniapia has wonderful views both of Hilo Bay and a magnificent 120-foot waterfall that tumbles into a 300-foot-wide swimming pond. The Pagoda, a private guesthouse with a kitchen and living room, sleeps four adults and two children for $175 a night. The only drawbacks are the slightly tacky decor and less than amazing service. The spa has a menu of eight different massages. All in all, this place is a good deal for those who aren't expecting four-star accommodations. **Pros:** waterfalls on property, good value. **Cons:** tacky decor, some complain of poor service. ⌂ *Box 11338, Hilo 96721* ☎ *808/935–8088 or 888/838–6373* ⊕ *www.waterfall.net* ↪ *4 rooms* ⚲ *In-room: no A/C* ▭ *AE, MC, V.*

$

Naniloa Volcanoes Resort. The Naniloa's newly renovated guest rooms in the Mauna Kea tower are a vast improvement over the old ones. Renovations are ongoing in the hotel's other two towers, pool, and lobby area, but Naniloa is still a great home base to explore the island's unspoiled east side. Remodeled rooms feature new beds, a tile bathroom with imported fixtures from Spain and Italy, flat-screen TVs, and original tropical oil paintings painted by the owner's daughter. All ocean-view rooms have a small lānai and great views of Hilo Bay. With wall-to-wall tiling and wood-panel sliding walls in the place of curtains, rooms don't feel particularly warm or "Hawaiian," but a look at true Hawai'i lies just outside your window. Suites are worth the added cost with two private balconies, panoramic views, a kitchenette, wine refrigerator, two flat-screen TVs, and a sitting area. The hotel has one restaurant that currently only serves breakfast, but dinner should be on the menu shortly. **Pros:** newly renovated rooms; great views of Hilo Bay, Mauna Kea, and Mauna Loa volcanoes from some rooms. **Cons:** ongoing renovations, limited dining options. ⊠ *93 Banyan Drive, Hilo* ☎ *808/969-3333* ⊕ *www.volcanohousehotel.com/naniloa_volcanoes_resort.htm* ↪ *313 rooms, 7 suites.* ⚲ *In-room: A/C, Internet, refrigerators. In-hotel: restaurant, golf course, pool, laundry facilities, Wi-Fi.* ▭ *AE, D, MC, V.*

9

\$\$
B&B/INN

Shipman House Bed & Breakfast Inn. You'll have a choice between three rooms in the mansion—the turreted main house dating from 1899—or two rooms in a separate cottage. The bed-and-breakfast is on 5½ verdant acres on Reed's Island; the house is furnished with antique koa and period pieces, some dating from the days when Queen Liliʻuokalani came to tea. On Wednesday night, a hula class practices Hawaiʻi's dances out on the lānai. Guests are allowed to participate or just hang out and watch. Barbara (part of the Shipman family) and her husband Gary are friendly hosts with a vast knowledge of the area and the rest of the island. Don't miss the tropical breakfast buffet with macadamia-nut granola, special breads and muffins, and a variety of tropical fruits that are grown right on the property. Barbara will even teach you how to string a lei with sweet-smelling flowers from the garden. Two-night minimum. **Pros:** 10-minute walk to downtown Hilo, historic home, friendly and knowledgeable local hosts. **Cons:** chock-full of antiques, not a great spot for kids. ⊠ *131 Kaʻiulani St., Hilo* ☎ *808/934–8002 or 800/627–8447* ⊕ *www.hilo-hawaii.com* ➳ *3 rooms, 2 cottage rooms* ⚷ *In-room: no A/C, Wi-Fi, no in-room phones, no TVs in rooms, refrigerators* ▭ *AE, MC, V.*

PUNA

Puna is a world apart—wild jungles, volcanically heated hot springs, and not a resort for miles around. There are, however, a handful of vacation homes and bed-and-breakfasts, most of which are a great deal due to the fact that Puna doesn't attract nearly as many visitors as other regions on the island. This is not a typical vacation spot: there are a few black-sand beaches (some of them clothing-optional), very few dining or entertainment options, and quite a few, er, interesting locals. That said, for those who want to have a unique experience, get away from everything, and like the thought of rubbing shoulders with the locals, this is the place to do it. The volcano, Hilo, and the Hāmākua Coast are all within easy driving distance, and nearby Pahoa has a few restaurants.

¢–\$
B&B/INN

Bed & Breakfast Mountain View. This modern home is surrounded by rolling forest and farmland. The secluded 4-acre estate has extensive floral gardens and a fishpond. Owners Linus and Jane Chao are longtime Big Island art educators and have an art studio on the lower level where they teach classes. Some special packages include art lessons. The house itself is a virtual art gallery with varied displays in oil, acrylic, watercolor, and Oriental brush paintings. **Pros:** reasonable prices, local artist hosts, beautiful landscaping. **Cons:** rooms could use some updating, location is remote. ⊠ *South Kulani Rd., Kurtistown* ☎ *808/968–6868 or 888/698–9896* ⊕ *www.bbmtview.com* ➳ *4 rooms, 2 with shared bath* ⚷ *In-room: no A/C. In-hotel: no kids under 5* ▭ *MC, V.*

\$

Coconut Cottage Bed & Breakfast. New to the bed-and-breakfast scene, Coconut Cottage has quickly become a favorite among visitors for its beautiful grounds, hosts' attention to detail, and proximity to different island adventures. Owners Jerry and Todd refurbished the old Jade Garden B&B in 2007 to include two additional rooms with vintage, island-style furnishings. The Bali Spirit Suite is perhaps the most romantic, with an antique Balinese four-poster bed and windows that overlook the anthurium garden. The larger Garden Bungalow sleeps four and is great for families. Guests enjoy a full breakfast with popular dishes like coconut/macadamia-nut pancakes and quiche. This area of the island has little in the way of nightlife, so Coconut Cottage boasts a library of more than 500 DVDs that you can watch in the privacy of your room, or you can reach ultimate relaxation by soaking for hours in the outdoor hot tub. Inquire about special rates for extended stays. **Pros:** great breakfast, centrally located between Hilo and Volcanoes National Park. **Cons:** no nightlife nearby, some may have a hard time sleeping with the coqui frogs chirping. ⊠ *13-1139 Leilani Ave., Pahoa* ☎ *808/965-0973 or 866/204-7444* ⊕ *www.coconutcottagehawaii.com* ⌂ *3 rooms, 1 bungalow* ⌂ *In-room: no A/C, refrigerator, DVD, Wi-Fi (some). In-hotel: laundry facilities, Wi-Fi.* ⊟ *AE, MC, V.*

¢–$ 📷 **Yoga Oasis.** This center, on 26 tropical acres, has a bit of a commune
B&B/INN   feel. With its exposed redwood beams, Balinese doorways, and imported art, Yoga Oasis draws those who seek relaxation and rejuvenation, and perhaps a free yoga lesson or two. A 1,600-square-foot state-of-the-art yoga and gymnastics space, with 18-foot ceilings, crowns this friendly retreat. You're close to hot springs and black-sand beaches, and the volcano is a 45-minute drive away. **Pros:** daily yoga, focus on relaxation, very low prices. **Cons:** remote location, shared bathrooms in the main building. ⊠ *Pohoiki Rd., Box 1935, Pāhoa* ☎ *808/965–8460 or 800/274–4446* ⊕ *www.yogaoasis.org* ⌂ *4 rooms with shared bath, 3 deluxe cabins, 1 Bali house* ⌂ *In-room: no A/C, Wi-Fi, no in-room phones, no TVs in rooms. In-hotel: Internet Room, laundry service* ⊟ *MC, V.*

VOLCANO

If you are going to visit Volcanoes National Park, and we highly recommend that you do, stay the night in Volcano Village. This allows you to do the late-night lava hike—the best way to see lava—without worrying about driving an hour or more back to your condo, hotel, or bed-and-breakfast. Lucky for you, there are plenty of places to stay in the area, and many of them are both charming and reasonable. Volcano Village has just enough dining and shopping options to satisfy you for a day or two. From here you are also close to Hilo, the Puna region, and Punalu'u's black-sand beach, should you decide to make Volcano your home base for more than a day or two.

¢–$$ 📷 **Chalet Kīlauea Collection.** The Collection comprises three inns and
RENTAL   lodges and five vacation houses in and around Volcano Village. The rooms, suites, and vacation homes range from a historic lodge with no-frills, basic bedrooms to a deluxe inn with themed rooms and its own six-person hot tub. The Collection's showpiece property, the Inn at Volcano ($120–$299), along with the rest of the properties were refurbished recently with new flooring, fixtures, paint, mounted flat-screen TVs, imported linens, and custom-made wooden bed frames. The **Lokahi Lodge** ($115–$135) provides cozy rooms in a country lodge with plenty of exposed beams and wood, and comfy beds. A large kitchen is available for guest use, as is an on-site hot tub. For those looking for a

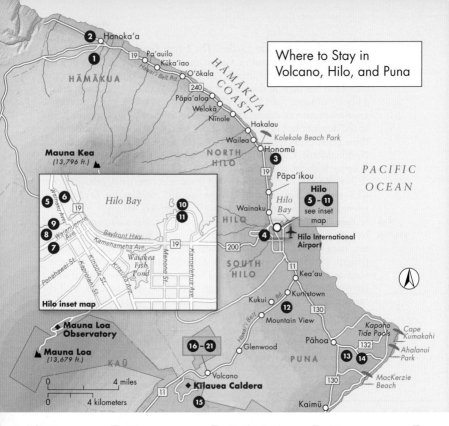

Where to Stay in Volcano, Hilo, and Puna

Hilo inset map

bit more privacy, the **Volcano Cottages** are dispersed vacation homes and cottage rentals around Volcano Village. Each of the six one-, two-, or three-bedroom rentals has a different layout and decor; our favorites are the Ohia Hideaway ($135/night) for couples or small groups, and Pele's Plantation ($225/night) for large groups. The Collection's most reasonably priced offering is

the **Volcano Hale** ($55–$69 double-occupancy room), which has a communal kitchen and fireplace. **Pros:** free afternoon tea at main office, large variety of lodging types to choose from, hot tub, fireplace. **Cons:** Wi-Fi only available at main office, self-check-in after 6 PM ⊠ *Wright Rd., Volcano* ☎ *808/967–7786 or 800/937–7786* ⊕ *www.volcanohawaii.com* ↩ *14 rooms, 3 suites, 5 houses* ⚷ *In-room: no A/C, no phones in some rooms. In-hotel: Wi-Fi* ▤ *D, DC, MC, V.*

$ 🏠 **Hale Ohia Cottages.** A stately and comfortable Queen Anne–style mansion, Hale Ohia was built in the 1930s as a summer place for a wealthy Scotsman. All the rooms have been recently refurbished except for the largest 3-bedroom unit, which was partially redone. The namesake Ohia cottage, large enough for a family, has a full kitchen. Cottage 44 is the cushiest of the group; built into an old water tank, it's naturally lighted, elegantly designed, and completely private. Breakfast (including homemade banana bread, macadamia nuts, and cranberries) is left in your refrigerator while you're away in the afternoon so that you can enjoy it at your leisure in the morning. This place does everything possible to make everyone, from couples to families to solo travelers, feel at home. **Pros:** unique architecture, plenty of props like umbrellas and flashlights for volcano excursions. **Cons:** no TVs; property cat roams around, which could be a problem for allergic guests. ⊠ *Hale Ohia Rd., off Hwy. 11, Volcano* ☎ *808/967–7986* ⊕ *www.haleohia.com* ↩ *4 rooms, 3 cottages, 1 suite* ⚷ *In-room: A/C, Wi-Fi, no room phones, no TVs in rooms, kitchen (some), refrigerators* ▤ *MC, V.*

$$ 🏠 **Kīlauea Lodge.** A mile from the entrance of Hawai'i Volcanoes National
HOTEL Park, this lodge was initially built as a YMCA camp in the 1930s. Now it is a pleasant inn, tastefully furnished with European antiques. Rooms have rich quilts and Hawaiian photographs, and some have their own wood-burning or gas fireplace. A charming one-bedroom cottage with a gas fireplace and a porch is perfect for romance. Cottages off the main property include Pi'i Mauna House, on the fairway of the Volcano Golf Course. Rates include a full hot breakfast at the lodge's restaurant, which has an excellent and unusual dinner menu that includes braised rabbit, medallions of venison, ostrich, and leg of antelope. The duck l'orange is a customer favorite. The restaurant is open to the public for breakfast, lunch, and dinner. **Pros:** great restaurant, close to volcano, fireplaces. **Cons:** overpriced for area, limited breakfast selection. ⊠ *19-3948 Old Volcano Rd., 1 mi northeast of Volcano Store* ⬡ *Box 116, Volcano 96785* ☎ *808/967–7366* ⊕ *www.kilaualodge.com* ↩ *12*

9

rooms, 2 cottages (off property) ⚿ In-room: no A/C, Wi-Fi, no TV in some rooms. In-hotel: restaurant ▤ AE, MC, V.

¢–$ 🏨 **My Island Bed & Breakfast Inn.** Gordon and Joann Morse, along with
B&B/INN   their daughter Ki'i, opened their historic home and 7-acre botanical estate to visitors in 1985. The oldest in Volcano, it was built in 1886 by the Lyman missionary family. Three rooms, one with a private bath, are in the main house. Also on the property are three garden units with private entrances and bathrooms, and one guesthouse. You won't start the day hungry after a deluxe all-you-can-eat breakfast. **Pros:** historic home, full breakfast. **Cons:** remote location, some shared bathrooms. ✉ 19-3896 Old Volcano Hwy. ◫ Box 100, Volcano 96785 ☎ 808/967–7216 or 808/967–7110 ⊕ www.myislandinnhawaii.com ⇆ 6 rooms, 4 with bath; 1 guesthouse ⚿ In-room: no A/C, no phones in some rooms, no TVs in some rooms. ▤ D, MC, V.

¢   🏨 **Nāmakani Paio Cabins.** These A-frame cabins at the end of a long,
☾   deserted road look like little birdhouses. Though recently remodeled,
CABINS   and managed by Volcano House, the cabins are definitely for those who are into roughing it. Inexpensive and clean, each has a double bed, two bunk beds, and electric lights, but no outlets. Bring extra blankets, as it gets cold at night. Each cabin also has a grill outside, but you must bring your own firewood. A communal bathroom facility provides toilets and hot showers for all cabin guests. **Pros:** camping in Volcanoes National Park, unique design. **Cons:** cold nights with no insulation, price is high for rustic cabins. ◫ Volcano House, Box 53, Hawai'i Volcanoes National Park, Volcano 96785 ☎ 808/967–7321 ⊕ www.volcanohousehotel.com/cabins.htm ⇆ 10 cabins ⚿ In-room: no A/C, no in-room phones, no room TVs ▤ AE, D, DC, MC, V.

¢–$$ 🏨 **Volcano Places.** A collection of lovely vacation homes, these accom-
RENTAL   modations range from a simple cottage in the rain forest to a stunning Craftsman-style house with its own spa room. Many can accommodate up to eight people comfortably. All come equipped with full kitchens. **Pros:** unique architecture, rain-forest location, total privacy. **Cons:** can't always select the exact property you want, prices of more expensive units is high for the area. ◫ Box 159, Volcano 96785 ☎ 808/967–7990 ⊕ www.volcanoplaces.com ⇆ 3 cottages ⚿ In-room: A/C, kitchen ▤ MC, V.

$$ 🏨 **Volcano Teapot Cottage.** A near-perfect spot for couples seeking a romantic getaway, this cute red-and-white cottage is completely private. The claw-foot bathtub, hot tub, and fireplace add to the general coziness. The owners recently added a shower. Breakfast is included and the restaurants in Volcano Village are nearby. **Pros:** claw-foot tub, hot tub, fireplace, laundry facilities. **Cons:** isolated location, single or double occupancy only. ✉ 19-3820 Old Volcano Hwy. ◫ Box 511, Volcano 96785 ☎ 808/967–7112 ⊕ www.volcanoteapot.com ⇆ 1 cottage ⚿ In-room: A/C, Wi-Fi, in-room DVD players, kitchen ▤ AE, MC, V.

UNDERSTANDING
BIG ISLAND

Hawaiian Vocabulary

HAWAIIAN VOCABULARY

Although an understanding of Hawaiian is by no means required on a trip to the Aloha State, a *malihini,* or newcomer, will find plenty of opportunities to pick up a few of the local words and phrases. Traditional names and expressions are widely used in the Islands. You're likely to read or hear at least a few words each day of your stay.

With a basic understanding and some uninhibited practice, anyone can have enough command of the local tongue to ask for directions and to order from a restaurant menu. One visitor announced she would not leave until she could pronounce the name of the state fish, the *humuhumunukunukuāpua'a.*

Simplifying the learning process is the fact that the Hawaiian language contains only eight consonants—H, K, L, M, N, P, W, and the silent *'okina,* or glottal stop, written '—plus one or more of the five vowels. All syllables, and therefore all words, end in a vowel. Each vowel, with the exception of a few diphthongized double vowels such as *au* (pronounced "ow") or *ai* (pronounced "eye"), is pronounced separately. Thus *'Iolani* is four syllables (ee-oh-la-nee), not three (yo-la-nee). Although some Hawaiian words have only vowels, most also contain some consonants, but consonants are never doubled.

Pronunciation is simple. Pronounce *A* "ah" as in *father; E* "ay" as in *weigh; I* "ee" as in *marine; O* "oh" as in *no; U* "oo" as in *true.*

Consonants mirror their English equivalents, with the exception of *W.* When the letter begins any syllable other than the first one in a word, it is usually pronounced as a *V. 'Awa,* the Polynesian drink, is pronounced "ava," *'ewa* is pronounced "eva."

Almost all long Hawaiian words are combinations of shorter words; they are not difficult to pronounce if you segment them. *Kalaniana'ole,* the highway running east from Honolulu, is easily understood as *Kalani ana 'ole.* Apply the standard pronunciation rules—the stress falls on the next-to-last syllable of most two- or three-syllable Hawaiian words—and Kalaniana'ole Highway is as easy to say as Main Street.

Now about that fish. Try *humu-humu nuku-nuku āpu a'a.*

The other unusual element in Hawaiian language is the *kahakō,* or macron, written as a short line (¯) placed over a vowel. Like the accent (´) in Spanish, the kahakō puts emphasis on a syllable that would normally not be stressed. The most familiar example is probably *Waikīkī.* With no macrons, the stress would fall on the middle syllable; with only one macron, on the last syllable, the stress would fall on the first and last syllables. Some words become plural with the addition of a macron, often on a syllable that would have been stressed anyway. No Hawaiian word becomes plural with the addition of an *S,* since that letter does not exist in the language.

What follows is a glossary of some of the most commonly used Hawaiian words. Hawaiian residents appreciate visitors who at least try to pick up the local language.

'a'ā: rough, crumbling lava, contrasting with *pāhoehoe,* which is smooth.

'ae: yes.

aikane: friend.

āina: land.

akamai: smart, clever, possessing savoir faire.

akua: god.

ala: a road, path, or trail.

ali'i: a Hawaiian chief, a member of the chiefly class.

aloha: love, affection, kindness; also a salutation meaning both greetings and farewell.

'ānuenue: rainbow.

'a'ole: no.

'apōpō: tomorrow.

'auwai: a ditch.

auwē: alas, woe is me!

'ehu: a red-haired Hawaiian.

'ewa: in the direction of 'Ewa plantation, west of Honolulu.

hala: the pandanus tree, whose leaves (*lau hala*) are used to make baskets and plaited mats.

hālau: school.

hale: a house.

hale pule: church, house of worship.

ha mea iki or **ha mea 'ole:** you're welcome.

hana: to work.

haole: ghost. Since the first foreigners were Caucasian, *haole* now means a Caucasian person.

hapa: a part, sometimes a half; often used as a short form of *hapa haole,* to mean a person who is part-Caucasian.

hau'oli: to rejoice. *Hau'oli Makahiki Hou* means Happy New Year. *Hau'oli lā hānau* means Happy Birthday.

heiau: an outdoor stone platform; an ancient Hawaiian place of worship.

holo: to run.

holoholo: to go for a walk, ride, or sail.

holokū: a long Hawaiian dress, somewhat fitted, with a yoke and a train. Influenced by European fashion, it was worn at court, and at least one local translates the word as "expensive mu'umu'u."

holomū: a post–World War II cross between a *holokū* and a mu'umu'u, less fitted than the former but less voluminous than the latter, and having no train.

honi: to kiss; a kiss. A phrase that some tourists may find useful, quoted from a popular hula, is *Honi Ka'ua Wikiwiki:* Kiss me quick!

honu: turtle.

ho'omalimali: flattery, a deceptive "line," bunk, baloney, hooey.

huhū: angry.

hui: a group, club, or assembly. A church may refer to its congregation as a *hui* and a social club may be called a *hui.*

hukilau: a seine; a communal fishing party in which everyone helps to drive the fish into a huge net, pull it in, and divide the catch.

hula: the dance of Hawai'i.

iki: little.

ipo: sweetheart.

ka: the. This is the definite article for most singular words; for plural nouns, the definite article is usually *nā.* Since there is no *S* in Hawaiian, the article may be your only clue that a noun is plural.

kahuna: a priest, doctor, or other trained person of old Hawai'i, endowed with special professional skills that often included prophecy or other supernatural powers; the plural form is *kāhuna.*

kai: the sea, saltwater.

kalo: the taro plant from whose root *poi* (paste) is made.

kamā'aina: literally, a child of the soil; it refers to people who were born in the Islands or have lived there for a long time.

kanaka: originally a man or humanity, it is now used to denote a male Hawaiian or part-Hawaiian, but is occasionally taken as a slur when used by non-Hawaiians. *Kanaka maoli,* originally a full-blooded Hawaiian person, is used by some native Hawaiian rights activists to embrace part-Hawaiians as well.

kāne: a man, a husband. If you see this word on a door, it's the men's room. If you see *kane* on a door, it's probably a misspelling; that is the Hawaiian name for the skin fungus tinea.

kapa: also called by its Tahitian name, *tapa,* a cloth made of beaten bark and usually dyed and stamped with a repeat design.

kapakahi: crooked, cockeyed, uneven. You've got your hat on *kapakahi.*

kapu: keep out, prohibited. This is the Hawaiian version of the more widely known Tongan word *tabu* (taboo).

kapuna: grandparent; elder.

kēia lā: today.

keiki: a child; *keikikāne* is a boy, *keikiwahine* a girl.

kona: the leeward side of the Islands, the direction (south) from which the *kona* wind and *kona* rain come.

kula: upland.

kuleana: a homestead or small plot of ground on which a family has been installed for some generations without necessarily owning it. By extension, *kuleana* is used to denote any area or department in which one has a special interest or prerogative. You'll hear it used this way: If you want to hire a surfboard, see Moki; that's his *kuleana*.

lā: sun.

lamalama: to fish with a torch.

lānai: a porch, a balcony, an outdoor living room. Almost every house in Hawai'i has one. Don't confuse this two-syllable word with the three-syllable name of the island, Lāna'i.

lani: heaven, the sky.

lau hala: the leaf of the *hala*, or pandanus tree, widely used in handicrafts.

lei: a garland of flowers.

limu: sun.

lolo: stupid.

luna: a plantation overseer or foreman.

mahalo: thank you.

makai: toward the ocean.

malihini: a newcomer to the Islands.

mana: the spiritual power that the Hawaiian believed inhabited all things and creatures.

manō: shark.

manuwahi: free, gratis.

mauka: toward the mountains.

mauna: mountain.

mele: a Hawaiian song or chant, often of epic proportions.

Mele Kalikimaka: Merry Christmas (a transliteration from the English phrase).

Menehune: a Hawaiian pixie. The *Menehune* were a legendary race of little people who accomplished prodigious work, such as building fishponds and temples in the course of a single night.

moana: the ocean.

mu'umu'u: the voluminous dress in which the missionaries enveloped Hawaiian women. Now made in bright printed cottons and silks, it is an indispensable garment. Culturally sensitive locals have embraced the Hawaiian spelling but often shorten the spoken word to "mu'u." Most English dictionaries include the spelling "muumuu."

nani: beautiful.

nui: big.

ohana: family.

'ono: delicious.

pāhoehoe: smooth, unbroken, satiny lava.

Pākē: Chinese. This *Pākē* carver makes beautiful things.

palapala: document, printed matter.

pali: a cliff, precipice.

pānini: prickly pear cactus.

paniolo: a Hawaiian cowboy, a rough transliteration of *español,* the language of the Islands' earliest cowboys.

pau: finished, done.

pilikia: trouble. The Hawaiian word is much more widely used here than its English equivalent.

puka: a hole.

pupule: crazy, like the celebrated Princess Pupule. This word has replaced its English equivalent in local usage.

pu'u: volcanic cinder cone.

waha: mouth.

wahine: a female, a woman, a wife, and a sign on the ladies' room door; the plural form is *wāhine.*

wai: freshwater, as opposed to saltwater, which is *kai.*

wailele: waterfall.

wikiwiki: to hurry, hurry up (since this is a reduplication of *wiki,* quick, neither *W* is pronounced as a *V*).

Note: Pidgin is the unofficial language of Hawai'i. It is a Creole language, with its own grammar, evolved from the mixture of English, Hawaiian, Japanese, Portuguese, and other languages spoken in 19th-century Hawai'i, and it is heard everywhere.

Travel Smart
Big Island

WORD OF MOUTH

"Yes, do visit Akaka Falls if time permits. The walk down to the viewing platform takes you on a paved footpath, surrounded by bamboo, wild orchids, etc. When you pick up your rental car, they'll give you an island map. Ask the clerk to highlight the roads you'll need to take to view Volcanoes National Park and Akaka Falls."

—auntiemaria

GETTING HERE AND AROUND

Unless your cousin is a travel agent, you're probably among the millions of people who make most of their travel arrangements online. But have you ever wondered just what the differences are between an online travel agent (a Web site through which you make reservations instead of going directly to the airline, hotel, or car-rental company), a discounter (a firm that does a high volume of business with a hotel chain or airline and accordingly gets good prices), a wholesaler (one that makes cheap reservations in bulk and then resells them to people like you), and an aggregator (one that compares all the offerings so you don't have to)? Is it truly better to book directly on an airline or hotel Web site? And when does a real live travel agent come in handy?

▌ AIR TRAVEL

Flying time to the Big Island is about 10 hours from New York, eight hours from Chicago, five hours from Los Angeles, and 15 hours from London, not including layovers. Some of the major airline carriers serving Hawai'i fly direct to the Big Island, allowing you to bypass connecting flights out of Honolulu. For the more spontaneous traveler, island-hopping is easy; flights depart every 20 to 30 minutes daily until midevening.

Although the Big Island's airports are smaller and more casual than Honolulu International, during peak times they can also be quite busy. Allot extra travel time to all airports during morning and afternoon rush-hour traffic periods. Plan to arrive at the airport 45 to 60 minutes before departure for interisland flights.

Plants and plant products are subject to regulation by the Department of Agriculture, both on entering and leaving Hawai'i. Upon leaving the Islands, you'll have to have your bags X-rayed and tagged at one of the airport's agricultural inspection stations before you proceed to check-in. Pineapples and coconuts with the packer's agricultural inspection stamp pass freely; papayas must be treated, inspected, and stamped. All other fruits are banned for export to the U.S. mainland. Flowers pass except for gardenia, rose leaves, jade vine, and mauna loa. Also banned are insects, snails, soil, cotton, cacti, sugarcane, and all berry plants.

You'll have to leave dogs and other pets at home. A 120-day quarantine is imposed to keep out rabies, which is nonexistent in Hawai'i. If specific pre- and post-arrival requirements are met, animals may qualify for a 30-day or five-day-or-less quarantine.

Airlines and Airports Airline and Airport Links.com (⊕ *www.airlineandairportlinks.com*) has links to many of the world's airlines and airports.

Airline Security Issues Transportation Security Administration (⊕ *www.tsa.gov*) has answers for almost every question that might come up.

Air Travel Resources in Hawai'i State of Hawai'i Airports Division Offices (☎ *808/836–6417* ⊕ *hawaii.gov/hnl*).

AIRPORTS

Honolulu International Airport (HNL) is the main stopover for most domestic and international flights. From Honolulu, there are departing interisland flights to the Big Island departing regularly from early morning until evening. Some carriers now offer nonstop service directly from the mainland to the Kona International Airport at Keāhole (KOA) and Hilo International Airport (ITO) on a limited basis. Like all of Hawai'i's airports, the two Big Island airports are "open-air," meaning you can enjoy those trade-wind breezes until the moment you step on the plane.

HONOLULU/O'AHU AIRPORT

Hawai'i's major airport is Honolulu International, on O'ahu, 20 minutes (9 mi) west of Waikīkī. To travel to the Big Island from Honolulu, you can depart from either the interisland terminal or the commuter-airline terminal, located in two separate structures adjacent to the main overseas terminal building. A free bus service, the Wiki Wiki Shuttle, operates between terminals.

Information Honolulu International Airport (HNL) (☎ 808/836–6413 ⊕ www. honoluluairport.com).

BIG ISLAND AIRPORTS

Those flying to the Big Island of Hawai'i regularly land at one of two fields. Kona International Airport at Keāhole, on the west side, best serves Kailua-Kona, Keauhou, and the Kohala Coast. There are two Visitor Information Program (VIP) booths located at baggage claims A and B to assist travelers at the Kona International Airport. Additionally, there are news and lei stands, Maxwell's Landing restaurant and a gift shop.

Hilo International Airport is more appropriate for those going to the east side of the island. Here, visitors will find VIP booths across from the Centerplate Coffee Shop & Lounge near the departure lobby and in the arrival areas at each end of the terminal. In addition to the coffee shop, services include a Bank of Hawai'i automatic teller machine, a gift shop, and news and lei stands. Waimea-Kohala Airport, called Kamuela Airport by residents, is used primarily for commuting among the Islands.

Information Hilo International Airport (ITO) (☎ 808/934–5838). **Kona International Airport at Keāhole (KOA)** (☎ 808/329–3423). **Waimea-Kohala Airport (MUE)** (☎ 808/887–8126).

GROUND TRANSPORTATION

Only Arnott's Lodge and the Hawai'i Naniloa Hotel provide airport shuttles to and from the Hilo International Airport. If you're not renting a car, you'll need to take a taxi. There are 13 taxi companies serving the Hilo Airport. The approximate taxi rate is $3 flip, plus $.30 every [1/8] mile, with surcharges for waiting time at $.30 per minute and $1 per bag. Cab fares to locations around the island are estimated as follows: Banyan Drive hotels $11, Hilo town $12, Hilo Pier $13, Volcano $75, Kea'au $22, Pāhoa $50, Honoka'a $105, Kamuela/Waimea $148, Waikoloa $188, and Kailua town $240.

At the Kona International Airport, Speedi-Shuttle offers transportation between the airport and hotels, resorts, and condominium complexes from Waimea to Keauhou. There is an online reservation and fare quote system for information and bookings.

Contacts SpeediShuttle (☎ 877/242–5777 ⊕ www.speedishuttle.com).

FLIGHTS

America West, American, and United fly into O'ahu, Maui, Kaua'i, and the Big Island. Alaska flies into O'ahu and Kaua'i. Delta and Northwest serve O'ahu (Honolulu), Maui, and the Big Island. Continental flies into Honolulu.

Most domestic airline tickets are electronic; international tickets may be either electronic or paper. With an e-ticket the only thing you receive is an e-mail receipt citing your itinerary, and reservation and ticket numbers. The greatest advantage of an e-ticket is that if you lose your receipt, you can simply print out another copy or ask the airline to do it for you at check-in. You usually pay a surcharge (up to $50) to get a paper ticket, if you can get one at all.

Airline Contacts America West/US Airways (☎ 800/428–4322 ⊕ www.usairways. com). **American Airlines** (☎ 800/433–7300 ⊕ www.aa.com). **Continental Airlines** (☎ 800/523—3273 for U.S. and Mexico reservations, 800/231–0856 for international reservations ⊕ www.continental.com). **Delta Airlines** (☎ 800/221–1212 for U.S. reservations ⊕ www. delta.com). **United Airlines** (☎ 800/864–8331

FOR INTERNATIONAL TRAVELERS

CURRENCY

The dollar is the basic unit of U.S. currency. It has 100 cents. Coins are the penny (1¢); the nickel (5¢), dime (10¢), quarter (25¢), half-dollar (50¢), and the very rare golden $1 coin and even rarer silver $1. Bills are denominated $1, $5, $10, $20, $50, and $100, all mostly green and identical in size; designs and background tints vary. You may come across a $2 bill, but the chances are slim.

CUSTOMS

Information **U.S. Customs and Border Protection** (⊕ www.cbp.gov).

DRIVING

Gas costs range from $2.50 to $3.50 a gallon.

Driving in the United States is on the right. Speed limits are posted in miles per hour (usually 50–55 mph on major highways). Watch for lower limits in small towns and on back roads (usually 30–40 mph). Most states require front-seat passengers to wear seat belts; many states require children to sit in the backseat and to wear seat belts. In major cities rush hour is between 7 and 10 AM; afternoon rush hour is between 4 and 7 PM.

Highways are well paved.

Gas stations are fairly far apart and those in rural towns may close early, especially on Sundays. If your car breaks down on the highway, pull onto the shoulder and wait for help, or have your passengers wait while you walk to an emergency phone (available in most states). If you carry a cell phone, dial *55, noting your location on the small green roadside mileage marker.

ELECTRICITY

The U.S. standard is AC, 110 volts/60 cycles. Plugs have two flat pins set parallel to each other.

EMBASSIES

Contacts **Australia** (☎ 202/797–3000 ⊕ www.austemb.org). **Canada**

(☎ 202/682–1740 ⊕ www.canadianembassy. org). **United Kingdom** (☎ 202/588–7800 ⊕ www.britainusa.com).

EMERGENCIES

For police, fire, or ambulance, dial 911 (0 in rural areas).

HOLIDAYS

New Year's Day (Jan. 1); Martin Luther King Day (3rd Mon. in Jan.); Presidents' Day (3rd Mon. in Feb.); Memorial Day (last Mon. in May); Independence Day (July 4); Labor Day (1st Mon. in Sept.); Columbus Day (2nd Mon. in Oct.); Thanksgiving Day (4th Thurs. in Nov.); Christmas Eve and Christmas Day (Dec. 24 and 25); and New Year's Eve (Dec. 31).

MAIL

You can buy stamps and aerograms, and send letters and parcels in post offices. Stamp-dispensing machines can occasionally be found in airports, bus and train stations, office buildings, drugstores, and convenience stores. U.S. mailboxes are stout, dark blue steel bins; pickup schedules are posted inside the bin (pull down the handle to see them). Parcels weighing more than a pound must be mailed at a post office or at a private mailing center.

Within the United States a first-class letter weighing 1 ounce or less costs 41¢; each additional ounce costs 17¢ up to 3.5 ounces. Postcards cost 26¢. A 1-ounce airmail letter or postcard to most countries costs 90¢, a 1-ounce letter or postcard to Canada or Mexico costs 69¢.

To receive mail on the road, have it sent c/o General Delivery at your destination's main post office (use the correct five-digit ZIP code). You must pick up mail in person within 30 days, with a driver's license or passport for identification.

Contacts **DHL** (☎ 800/225–5345 ⊕ www. dhl.com). **Federal Express** (☎ 800/463–3339 ⊕ www.fedex.com). **Mail Boxes, Etc./**

The UPS Store (☎ *800/789–4623* ⊕ *www. mbe.com*). **United States Postal Service** (⊕ *www.usps.com*).

PASSPORTS AND VISAS

Visitor visas aren't necessary for citizens of Australia, Canada, the United Kingdom, or most citizens of European Union countries coming for tourism and staying for fewer than 90 days. If you require a visa, the cost is $100, and waiting time can be substantial, depending on where you live. Apply for a visa at the U.S. consulate in your place of residence; check the U.S. State Department's special Visa Web site for further information.

Visa Information **Destination USA** (⊕ *travel.state.gov/visa*).

PHONES

Numbers consist of a three-digit area code and a seven-digit local number. The area code for all calls within the state of Hawai'i is 808. Within many local calling areas you dial only the seven digits; in others you dial "1" first and all 10 digits—just as you would for calls between area-code regions. The same is true for calls to numbers prefixed by "800," "888," "866," and "877"—all toll free. For calls to numbers prefixed by "900" you must pay—usually dearly.

For international calls, dial "011" followed by the country code and the local number. For help, dial "0" and ask for an overseas operator. Most phone books list country codes and U.S. area codes. The country code for Australia is 61, for New Zealand 64, for the United Kingdom 44. Calling Canada is the same as calling within the United States, whose country code, by the way, is 1.

For operator assistance, dial "0." For directory assistance, call 555–1212 or occasionally 411 (free at many public phones). You can reverse long-distance charges by calling "collect"; dial "0" instead of "1" before the 10-digit number.

Instructions are generally posted on pay phones. Usually you insert coins in a slot (usually 25¢–50¢ for local calls) and wait for a steady tone before dialing. On long-distance calls the operator tells you how much to insert; prepaid phone cards, widely available in various denominations, can be used from any phone. Follow the directions to activate the card (there's usually an access number, then an activation code), then dial your number.

CELL PHONES

The United States has several GSM (Global System for Mobile Communications) networks, so multiband mobiles from most countries (except for Japan) work here. Unfortunately, it's almost impossible to buy a pay-as-you-go mobile SIM card in the U.S.—which allows you to avoid roaming charges—without also buying a phone. That said, cell phones with pay-as-you-go plans are available for well under $100. AT&T, T-Mobile, and Virgin Mobile offer affordable, pay-as-you-go service.

Contacts **AT&T** (☎ *800/331–0500* ⊕ *www. att.com*). **T Mobile** (☎ *800/937–8997* ⊕ *www.t-mobile.com*). **Virgin Mobile** (☎ *No phone* ⊕ *www.virginmobileusa.com*).

for U.S. reservations, 800/538–2929 for international reservations ⊕ www.united.com).

INTERISLAND FLIGHTS

Check local and community newspapers when you're on the Big Island for deals and coupons on interisland flights, should you wish to visit neighboring islands. Go! Airlines, Hawaiian Airlines, IslandAir, Mokulele Airlines and PW Express offer regular service between the islands. In addition to offering very competitive rates and online specials, all have free frequent-flier programs which will entitle you to rewards and upgrades the more you fly. Be sure to compare prices offered by all the interisland carriers. If you are somewhat flexible with your dates and times for island-hopping, you should have no problem getting a very affordable round-trip ticket.

Interisland Carriers go! Airlines (☎ 888/435–9462 ⊕ www.iflygo.com). **Hawaiian Airlines** (☎ 800/367–5320 ⊕ www.hawaiianair.com). **IslandAir** (☎ 800/652–6541 ⊕ www.islandair.com). **Mokulele Airlines** (☎ 808/326–7070 ⊕ www.mokuleleairlines.com). **PW Express** (☎ 888/866–5022 ⊕ www.flypwx.com).

CHARTER FLIGHTS

In addition to its regular service between the Big Island and Maui, Mokulele Airlines also provides charter service from the Kona airport to Maui, MolokaʻI, and Lānaʻi. In business since 1998, the Kona-based company also offers air tours of the Big Island. Pacific Wings offers a variety of charter options at the Hilo, Kamuela, and Kona airports and also serves Lānaʻi, Maui, Molokaʻi, and Oʻahu. Services include premiere (same-day departures on short notice), premium (24-hour notice), priority (48-hour notice), group, and cargo/courier services. The company also has a frequent-flier program. The cost of a round-trip between Honolulu and Kamuela purchased in advance through the company's Web site is about $600.

Paragon Air offers 24-hour private charter service to and from the Hilo, Kamuela,

and Kona airports. In business since 1980, the company prides itself on its perfect safety record and has served a number of celebrities including Bill Gates, Michael Douglas, and Kevin Costner, among others. You can arrange a customized tour of the Big Island or neighboring islands, as well as air service from any airport in Hawaiʻi. Charter prices start at $475.

Charter Companies Mokulele Airlines (☎ 808/326–7070 ⊕ www.mokuleleairlines.com). **Pacific Wings** (☎ 888/575–4546 ⊕ www.pacificwings.com).

▎ BUS TRAVEL

Travelers can take advantage of the Hawaiʻi County Mass Transit Agency's free Hele-On Bus, which travels routes throughout the island. A one-way journey between Hilo and Kona will take about four hours. There's regular service in and around downtown Hilo, Kailua-Kona, Waimea, North and South Kohala, Honokaʻa, and Pāhoa. There is a charge of $1 per piece for bicycles, luggage, and large backpacks that can't fit under a seat. Visitors staying in Hilo can take advantage of the Transit Agency's Shared Ride Taxi program, which provides door-to-door transportation in the area. A one-way fare is $2 and a book of 15 coupons can be purchased for $30.

Information Hele-On Bus (☎ 808/961–8744 ⊕ www.co.hawaii.hi.us/mass_transit/heleonbus.html).

▎ CAR TRAVEL

Technically, the Big Island of Hawaiʻi is the only island you can completely circle by car, and driving is the best way to enjoy the sightseeing opportunities afforded by the miles of scenic roadway.

Instead of using compass directions, remember that Hawaiʻi residents refer to places as being either *mauka* (toward the mountains) or *makai* (toward the ocean) from one another. Hawaiʻi has a strict seat belt law. Those riding in the front seat

Car Rental Resources

Automobile Associations		
American Automobile Association	☎ 315/797–5000	⊕ www.aaa.com
National Automobile Club	☎ 650/294–7000	⊕ www.thenac.com; CA residents only
Local Agencies		
AA Aloha Cars-R-Us	☎ 800/655–7989	⊕ www.hawaiicarrental.com
Discount Hawai'i Car Rentals	☎ 888/292–3307	⊕ www.discounthawaiicarrental.com
Harper Car and Truck Rental (Big Island)	☎ 800/852–9993	⊕ www.harpershawaii.com
Hawaiian Discount Car Rentals	☎ 800/882–9007	⊕ www.hawaiidrive-o.com
Kona Harley-Davidson	☎ 866/326–9887	⊕ www.hawaiiharleyrental.com
Oahu Camping Vans	☎ 808/261–9393	⊕ www.oahucampingvans.com
Major Agencies		
Alamo	☎ 800/462–5266	⊕ www.alamo.com
Avis	☎ 800/331–1212	⊕ www.avis.com
Budget	☎ 800/527–0700	⊕ www.budget.com
Hertz	☎ 800/654–3131	⊕ www.hertz.com
National Car Rental	☎ 800/227–7368	⊕ www.nationalcar.com
Thrifty	☎ 800/847–4389	⊕ www.thrifty.com

must wear a seat belt and children under the age of 17 in the back seats must be belted. The fine for not wearing a seat belt is $92. Jaywalking is also very common in the islands so please pay careful attention to the roads, especially while driving in downtown Hilo, Kailua-Kona, and the smaller towns around the island.

GASOLINE

You can count on having to pay more at the pump for gasoline on the Big Island than on the U.S. mainland.

PARKING

Parking can be a challenge in downtown Kona. If you're willing to walk several blocks, you should be able to find free parking off Ali'i Drive on some of the residential streets. Otherwise, there are municipal lots just off Ali'i Drive with an honor system. You will be ticketed if you don't pay. In Hilo, there is a good availability of free parking.

ROAD CONDITIONS

It's difficult to get lost in most of Hawai'i. Roads and streets, although they may challenge the visitor's tongue, are well marked. Free publications containing good-quality road maps can be found on all the Islands.

Roads on the Big Island are generally well-maintained and can be easily negotiated. Most of the roads are two-lane highways with limited shoulders—and yes, even in paradise, there is traffic, especially during the morning and afternoon rush hours. Unless you have a four-wheel drive vehicle, do not attempt Saddle Road between Hilo and Waimea; it's narrow, windy, and poor in many areas. Most rental car agencies do not allow driving on Saddle Road, and several companies make you sign a statement that you won't, even if you rent a four-wheel-drive vehicle.

Gas stations are fairly far apart and in rural areas it's not unusual for the stations to close early. If you see that your tank is getting low, don't take any chances; fill up when you see a station. In Hawai'i, turning right on a red light is legal, except where noted. Use caution during heavy downpours, especially if you see signs warning of falling rocks. The road to Ka Lae, the southernmost tip of the U.S., provides gorgeous views, but is narrow: if you want to enjoy the views, pull over to the side.

RENTALS

Should you plan to do any sightseeing on the Big Island, it is best to rent a car due to the size of the island. With more than 260 mi of coastline—and attractions as varied as the Hawai'i Volcanoes National Park, 'Akaka Falls State Park, and Pu'ukoholā Heiau National Historic Site—ideally you should split up your stay between the east and west coasts of the island. Even if all you want to do is relax at your resort, you may want to hop in the car to check out one of the island's popular restaurants.

While on the Big Island, you can rent anything from an econobox to a Ferrari to a motor home. Rates are usually better if you reserve though a rental agency's Web site. It's wise to make reservations far in advance and make sure that a confirmed reservation guarantees you a car, especially if visiting during peak seasons or for major conventions or sporting events. It's not uncommon to find several car categories sold out during major events on the island like the Merrie Monarch Festival in Hilo in April or the Ironman Triathlon World Championship in Kailua-Kona in October. ■ TIP➔ If you're planning on driving to the 13,796-foot summit of Mauna Kea for stargazing, you'll need a four-wheel drive vehicle. Harper Car and Truck Rental, with offices in Hilo and Kona, is a good source for 4x4 vehicles.

For some, renting an RV or motor home might be an appealing way to see the island. Harper's has motor homes available and Oahu Camping Vans rents out Volkswagon Westfalia camping vans. And if exploring the island on two wheels is more your speed, Kona Harley-Davidson rents motorcycles.

Rates begin at about $25 to $35 a day for an economy car with air-conditioning, automatic transmission, and unlimited mileage. This does not include the airport concession fee, general excise tax, rental vehicle surcharge, or vehicle license fee. When you reserve a car, ask about cancellation penalties and drop-off charges should you plan to pick up the car in one location and return it to another. Many rental companies in Hawai'i offer coupons for discounts at various attractions that could save you money later on in your trip.

In Hawai'i you must be 21 years of age to rent a car and you must have a valid driver's license and a major credit card. Those under 25 will pay a daily surcharge of $15–$25. Request car seats and extras such as GPS when you book. Hawai'i's Child Restraint Law requires that all children three years and younger be in an approved child safety seat in the backseat of a vehicle. Children ages four to seven must be seated in a rear booster seat or child restraint such as a lap and shoulder belt. Car seats and boosters range from $5 to $8 per day.

In Hawai'i, a valid mainland driver's license is valid for rental for up to 90 days.

Since the road circling the Big Island is mostly two lanes, be sure to allow plenty of time to return your vehicle so that you can make your flight. Traffic can be bad during morning and afternoon rush hours, especially in the Kona area. Give yourself about 3½ hours before departure time to return your vehicle.

CAR-RENTAL INSURANCE

Everyone who rents a car wonders whether the insurance that the rental companies offer is worth the expense. No one—including us—has a simple answer. It all depends on how much regular insurance you have, how comfortable you are with risk, and whether or not money is an issue.

If you own a car and carry comprehensive car insurance for both collision and liability, your personal auto insurance will probably cover a rental, but read your policy's fine print to be sure. If you don't have auto insurance, then you should probably buy the collision- or loss-damage waiver (CDW or LDW) from the rental company. This eliminates your liability for damage to the car. Some credit cards offer CDW coverage, but it's usually supplemental to your own insurance and rarely covers SUVs, minivans, luxury models, and the like. If your coverage is secondary, you may still be liable for loss-of-use costs from the car-rental company (again, read the fine print). But no credit-card insurance is valid unless you use that card for *all* transactions, from reserving to paying the final bill.

■TIP➔ Diners Club offers primary CDW coverage on all rentals reserved and paid for with the card. This means that Diners Club's company—not your own car insurance—pays in case of an accident. It *doesn't* mean that your car-insurance company won't raise your rates once it discovers you had an accident.

You may also be offered supplemental liability coverage; the car-rental company is required to carry a minimal level of liability coverage insuring all renters, but it's rarely enough to cover claims in a really serious accident if you're at fault. Your own auto-insurance policy will protect you if you own a car; if you don't, you have to decide whether you are willing to take the risk.

U.S. rental companies sell CDWs and LDWs for about $15 to $25 a day; supplemental liability is usually more than $10 a day. The car-rental company may offer you all sorts of other policies, but they're rarely worth the cost. Personal accident insurance, which is basic hospitalization coverage, is an especially egregious rip-off if you already have health insurance.

■TIP➔ You can decline the insurance from the rental company and purchase it through a third-party provider such as Travel Guard (⊕ *www.travelguard.com*)—$9 per day for $35,000 of coverage. That's sometimes just under half the price of the CDW offered by some car-rental companies.

ESSENTIALS

We're really proud of our Web site: Fodors.com is a great place to begin any journey. Scan Travel Wire for suggested itineraries, travel deals, restaurant and hotel openings, and other up-to-the-minute info. Check out Booking to research prices and book plane tickets, hotel rooms, rental cars, and vacation packages. Head to Talk for on-the-ground pointers from travelers who frequent our message boards. You can also link to loads of other travel-related resources.

▌ COMMUNICATIONS

INTERNET

If you've brought your laptop with you to the Big Island, you should have no problem checking e-mail or connecting to the Internet. Most of the major hotels and resorts offer high-speed access in rooms and/or lobbies. You should check with your hotel in advance to confirm that access is wireless; if not, ask whether in-room cables are provided. In some cases there will be an hourly or daily charge posted to your room. If you're staying at a small inn or bed-and-breakfast without Internet access, ask the proprietor for the nearest café or coffee shop with wireless access.

Contacts Cybercafes (⊕ www.cybercafes. com) lists over 4,000 Internet cafés worldwide.

▌ HEALTH

Hawai'i is known as the Health State. The life expectancy here is 79 years, the longest in the nation. Balmy weather makes it easy to remain active year-round, and the low-stress aloha attitude certainly contributes to general well-being. When visiting the Islands, however, there are a few health issues to keep in mind.

The Hawai'i State Department of Health recommends that you drink 16 ounces of water per hour to avoid dehydration when hiking or spending time in the sun. Use sunblock, wear UV-reflective sunglasses, and protect your head with a visor or hat for shade. If you're not acclimated to warm, humid weather you should allow plenty of time for rest stops and refreshments. When visiting freshwater streams, be aware of the tropical disease leptospirosis, which is spread by animal urine and carried into streams and mud. Symptoms include fever, headache, nausea, and red eyes. If left untreated it can cause liver and kidney damage, respiratory failure, internal bleeding, and even death. To avoid this, don't swim or wade in freshwater streams or ponds if you have open sores and don't drink from any freshwater streams or ponds.

On the Islands, fog is a rare occurrence, but there can often be "vog," an airborne haze of gases released from volcanic vents at Kīlauea. During certain weather conditions such as "Kona Winds," the vog can settle over the Islands and wreak havoc with respiratory and other health conditions, especially asthma or emphysema. If susceptible, stay indoors and get emergency assistance if needed.

The Islands have their share of bugs and insects that enjoy the tropical climate as much as visitors do. Most are harmless but annoying. When planning to spend time outdoors in hiking areas, wear long-sleeve clothing and pants and use mosquito repellent containing DEET. In very damp places you may encounter the dreaded local centipede. On the Islands they usually come in two colors, brown and blue, and they range from the size of a worm to an 8-inch cigar. Their sting is very painful, and the reaction is similar to bee- and wasp-sting reactions. When camping, shake out your sleeping bag before climbing in, and check your shoes in the morning, as the centipedes like cozy places. If planning on hiking or traveling in remote areas, always carry a first-aid kit and appropriate medications for sting reactions.

■ HOURS OF OPERATION

Even people in paradise have to work. Generally local business hours are weekdays 8–5. Banks are usually open Monday–Thursday 8:30–3 and until 6 on Friday. Some banks have Saturday-morning hours.

Many self-serve gas stations stay open around-the-clock, with full-service stations usually open from around 7 AM until 9 PM. U.S. post offices are open weekdays 8:30 AM–4:30 PM and Saturday 8:30–noon.

Most museums generally open their doors between 9 AM and 10 AM and stay open until 5 PM Tuesday–Saturday. Many museums operate with afternoon hours only on Sunday and close on Monday. Visitor-attraction hours vary throughout the state, but most sights are open daily with the exception of major holidays such as Christmas. Check local newspapers upon arrival for attraction hours and schedules if visiting over holiday periods. The local dailies carry a listing of "What's Open/ What's Not" for those time periods.

Stores in resort areas sometimes open as early as 8 AM, with shopping-center opening hours varying from 9:30 to 10 AM on weekdays and Saturday, a bit later on Sunday. Bigger malls stay open until 9 PM weekdays and Saturday and close at 5 PM on Sunday. Boutiques in resort areas may stay open as late as 11 PM.

■ MONEY

Automatic teller machines for easy access to cash are everywhere on the Islands. ATMs can be found in shopping centers, small convenience and grocery stores, inside hotels and resorts, as well as outside most bank branches. For a directory of locations, call ☎ 800/424–7787 for the MasterCard/Cirrus/Maestro network or ☎ 800/843–7587 for the Visa/Plus network.

CREDIT CARDS

Throughout this guide, the following abbreviations are used: **AE**, American Express; **D**, Discover; **DC**, Diners Club; **MC**, MasterCard; and **V**, Visa.

It's a good idea to inform your credit-card company before you travel, especially if you're going abroad and don't travel internationally very often. Otherwise, the credit-card company might put a hold on your card owing to unusual activity—not a good thing halfway through your trip. Record all your credit-card numbers—as well as the phone numbers to call if your cards are lost or stolen—in a safe place, so you're prepared should something go wrong. Both MasterCard and Visa have general numbers you can call (collect if you're abroad) if your card is lost, but you're better off calling the number of your issuing bank, since MasterCard and Visa usually just transfer you to your bank. Your bank's number is usually printed on your card.

Reporting Lost Cards American Express (☎ 800/528–4800 in the U.S., 336/393–1111 collect from abroad ⊕ www.americanexpress. com). **Diners Club** (☎ 800/234–6377 in the U.S., 303/799–1504 collect from abroad ⊕ www.dinersclub.com). **Discover** (☎ 800/347–2683 in the U.S., 801/902–3100 collect from abroad ⊕ www.discovercard.com). **MasterCard** (☎ 800/622–7747 in the U.S., 636/722–7111 collect from abroad ⊕ www. mastercard.com). **Visa** (☎ 800/847–2911 in the U.S., 410/581–9994 collect from abroad ⊕ www.visa.com).

LOCAL DO'S & TABOOS

GREETINGS

Hawai'i is a very friendly place and this is reflected in the day-to-day encounters with friends, family, and even business associates. Women will often hug and kiss one another on the cheek and men will shake hands and sometimes combine that with a friendly hug. When a man and woman are greeting each other and are good friends, it is not unusual for them to hug and kiss on the cheek. Children are taught to call any elders "auntie" or "uncle," even if they aren't related. It's a way to show respect and can result in a local Hawaiian child having dozens of aunties or uncles. It's also reflective of the strong sense of family that exists in the Islands.

When you walk off a long flight, perhaps a bit groggy and stiff, nothing quite compares with a Hawaiian lei greeting. The casual ceremony ranks as one of the fastest ways to make the transition from the worries of home to the joys of your vacation. Though the tradition has created an expectation that everyone receives this floral garland when they step off the plane, the state of Hawai'i cannot greet each of its nearly seven million annual visitors.

If you've booked a vacation with a wholesaler or tour company, a lei greeting might be included in your package, so check before you leave. If not, it's easy to arrange a lei greeting for yourself or for your companions before you arrive. Contact Kama'āina Leis, Flowers & Greeters if you're arriving into Kona International Airport. To be really wowed by the experience, request a lei of plumeria, some of the most divine-smelling blossoms on the planet. A plumeria or dendrobium orchid lei are considered standard and cost $20/person. Hilo International Airport does not allow companies to provide lei greeting services, but there are lei vendors at the airport should you wish to purchase lei upon arrival.

Information Kama'āina Leis, Flowers & Greeters (☎ *800/367–5183* or *808/836–3246* ⊕ *www.alohaleigreetings. com*).

LANGUAGE

Hawai'i was admitted to the Union in 1959, so residents can be sensitive when visitors refer to their own hometowns as "back in the States." Remember, when in Hawai'i, refer to the contiguous 48 states as "the mainland" and not as the United States. When you do, you won't appear to be such a *malahini* (newcomer).

English is the primary language on the Islands. Making the effort to learn some Hawaiian words can be rewarding, however. Despite the length of many Hawaiian words, the Hawaiian alphabet is actually one of the world's shortest, with only 12 letters: the five vowels, *a, e, i, o, u*, and seven consonants, *h, k, l, m, n, p, w*. Hawaiian words you're most likely to encounter during your visit to the Islands are *aloha, mahalo* (thank you), *keiki* (child), *haole* (Caucasian or foreigner), *mauka* (toward the mountains), *makai* (toward the ocean), and *pau* (finished, all done).

Hawaiian history includes waves of immigrants, each bringing their own languages. To communicate with each other, they developed a sort of slang known as "pidgin." If you listen closely, you'll know what is being said by the inflections and by the extensive use of body language. For example, when you know what you want to say but don't know how to say it, just say "you know, da kine." For an informative and somewhat-hilarious view of things Hawaiian, check out Jerry Hopkins's series of books titled *Pidgin to the Max* and *Fax to the Max*, available at most local bookstores in the Hawaiiana sections.

TRAVELER'S CHECKS

Some consider this the currency of the caveman, and it's true that fewer establishments accept traveler's checks these days. Nevertheless, they're a cheap and secure way to carry extra money, particularly on trips to urban areas. Both Citibank (under the Visa brand) and American Express issue traveler's checks in the United States, but Amex is better known and more widely accepted; you can also avoid hefty surcharges by cashing Amex checks at Amex offices. Whatever you do, keep track of all the serial numbers in case the checks are lost or stolen.

Contacts American Express (☎ 888/412–6945 in the U.S., 801/945–9450 collect outside of the U.S. to speak to customer service ⊕ www.americanexpress.com).

▮ PACKING

Hawai'i is casual: sandals, bathing suits, and comfortable, informal clothing are the norm. In summer synthetic slacks and shirts, although easy to care for, can be uncomfortably warm.

One of the most important things to tuck into your suitcase is sunscreen. Hats and sunglasses offer important sun protection, too. Both are easy to find in island shops, but if you already have a favorite packable hat or sun visor, bring it with you. All major hotels in Hawai'i provide beach towels.

As for clothing in the Hawaiian Islands, there's a saying that when a man wears a suit during the day, he's either going for a loan or he's a lawyer trying a case. Only a few upscale restaurants require a jacket for dinner. The *aloha* shirt is accepted dress in Hawai'i for business and most social occasions. Shorts are acceptable daytime attire, along with a T-shirt or polo shirt. There's no need to buy expensive sandals on the mainland—here you can get flip-flops for a couple of dollars and off-brand sandals for $20. Golfers should remember that many courses have dress codes requiring a collared shirt; call courses you're interested in for details. If you're not prepared, you can pick up appropriate clothing at resort pro shops. If you're visiting in winter, bring a sweater or light- to medium-weight jacket. A polar fleece pullover is ideal, and makes a great impromptu pillow.

If your vacation plans include Hilo, especially during the spring and winter months, you'll want to pack a folding umbrella and light raincoat. And if you'll be exploring Hawai'i Volcanoes National Park, make sure you pack appropriately as weather ranges from hot and dry along the shore to cool and rainy at the summit. Good boots are recommended if you'll be hiking or camping in the Park.

▮ SAFETY

Hawai'i is generally a safe tourist destination, but it's still wise to follow the same common sense safety precautions you would normally follow in your own hometown. Hotel and visitor-center staff can provide information should you decide to head out on your own to more remote areas. Rental cars are magnets for break-ins, so don't leave any valuables in the car, not even in a locked trunk. Avoid poorly lighted areas, beach parks, and isolated areas after dark as a precaution. When hiking, stay on marked trails, no matter how alluring the temptation might be to stray. Weather conditions can cause landscapes to become muddy, slippery, and tenuous, so staying on marked trails will lessen the possibility of a fall or getting lost.

Ocean safety is of the utmost importance when visiting an island destination. Don't swim alone, and follow the international signage posted at beaches that alerts swimmers to strong currents, man-of-war jellyfish, sharp coral, high surf, sharks, and dangerous shore breaks. At coastal lookouts along cliff tops, heed the signs indicating that waves can climb over the ledges. Check with lifeguards at each beach for current conditions, and if the red flags are up, indicating swimming and surfing are not allowed, don't go in. Waters that look calm on the surface can harbor strong currents and undertows, and not a few people who were just wading have been dragged out to sea.

Women traveling alone are generally safe on the Islands, but always follow the safety precautions you would use in any major destination. When booking hotels, request rooms closest to the elevator, and always keep your hotel-room door and balcony doors locked. Stay away from isolated areas after dark; camping and hiking solo are not advised. If you stay out late visiting nightclubs and bars, use caution when exiting night spots and returning to your lodging.

▮ TAXES

There's a 4.16% state sales tax on all purchases, including food. A hotel room tax of 7.25%, combined with the sales tax of 4%, equals an 11.41% rate added onto your hotel bill. A $3-per-day road tax is also assessed on each rental vehicle.

▮ TIME

Hawai'i is on Hawaiian Standard Time, five hours behind New York, two hours behind Los Angeles, and 10 hours behind London.

When the U.S. mainland is on daylight saving time, Hawai'i is not, so add an extra hour of time difference between the Islands and U.S. mainland destinations.

▮ TIPPING

Hawai'i is a major vacation destination and many of the people who work at the hotels and resorts rely on tips to supplement their wages, so tipping is common. Tip cabdrivers 15% of the fare. Standard tips at restaurants and spas run from 15% to 20% of the bill, depending on the quality of service; bartenders expect about $1 per drink. Bellhops at hotels usually receive $1 per bag, more if you have bulky

items like bicycles or surfboards. Tip the hotel maid $1 per night, paid daily. Tip doormen $1 to $5 for assistance with taxis, bags, or golf clubs; tips for concierges vary depending on the service.

▮ TOURS

Guided tours are a good option when you don't want to do it all yourself. You travel along with a group (sometimes large, sometimes small), stay in prebooked hotels, eat with your fellow travelers (the cost of meals is sometimes included in the price of your tour), and follow a schedule. But not all guided tours are an if-it's-Tuesday-this-must-be-Belgium experience. A knowledgeable guide can take you places that you might never discover on your own, and you may be pushed to see more than you would have otherwise.

Tours aren't for everyone, but they can be just the thing for first-time travelers to the Big Island or those who enjoy the group traveling experience. Whenever you book a guided tour, find out what's included and what isn't. A "land-only" tour includes all your travel (by bus, in most cases) in the destination, but not necessarily your flights to and from or even within it. Also, in most cases prices in tour brochures don't include fees and taxes. And remember that you'll be expected to tip your guide (in cash) at the end of the tour.

GENERAL-INTEREST TOURS

Globus has three Hawai'i itineraries that include the Big Island, one of which is an escorted cruise on Norwegian Cruise Lines' *Pride of America* that includes one day each in Kona and Hilo. Tauck Travel and Trafalgar offer several land-based Hawai'i itineraries that include two to three nights on the Big Island, depending on the tour. Both companies offer similar itineraries. Tauck offers seven- and 11-night multi-island tours with two and three nights on the Big Island, respectively, including a Magical Hawai'i trip for families. Trafalgar has seven-, nine-, 10-, and 12-night multi-island tours with two nights on the Big Island. In all cases, visits to Hawai'i Volcanoes National Park are included.

EscortedHawaiiTours.com, owned and operated by Atlas Cruises & Tours, sells more than a dozen Hawai'i trips ranging from seven to 12 nights operated by various guided tour companies including Globus, Tauck, and Trafalgar.

Recommended Companies Atlas Cruises & Tours (☎ 800/942–3301 ⊕ www.escortedhawaiitours.com). **Globus** (☎ 866/755–8581 ⊕ www.globusjourneys.com). **Tauck Travel** (☎ 800/788–7885 ⊕ www.tauck. com). **Trafalgar** (☎ 866/544–4434 ⊕ www. trafalgar.com).

SPECIAL-INTEREST TOURS

ADVENTURE STUDY

Want to discover the incredible geologic treasures of Kīlauea Volcano? If so, you'll want to book a tour with Volcano Discovery, a company founded by volcanologist Tom Pfeiffer and photographer Tobias Schorr in Germany in 2005. Along with Hawai'i geologic specialist Philip Ong, who lives on the Big Island, the company offers exciting expeditions for travelers who want to get an up-close look at Kīlauea. Heartbeat of the Earth is a 13-night study and walking tour where participants will spend four days learning all about Kīlauea Volcano, followed by further exploration of the island's many other natural highlights. Kīlauea Volcano is a five-night study tour of the geologic features of this amazing volcano. These tours can be scheduled at any time of the year for groups ranging from two to eight people. In addition, the company usually offers a fixed-date hiking and geology tour of the Big Island.

Contact Volcano Discovery (☎ 011/49–2241-2080175 [Germany] ⊕ www. volcanodiscovery.com).

ART

Whether you want to learn about Hawaiian arts, history, and culture; astronomy, ecology, or botany; or the geology of the Hawaiian volcanoes, Volcano Art Center can design a program for your group that utilizes the talents of local artists, scientists, performers, historians, park rangers, storytellers, and guides. You choose the length of the vacation and the Art Center staff packages all the components, including transportation, accommodations, meals, field trips, hikes, demonstrations, entertainment, classes, and lectures. The Art Center also features workshops and performances throughout the year that you may want to incorporate into your vacation.

Contact Volcano Art Center (☎ 866/967–7565 ⊕ www.volcanoartcenter.org).

BIKING

If you're a bicycling enthusiast, you've got exciting options on the Big Island. Bicycle Adventures has a seven-day Hawai'i tour and a six-day budget tour. You'll ride about 45 mi per day. Priced at about $2,900 per person, the Hawai'i tour incorporates biking, hiking, snorkeling, sailing, and whale watching. The budget tour is priced at about $2,100 per person, and accommodations are in moderately priced hotels; only biking, hiking, and snorkeling are included. Both tour prices include accommodations, meals, snacks, maps, van support, guide, activity fees and park admissions, taxes, and gratuities. Bicycle rental, pre- or post-lodging, and singles supplements are extra.

WomanTours has a seven-night bike tour for women only that circumnavigates the entire island. Included in the $2,190 per person price are seven nights' accommodations (some triple occupancy rooms), some meals (five breakfasts, picnic lunches, five dinners, and snacks), van support, and trained guides. Rental bikes and upgrades to single or double rooms are available for an additional cost.

Airfare must be purchased separately for these bike tours.

■ TIP→ Most airlines accommodate bikes as luggage, provided they're dismantled and boxed.

Contacts **Bicycle Adventures** (☎ 800/443–6060 ⊕ www.bicycleadventures.com). **Woman-Tours** (☎ 800/247–1444 ⊕ www.womantours.com).

BIRD-WATCHING

Hawai'i boasts more than 150 species of birds that live in the Hawaiian Islands. Field Guides has a three-island, 11-day guided bird-watching trip that focuses on endemic land birds and specialty seabirds. While on the Big Island, birders will visit Hawai'i Volcanoes National Park, Haka-lau Preserve and Mauna Kea to see forest birds including the Hawaiian hawk, *oma'o* (Hawaiian thrush), nēnē (Hawaiian goose), and the Hawai'i creeper. Participants might also get a glimpse of the rare *palila*, the only finch-like Hawaiian honeycreeper that remains on the main islands. The trip costs about $4,200 per person and includes accommodations, meals, ground transportation, interisland air, an eight-hour pelagic boat trip, and guided bird-watching excursions. Travelers must purchase their own airfare from/to their gateway city.

Victor Emanuel Nature Tours has two nine-day trips that include the Big Island. The guide for both tours is Bob Sundstrom, a skilled birder with a special interest in birdsong who has been leading birding tours in Hawai'i and other destinations since 1989. "Kaua'i and Hawai'i" is the theme of the March birding trip. Birders will see indigenous Hawaiian birds including the *'amakihi*, *'apapane*, *'elepaio*, and the comical scarlet *'i'iwi*, as well as endemic birds such as the *ōma'o*, *palila*, and *'ākepa* honey creepers. Participants in the Fall Hawai'i birding trip will visit O'ahu, Kaua'i, and the Big Island in October. Birders will spend two nights at the Volcano House, which is perched alongside the Kīlauea Caldera. The Kaua'i and Hawai'i tour costs about $3,300/person and the Fall Hawai'i tour is priced at about $4,000/person. Both trips include accommodations, meals, interisland air, ground transportation, and guided excursions. Travelers must purchase their own airline ticket from/to their gateway city.

Contacts **Field Guides** (☎ 800/728–4953 ⊕ www.fieldguides.com). **Victor Emanuel Nature Tours** (☎ 800/328–8368 ⊕ www.ventbird.com).

CULTURE

Exploritas, a nonprofit educational travel organization which has been leading all-inclusive learning adventures around the world for more than 20 years, offers several land-only cultural and educational tours. Big Island of Hawai'i: History, Volcanoes, and Marine Life is a 14-night tour presented in association with Lyman Mission House and Museum and the University of Hawai'i-Hilo. You'll spend five nights in Hilo, five nights at Hawai'i Volcanoes National Park, and four nights in Kona, learning about Hawaiian history, geology, star navigation, language, arts and crafts, and medicine from local cultural historians. You'll visit Rainbow and 'Akaka Falls, Waipi'o, orchid and macadamia-nut factories, Pu'uhonua O Hōnaunau National Historic Park, Hulihe'e Palace, and Moku'aikaua Church—and you'll walk through rain forests, and lava and petroglyph fields. Free time and visits to beaches are also included. The cost of this tour starts at $2,631 per person and includes accommodations, meals, ground transportation, and admission fees.

Big Island of Hawai'i Odyssey: Earth, Sky, and Sea is an 11-night tour designed for children ages nine to 12 accompanied by an adult. Highlights include Hawaiian storytelling, an astronomy presentation at the Onizuka Visitor Center at Mauna Kea, horseback riding in Waimea, and a hike to a black-sand beach, among others. Prices start at $1,956 per person.

The Big Island also is included in several multi-island tours; check out the Exploritas Web site for information.

Contacts **Exploritas** (☎ 800/454–5768 ⊕ www.exploritas.org).

CULINARY

A Taste of Paradise: Hawaiian Style, another land-only Exploritas tour, visits the Big Island (three nights each in Kīlauea and Kona) and Maui. Travelers will wander the stalls of the Hilo Farmers Market where they'll find exotic fresh fruit like rambutan, soursop, jackfruit, and jaboticaba; vegetables such as hydroponic lettuce, organic spinach, eggplant, and baby ginger; anthuriums, protea, bonsai plants, herbs, and orchids; locally made crafts and gift items including Hawaiian hardwood bowls, clothing, and shell jewelry; and specialty food items such as dried fish, breads and pastries, jams, and jellies (including the incredibly delicious ʻōhiʻa berry jam). There are visits to banana, papaya, coffee, cocoa, lettuce, vanilla, and anthurium farms, as well as the macadamia-nut factory.

Contacts Exploritas (☎ 800/454–5768 ⊕ www.exploritas.org).

ECO TOURS

Hawaiʻi Forest & Trail's mission is to educate, inspire, and entertain visitors. For the past 15 years, the company has showcased the island's amazing diversity with adventures to waterfalls, rain forests, nature preserves, Mauna Kea and Hawaiʻi Volcanoes National Park. In 2006, Hawaiʻi Forest & Trail was awarded Ecotour Operator of the Year by the Hawaiʻi Ecotourism Association. The company can customize a multiday adventure tour for your group, including everything from caving in lava tubes and hiking to a secluded waterfall for a private picnic lunch to marveling at the nighttime lava flow of Kīlauea. Prices vary depending on activities chosen and size of group.

Want to hike and paddle on the Big Island? Since 1992, Betsy Morrigan has been guiding multisport adventure tours on the Big Island. The Hawaiʻi Pack and Paddle camping trips showcase the entire island and are billed as "low-key and relaxing." All guides are lifeguards and certified in first aid and CPR. There is a guided four-day kayak/hiking trip suitable for beginners to advanced hikers that features three nights at bed-and-breakfasts in Kona and in Hawaiʻi Volcanoes National Park. Included in the price ($300 per day per person, for four days; children ages six to 12 are half price) are kayak and group camping equipment, lightweight sleeping gear, food, tents, snorkel gear, and guide services. A seven-day adventure that includes two nights camping and four nights in a bed-and-breakfast is also available. Airfare is extra with both tours. Morrigan, a college professor of Hawaiian literature, also offers seven- to 10-day specialized educational tours for teachers to earn graduate credits. She can also custom-design a tour program for your group.

"Under Hawaiian Skies: Big Island Adventure" is the theme of an eight-night trip sponsored by Sierra Club Outings. Highlights include swimming, snorkeling, and kayaking along the Kona coast; exploring Hawaiʻi Volcanoes National Park by hiking through crater trails, lava tubes, and rain forests; attending a "Star Party" at the Onizuka Center for International Astronomy located at the 9,300-foot level of Mauna Kea; touring ʻImiloa Astronomy Center in Hilo; and watching the 4th of July fireworks over Hilo Bay. Participants will also have opportunities to discover the uniqueness of Hawaiʻi's cultural heritage as they learn the hula and other ancient Hawaiian games; weave with coconut palm fronts; ride outrigger canoes; make a Hawaiian instrument; and taste traditional Hawaiian foods. Priced at around $1,600 per person, the tour includes accommodations, most meals, activities, and ground transportation.

Travelers must purchase their own airfare between the Big Island and their gateway city for all these tours.

Contacts Hawaiʻi Forest & Trail (☎ 800/464–1993 ⊕ www.hawaii-forest.com). **Hawaiʻi Pack and Paddle** (☎ 808/328–8911 ⊕ www.hawaiipackandpaddle.com). **Sierra Club Outings** (☎ 415/977–5522 ⊕ www.sierraclub.org/outings).

HIKING

Sierra Club Outings offers a seven-night, hotel-based hiking tour, Day Hikes & Creature Comforts. Off-the-beaten-path adventurers will explore many of the same trails once walked by ancient Hawaiians, beaches frequented by green sea turtles, rain forests, taro fields, extinct craters, and vast lava fields. Participants will assist in a conservation activity and help prepare meals using fresh, local ingredients. The trip is designed for travelers who hike on a regular basis, as each day the group will log anywhere from four to eight miles. Priced at about $1,500 per person, the tour includes accommodations, most meals, ground transportation, and activities.

Hawai'i Three Island Hiker is a seven-night hiking tour to the Big Island, Kaua'i, and Maui. Included in the per-person price of about $3,300 are accommodations, meals, interisland airfare, shuttle transportation, support vehicle, professional guides, and a T-shirt and water bottle. Hikers will spend two nights on the Big Island exploring Hawai'i Volcanoes National Park including hikes into Kīlauea Iki crater and along the Crater Rim trail, which encircles Kīlauea's summit caldera, and a coastline lava trail. The trip is rated moderately easy to moderate. The World Outdoors has been organizing and leading adventure trips around the world for 20 years.

Timberline Adventures has a five-night hiking tour, Hawai'i: Volcanoes & the Kailua-Kona Coast, designed to showcase the island's unique diversity. Highlights include hikes throughout Hawai'i Volcanoes National Park, Waipi'o Valley, Pu'uhonua O Hōnaunau, Captain Cook Trail, and along the coast from Miloli'i to Aholi Holua, an ancient slide used by Hawaiians as a form of athletic competition. The trip costs about $2,200 per person and includes accommodations (three nights at Kīlauea Lodge, and two nights at Outrigger Keauhou Beach Resort), meals, ground transportation, and activities.

Travelers must purchase their own airfare between the Big Island and their gateway city for all these hiking tours.

Contact Sierra Club Outings (☏ 415/977–5522 ⊕ www.sierraclub.org/outings). **The World Outdoors** (☏ 800/488–8483 ⊕ www.theworldoutdoors.com). **Timberline Adventures** (☏ 800/417–2453 ⊕ www.timbertours.com).

WELLNESS

Licensed massage therapist Nancy Kahalewai leads retreats on the art of *lomilomi* massage. This traditional Hawaiian massage uses kneading and gliding strokes to increase circulation, soothe nerves, and loosen muscle tissue. And, because it is also designed to improve energy levels in the recipient by encouraging *pono* (righteous emotions and thoughts), it is considered a holistic treatment. The author of *Hawaiian Lomilomi, Big Island Massage,* and the former director of two massage businesses, Kahalewai has been teaching massage therapy on the island since 1976.

Organic fitness trainer KeibaDawn Blacklidge owns and operates BodyTemple Boot Camp, "a metamorphosis program designed to create and manifest the ultimate ideal live body life force." Designed to strengthen body, mind, and spirit, BodyTemple Boot Camp is a six-night customized program for one to three people priced at $1,000–$1,500 per week. Blacklidge has more than 20 years of fitness training experience and has competed and placed in several natural bodybuilding competitions. The program includes eco-cabin lodging; daily meals and snacks (participants choose either a raw vegan, raw nonvegan, or fruitarian meal plan); daily personal fitness sessions and outdoor adventures; three massages and yoga sessions; and airport shuttle transportation.

Yoga practitioners might want to book one of the *nai'a* (dolphin) retreats offered by the Lotus Way. Certified instructor Heather George has been teaching yoga for more than 15 years. Held at a private home alongside Kealakekua Bay, the retreats include six-night accommodations, daily yoga and meditation sessions, most meals, and free time for snorkeling, kayaking, and other activities. Rates are dependent on the size and needs of the group. George also can facilitate workshops in the healing art of Thai yoga therapy at Ramashala, a Balinese-inspired vacation retreat in the Puna district, across from the black-sand Kehena Beach.

Ramashala also can create customized group fitness and body tonics programs for families and groups. With its lush, tropical gardens and architecture that combines Asian and Eastern influences, Ramashala is ideal for vacationers seeking a luxurious, peaceful, and healthy getaway. There is an in-house vegetarian chef with more than 20 years experience as a personal chef, restaurant owner, and cookbook author.

Yoga Oasis, a solar-powered eco-retreat located in a rain forest five miles from the village of Pāhoa on the Big Island's eastern tip, offers a number of yoga retreats. Prices vary depending on the retreats selected, but all include accommodations, meals, and yoga/workshop sessions.

Travelers must purchase their own airfare between the Big Island and their gateway city.

Contacts Big Island Massage (☎ 808/640–5755 ⊕ www.bigislandmassage.com). **BodyTemple Boot Camp** (☎ 808/965-9394 ⊕ www.bodytemplebootcamp.com). **The Lotus Way** (☎ 970/209-6723 ⊕ www.thelotusway.org). **Ramashala** (☎ 808/965-0068 ⊕ www.ramashala.com). **Yoga Oasis** (☎ 800/274-4446 ⊕ www.yogaoasis.com).

▌ VISITOR INFORMATION

Before you go, contact the Big Island Visitors Bureau to request a free official vacation planner with information on accommodations, transportation, sports and activities, dining, arts and entertainment, and culture. Take a virtual visit to the Big Island on the Web, which can be helpful in planning your vacation. The site also has a calendar section that allows you to see what local events coincide with your visit.

The Hawai'i Island Chamber of Commerce has links to dozens of museums, attractions, bed-and-breakfasts, and parks on its Web site. Volcano Art Center offers a host of activities at Kīlauea, including classes and workshops, music, dance, and theater performances, art shows, and volcano runs, which you may want to participate in while on the island.

Contacts Big Island Visitors Bureau (☎ 808/961–5797, 800/648-2441 for vacation planner and brochures ⊕ www.bigisland.org). **Hawai'i Island Chamber of Commerce** (☎ 808/935-7178 ⊕ www.hicc.biz). **Volcano Art Center** (☎ 866/967-7565 or 808/967-7565 ⊕ www.volcanoartcenter.org).

INDEX

PHOTO CREDITS

1 and 2, *Douglas Peebles/eStock Photo.* 5, *Polynesian Cultural Center.* **Chapter 1: Experience the Big Island:** 8-9, *Pacific Stock/SuperStock.* 10 and 11 (all), *Big Island Visitors Bureau.* 13 (left), *Photodisc.* 13 (right), WaterFrame/Alamy. 16 (top left), *Photo Resource Hawaii/Alamy.* 16 (bottom left), *Cornforth Images/Alamy.* 16 (top center), *Photo Resource Hawaii/Alamy.* 16 (bottom center), *Waterframe/Alamy.* 16 (right), *Douglas Peebles Photography/Alamy.* 17 (left), *Big Island Visitors Bureau.* 17 (top center), *Andre Seale/age fotostock.* 17 (bottom center), *Hemis/Alamy.* 17 (top right), *Photo Resource Hawaii/Alamy.* 17 (bottom right), *Stephen Frink Collection/Alamy.* 19 (left), *SuperStock/age fotostock.* 19 (right), *Photo Resource Hawaii/Alamy.* 21, Katja Govorushchenko/iStockphoto. 23, iStockphoto. 25, Jay Spooner/iStockphoto. 26, *Hilton Hawaii.* 27 (left), *Photo Resource Hawaii/Alamy.* 27 (right), Stephanie Horrocks/iStockphoto. 29, iStockphoto. 31, *Photo Resource Hawaii/Alamy.* 33 (left), *Douglas Peebles/age fotostock.* 33 (right), *Castle Resorts & Hotels.* 35, *Douglas Peebles/eStock Photo.* 37 (both), *Hilton Hawaii.* 38, *Bryan Lowry/Alamy.* **Chapter 2: Exploring the Big Island:** 39, *Douglas Peebles/eStock Photo.* 41, *Big Island Visitors Bureau.* 51, *Big Island Visitors Bureau.* 53-54, *Pacific Stock/SuperStock.* 57, *Greg Vaughn/Alamy.* 58, *Pacific Stock/SuperStock.* 63, *Pacific Stock/SuperStock.* 64, *Photo Resource Hawaii/Alamy.* 71, *Russ Bishop/Alamy.* 72, *Cornforth Images/Alamy.* 78, *SuperStock/age fotostock.* 86, *Interfoto Pressebildagentur/Alamy.* 88, *Big Island Visitors Bureau.* 89, *Russ Bishop/age fotostock.* 91, *Photo Resource Hawaii/Alamy.* 92, *Cornforth Images/Alamy.* 93 (top), *Pacific Stock/SuperStock.* 93 (bottom), *Linda Robshaw/Alamy.* **Chapter 3: Beaches:** 97, *Preferred Hotels & Resorts Worldwide.* 101, Luis Castanedox/agefotostock. 105, *Pacific Stock/SuperStock.* 109, *Cornforth Images/Alamy.* 110, *Douglas Peebles/eStock Photo.* **Chapter 4: Water Activities & Tours:** 113, *WaterFrame/Alamy.* 114, *Russ Bishop/Alamy.* 117, *Blaine Harrington III/Alamy.* 125, *Andre Seale/Alamy.* 127, *Ron Dahlquist/HVCB.* 128, *SuperStock/age fotostock.* 129 (all illustrations), *William Wu.* 130, *David Fleetham/Alamy.* 133, *Stephen Frink Collection/Alamy.* **Chapter 5: Golf, Hiking & Outdoor Activities:** 135, *HTJ.* 137, *Douglas Peebles/eStock Photo.* 143, *Pacific Stock/SuperStock.* 147, *Luca Tettoni/viestiphoto.com.* 148, *Kaua'I Visitors Bureau.* 149 (top illustrations), *William Wu.* 149 (bottom), *Jack Jeffrey.* 150, *Pacific Stock/SuperStock.* 153, *Photo Resource Hawaii/Alamy.* **Chapter 6: Shops & Spas:** 155, *Hilton Hawaii.* 157, *Sri Maiava Rusden/HVCB.* 165 (top), *Linda Ching/HVCB.* 165 (bottom), *Sri Maiava Rusden/HVCB.* 166, *Michael Soo/Alamy.* 167 (top), *leisofhawaii.com.* 167 (2nd from top), *kellyalexanderphotography.com.* 167 (3rd, 4th, and 5th from top), *leisofhawaii.com.* 167 (bottom), *kellyalexanderphotography.com.* 171 (all), *Mauna Lani Spa.* **Chapter 7: Entertainment & Nightlife:** 177, *Hilton Hawaii.* 182, *Hawaii Visitors & Convention Bureau.* 183, *Thinkstock LLC.* 185, *Hawaii Visitors & Convention Bureau.* **Chapter 8: Where to Eat:** 189, *Four Seasons Hotels & Resorts.* 209, *Polynesian Cultural Center.* 210 (top), *Douglas Peebles Photography.* 210 (top center), *Douglas Peebles Photography/Alamy.* 210 (center), *Dana Edmunds/Polynesian Cultural Center.* 211 (bottom center), *Douglas Peebles Photography/Alamy.* 211 (bottom), *Purcell Team/Alamy.* 211 (top, top center, and bottom center), *HTJ/HVCB.* 212 (top), *Danita Delimont/Alamy.* 212 (bottom), *Douglas Peebles/Alamy.* **Chapter 9: Where to Stay:** 223, *Waianuhea.* 238 (all), *Kyle Rothenborg/Four Seasons Hualalai.* 245 (top), *Kona Village Resort.* 245 (bottom), *Ahu Pohaku Ho'omaluhia, hawaii-island-retreat.com.* 252 (all) *Waianuhea.*

NOTES

NOTES

ABOUT OUR WRITERS

Bill Harby is an award-winning writer, editor and photographer based in Volcano village on Hawai'i Island. As a freelancer and staff editor for several Hawai'i magazines, he has written and photographed for numerous local and national publications, Web sites and guidebooks, and has traveled widely throughout the Islands while on assignment. He also works as an editorial consultant. Bill may be reached through http://billharby.squarespace.com.

After six years as an editor, columnist and writer for *MidWeek* newspaper in Honolulu covering everything from arts and entertainment to island living, Katie Young Yamanaka now writes about Hawai'i for a variety of print media from her home base on the Big Island. Her articles have also been published in the *Honolulu Star-Bulletin,* Hawaiian Airlines' *Hana Hou!* Magazine and the *Hawaii Tribune-Herald.* In addition, she has worked in public relations, advertising copywriting and as a writing teacher. However, she considers her greatest achievement to be her one-year-old daughter, Ava, who accompanies her and husband, Garth, on their Island adventures.